INUYASHA™

VOL. 19
Action Edition

Story and Art by
RUMIKO TAKAHASHI

English Adaptation by Gerard Jones

Translation/Mari Morimoto
Touch-Up Art & Lettering/Bill Schuch
Cover and Interior Graphics & Design/Yuki Ameda
Editor/Avery Gotoh
Supervising Editor/Michelle Pangilinan

Managing Editor/Annette Roman
Editor in Chief/Alvin Lu
Production Manager/Noboru Watanabe
Sr. Dir. of Licensing and Acquisitions/Rika Inouye
VP of Sales/Joe Morici
VP of Sales & Marketing/Liza Coppola
Executive VP/Hyoe Narita
Publisher/Seiji Horibuchi

© 1997 Rumiko Takahashi/Shogakukan, Inc. First published
by Shogakukan, Inc. in Japan as "Inuyasha."

New and adapted artwork and text
© 2004 VIZ, LLC
All rights reserved.

The stories, characters and incidents mentioned in this
publication are entirely fictional. For the purposes of publication in English, the artwork in this publication is printed in
reverse from the original Japanese version.

Printed in Canada.

Published by VIZ, LLC
P.O. Box 77010
San Francisco, CA 94107

Action Edition
10 9 8 7 6 5 4 3 2 1
First printing, August 2004

www.viz.com

store.viz.com

InuYasha

VOL. 19   Action Edition

STORY AND ART BY
RUMIKO TAKAHASHI

CONTENTS

THE STORY THUS FAR

Long ago, in the "Warring States" era of Japan's Muromachi period (*Sengoku-jidai*, approximately 1467-1568 CE), a legendary dog-like half-demon called "Inu-Yasha" attempted to steal the Shikon Jewel, or "Jewel of Four Souls," from a village, but was stopped by the enchanted arrow of the village priestess, Kikyo. Inu-Yasha fell into a deep sleep, pinned to a tree by Kikyo's arrow, while the mortally wounded Kikyo took the Shikon Jewel with her into the fires of her funeral pyre. Years passed.

Fast-forward to the present day. Kagome, a Japanese high school girl, is pulled into a well one day by a mysterious centipede monster, and finds herself transported into the past, only to come face to face with the trapped Inu-Yasha. She frees him, and Inu-Yasha easily defeats the centipede monster.

The residents of the village, now 50 years older, readily accept Kagome as the reincarnation of their deceased priestess Kikyo, a claim supported by the fact that the Shikon Jewel emerges from a cut on Kagome's body. Unfortunately, the jewel's rediscovery means that the village is soon under attack by a variety of demons in search of this treasure. Then, the jewel is accidentally shattered into many shards, each of which may have the fearsome power of the entire jewel.

Although Inu-Yasha says he hates Kagome because of her resemblance to Kikyo, the woman who "killed" him, he is forced to team up with her when Kaede, the village leader, binds him to Kagome with a powerful spell. Now the two grudging companions must fight to reclaim and reassemble the shattered shards of the Shikon Jewel before they fall into the wrong hands...

THIS VOLUME It's a case of the protected needing protection from the protector as Sango vows to never give up little brother Kohaku, Kagome is entrusted to his care...and Inu-Yasha wonders if, in trusting him, he hasn't made a bad, *deadly* mistake...

CHARACTERS

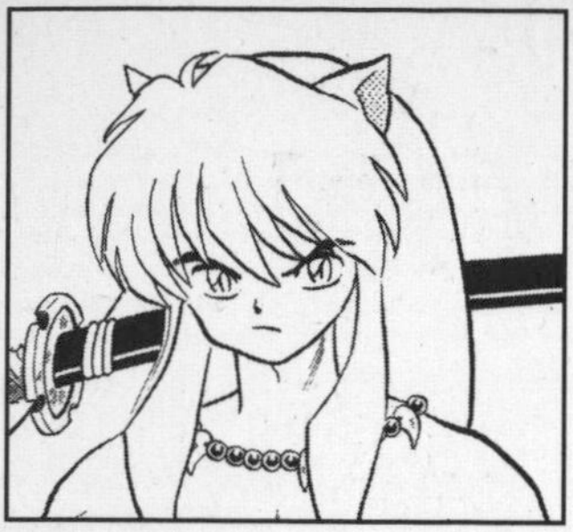

KAGOME
Modern-day Japanese schoolgirl who can travel back and forth between the past and present through an enchanted well.

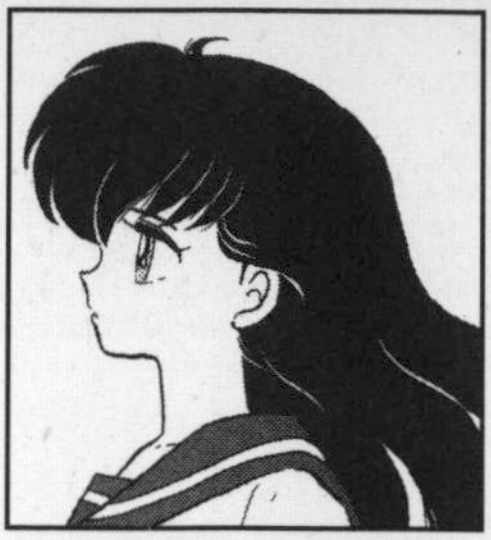

INU-YASHA
Half-demon hybrid, son of a human mother and demon father. His necklace is enchanted, allowing Kagome to control him with a word.

KOHAKU
Killed by Naraku—but not before first slaying both his own and Sango's father—now he's back again in a newer...if somewhat *slower*...form.

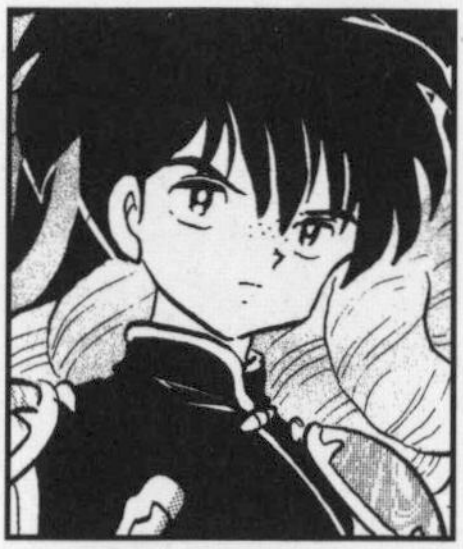

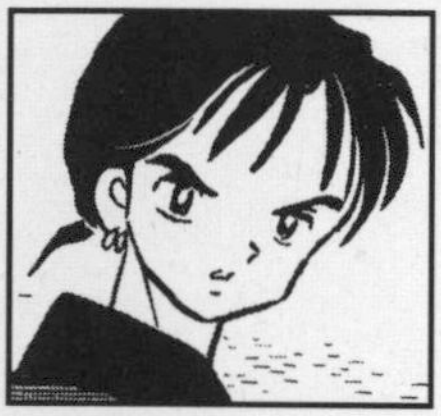

MIROKU
Lecherous Buddhist priest cursed with a mystical "hellhole" in his hand that's slowly killing him.

SANGO
"Demon Exterminator" or slayer from the village where the Shikon Jewel was first born.

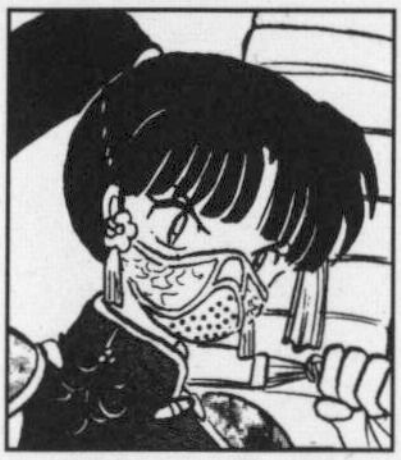

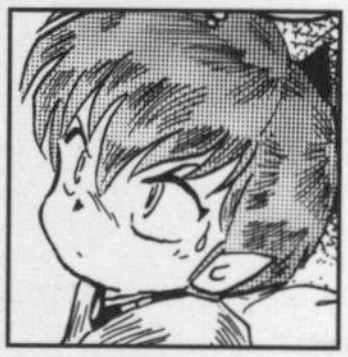

SHIPPO
Orphaned young fox-demon who likes to play shape-changing tricks.

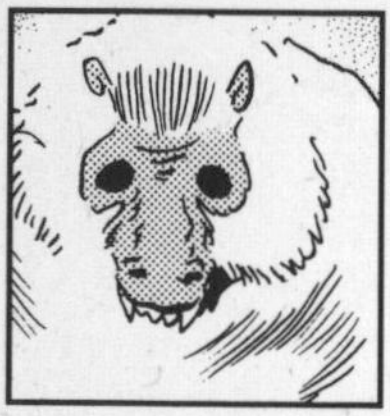

NARAKU
Enigmatic demon-mastermind behind the miseries of nearly everyone in the story.

TÔTÔSAI
Quirky (some might say "crazy") maker of swords—the genius-smith behind both Tetsusaiga and Tenseiga.

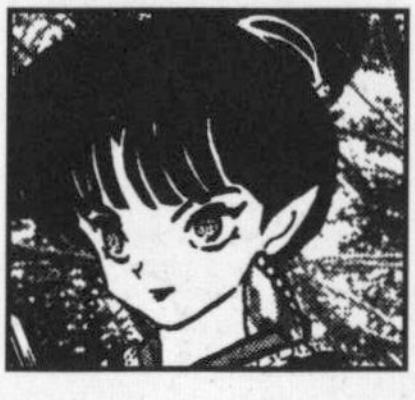

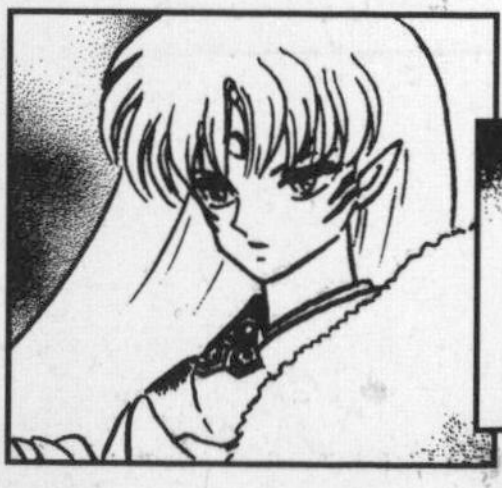

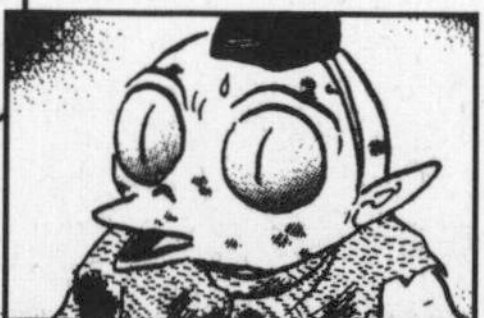

SESSHÔMARU and JAKEN
Inu-Yasha's half-brother, Sesshômaru is the full-demon son of the same father, while Jaken is Sesshômaru's toadying (and toad-ish) henchman.

SCROLL ONE
SUSPICION

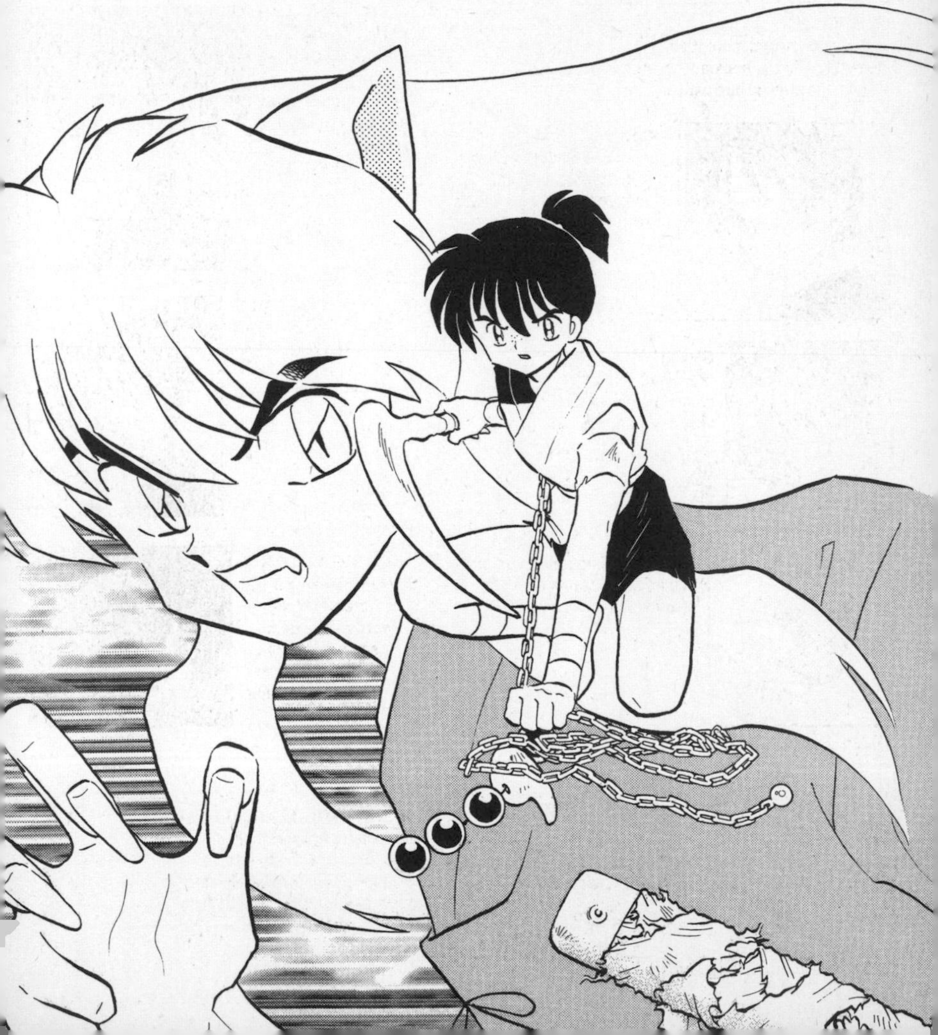

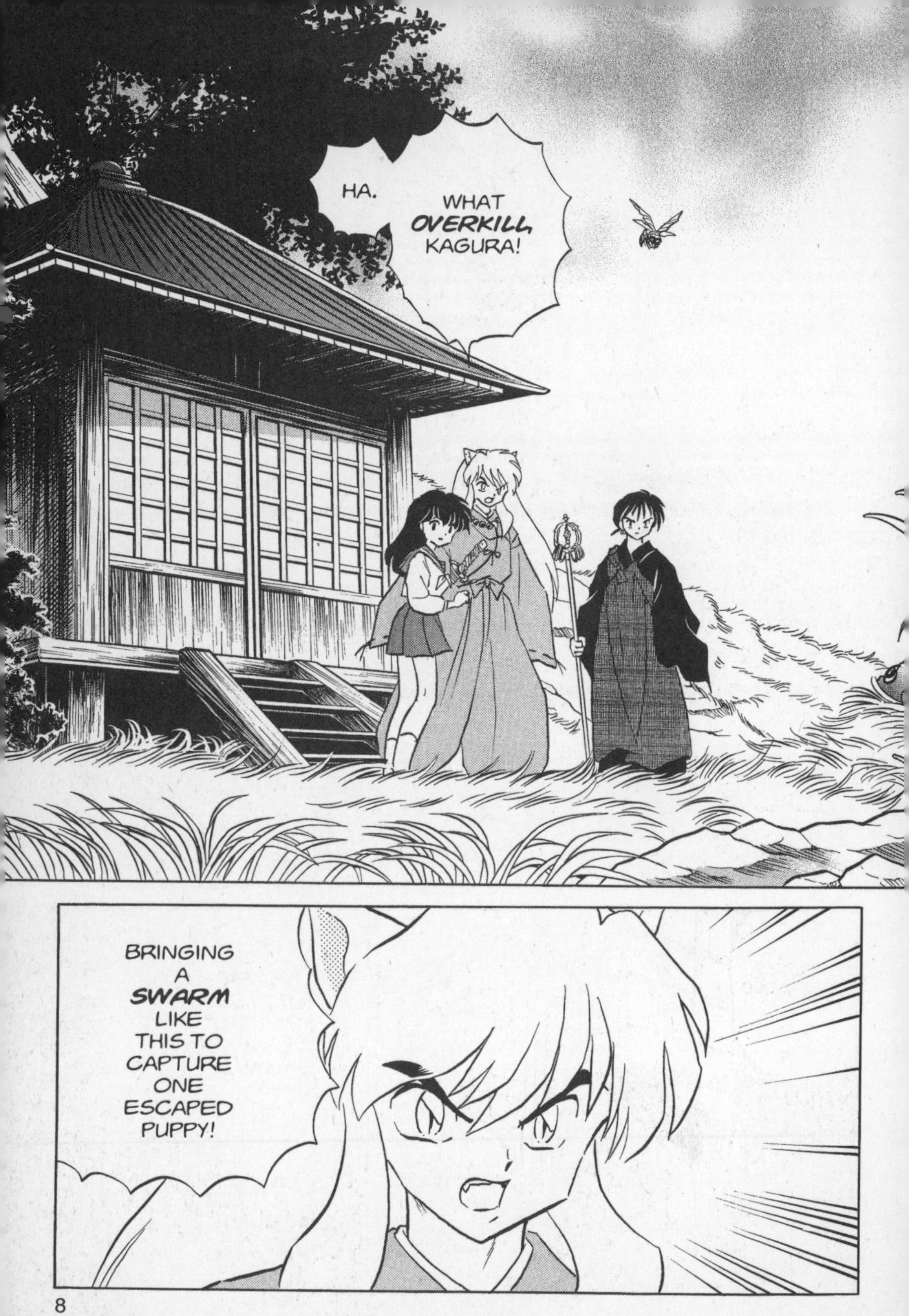
HA.
WHAT OVERKILL, KAGURA!
BRINGING A SWARM LIKE THIS TO CAPTURE ONE ESCAPED PUPPY!

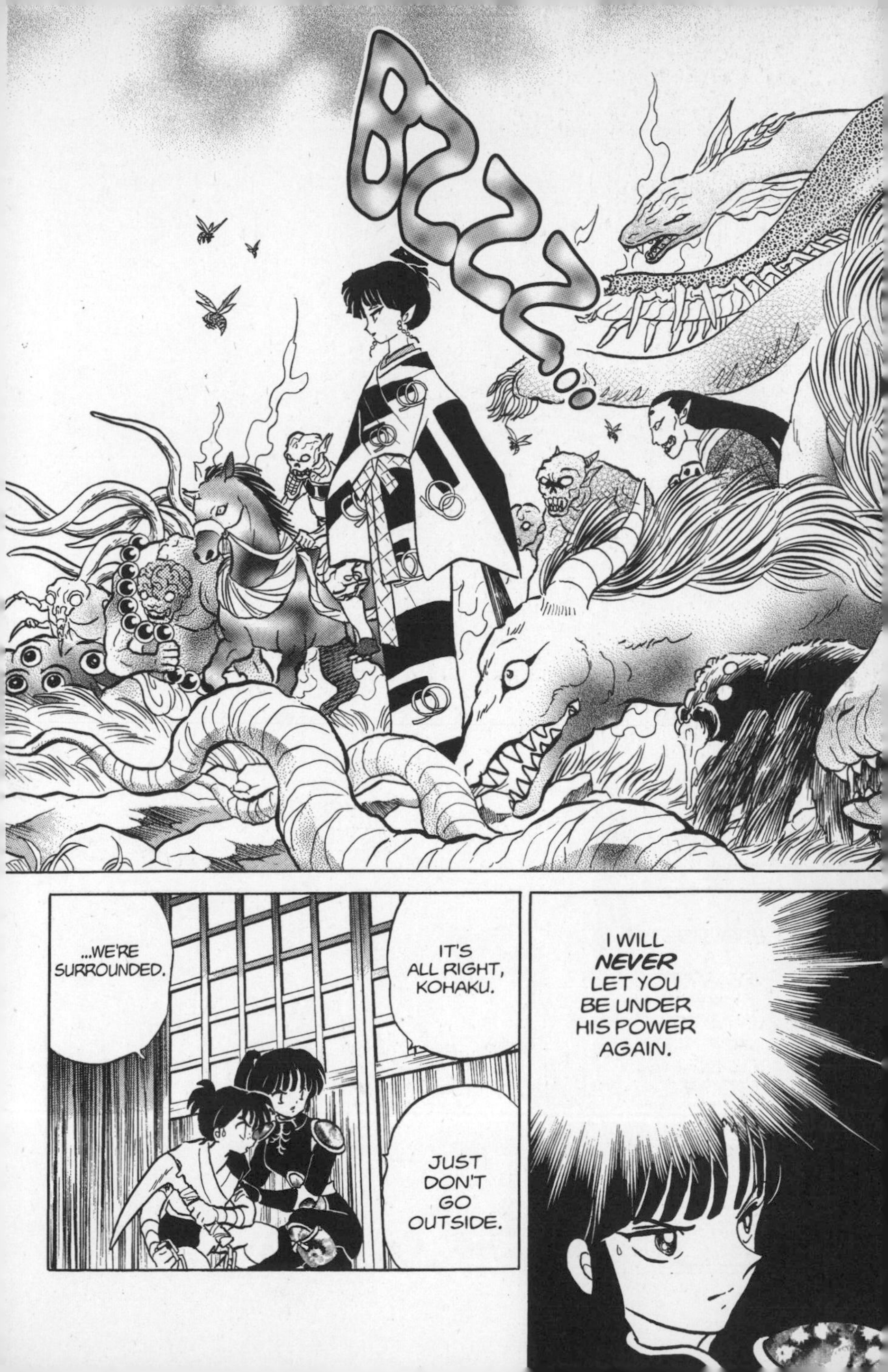
BZZZ...
...WE'RE SURROUNDED.
IT'S ALL RIGHT, KOHAKU.
JUST DON'T GO OUTSIDE.
I WILL NEVER LET YOU BE UNDER HIS POWER AGAIN.

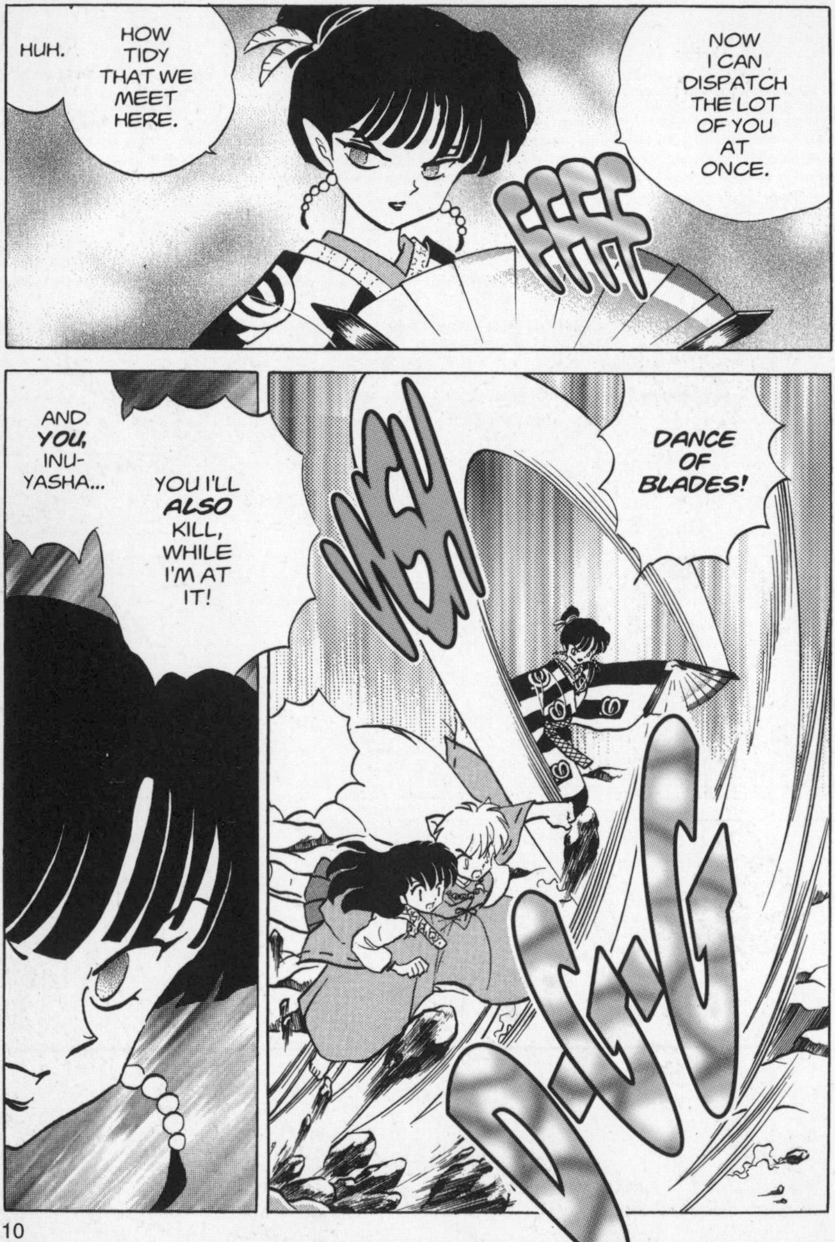
HUH.
HOW TIDY THAT WE MEET HERE.
NOW I CAN DISPATCH THE LOT OF YOU AT ONCE.
AND **YOU,** INU-YASHA...
YOU I'LL **ALSO** KILL, WHILE I'M AT IT!
DANCE OF BLADES!

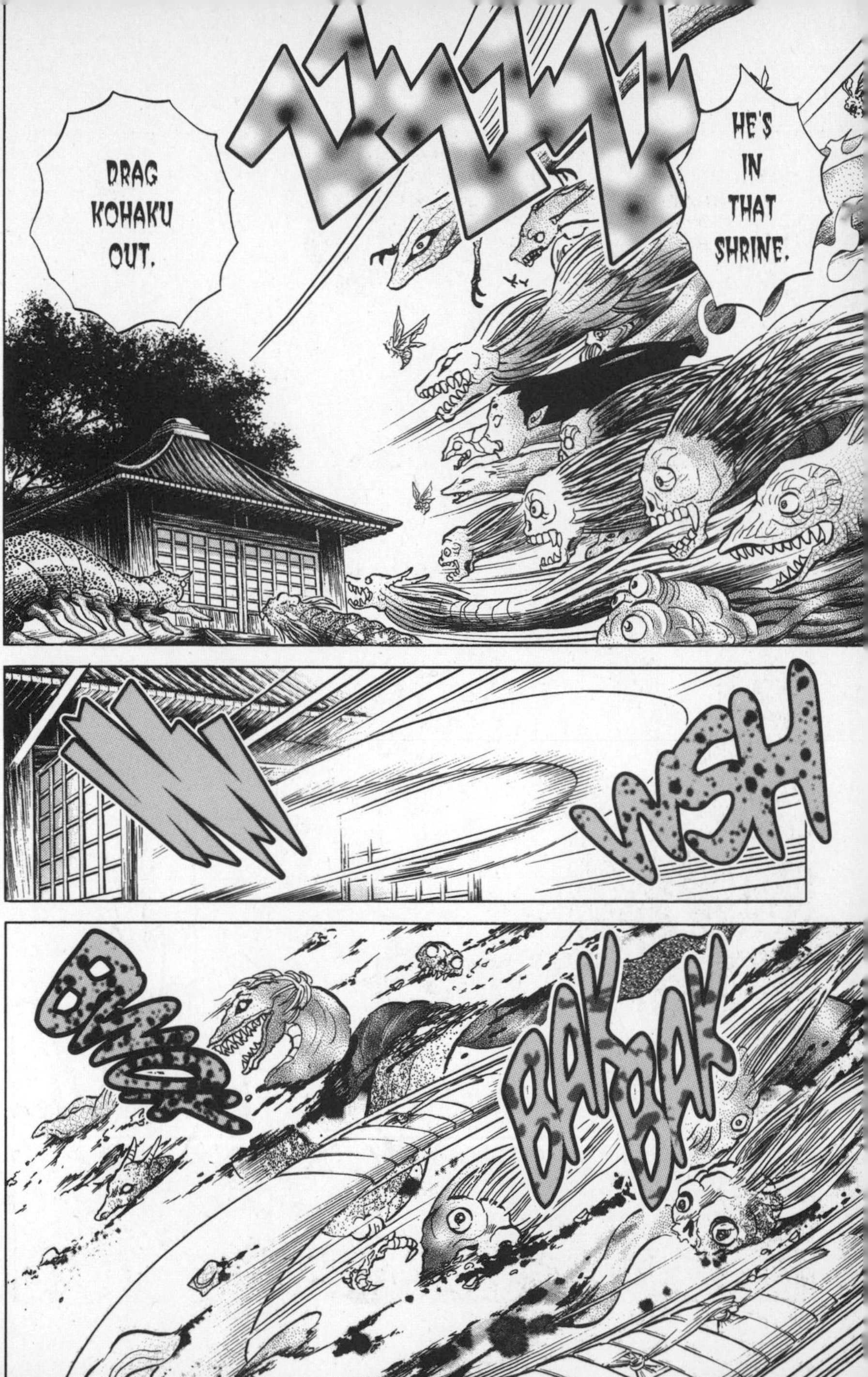
DRAG KOHAKU OUT.
HE'S IN THAT SHRINE.
WSH

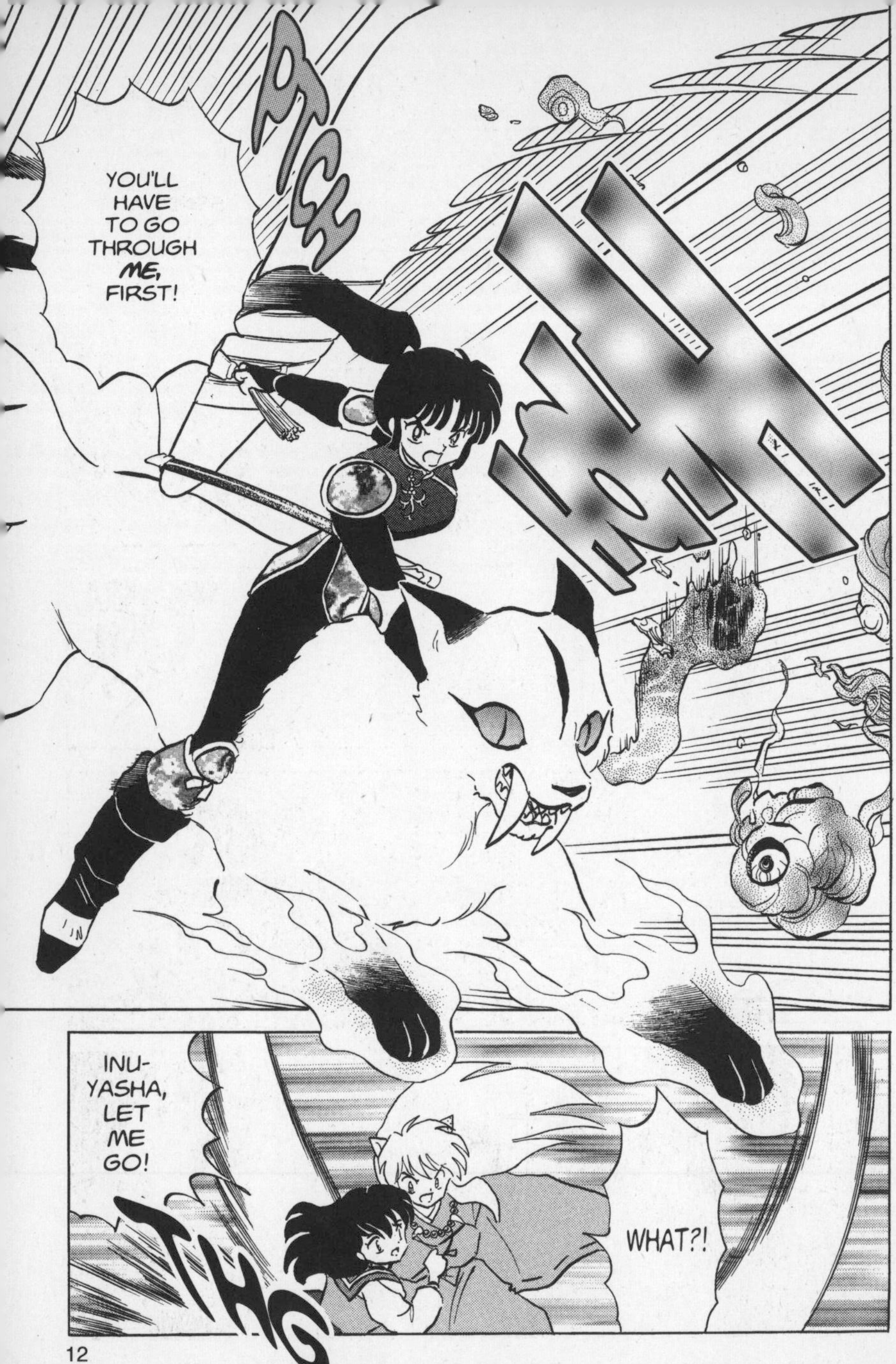
YOU'LL HAVE TO GO THROUGH *ME*, FIRST!
INU-YASHA, LET ME GO!
WHAT?!

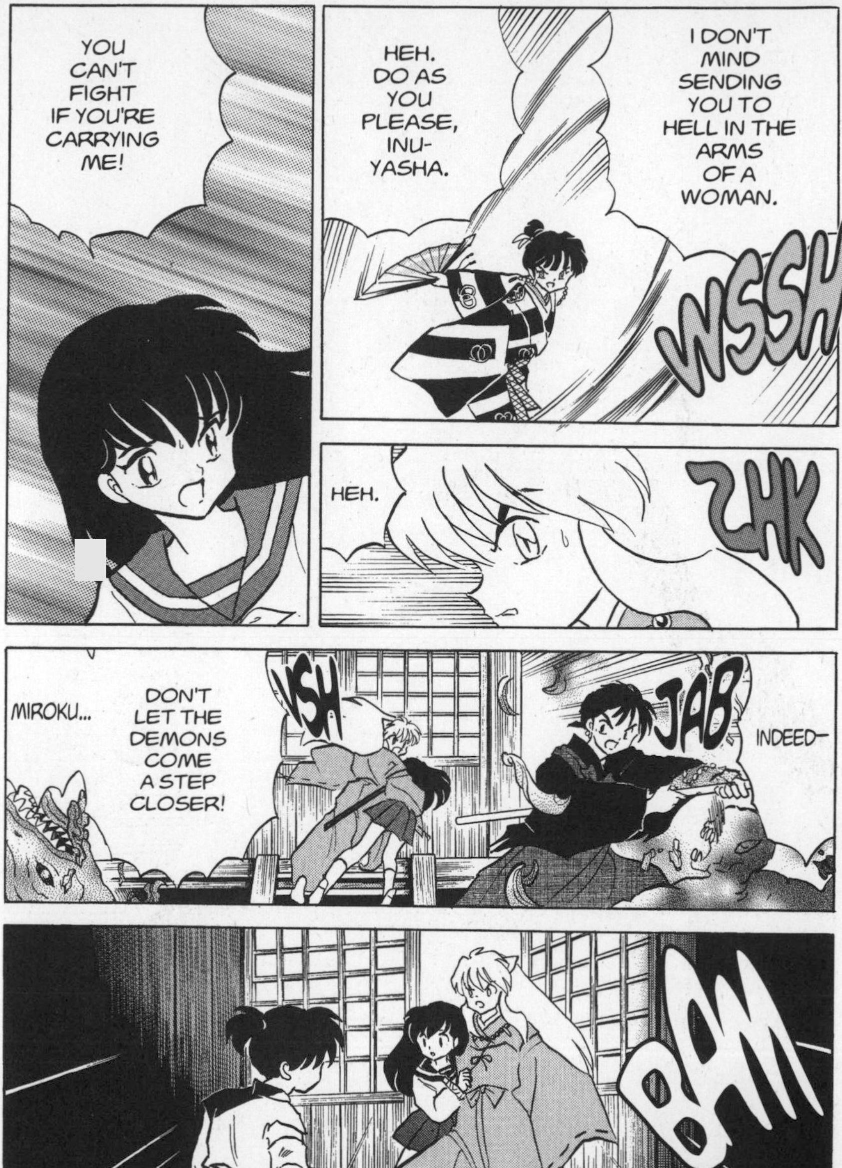
YOU CAN'T FIGHT IF YOU'RE CARRYING ME!
HEH. DO AS YOU PLEASE, INU-YASHA.
I DON'T MIND SENDING YOU TO HELL IN THE ARMS OF A WOMAN.
WSSH
HEH.
ZHK
MIROKU...
DON'T LET THE DEMONS COME A STEP CLOSER!
WSH
JAB
INDEED—
BAM

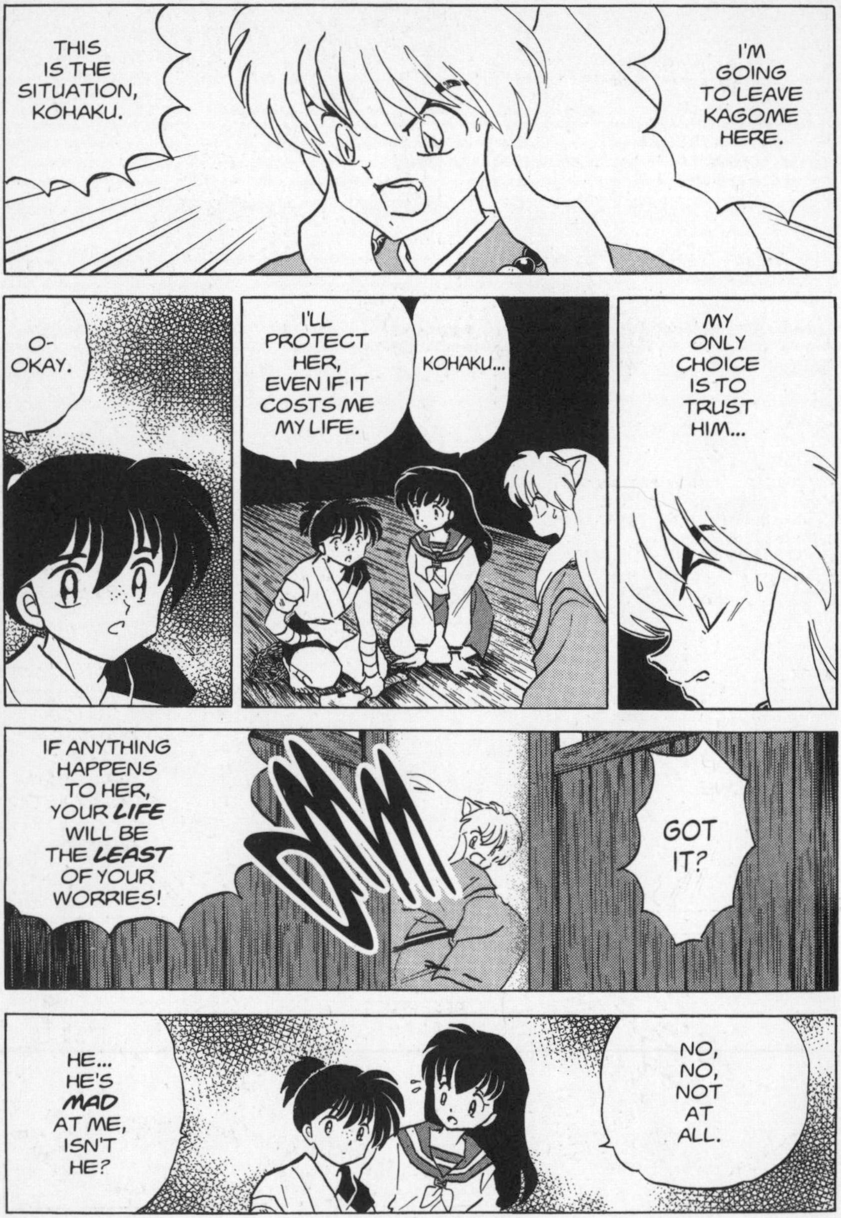
THIS IS THE SITUATION, KOHAKU.
I'M GOING TO LEAVE KAGOME HERE.
O-OKAY.
I'LL PROTECT HER, EVEN IF IT COSTS ME MY LIFE.
KOHAKU...
MY ONLY CHOICE IS TO TRUST HIM...
IF ANYTHING HAPPENS TO HER, YOUR *LIFE* WILL BE THE *LEAST* OF YOUR WORRIES!
GOT IT?
HE... HE'S *MAD* AT ME, ISN'T HE?
NO, NO, NOT AT ALL.

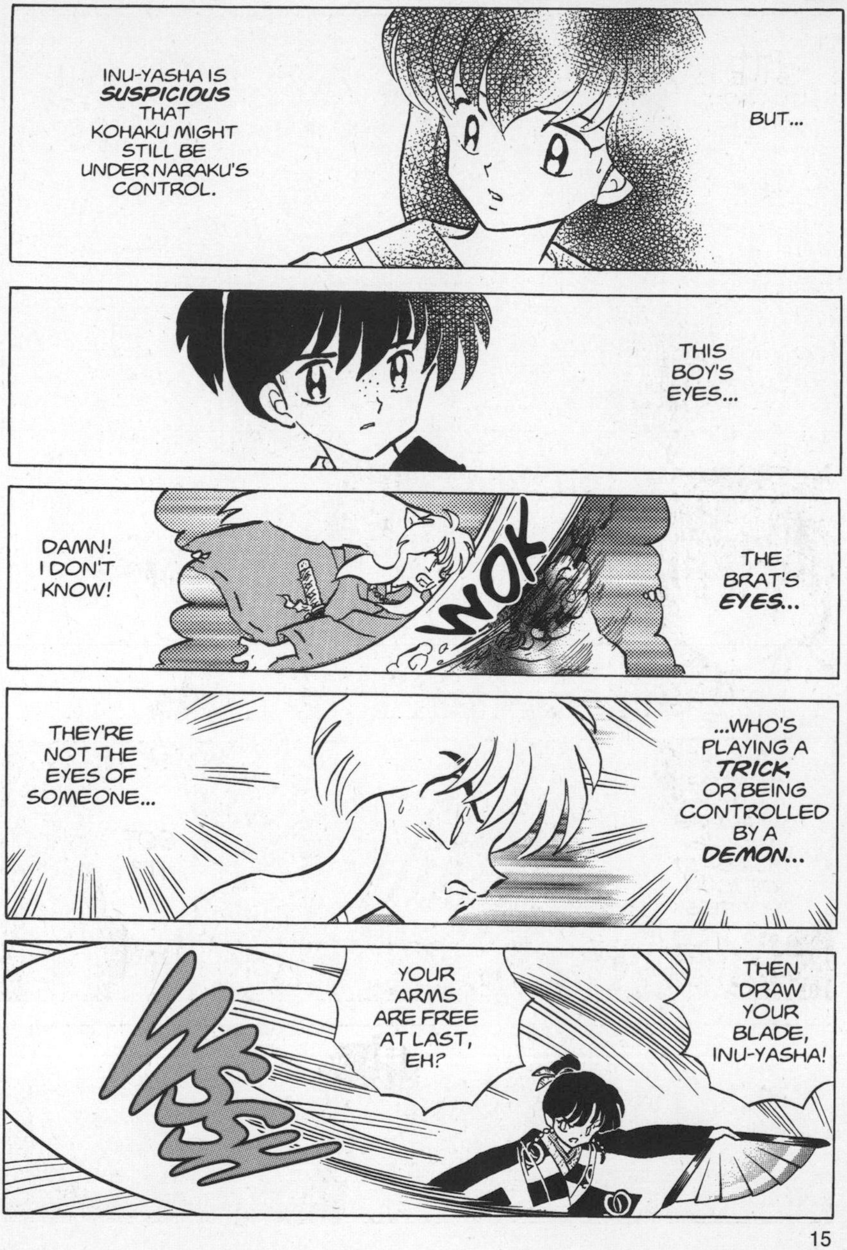
INU-YASHA IS SUSPICIOUS THAT KOHAKU MIGHT STILL BE UNDER NARAKU'S CONTROL.
BUT...
THIS BOY'S EYES...
DAMN! I DON'T KNOW!
WOK
THE BRAT'S EYES...
THEY'RE NOT THE EYES OF SOMEONE...
...WHO'S PLAYING A TRICK, OR BEING CONTROLLED BY A DEMON...
YOUR ARMS ARE FREE AT LAST, EH?
THEN DRAW YOUR BLADE, INU-YASHA!

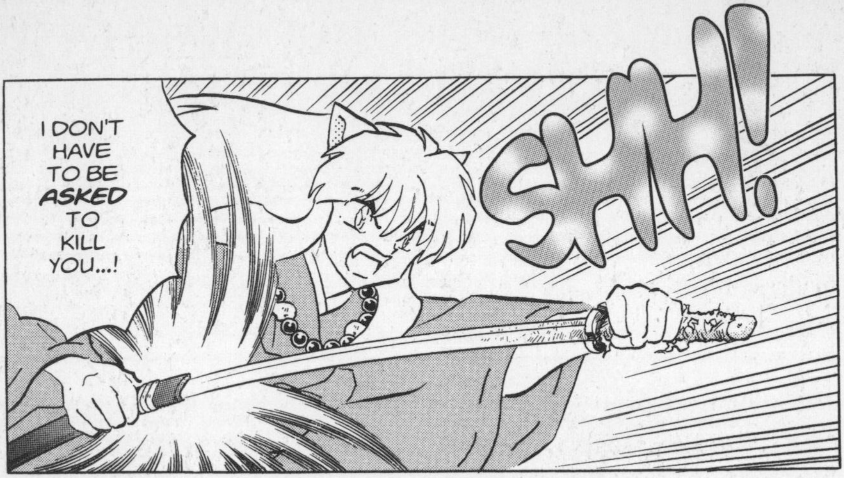
I DON'T HAVE TO BE ***ASKED*** TO KILL YOU...!
SHH!!

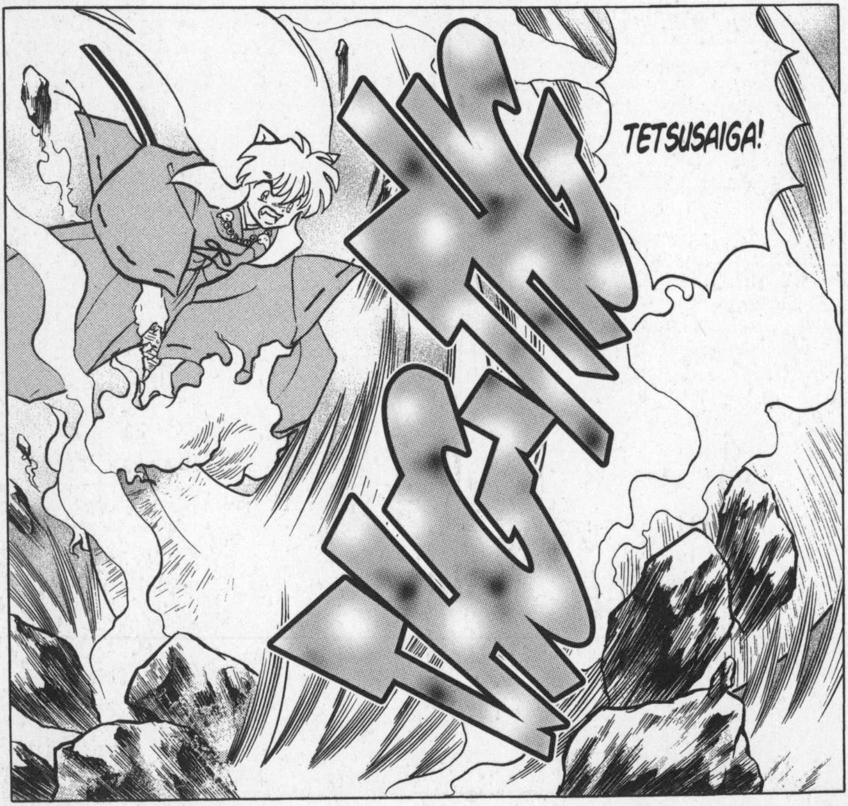
TETSUSAIGA!

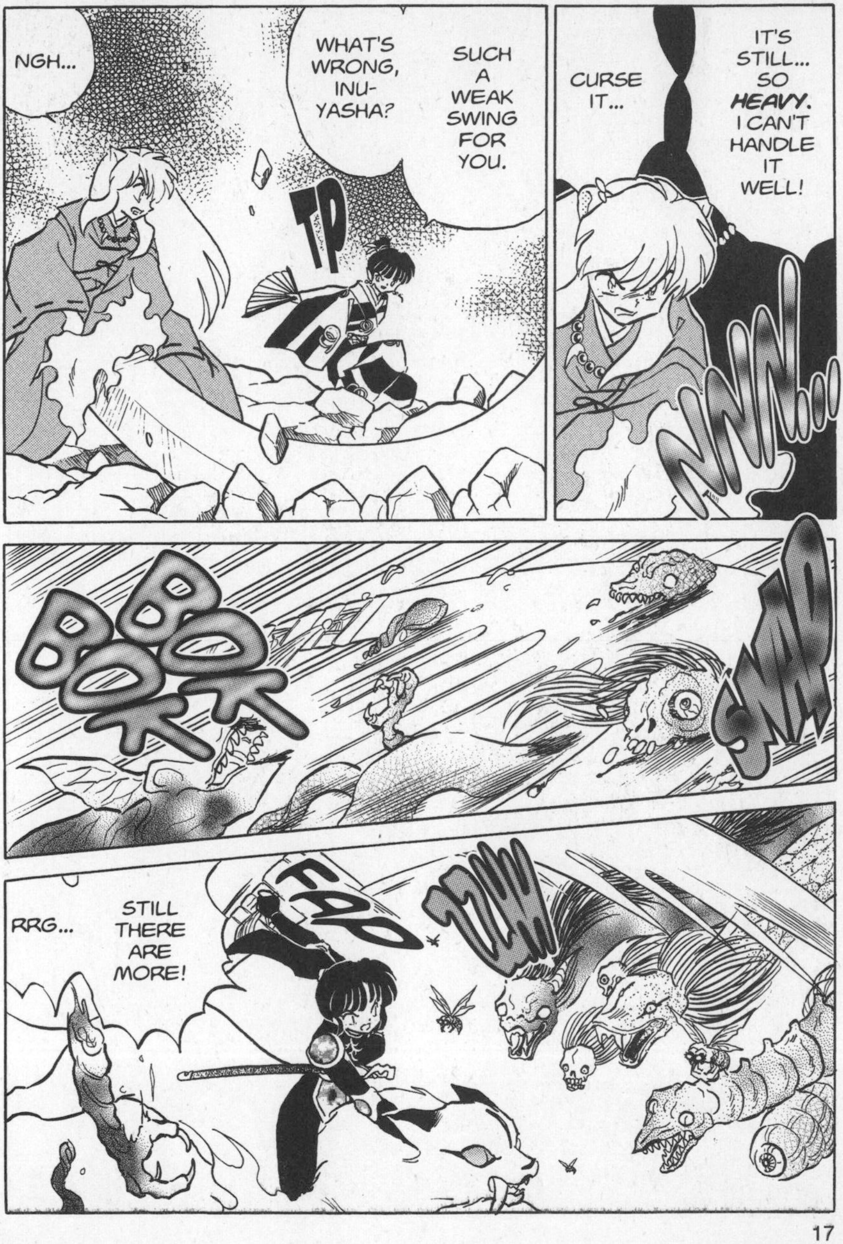
NGH...
WHAT'S WRONG, INU-YASHA?
SUCH A WEAK SWING FOR YOU.
TP
CURSE IT...
IT'S STILL... SO *HEAVY*. I CAN'T HANDLE IT WELL!
NNN...
BOK BOK
SNAP
RRG...
STILL THERE ARE MORE!
FAP
ZZWH

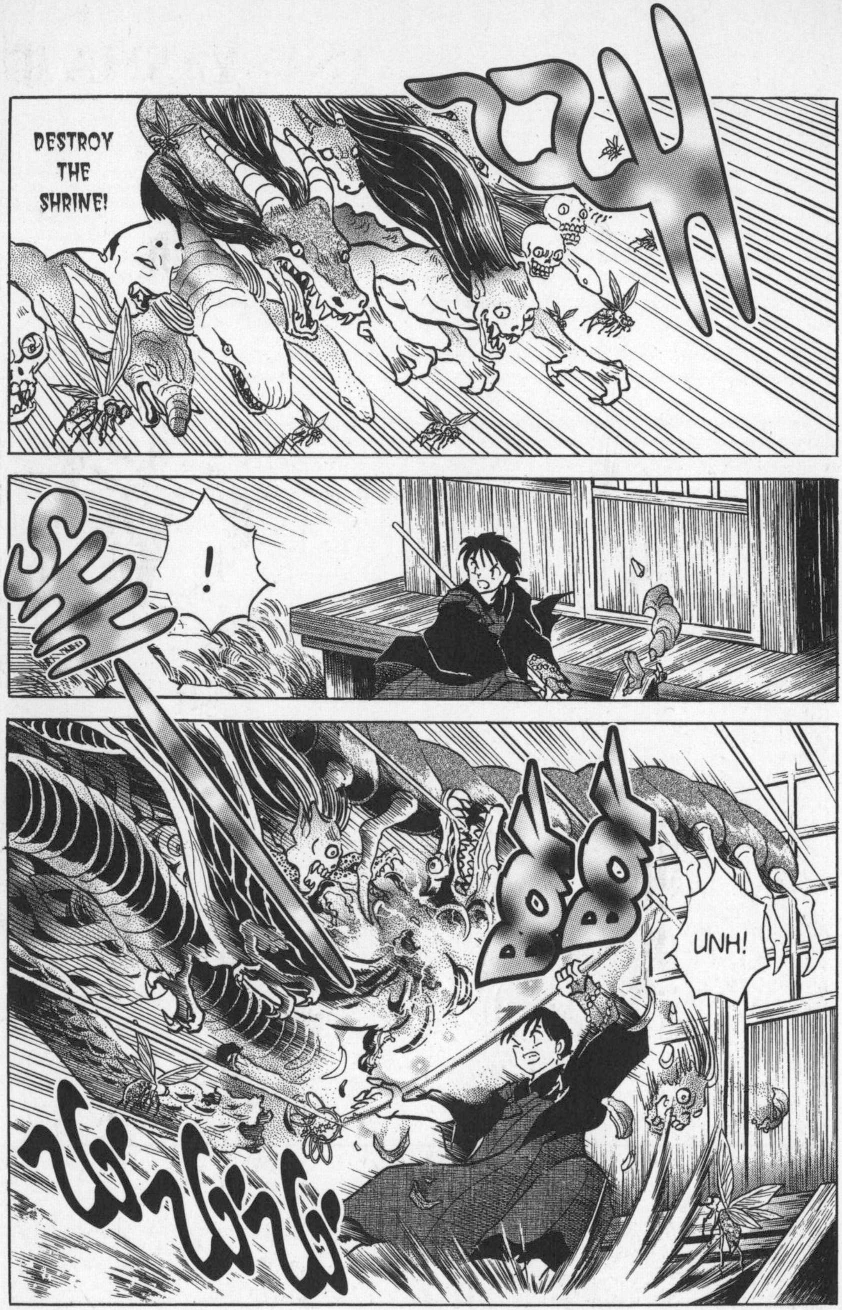
DESTROY THE SHRINE!
!
UNH!

MIROKU!

DON'T BE GETTING DISTRACTED!

VSH

NG!

D-DO

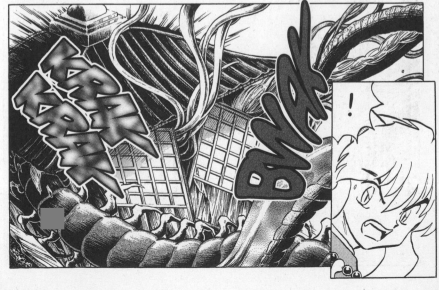

KRAK KRAK

BWAK

!

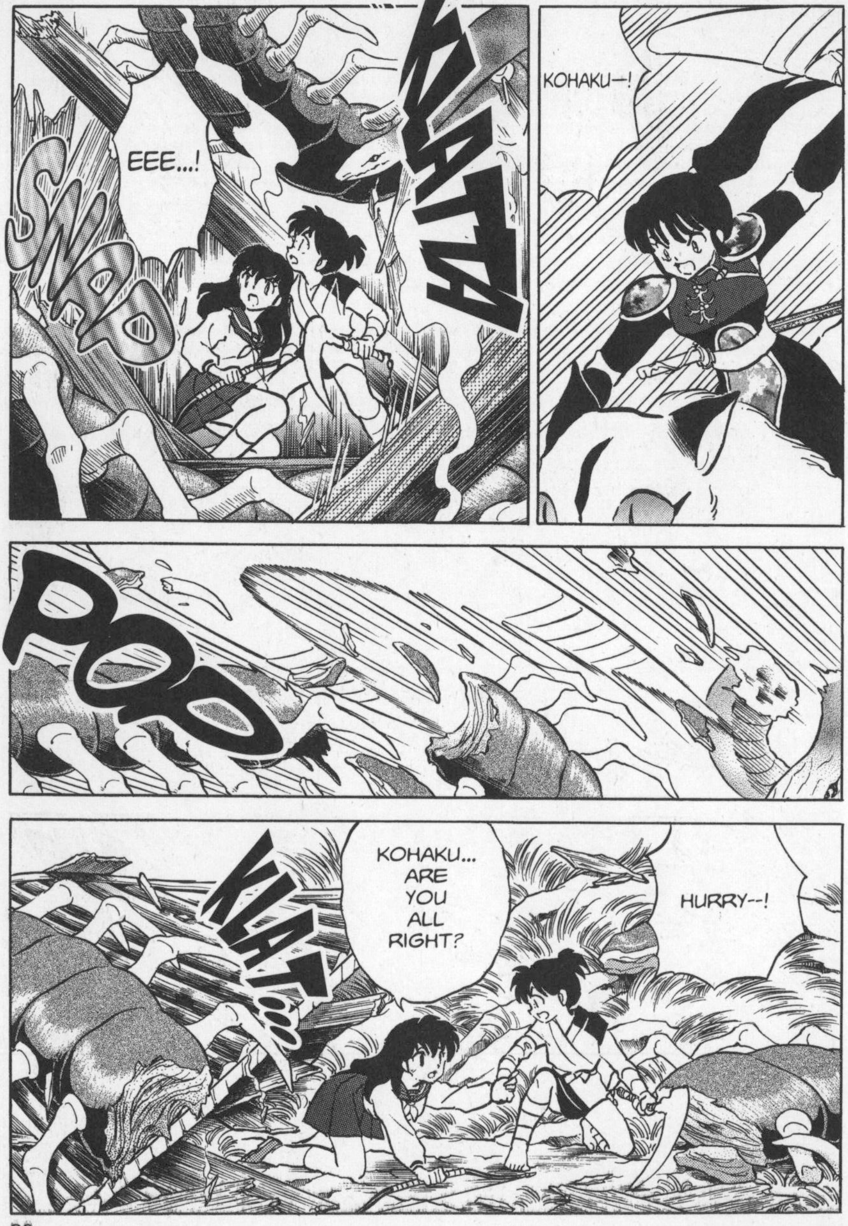
SNAP
EEE...!
KATATA
KOHAKU—!
POP
KLAT...
KOHAKU... ARE YOU ALL RIGHT?
HURRY--!

SSWP

YOU'LL NEVER ESCAPE US!

UGH!

ZSH

DON'T LET THEM GO...

ZSH

AFTER THEM!

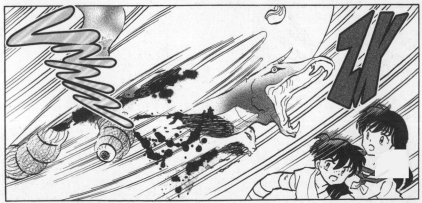

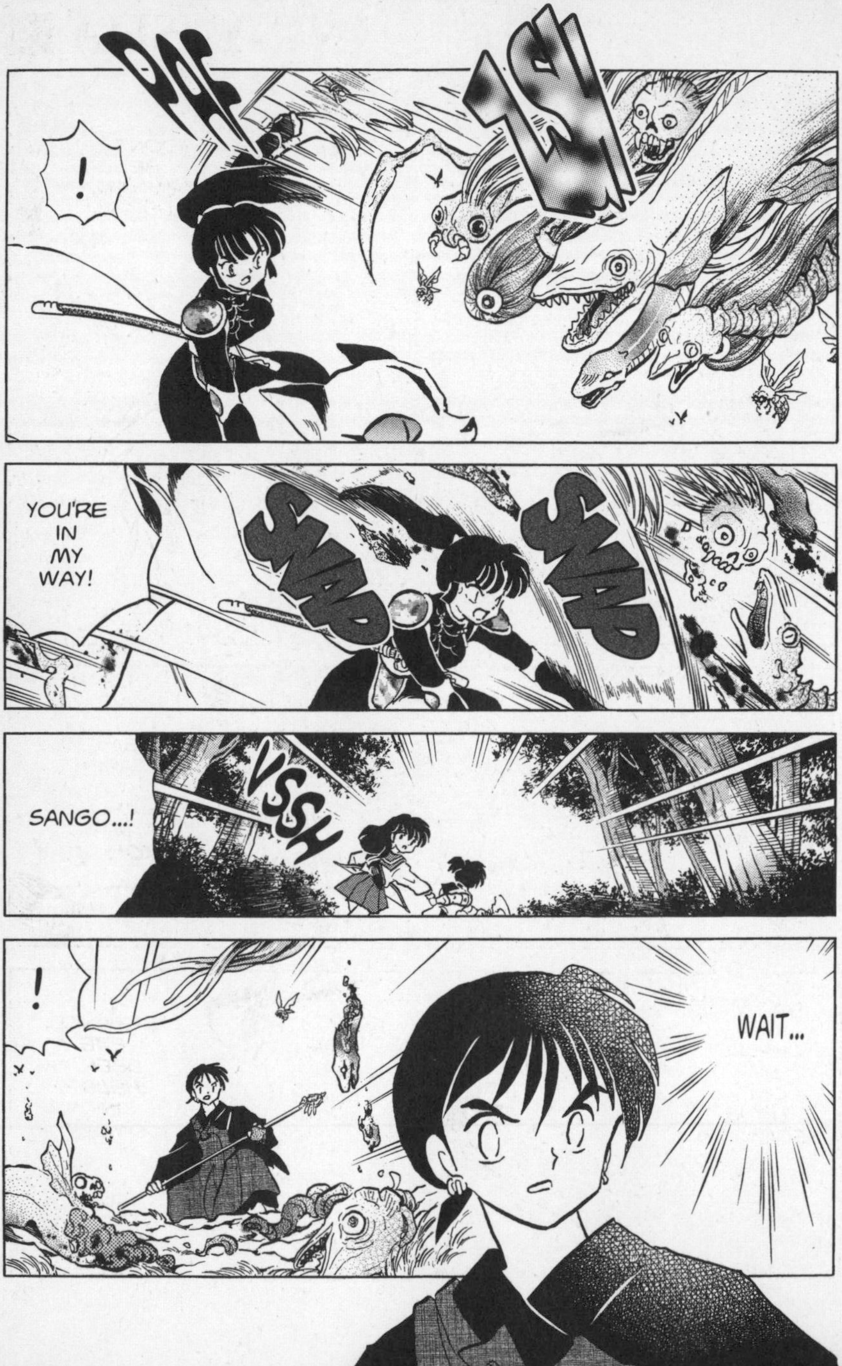
!
YOU'RE IN MY WAY!
SNAP
SNAP
SANGO...!
VSSH
!
WAIT...

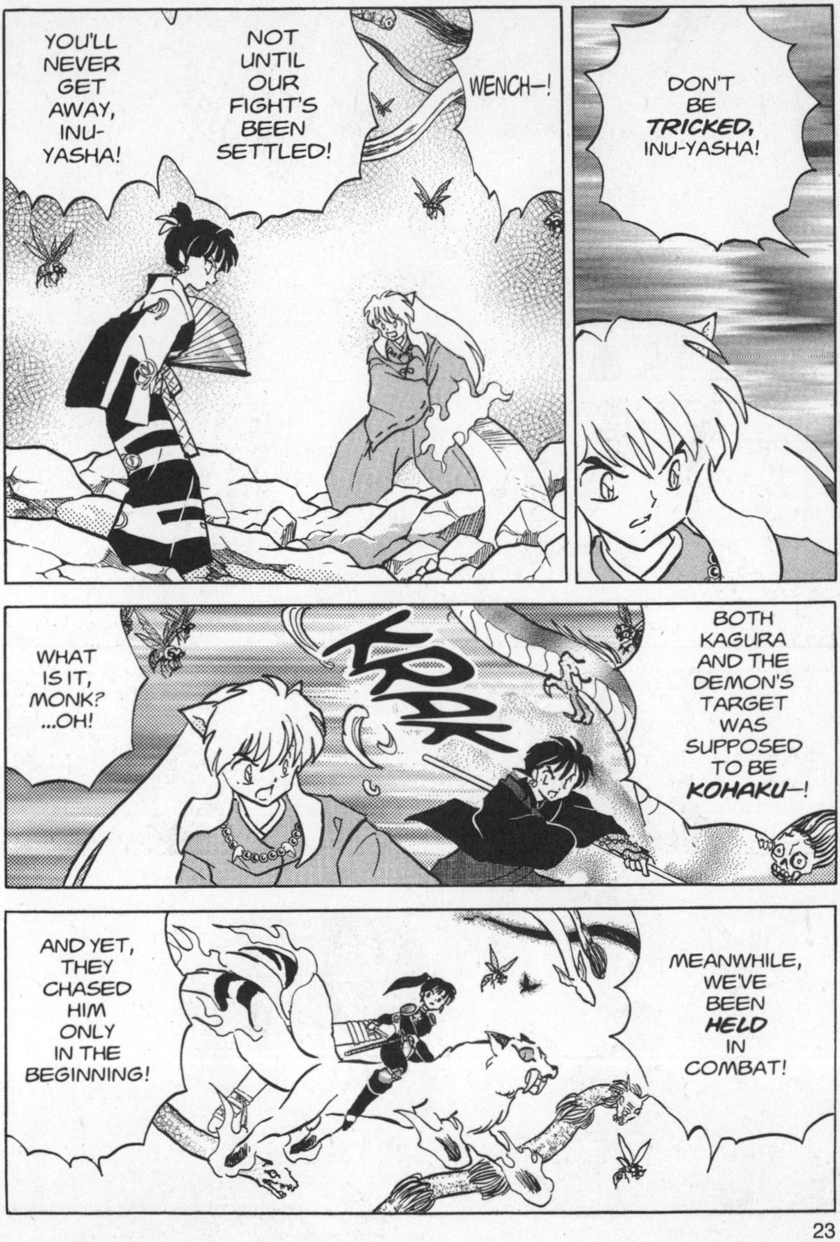
YOU'LL NEVER GET AWAY, INU-YASHA!
NOT UNTIL OUR FIGHT'S BEEN SETTLED!
WENCH—!
DON'T BE TRICKED, INU-YASHA!
WHAT IS IT, MONK? ...OH!
KRAK
BOTH KAGURA AND THE DEMON'S TARGET WAS SUPPOSED TO BE KOHAKU—!
AND YET, THEY CHASED HIM ONLY IN THE BEGINNING!
MEANWHILE, WE'VE BEEN HELD IN COMBAT!

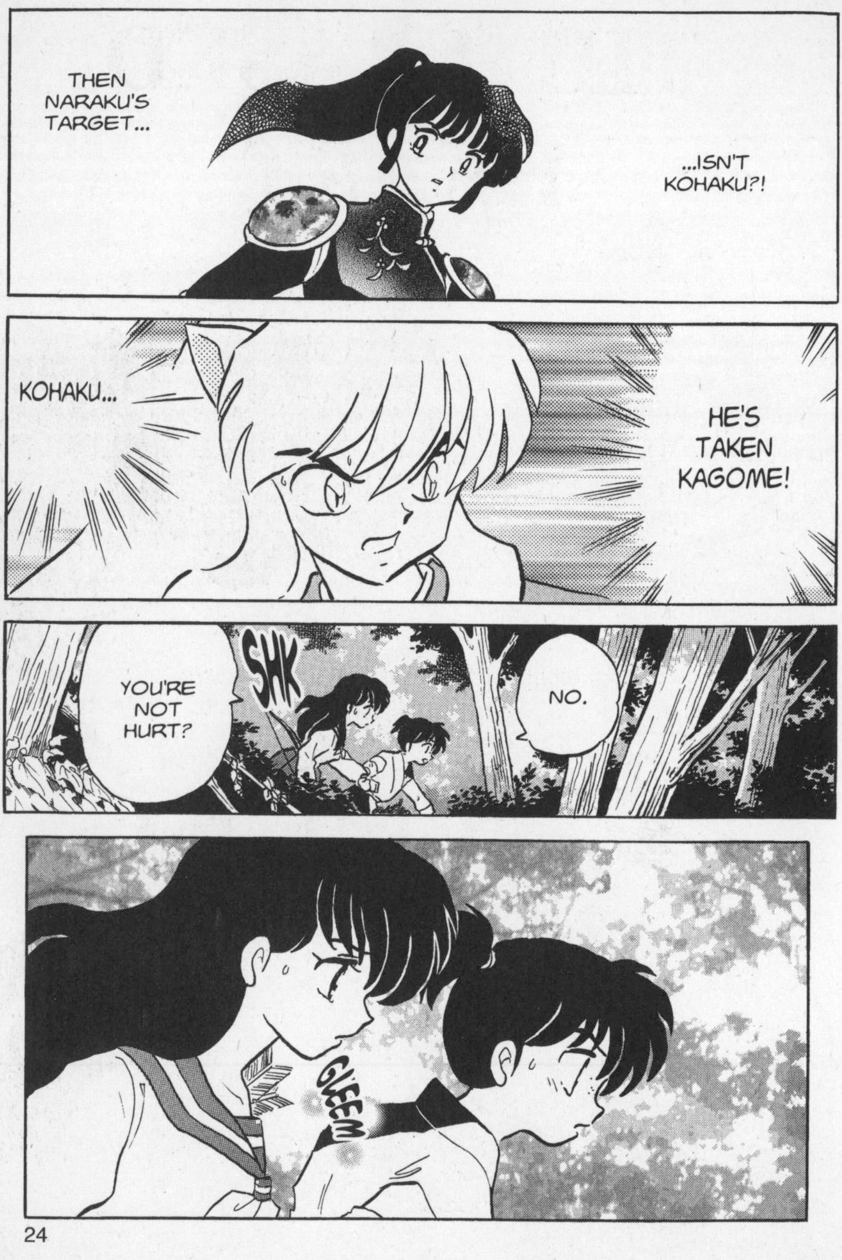

THEN NARAKU'S TARGET...
...ISN'T KOHAKU?!
KOHAKU...
HE'S TAKEN KAGOME!
YOU'RE NOT HURT?
SHK
NO.
GLEEM

SCROLL TWO

THE ERASED HEART

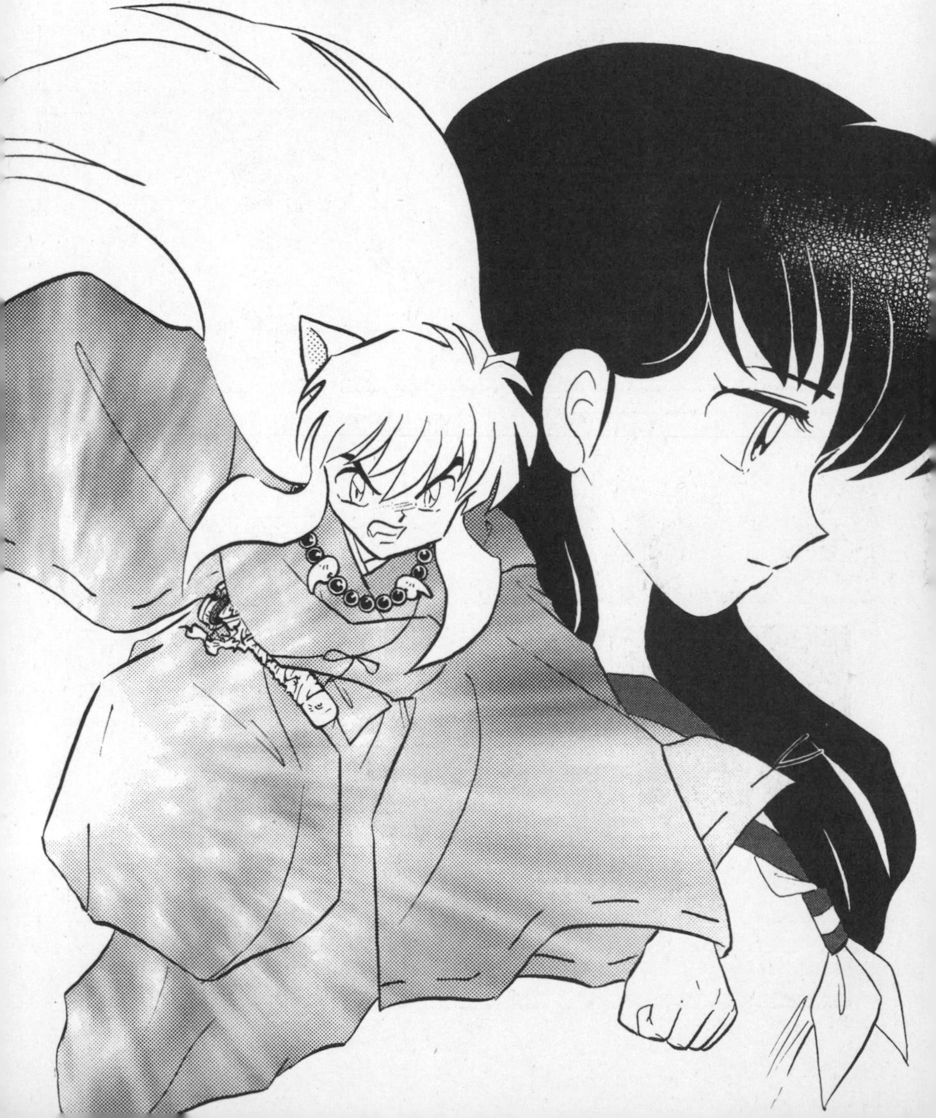

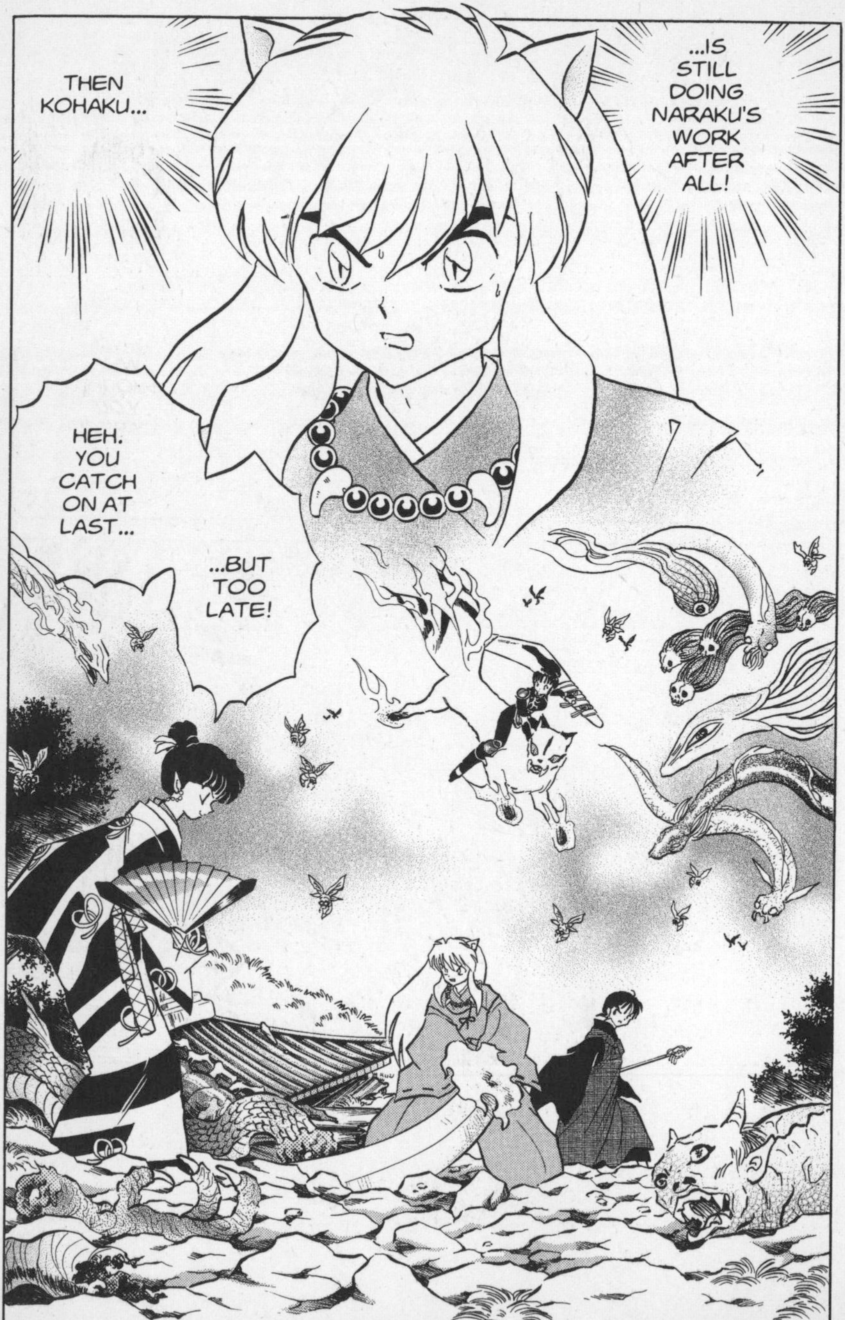
THEN KOHAKU...
...IS STILL DOING NARAKU'S WORK AFTER ALL!
HEH. YOU CATCH ON AT LAST...
...BUT TOO LATE!

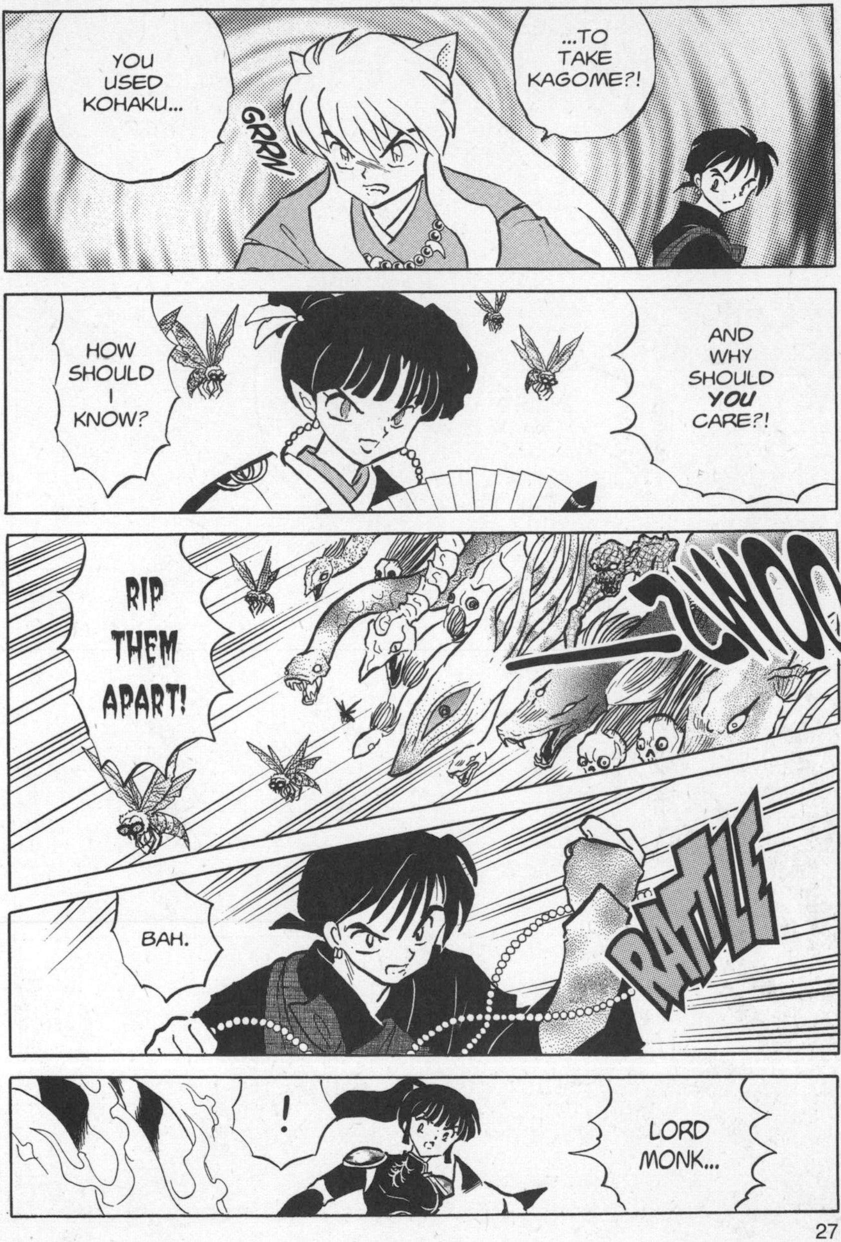
YOU USED KOHAKU...
GRRN
...TO TAKE KAGOME?!
HOW SHOULD I KNOW?
AND WHY SHOULD YOU CARE?!
RIP THEM APART!
ZWOO
BAH.
RATTLE
!
LORD MONK...

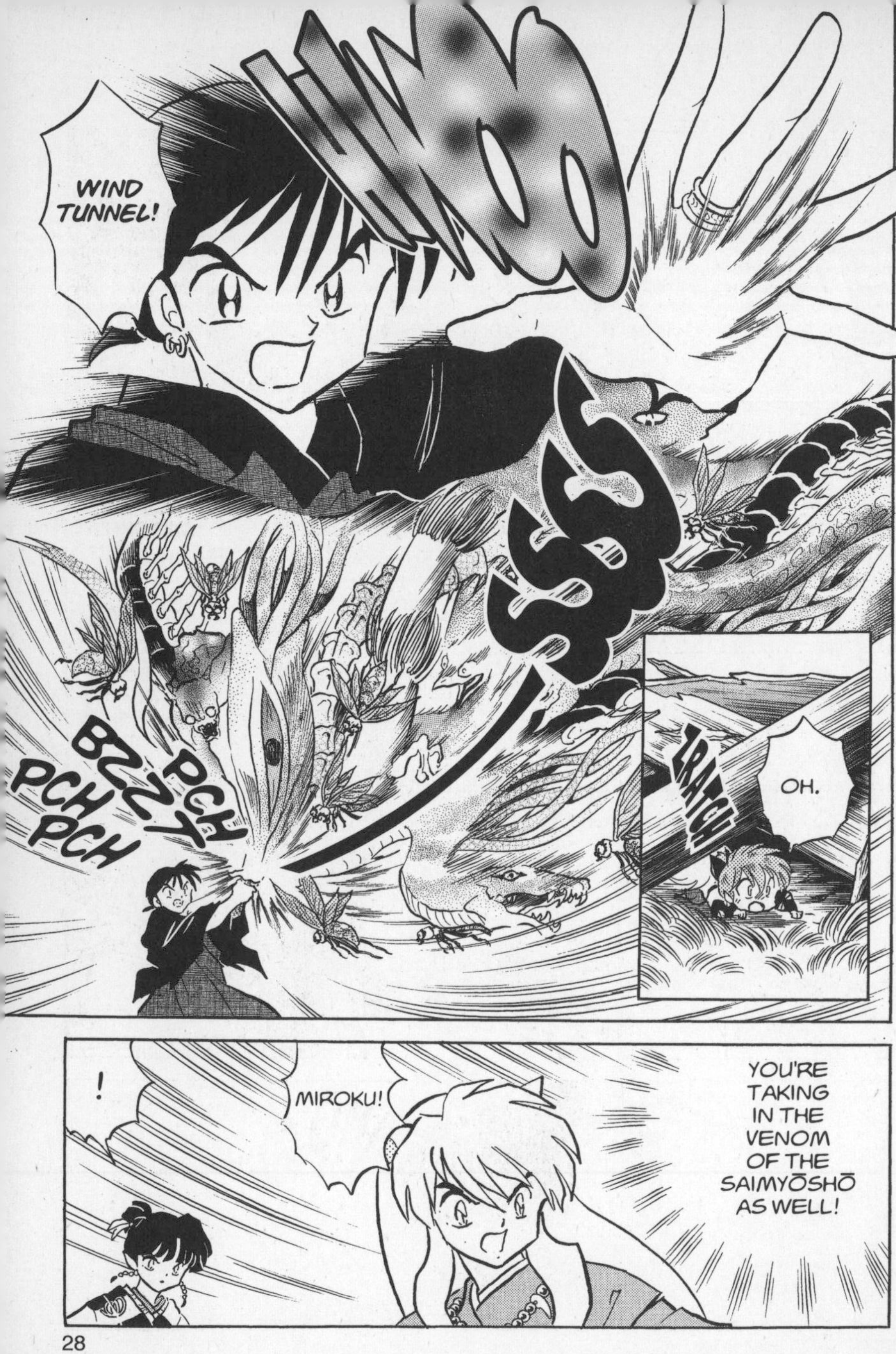
WIND TUNNEL!
PCH
BZZZT
PCH PCH
ZRATCH
OH.
!
MIROKU!
YOU'RE TAKING IN THE VENOM OF THE SAIMYŌSHŌ AS WELL!

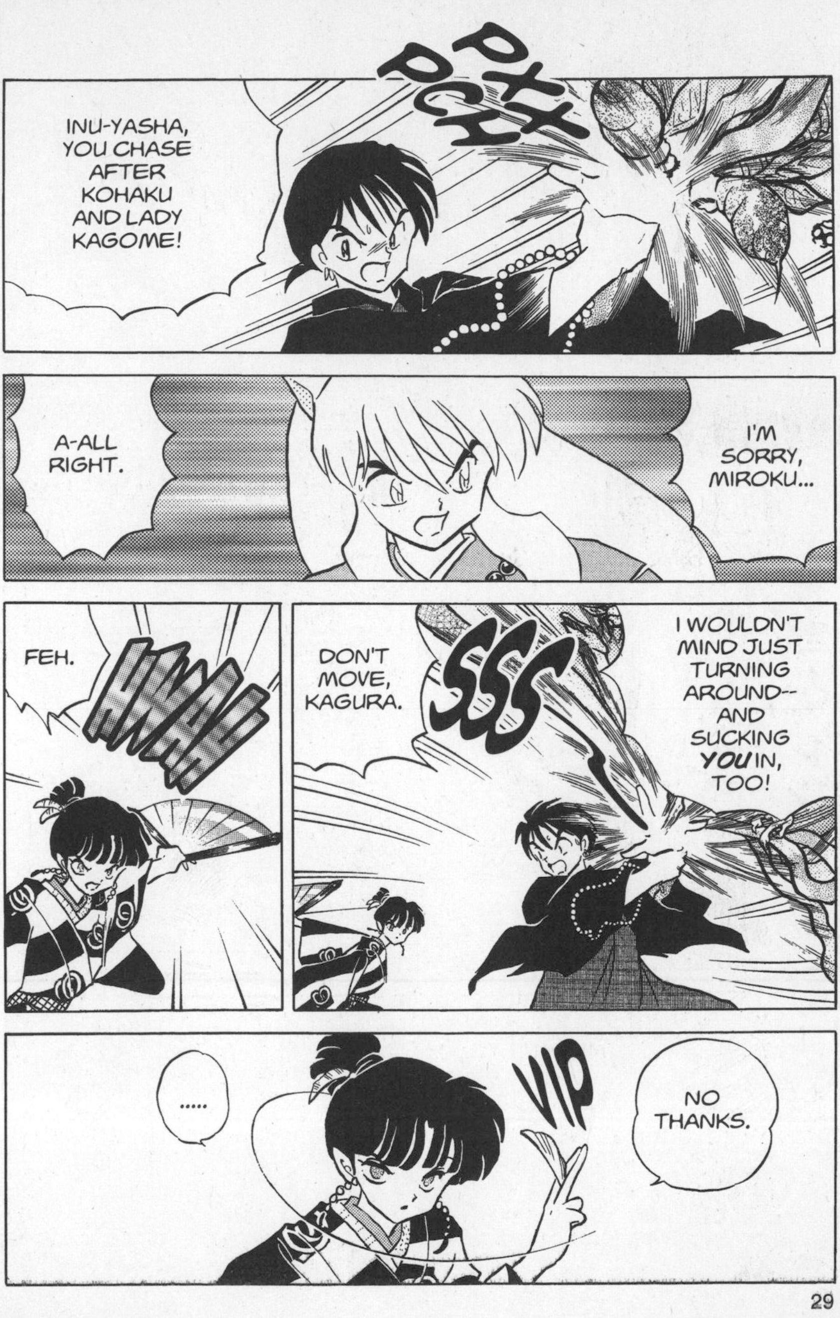
PCH
INU-YASHA, YOU CHASE AFTER KOHAKU AND LADY KAGOME!
A-ALL RIGHT.
I'M SORRY, MIROKU...
FEH.
DON'T MOVE, KAGURA.
SSS
I WOULDN'T MIND JUST TURNING AROUND--AND SUCKING YOU IN, TOO!
......
VIP
NO THANKS.

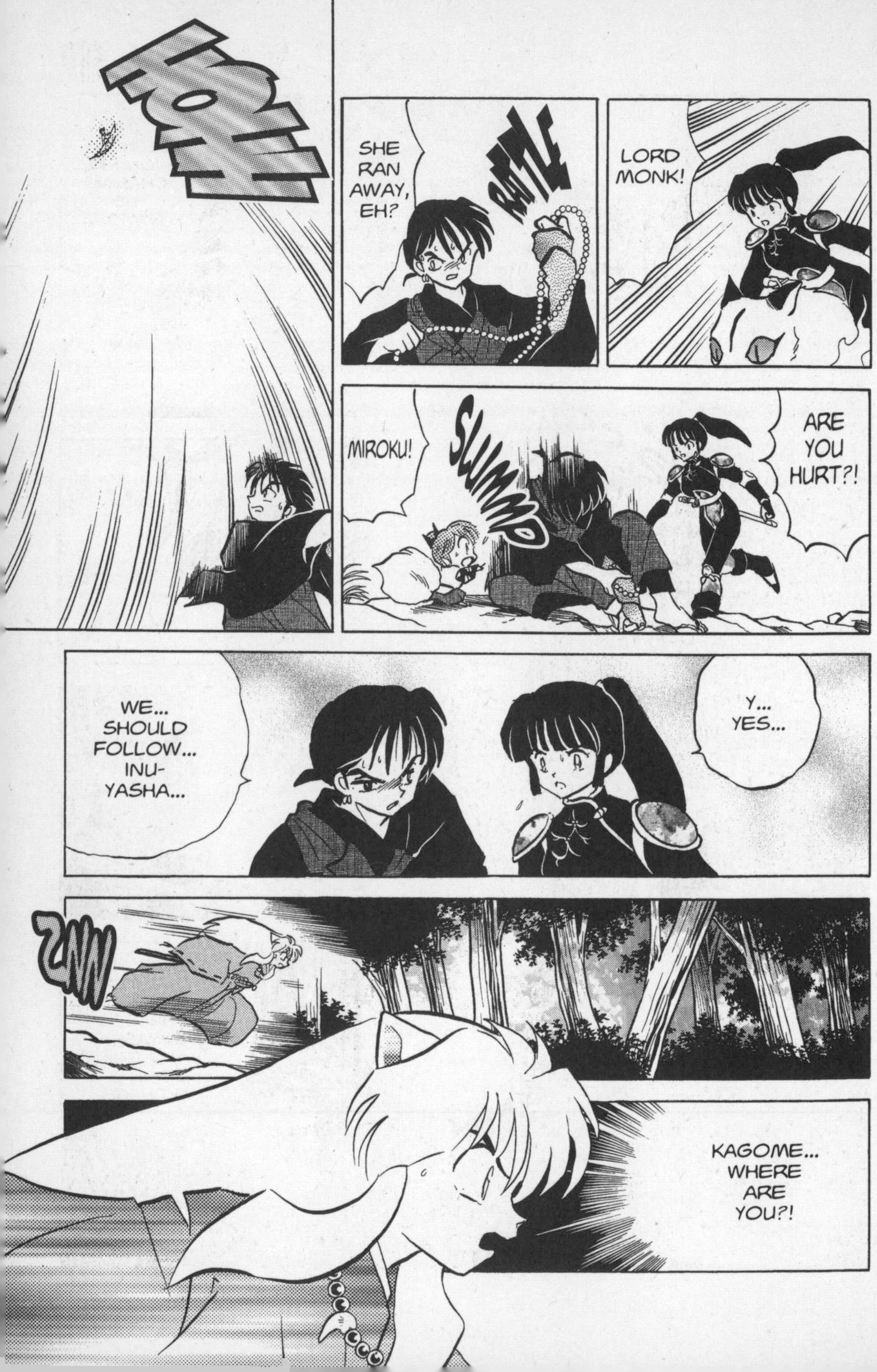
SHE RAN AWAY, EH?
RATTLE
LORD MONK!
MIROKU!
SLUMP
ARE YOU HURT?!
WE... SHOULD FOLLOW... INU-YASHA...
Y... YES...
KAGOME... WHERE ARE YOU?!

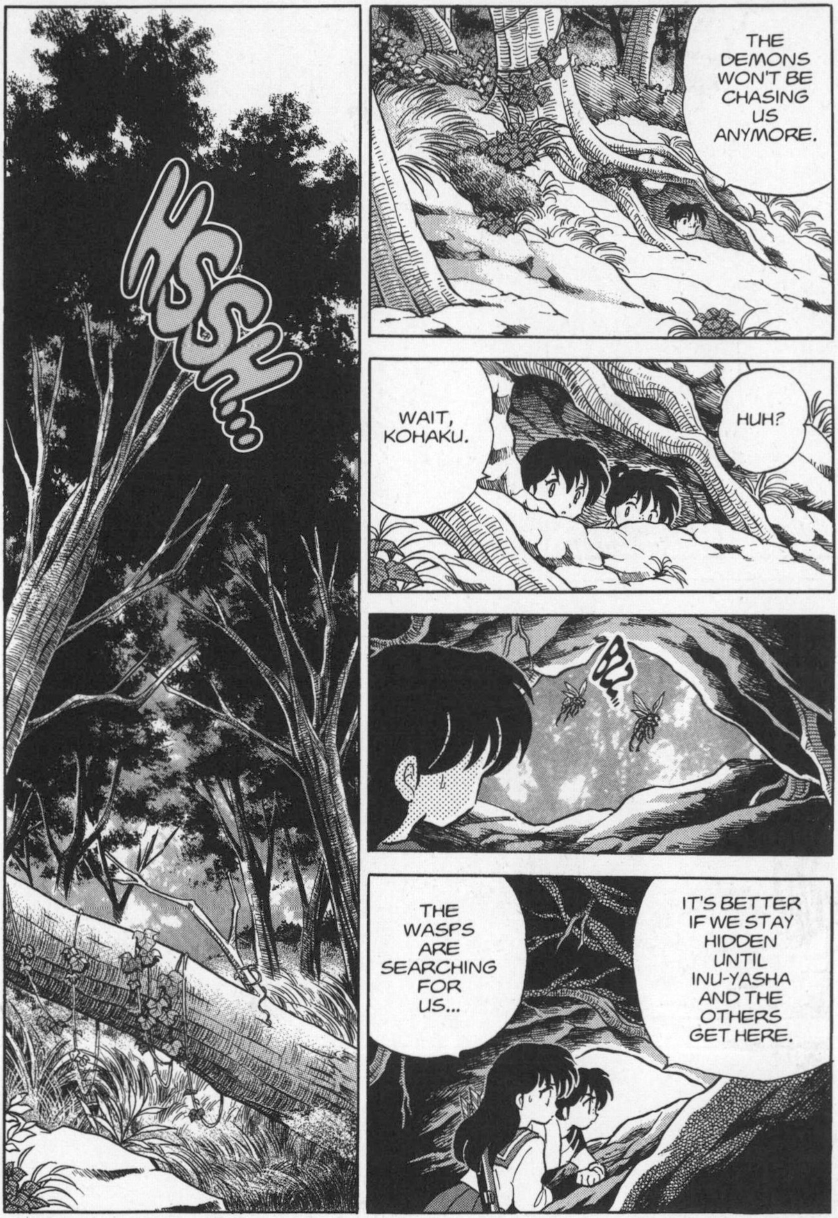
HSSH...
THE DEMONS WON'T BE CHASING US ANYMORE.
WAIT, KOHAKU.
HUH?
THE WASPS ARE SEARCHING FOR US...
IT'S BETTER IF WE STAY HIDDEN UNTIL INU-YASHA AND THE OTHERS GET HERE.

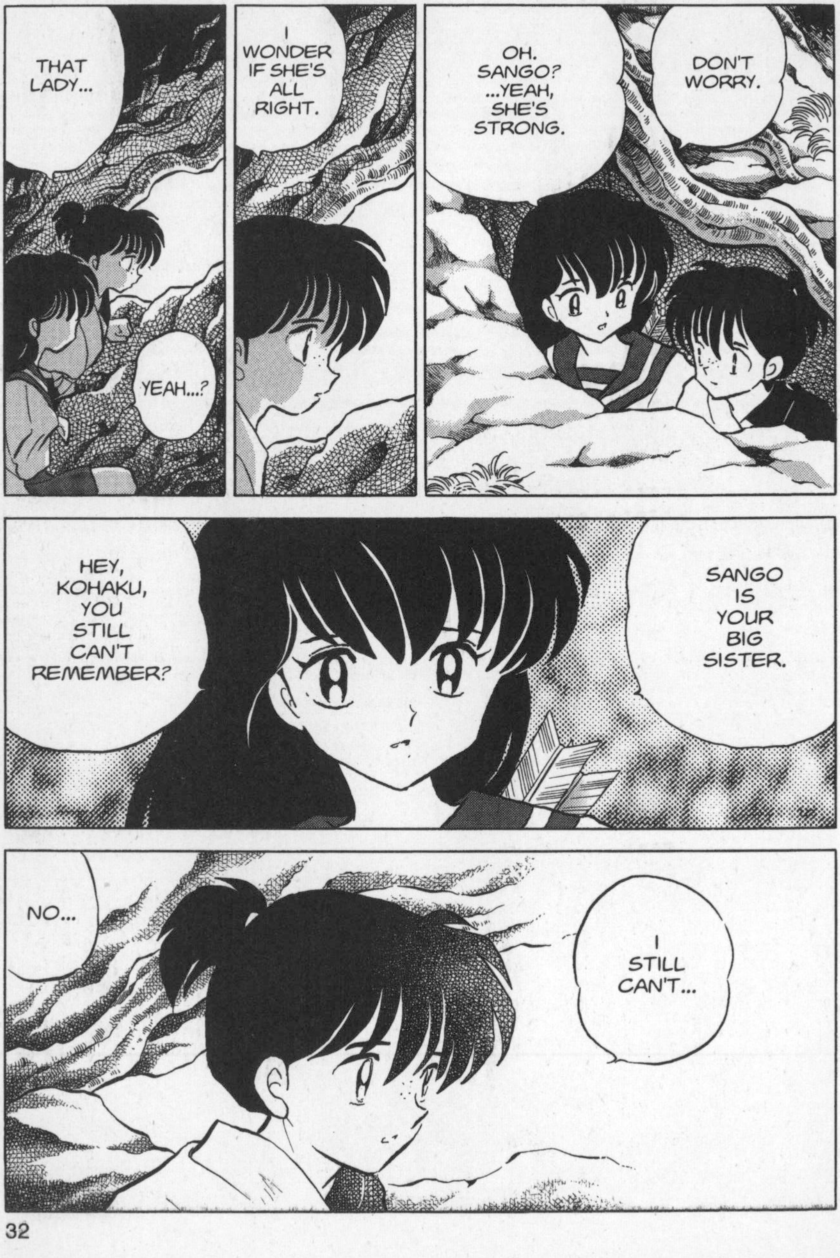
THAT LADY...
YEAH...?
I WONDER IF SHE'S ALL RIGHT.
OH. SANGO? ...YEAH, SHE'S STRONG.
DON'T WORRY.
HEY, KOHAKU, YOU STILL CAN'T REMEMBER?
SANGO IS YOUR BIG SISTER.
NO...
I STILL CAN'T...

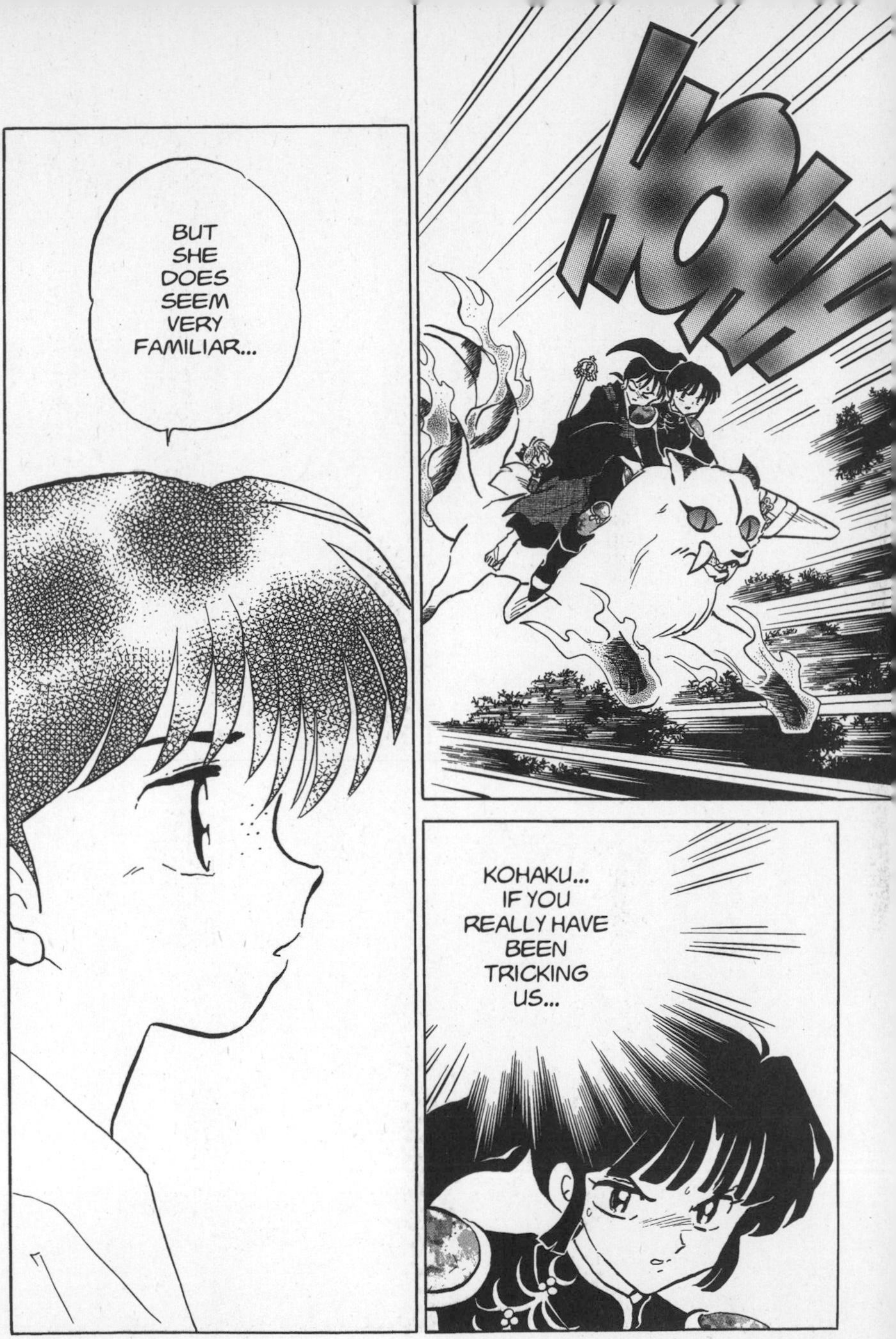
BUT SHE DOES SEEM VERY FAMILIAR...
KOHAKU... IF YOU REALLY HAVE BEEN TRICKING US...

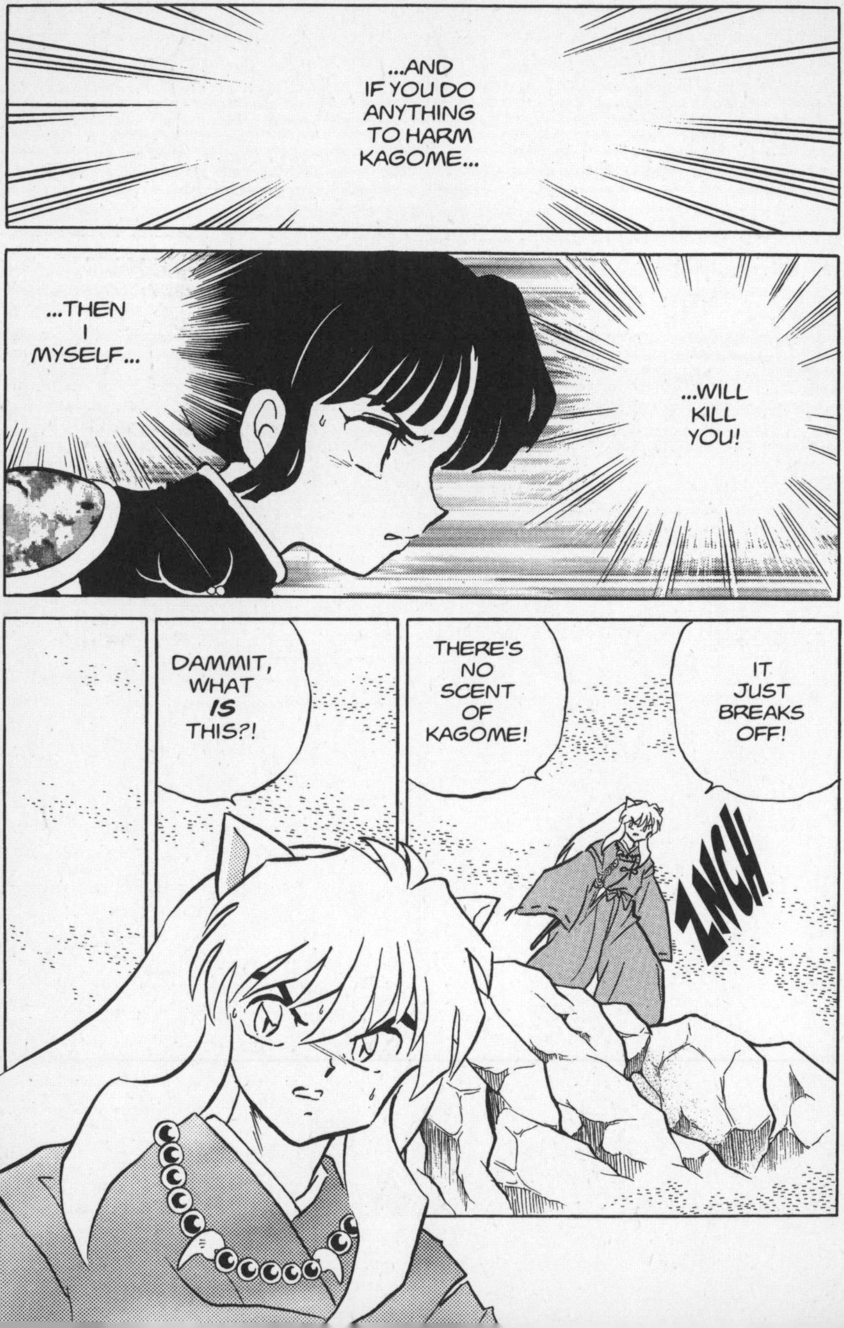
...AND IF YOU DO ANYTHING TO HARM KAGOME...
...THEN I MYSELF...
...WILL KILL YOU!
DAMMIT, WHAT *IS* THIS?!
THERE'S NO SCENT OF KAGOME!
IT JUST BREAKS OFF!
ZNCH

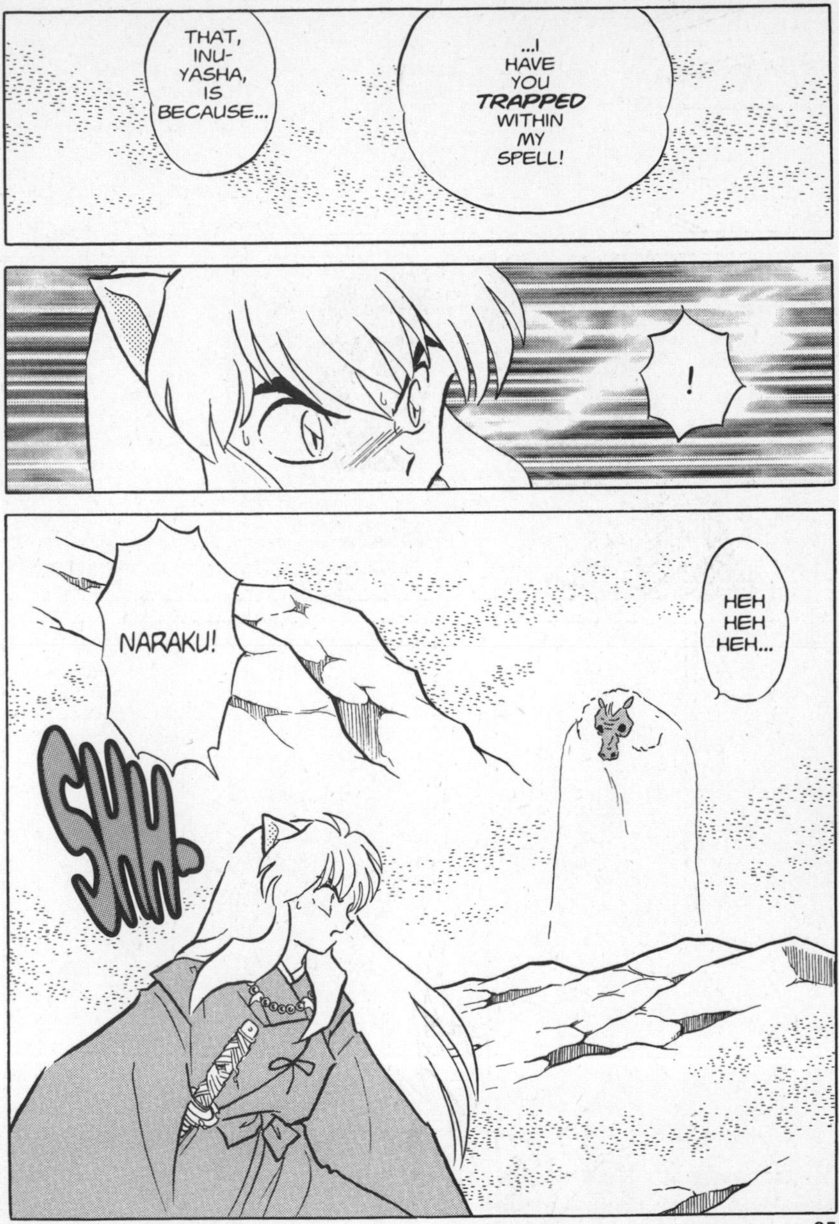
THAT, INU-YASHA, IS BECAUSE...
...I HAVE YOU *TRAPPED* WITHIN MY SPELL!
!
NARAKU!
HEH HEH HEH...
SHH

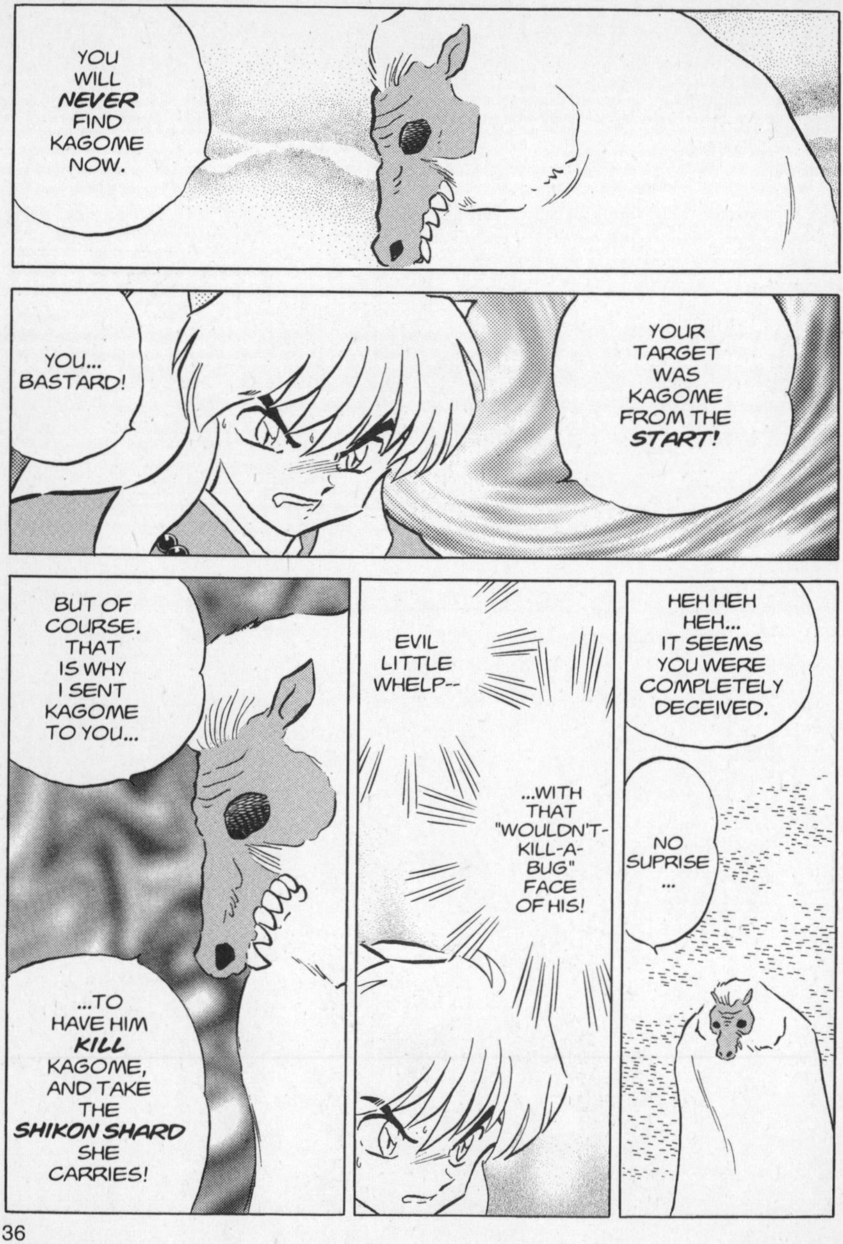
YOU WILL NEVER FIND KAGOME NOW.
YOU... BASTARD!
YOUR TARGET WAS KAGOME FROM THE START!
BUT OF COURSE. THAT IS WHY I SENT KAGOME TO YOU...
...TO HAVE HIM KILL KAGOME, AND TAKE THE SHIKON SHARD SHE CARRIES!
EVIL LITTLE WHELP--
...WITH THAT "WOULDN'T-KILL-A-BUG" FACE OF HIS!
HEH HEH HEH... IT SEEMS YOU WERE COMPLETELY DECEIVED.
NO SUPRISE ...

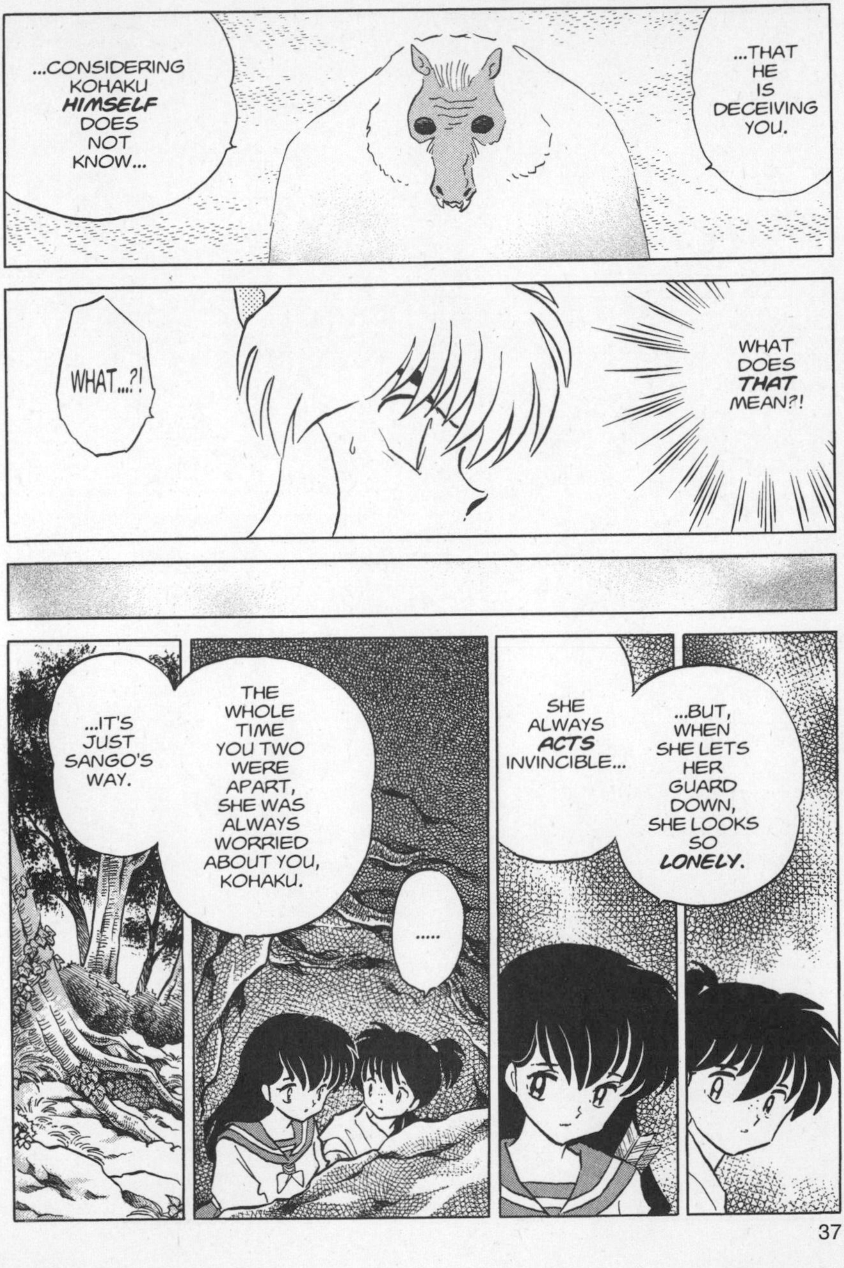
...CONSIDERING KOHAKU **HIMSELF** DOES NOT KNOW...
...THAT HE IS DECEIVING YOU.
WHAT...?!
WHAT DOES **THAT** MEAN?!
...IT'S JUST SANGO'S WAY.
THE WHOLE TIME YOU TWO WERE APART, SHE WAS ALWAYS WORRIED ABOUT YOU, KOHAKU.
.....
SHE ALWAYS **ACTS** INVINCIBLE...
...BUT, WHEN SHE LETS HER GUARD DOWN, SHE LOOKS SO **LONELY**.

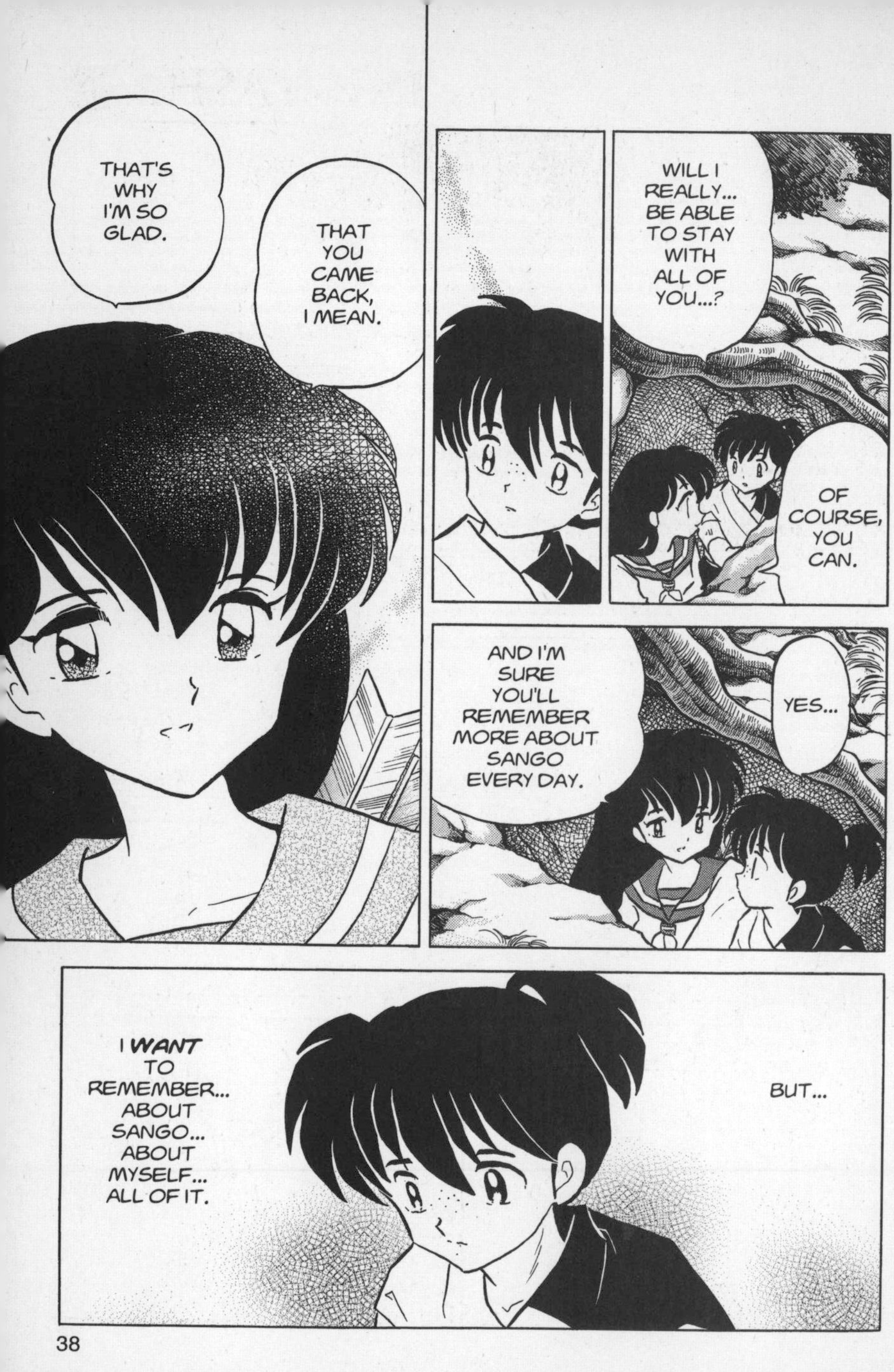
THAT'S WHY I'M SO GLAD.
THAT YOU CAME BACK, I MEAN.
WILL I REALLY... BE ABLE TO STAY WITH ALL OF YOU...?
OF COURSE, YOU CAN.
AND I'M SURE YOU'LL REMEMBER MORE ABOUT SANGO EVERY DAY.
YES...
I *WANT* TO REMEMBER... ABOUT SANGO... ABOUT MYSELF... ALL OF IT.
BUT...

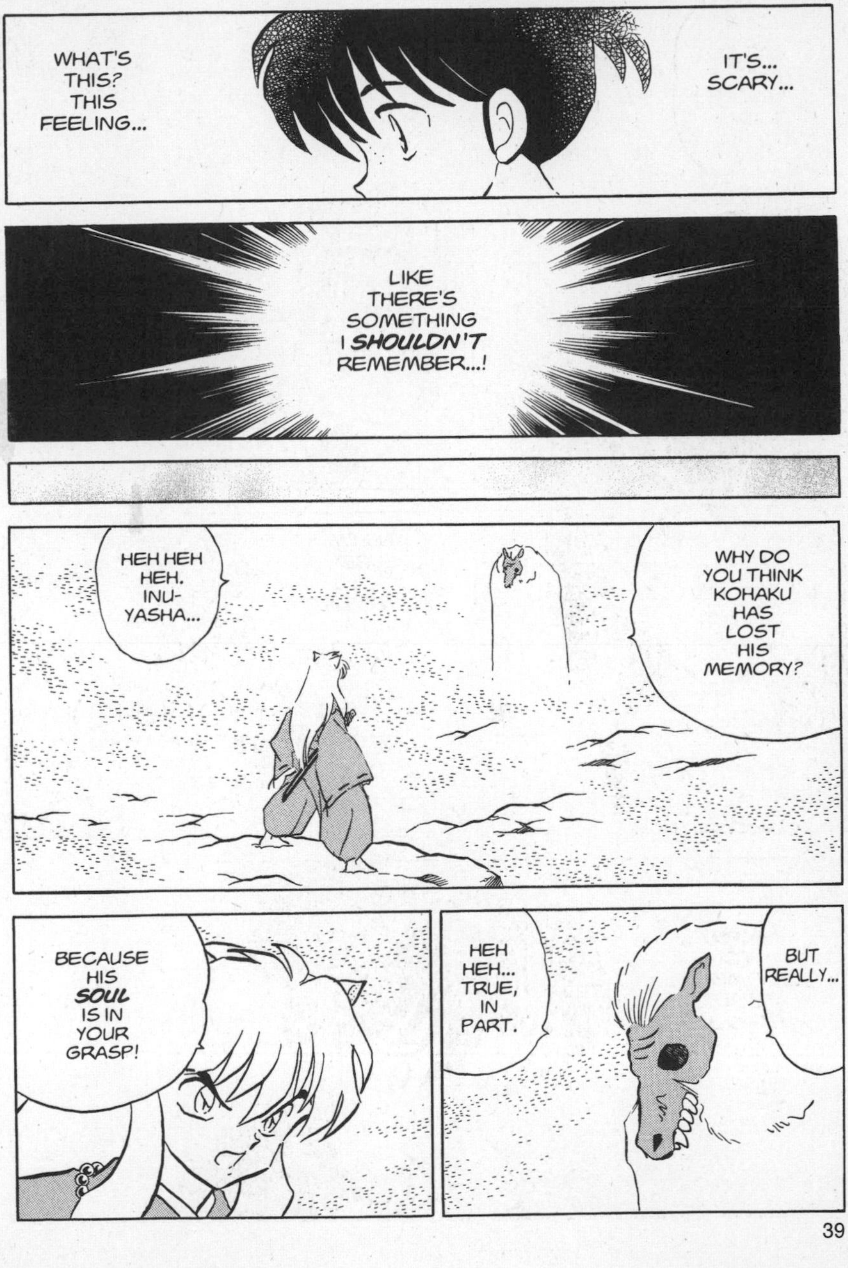
WHAT'S THIS? THIS FEELING...
IT'S... SCARY...
LIKE THERE'S SOMETHING I *SHOULDN'T* REMEMBER...!
HEH HEH HEH. INU-YASHA...
WHY DO YOU THINK KOHAKU HAS LOST HIS MEMORY?
BECAUSE HIS *SOUL* IS IN YOUR GRASP!
HEH HEH... TRUE, IN PART.
BUT REALLY...

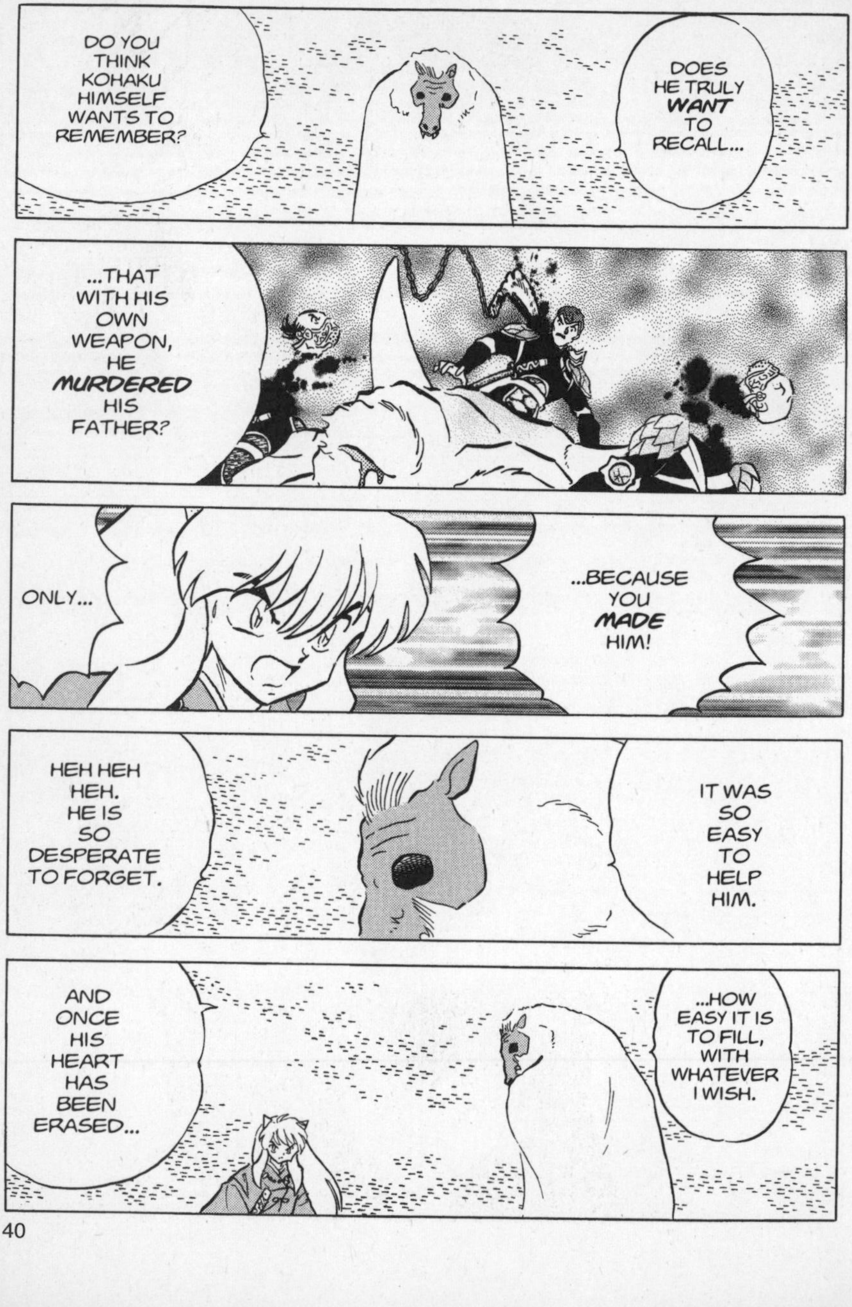
DO YOU THINK KOHAKU HIMSELF WANTS TO REMEMBER?
DOES HE TRULY WANT TO RECALL...
...THAT WITH HIS OWN WEAPON, HE MURDERED HIS FATHER?
ONLY...
...BECAUSE YOU MADE HIM!
HEH HEH HEH. HE IS SO DESPERATE TO FORGET.
IT WAS SO EASY TO HELP HIM.
AND ONCE HIS HEART HAS BEEN ERASED...
...HOW EASY IT IS TO FILL, WITH WHATEVER I WISH.

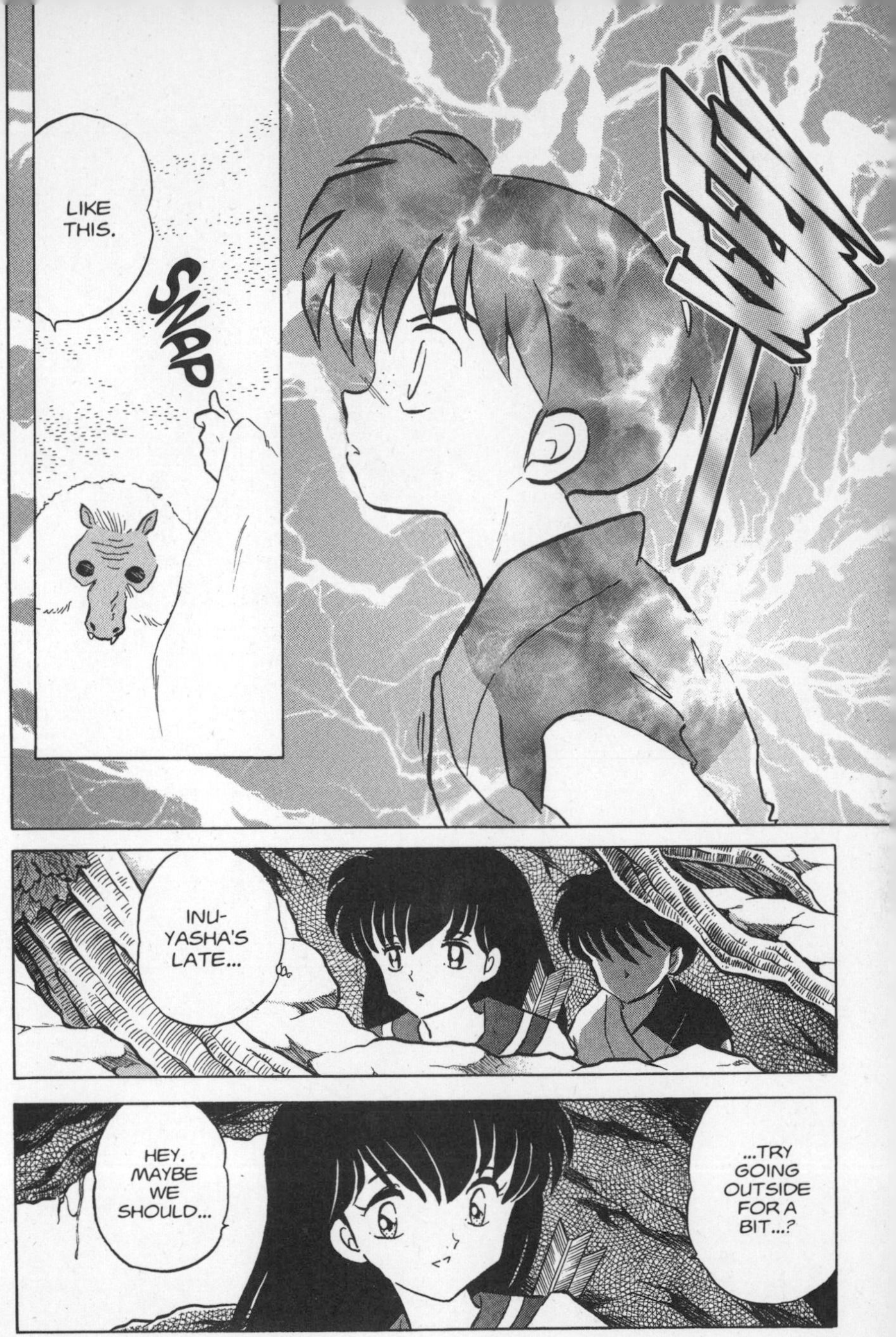
LIKE THIS.
SNAP
INU-YASHA'S LATE...
HEY. MAYBE WE SHOULD...
...TRY GOING OUTSIDE FOR A BIT...?

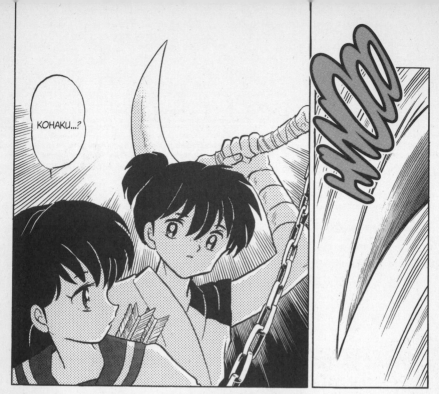

KOHAKU...?

KAGOME...

KOHAKU!

SCROLL THREE
SANGO'S DECISION

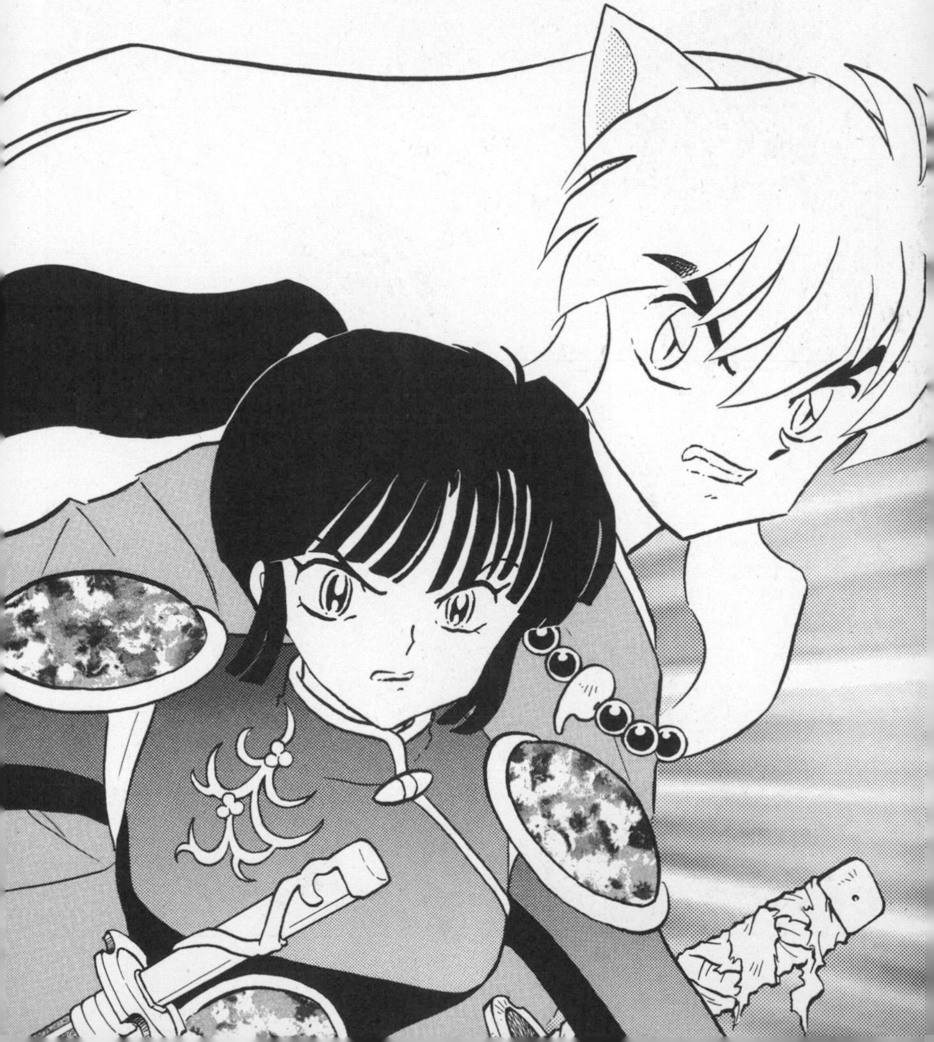

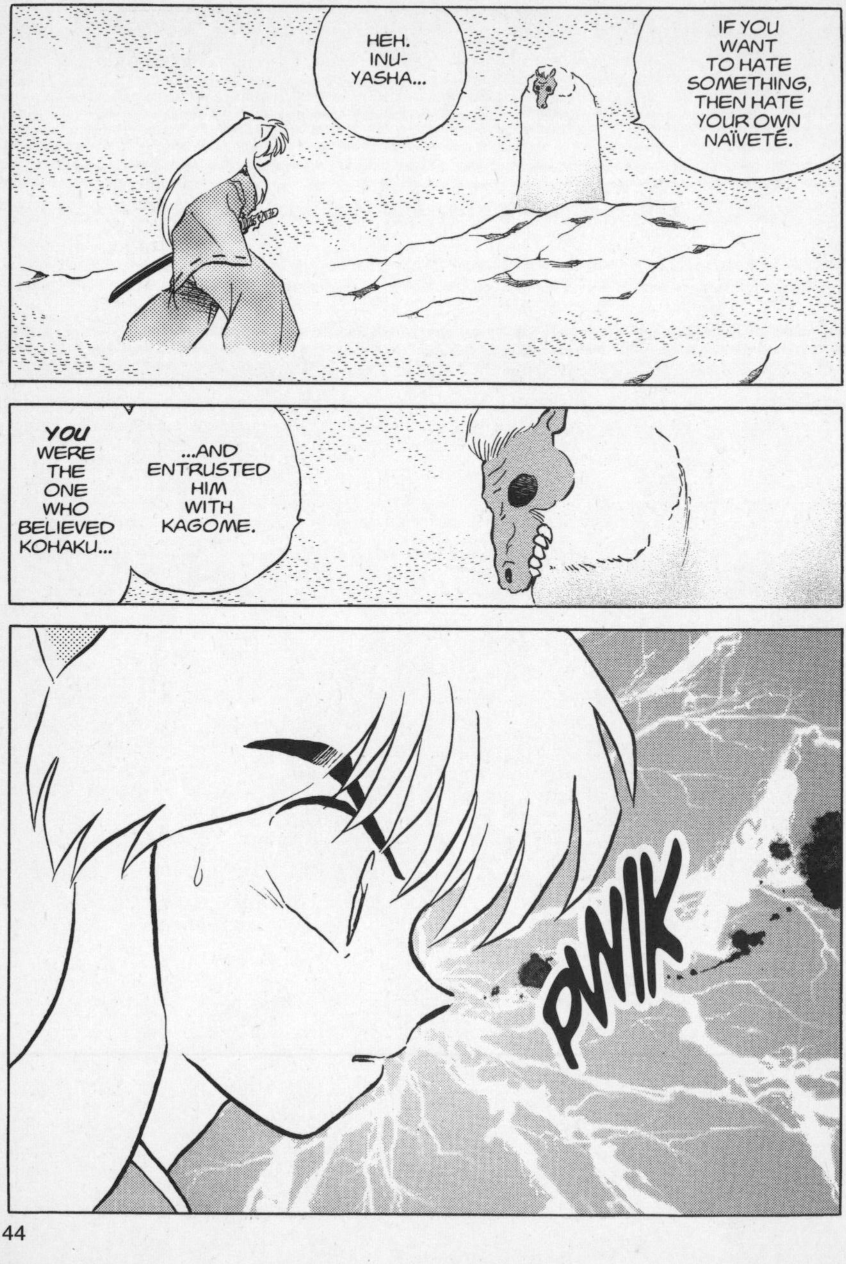
HEH. INU-YASHA...
IF YOU WANT TO HATE SOMETHING, THEN HATE YOUR OWN NAÏVETÉ.
YOU WERE THE ONE WHO BELIEVED KOHAKU...
...AND ENTRUSTED HIM WITH KAGOME.
PWIK

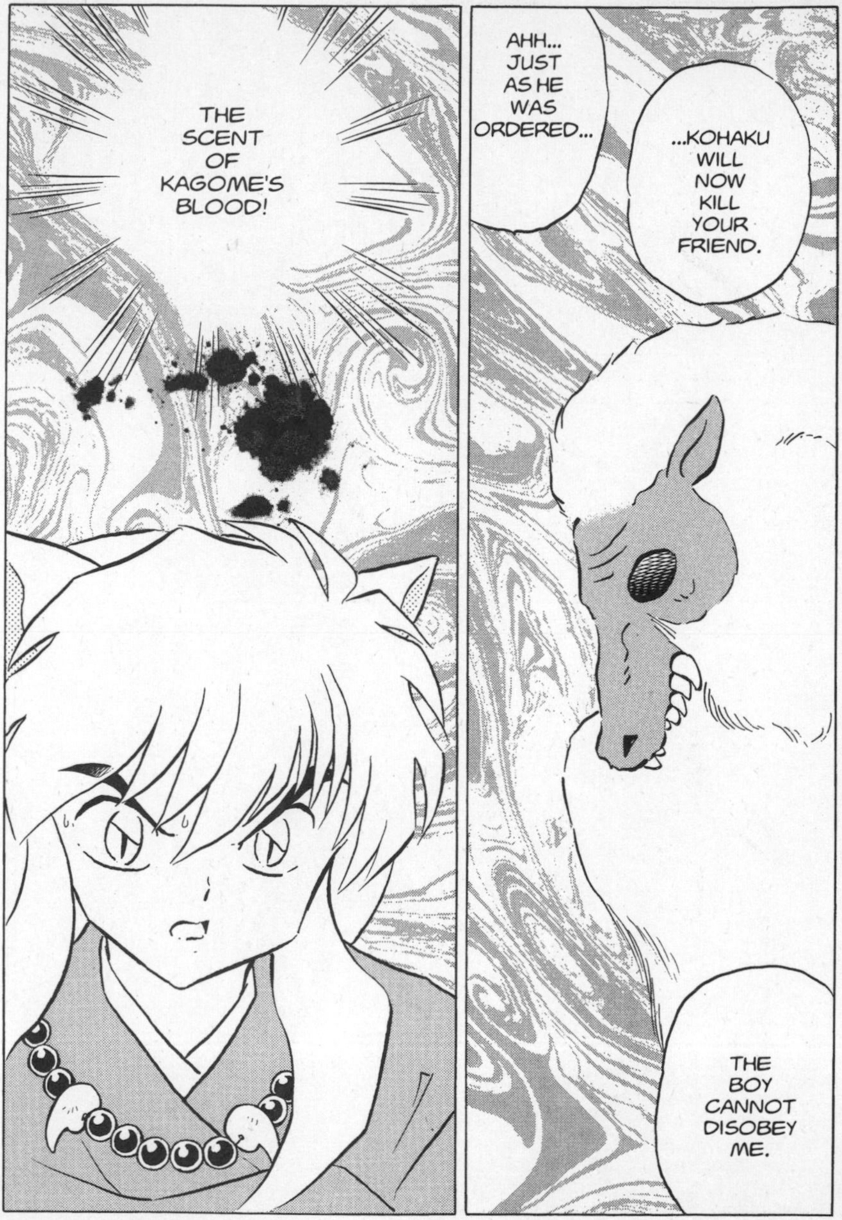
THE SCENT OF KAGOME'S BLOOD!
AHH... JUST AS HE WAS ORDERED...
...KOHAKU WILL NOW KILL YOUR FRIEND.
THE BOY CANNOT DISOBEY ME.

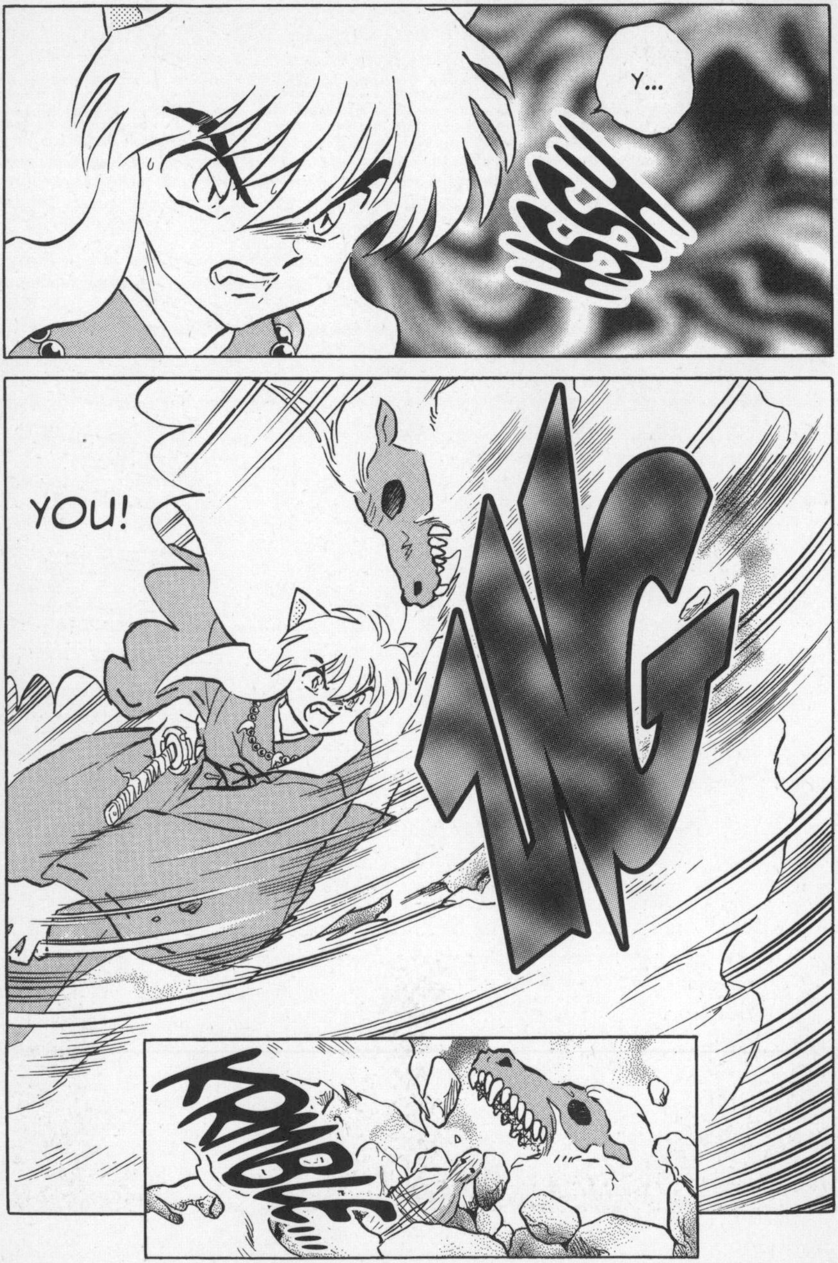
Y...
WSSH
YOU!
ZING
KRMBLE!!!

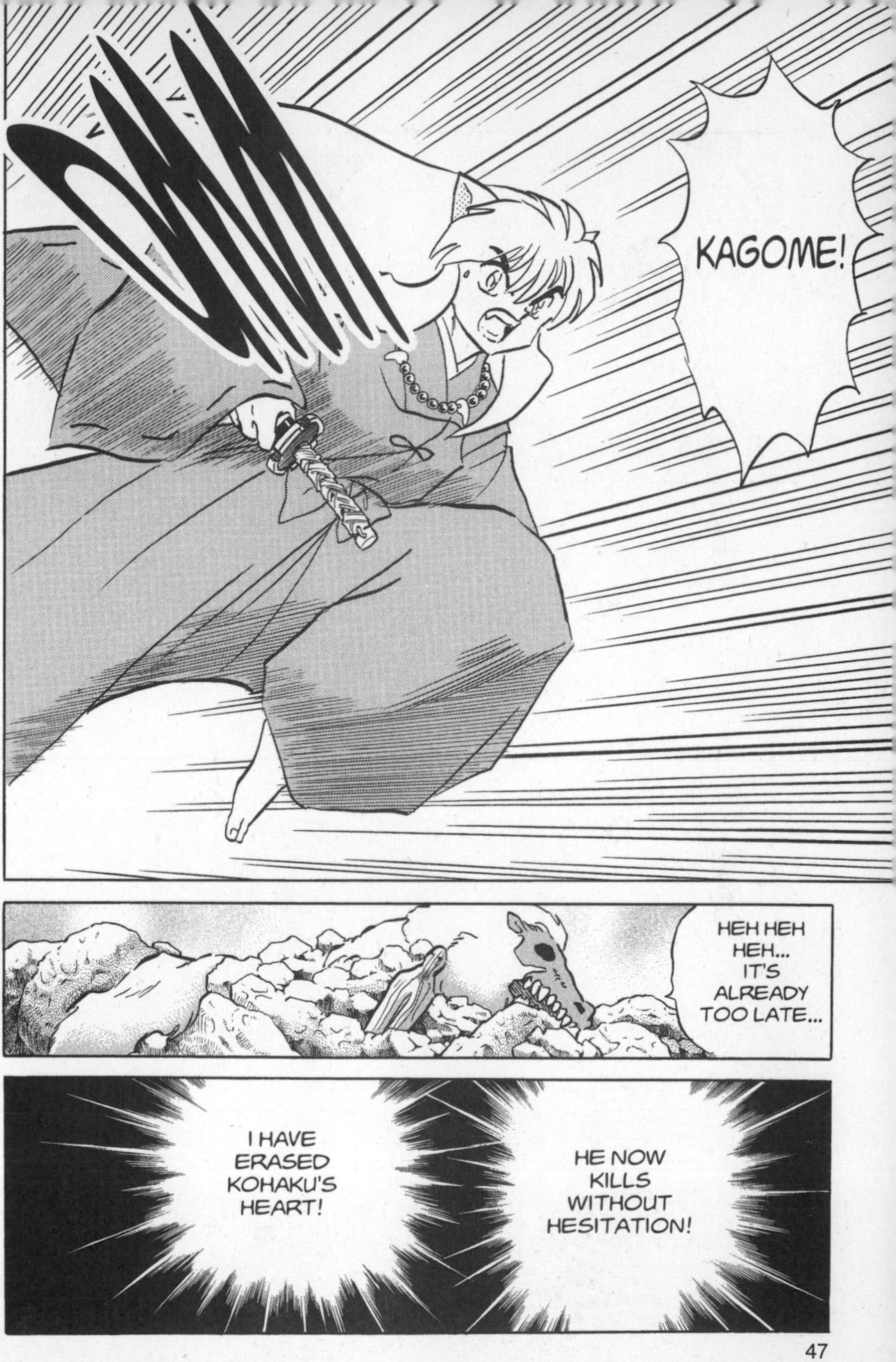
KAGOME!
HEH HEH HEH... IT'S ALREADY TOO LATE...
I HAVE ERASED KOHAKU'S HEART!
HE NOW KILLS WITHOUT HESITATION!

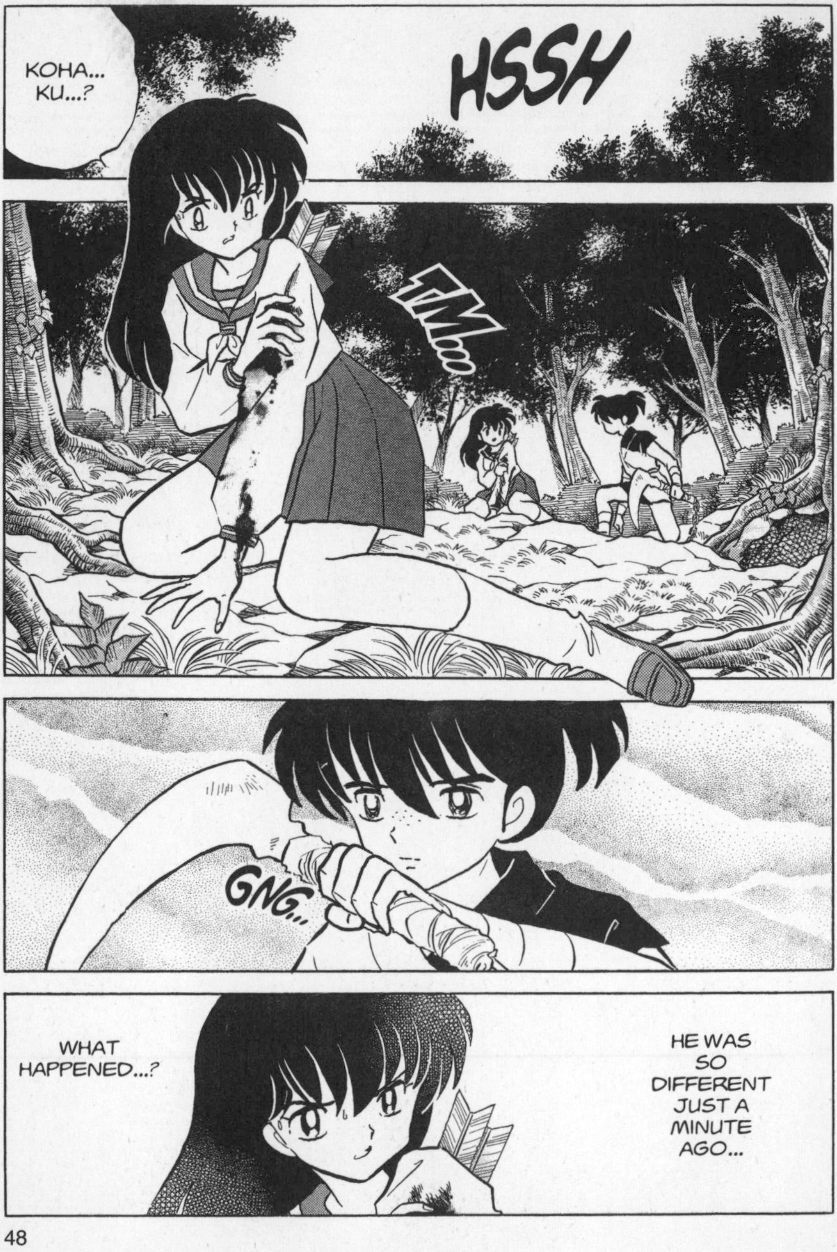
KOHA... KU...?
HSSH
TM...
GNG...
WHAT HAPPENED...?
HE WAS SO DIFFERENT JUST A MINUTE AGO...

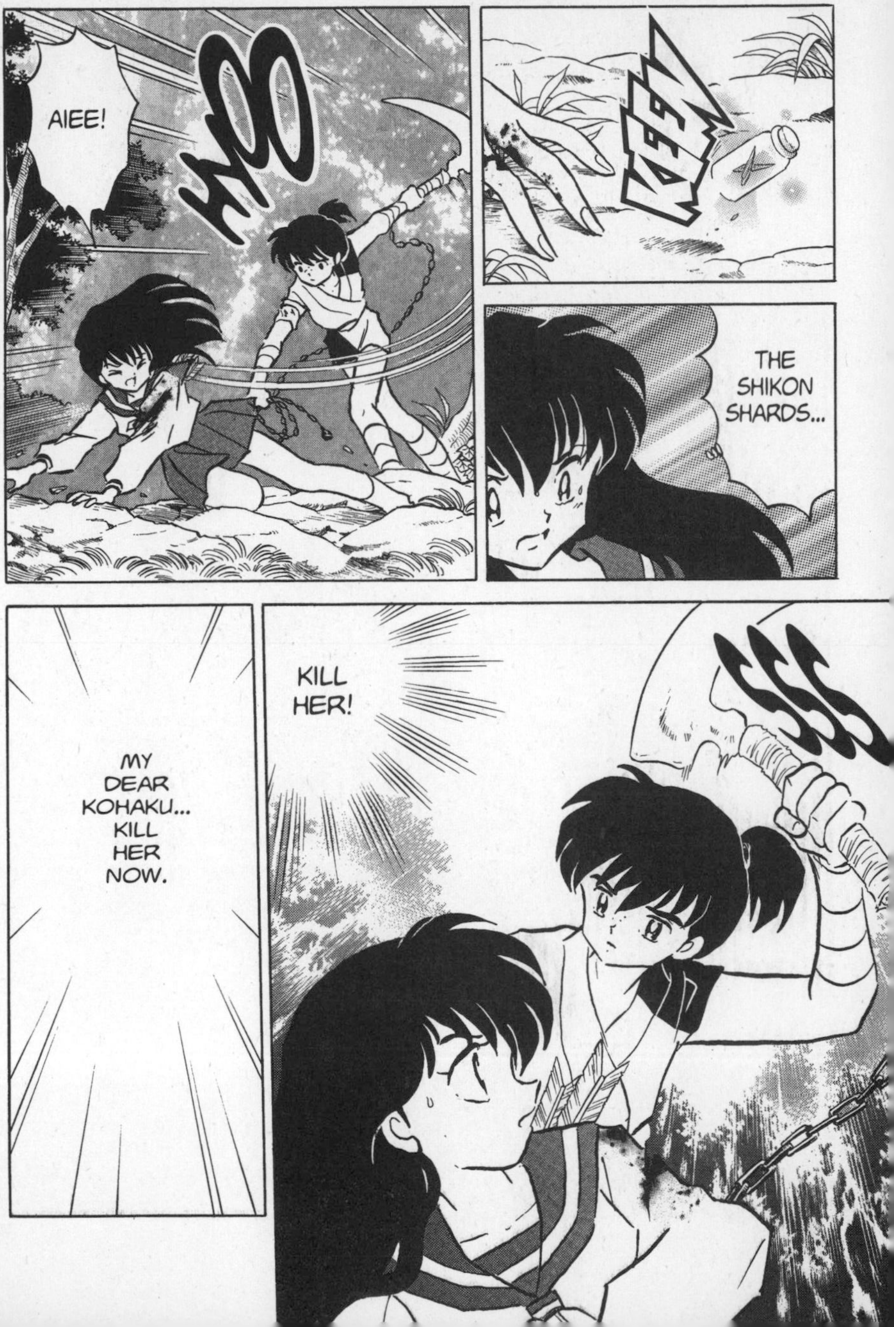
AIEE!
THE SHIKON SHARDS...
MY DEAR KOHAKU... KILL HER NOW.
KILL HER!

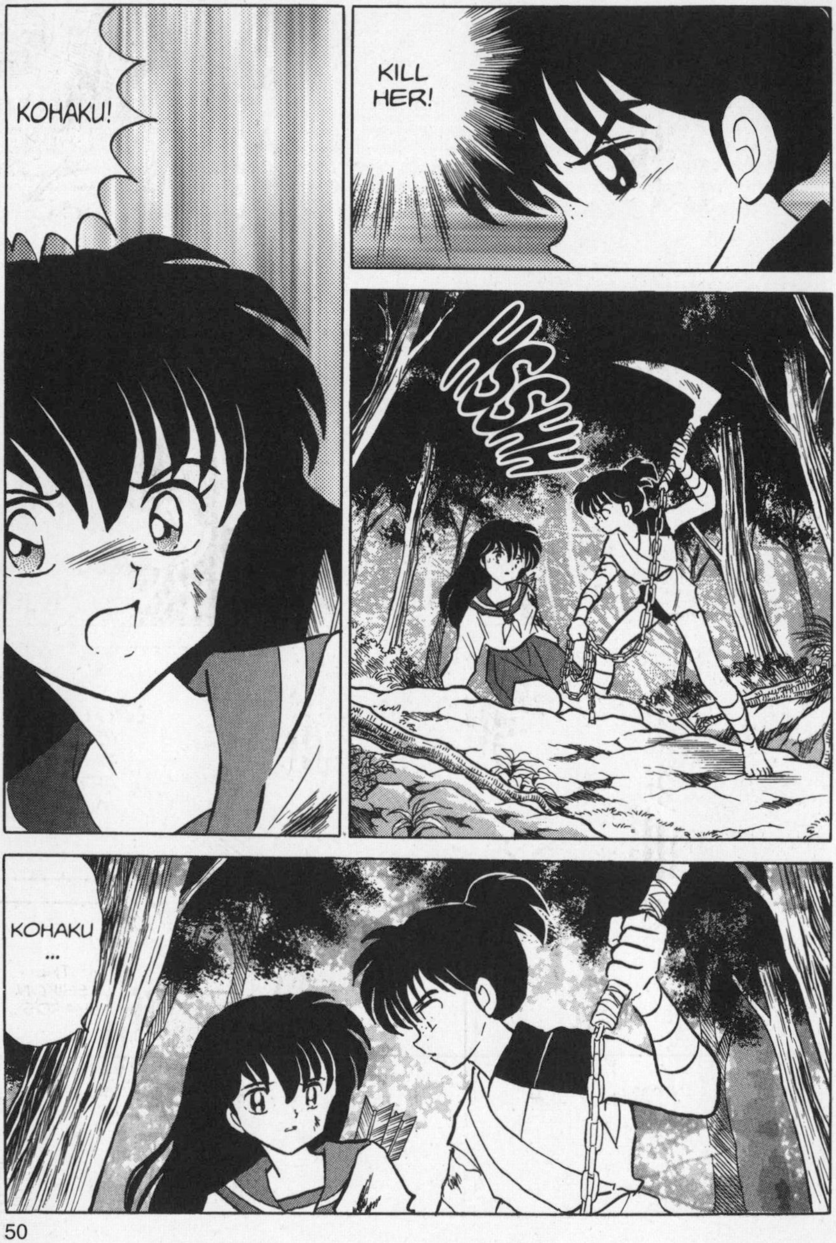
KOHAKU!
KILL HER!
HSSHH
KOHAKU ...

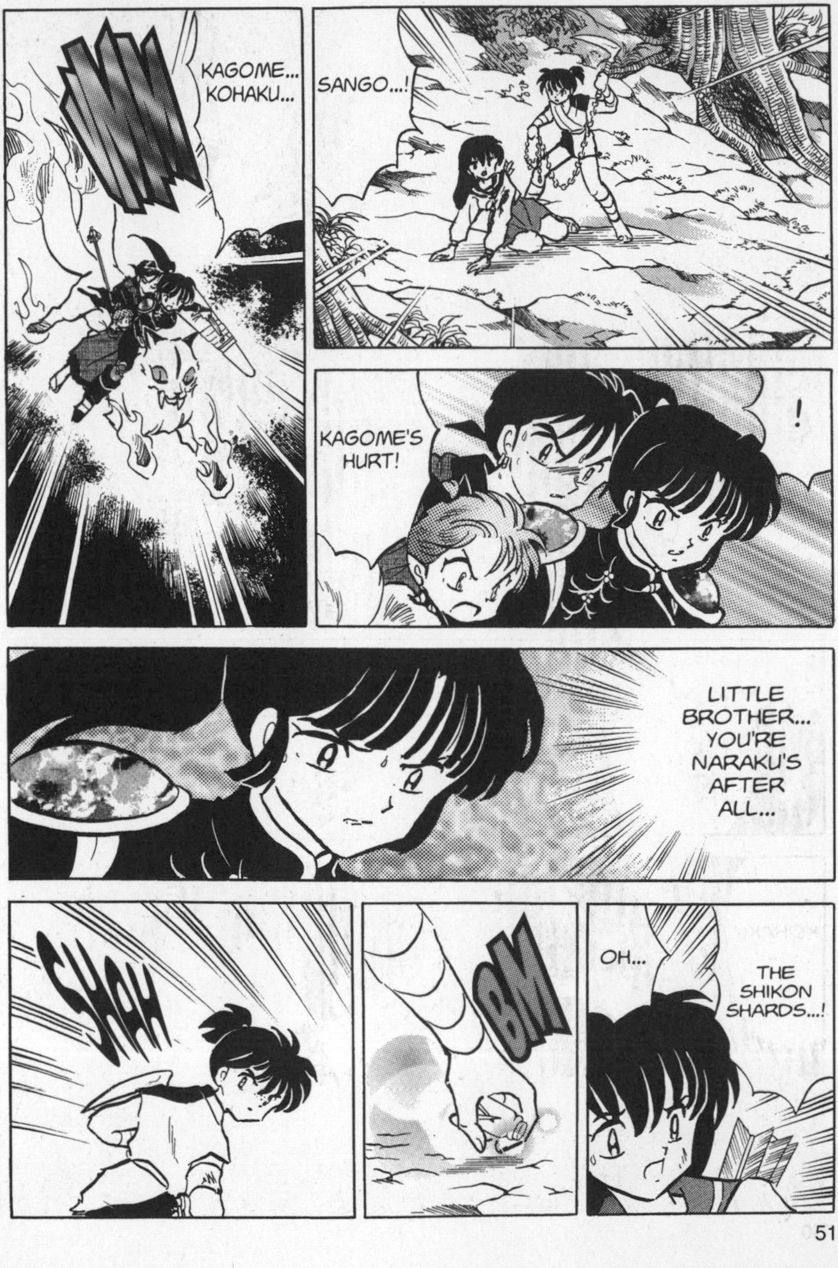
KAGOME... KOHAKU...
SANGO...!
KAGOME'S HURT!
!
LITTLE BROTHER... YOU'RE NARAKU'S AFTER ALL...
SHAH
BM
OH...
THE SHIKON SHARDS...!

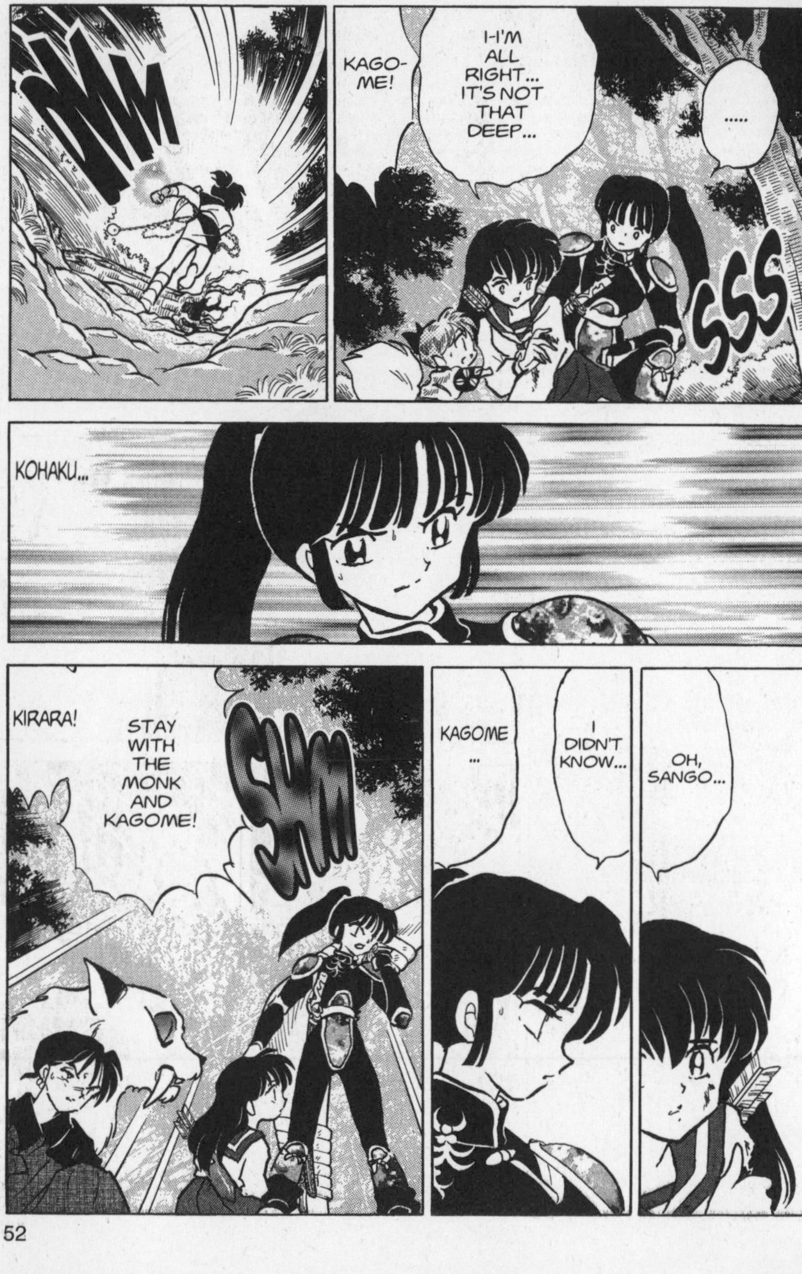
WHM
KAGO-
ME!
I-I'M
ALL
RIGHT...
IT'S NOT
THAT
DEEP...
.....
SSS
KOHAKU...
KIRARA!
STAY
WITH
THE
MONK
AND
KAGOME!
SHM
KAGOME
...
I
DIDN'T
KNOW...
OH,
SANGO...

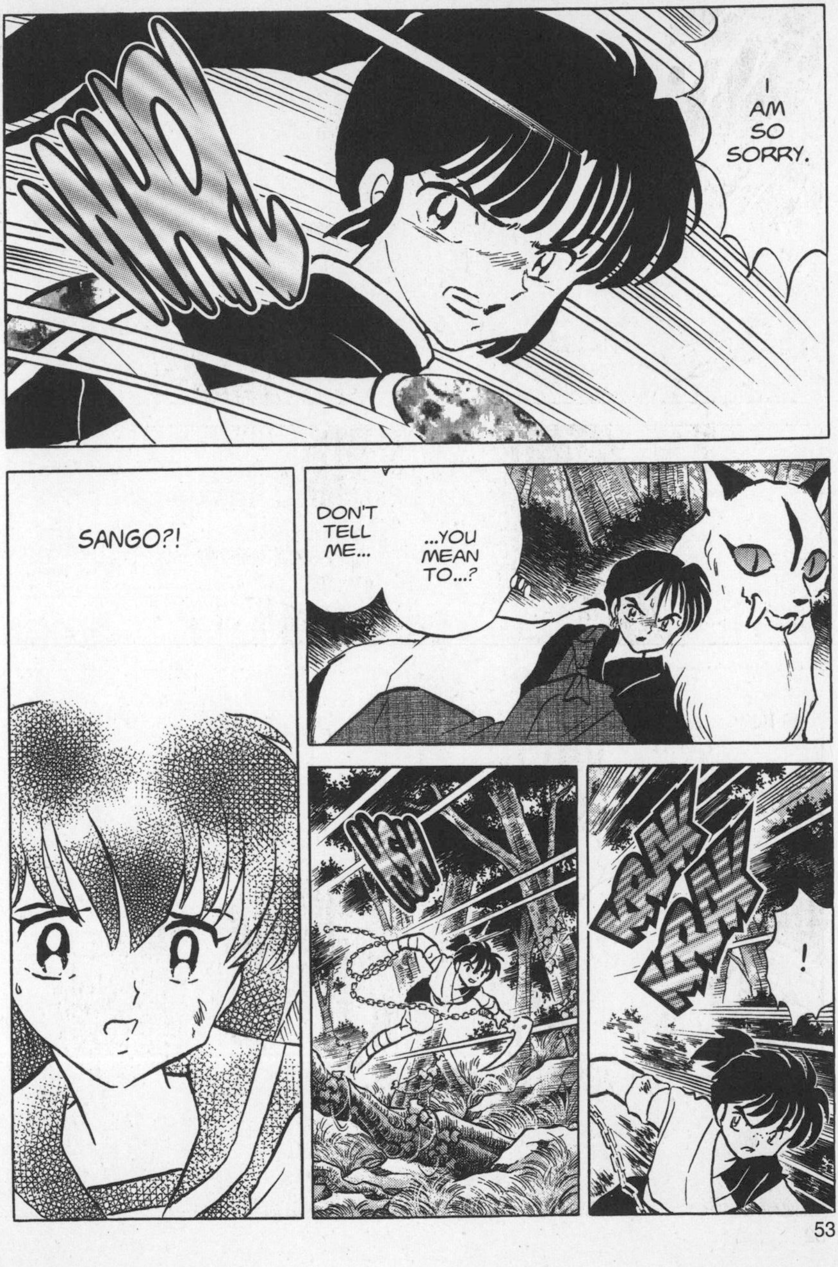
I AM SO SORRY.
SANGO?!
DON'T TELL ME...
...YOU MEAN TO...?
KRAK KRAK
!

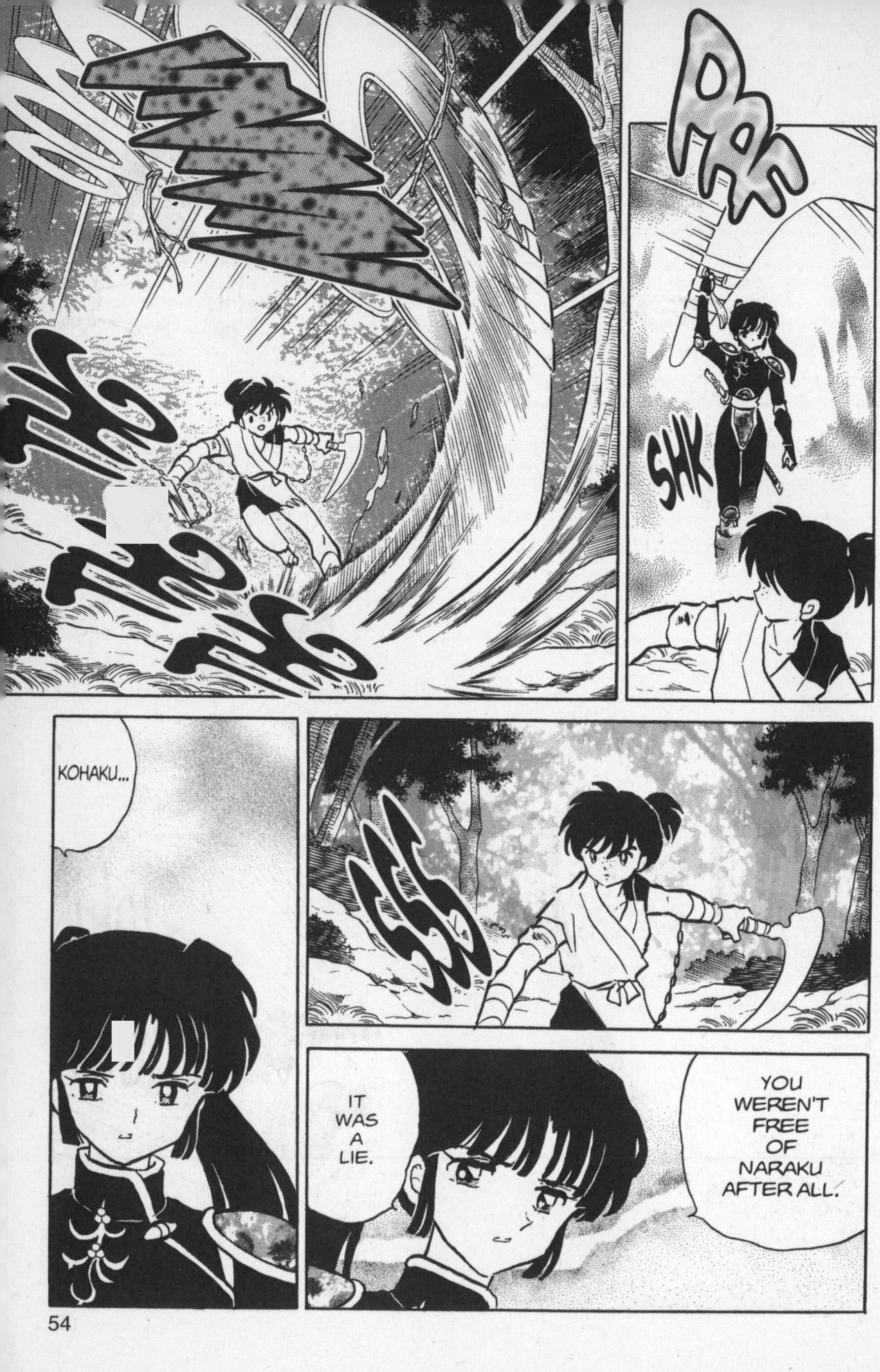
SHK
KOHAKU...
IT WAS A LIE.
YOU WEREN'T FREE OF NARAKU AFTER ALL.

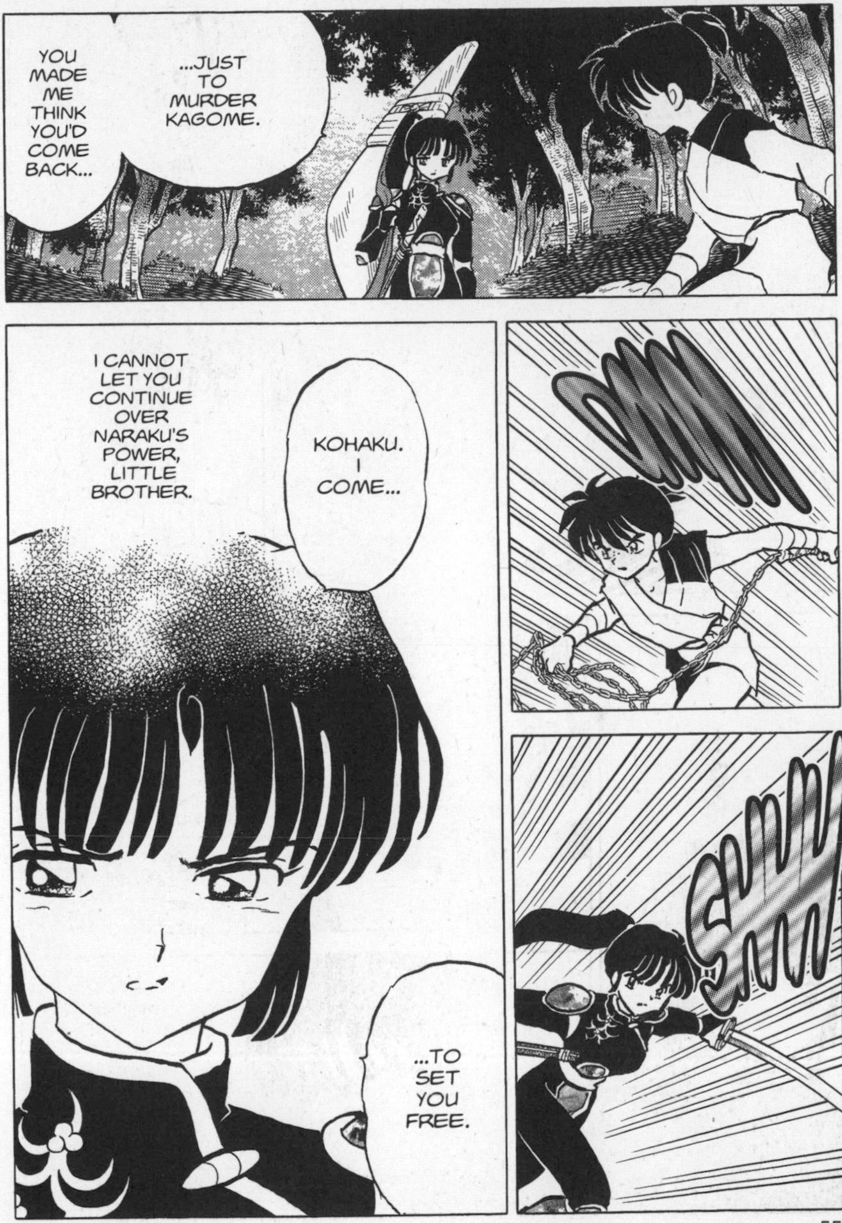
YOU MADE ME THINK YOU'D COME BACK...
...JUST TO MURDER KAGOME.
I CANNOT LET YOU CONTINUE OVER NARAKU'S POWER, LITTLE BROTHER.
KOHAKU. I COME...
...TO SET YOU FREE.

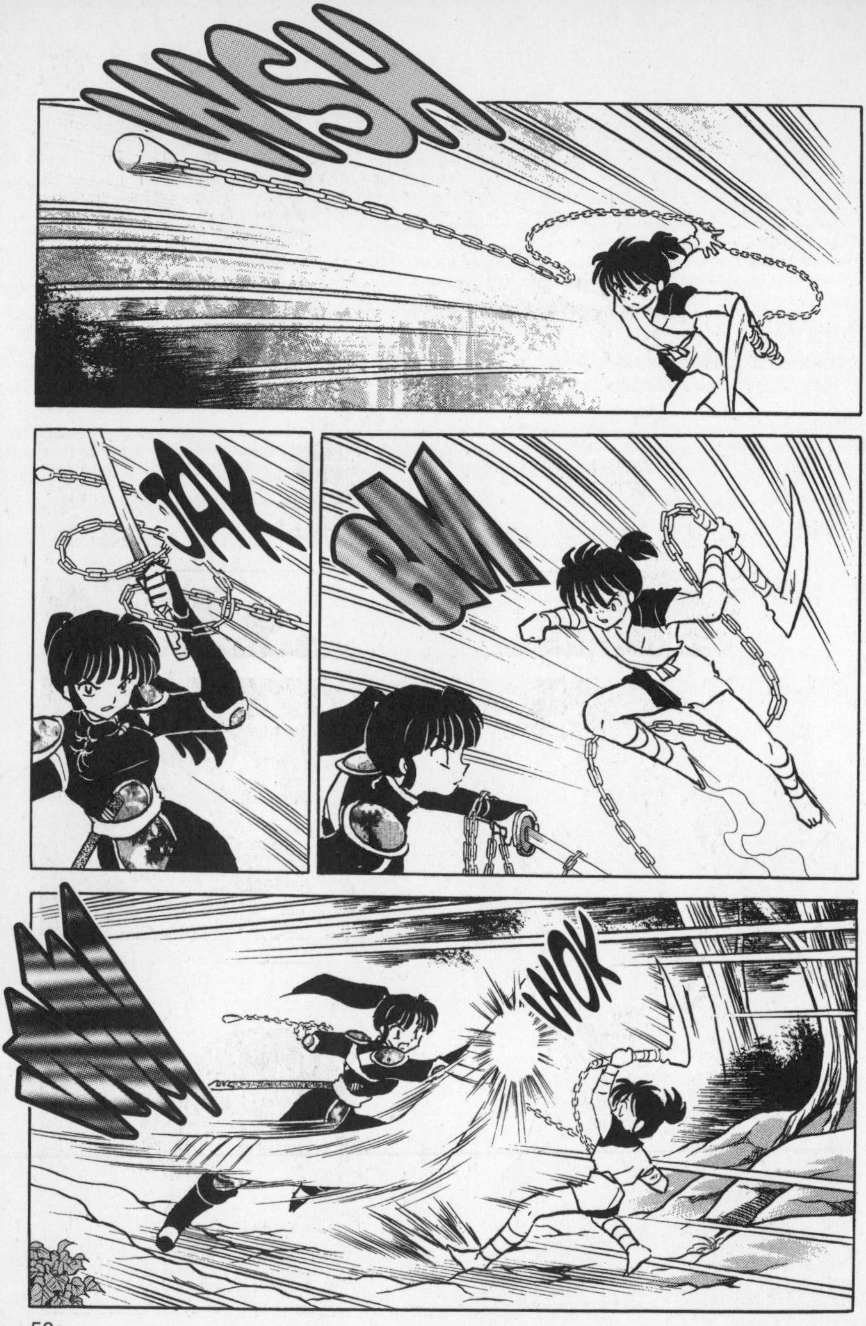
WHSH
JAK
BAM
WOK

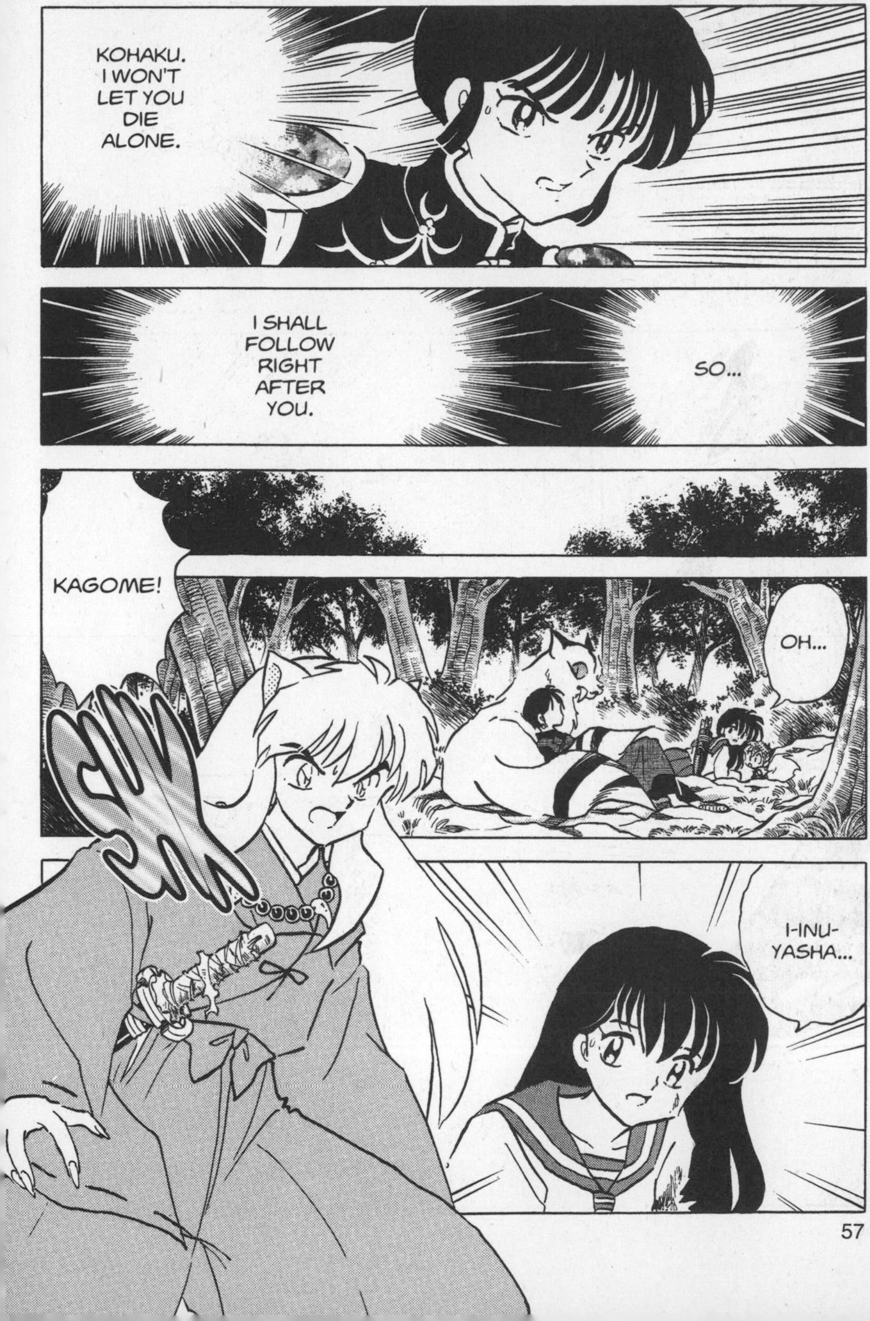
KOHAKU. I WON'T LET YOU DIE ALONE.
I SHALL FOLLOW RIGHT AFTER YOU.
SO...
KAGOME!
OH...
I-INU-YASHA...

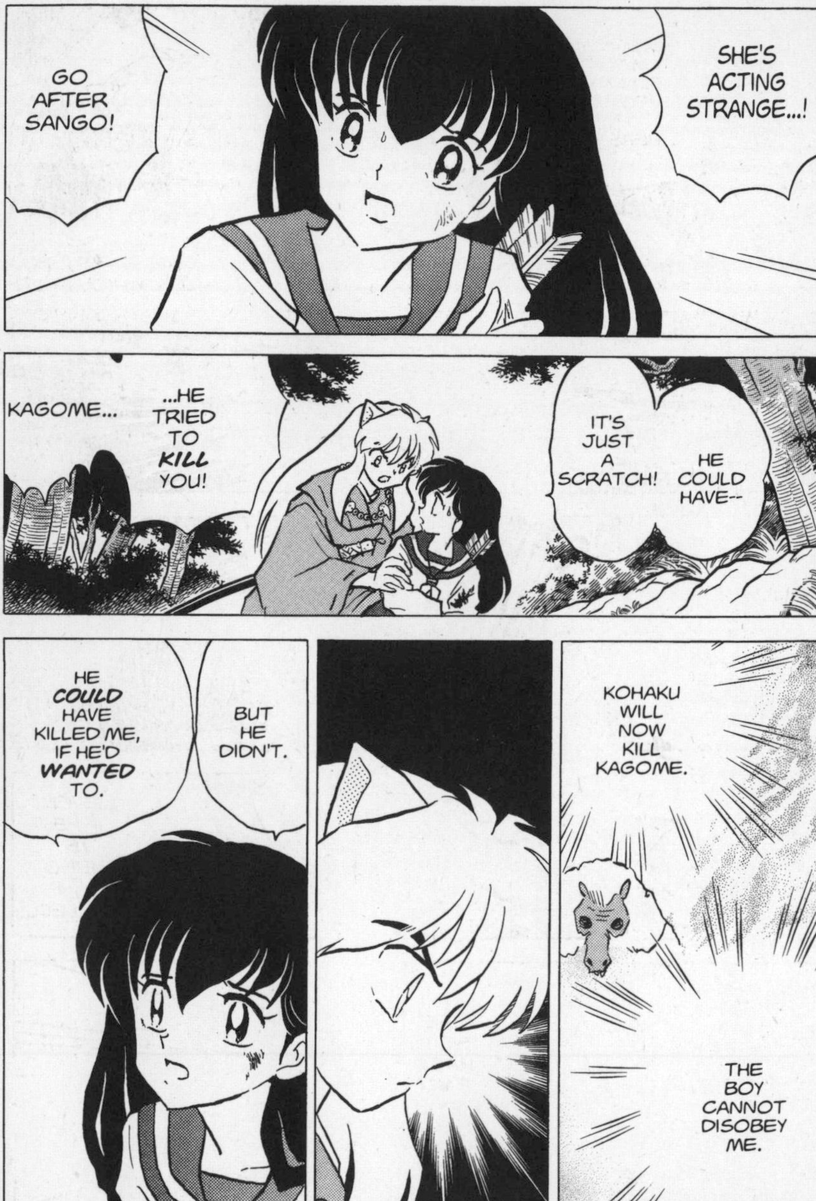
GO AFTER SANGO!
SHE'S ACTING STRANGE...!
KAGOME...
...HE TRIED TO **KILL** YOU!
IT'S JUST A SCRATCH!
HE COULD HAVE--
HE **COULD** HAVE KILLED ME, IF HE'D **WANTED** TO.
BUT HE DIDN'T.
KOHAKU WILL NOW KILL KAGOME.
THE BOY CANNOT DISOBEY ME.

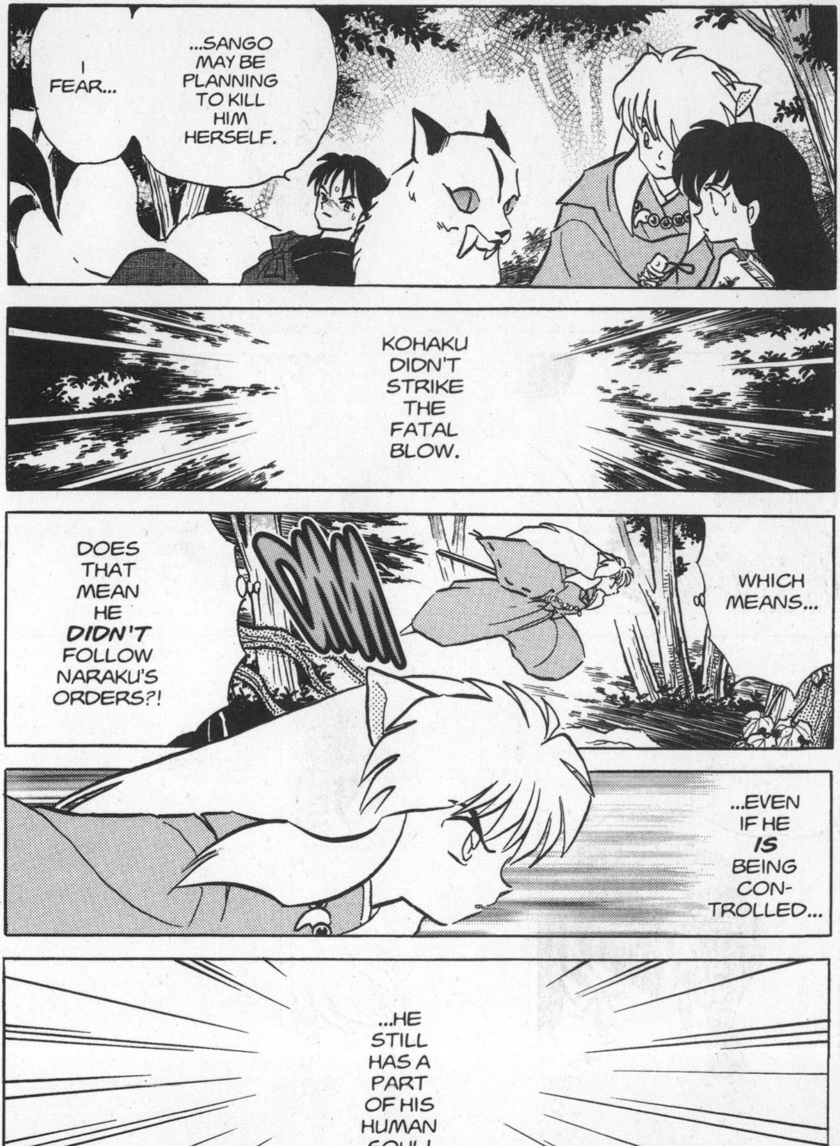
I FEAR...
...SANGO MAY BE PLANNING TO KILL HIM HERSELF.
KOHAKU DIDN'T STRIKE THE FATAL BLOW.
DOES THAT MEAN HE *DIDN'T* FOLLOW NARAKU'S ORDERS?!
WHICH MEANS...
...EVEN IF HE *IS* BEING CON-TROLLED...
...HE STILL HAS A PART OF HIS HUMAN SOUL!

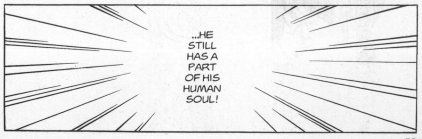

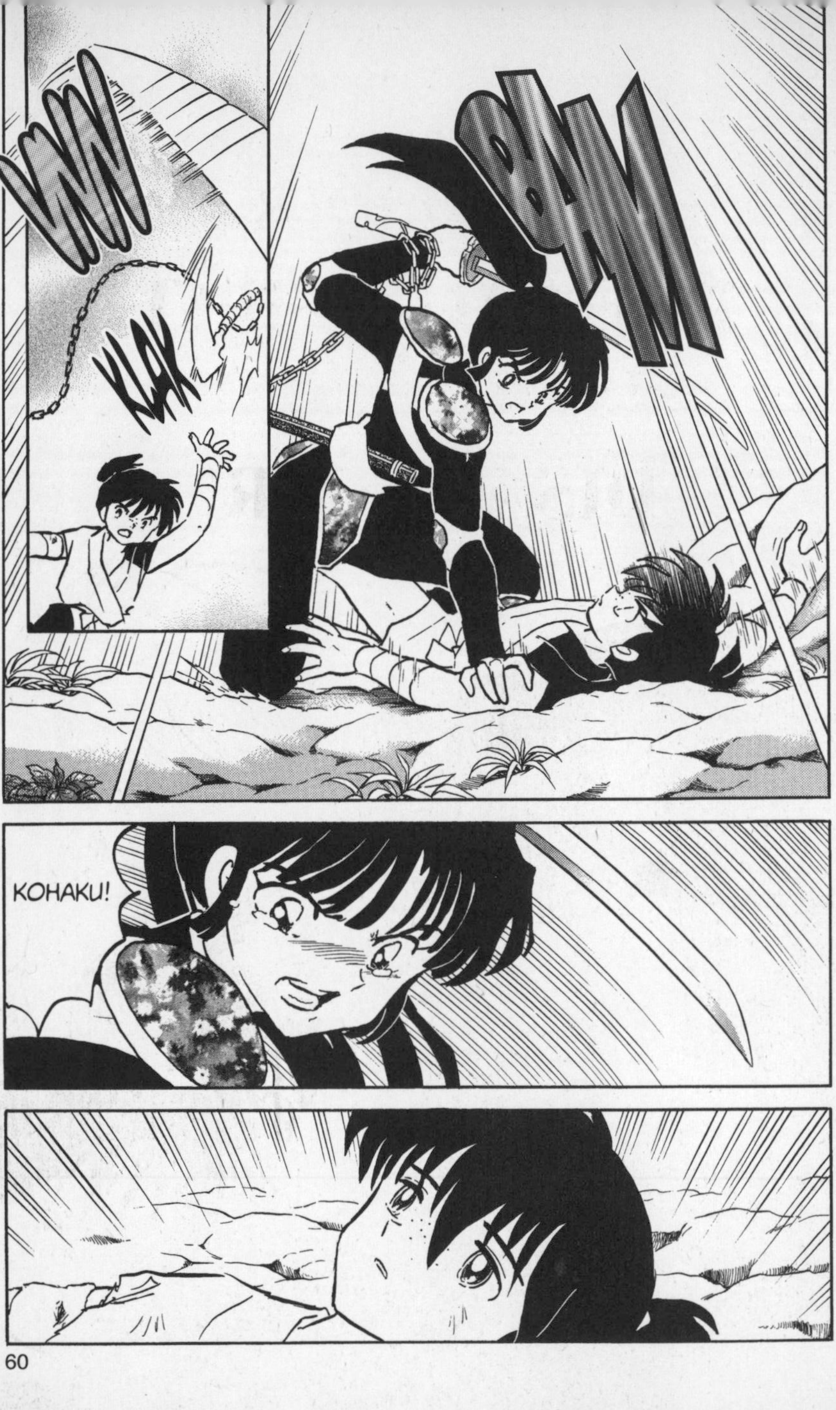
KLAK
BLAM
KOHAKU!

SCROLL FOUR

THE FACE THAT WOULDN'T DISAPPEAR

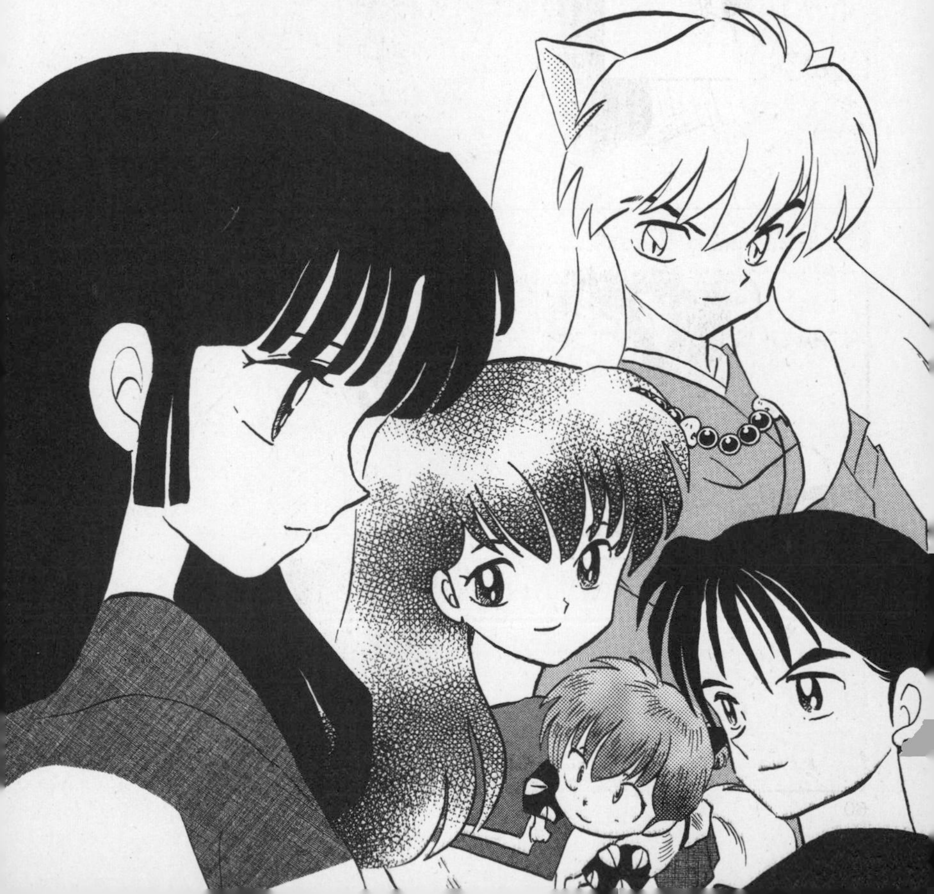

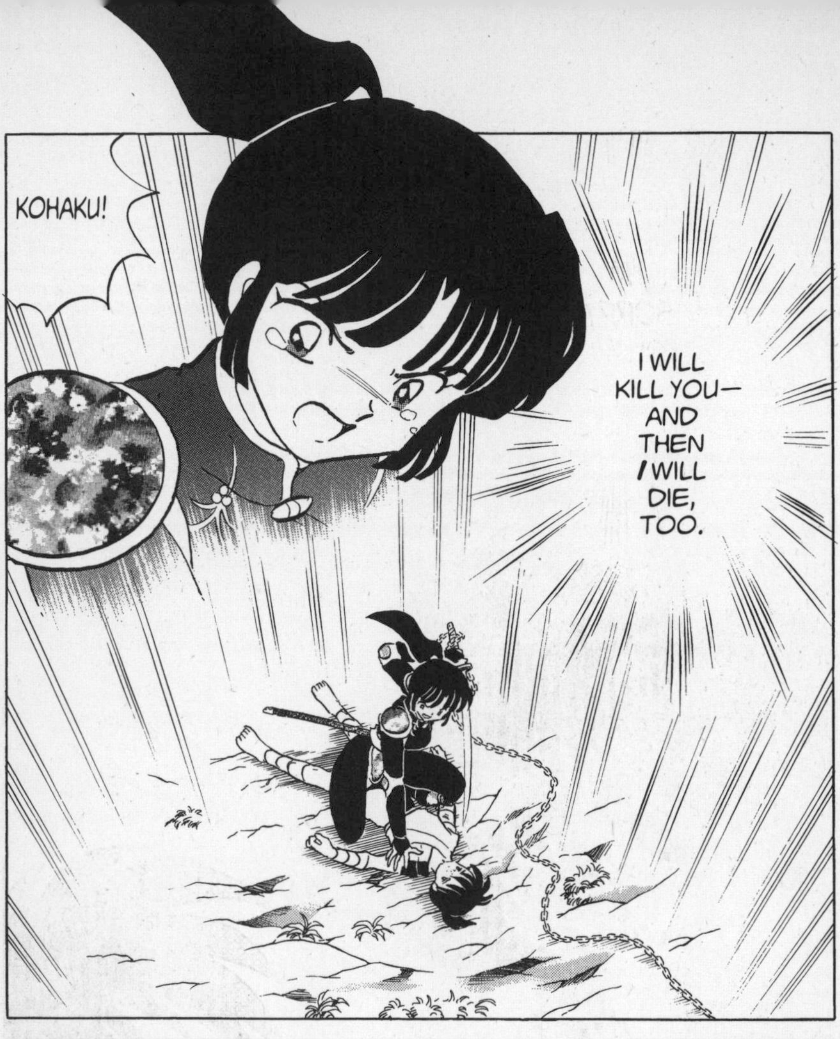
KOHAKU!
I WILL KILL YOU— AND THEN I WILL DIE, TOO.

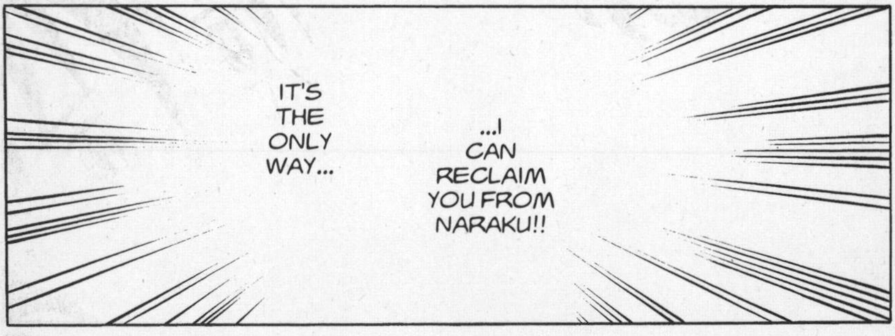
IT'S THE ONLY WAY...
...I CAN RECLAIM YOU FROM NARAKU!!

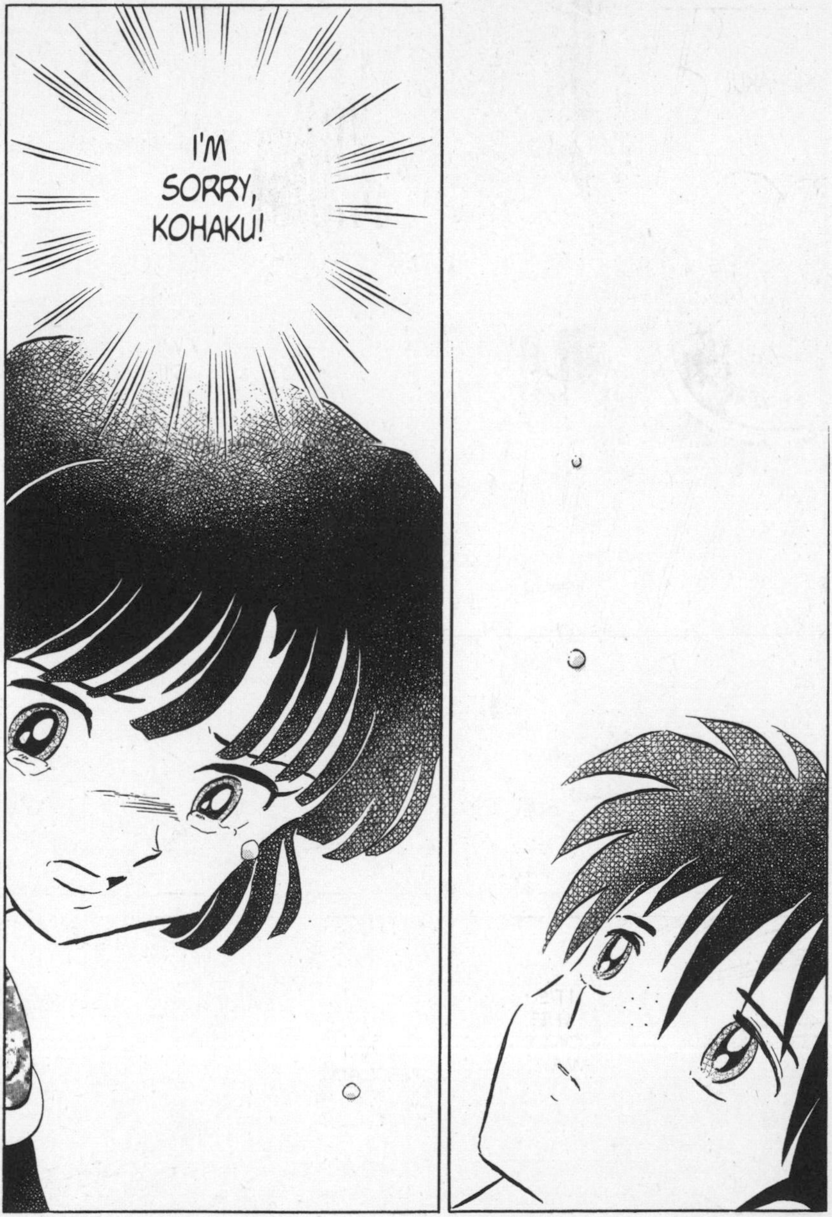
I'M SORRY, KOHAKU!

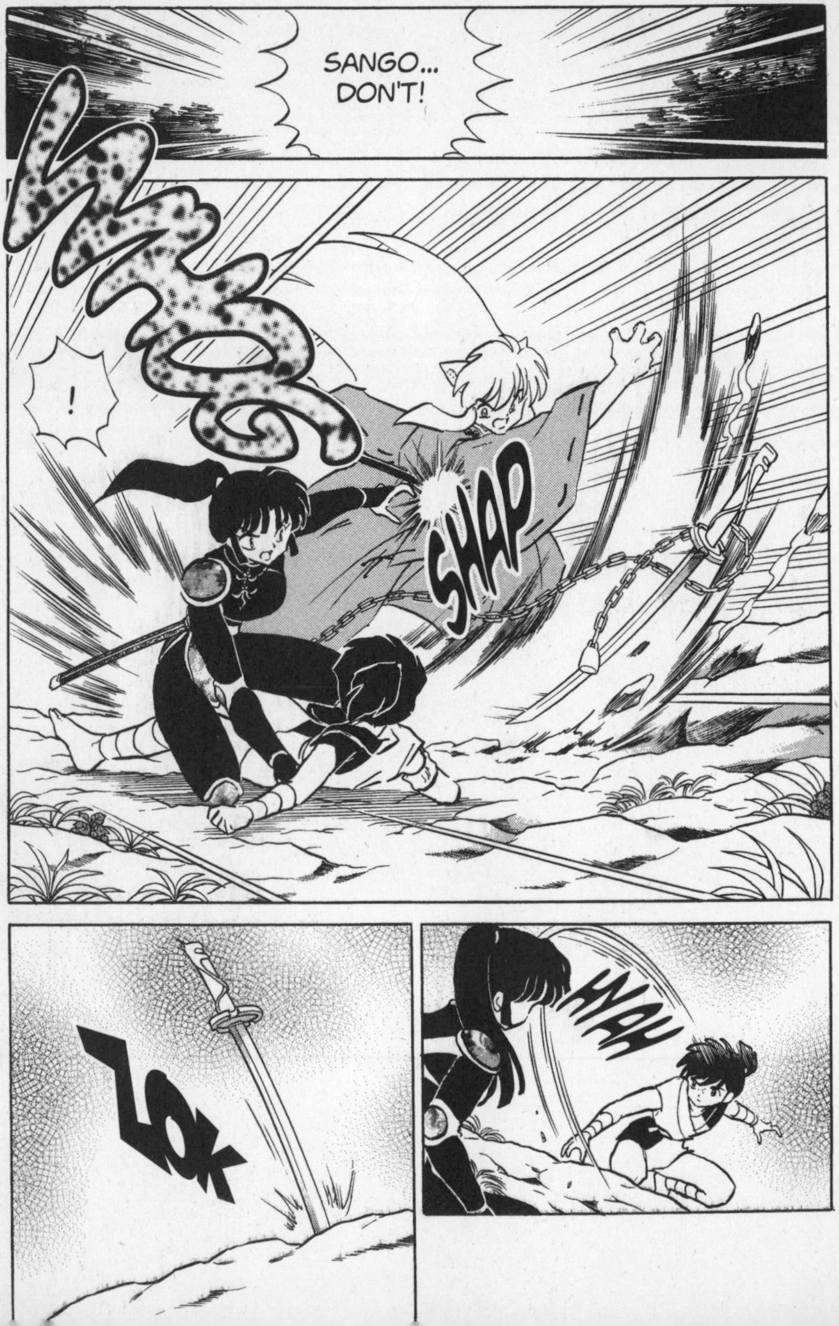
SANGO...
DON'T!
!
SHAP
ZOK
HYAH

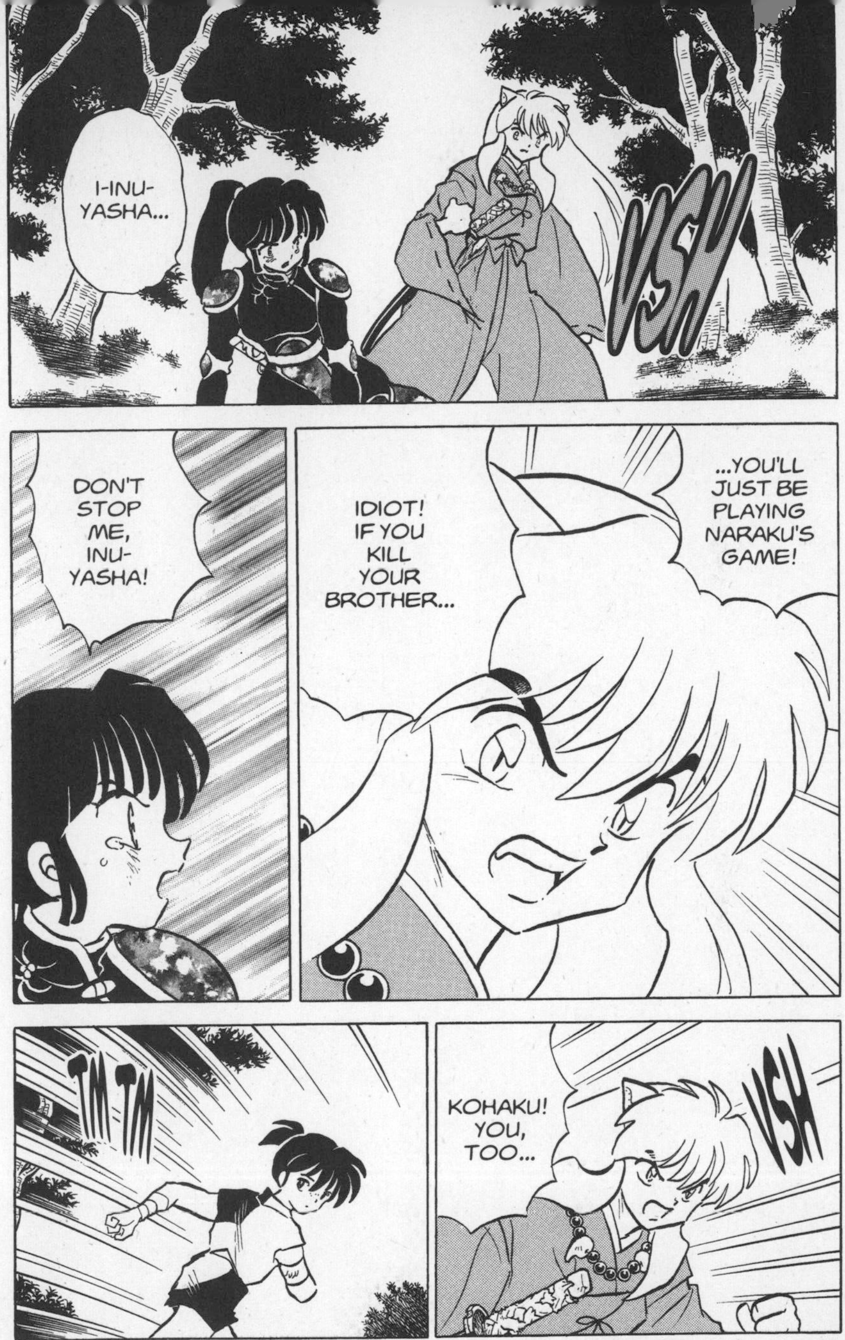
I-INU-YASHA...
VSH
DON'T STOP ME, INU-YASHA!
IDIOT! IF YOU KILL YOUR BROTHER...
...YOU'LL JUST BE PLAYING NARAKU'S GAME!
TM TM
KOHAKU! YOU, TOO...
VSH

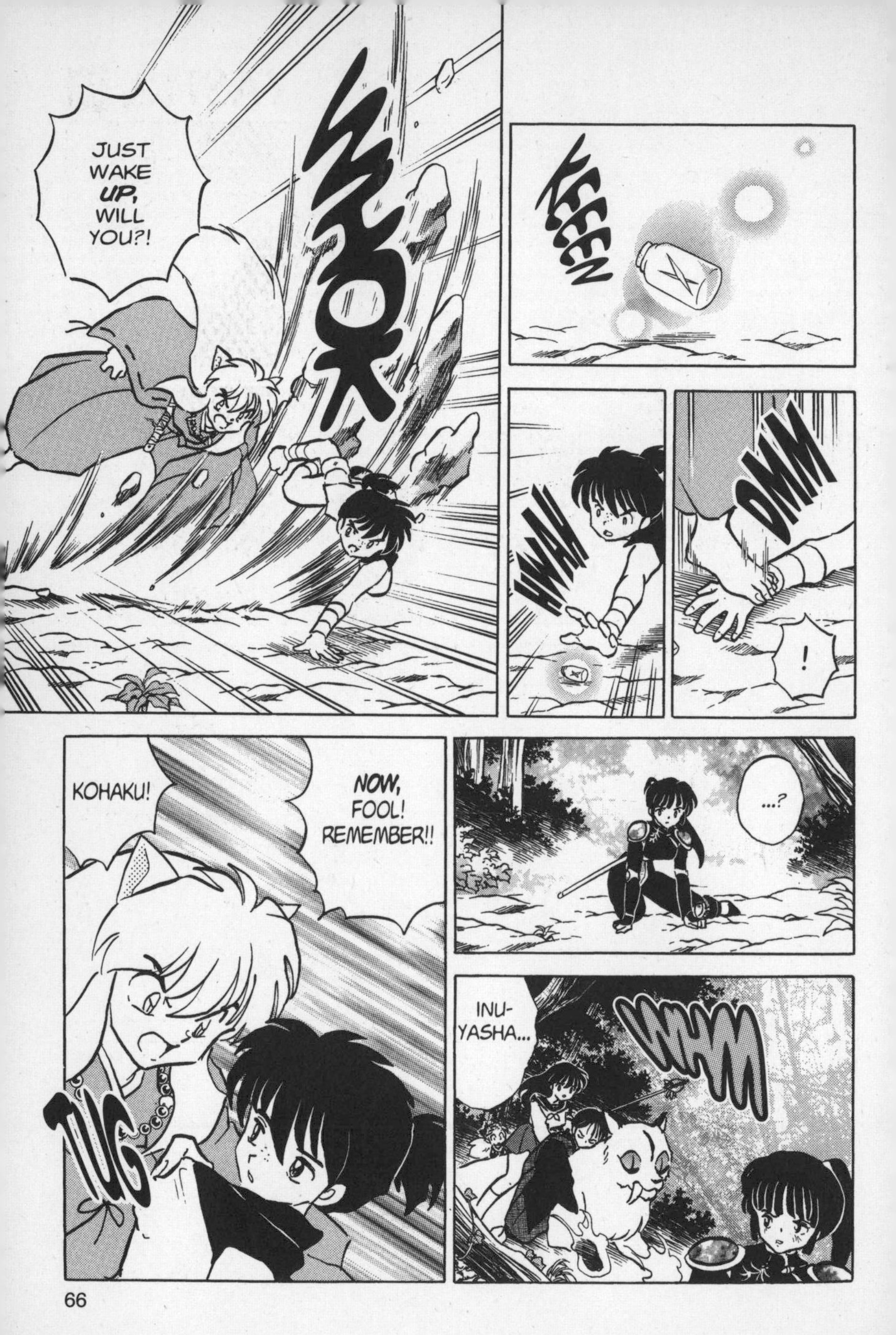
JUST WAKE UP, WILL YOU?!
KEEEN
WHAH
DMM
!
KOHAKU!
NOW, FOOL! REMEMBER!!
TUG
...?
INU-YASHA...

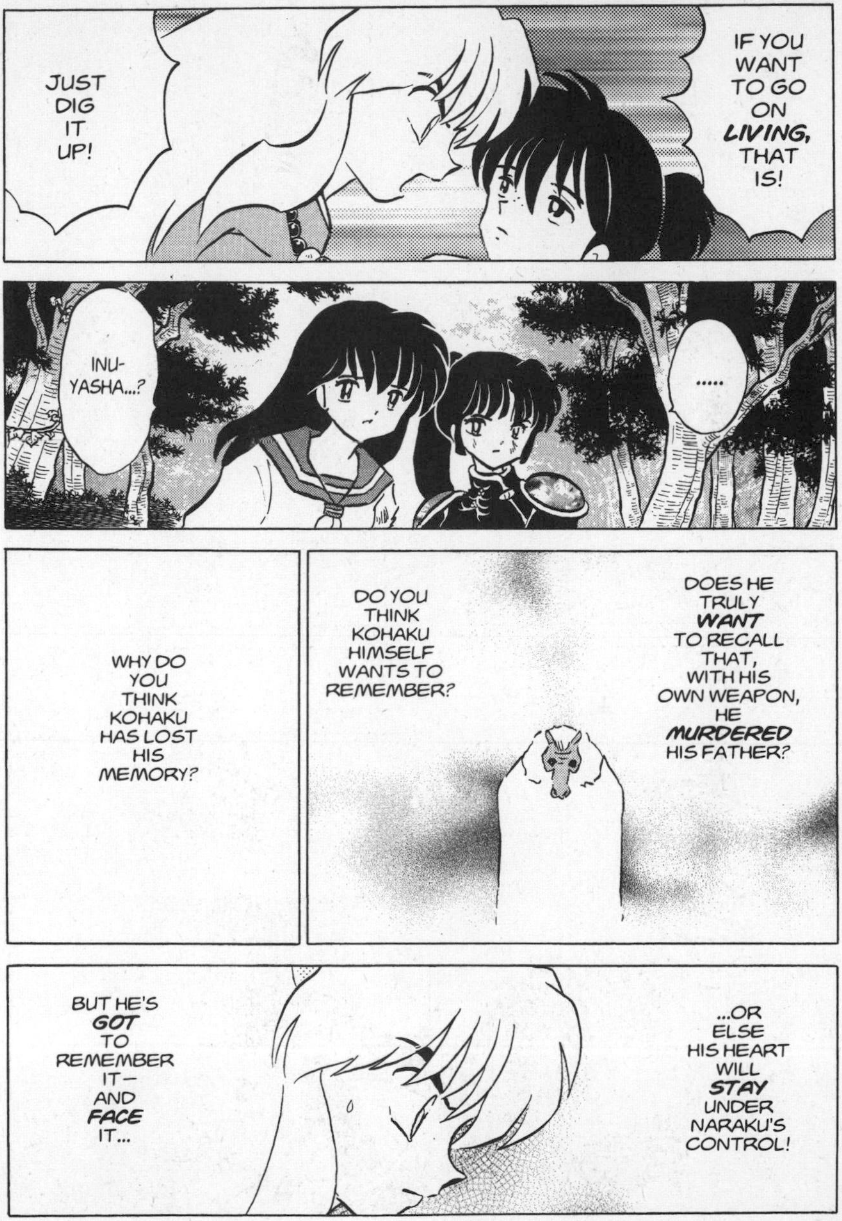
JUST DIG IT UP!
IF YOU WANT TO GO ON LIVING, THAT IS!
INU-YASHA...?
.....
WHY DO YOU THINK KOHAKU HAS LOST HIS MEMORY?
DO YOU THINK KOHAKU HIMSELF WANTS TO REMEMBER?
DOES HE TRULY WANT TO RECALL THAT, WITH HIS OWN WEAPON, HE MURDERED HIS FATHER?
BUT HE'S GOT TO REMEMBER IT— AND FACE IT...
...OR ELSE HIS HEART WILL STAY UNDER NARAKU'S CONTROL!

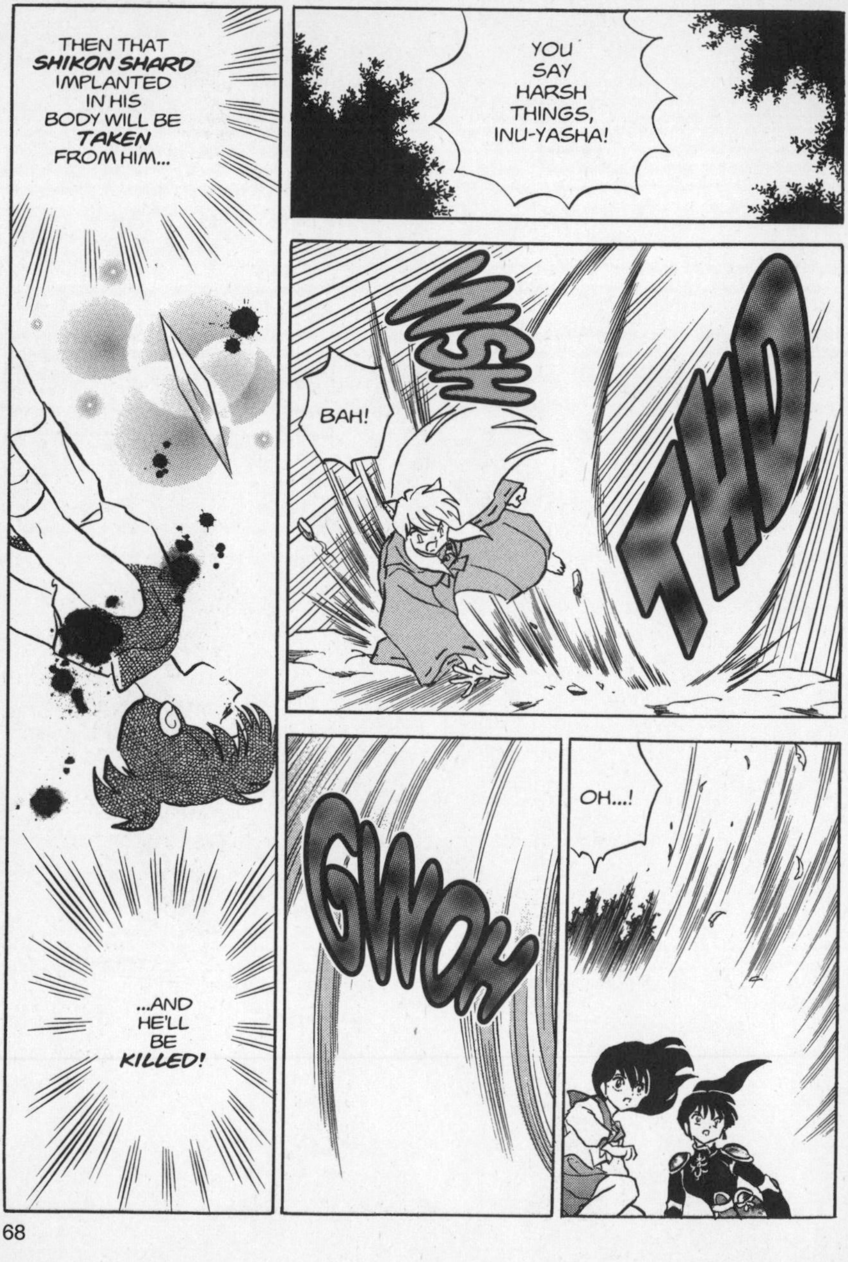
THEN THAT SHIKON SHARD IMPLANTED IN HIS BODY WILL BE TAKEN FROM HIM...
...AND HE'LL BE KILLED!
YOU SAY HARSH THINGS, INU-YASHA!
WSH
BAH!
THD
GWOH
OH...!

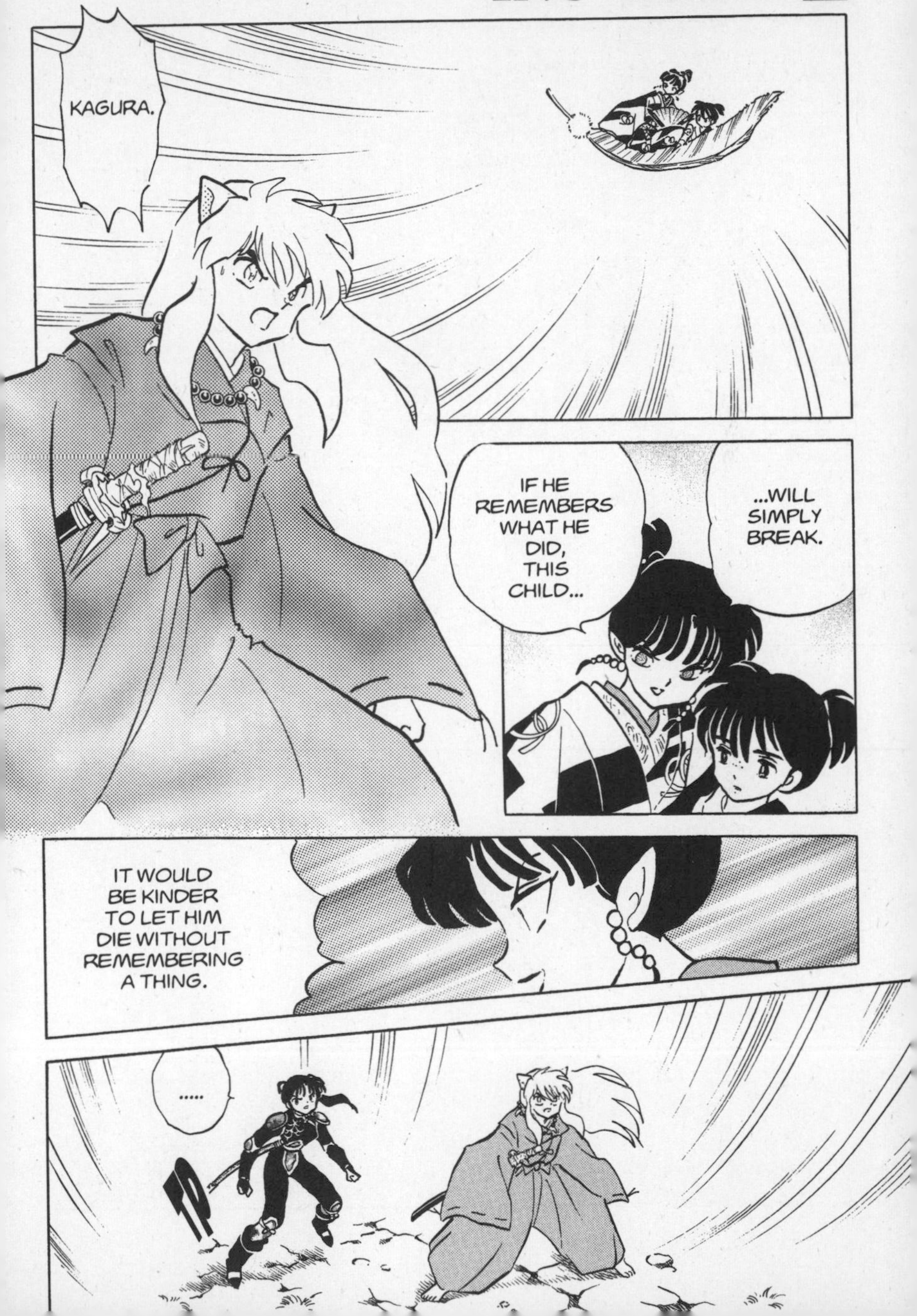
KAGURA.
IF HE REMEMBERS WHAT HE DID, THIS CHILD...
...WILL SIMPLY BREAK.
IT WOULD BE KINDER TO LET HIM DIE WITHOUT REMEMBERING A THING.
.....
TP

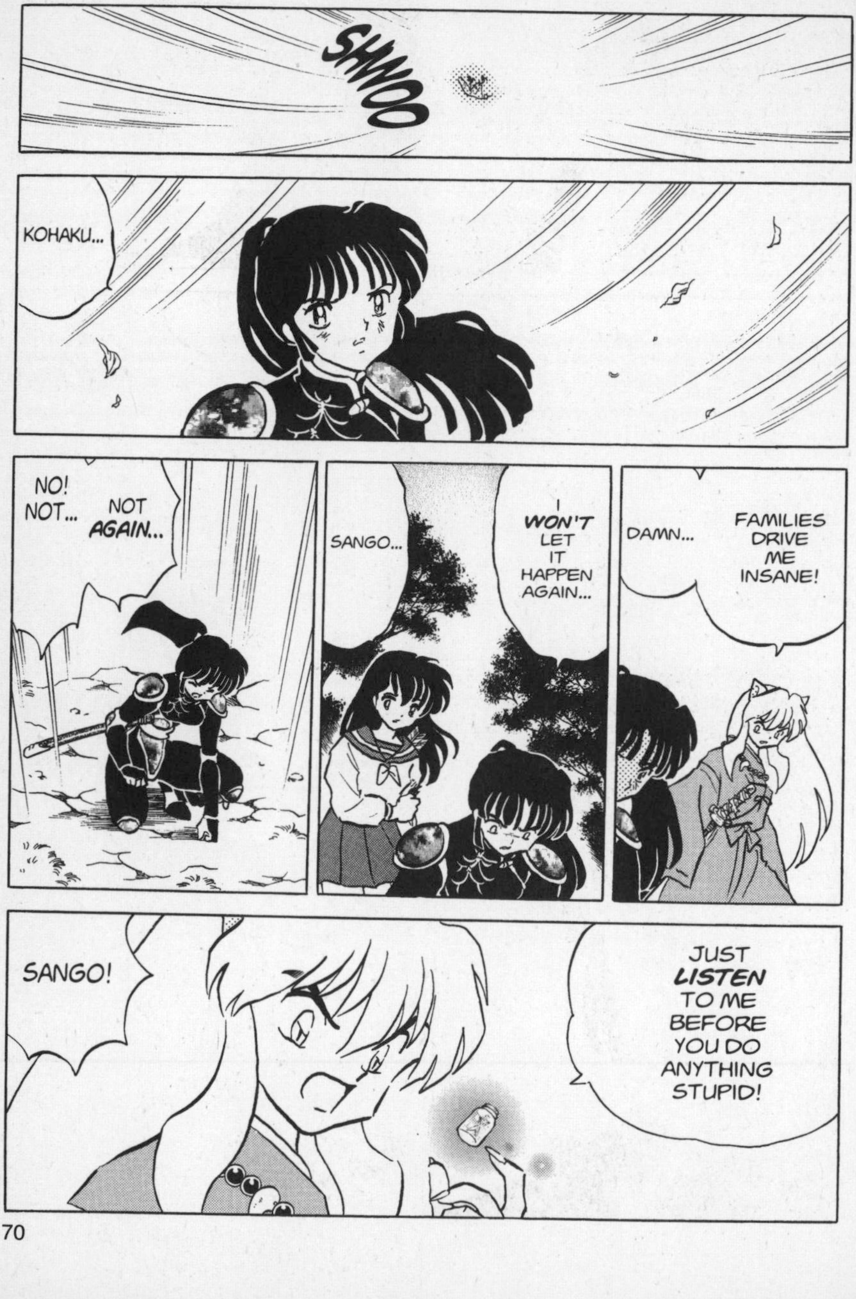
SHWOO
KOHAKU...
NO! NOT... NOT AGAIN...
SANGO...
I WON'T LET IT HAPPEN AGAIN...
DAMN...
FAMILIES DRIVE ME INSANE!
SANGO!
JUST LISTEN TO ME BEFORE YOU DO ANYTHING STUPID!

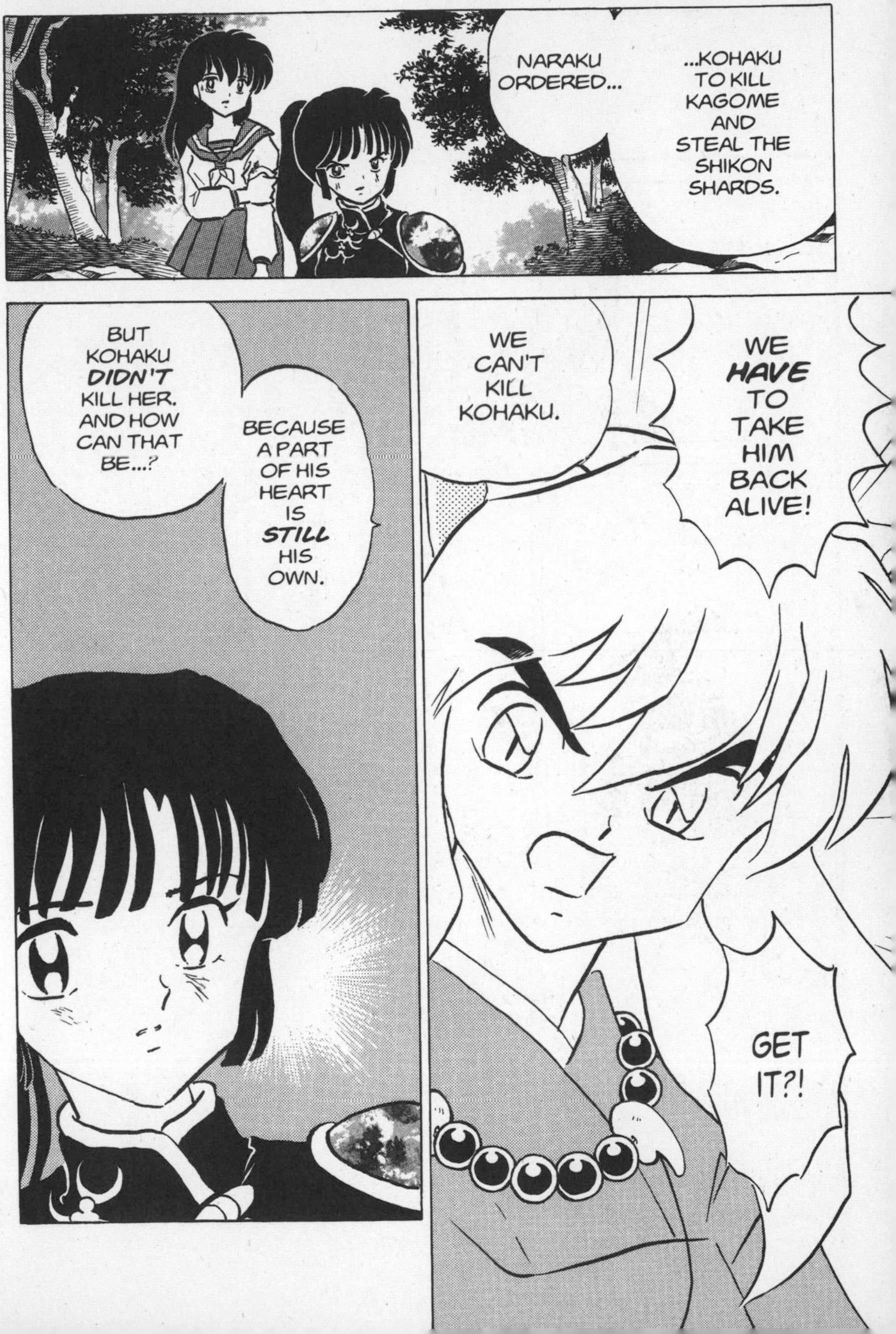
NARAKU ORDERED...
...KOHAKU TO KILL KAGOME AND STEAL THE SHIKON SHARDS.
BUT KOHAKU **DIDN'T** KILL HER. AND HOW CAN THAT BE...?
BECAUSE A PART OF HIS HEART IS **STILL** HIS OWN.
WE CAN'T KILL KOHAKU.
WE **HAVE** TO TAKE HIM BACK ALIVE!
GET IT?!

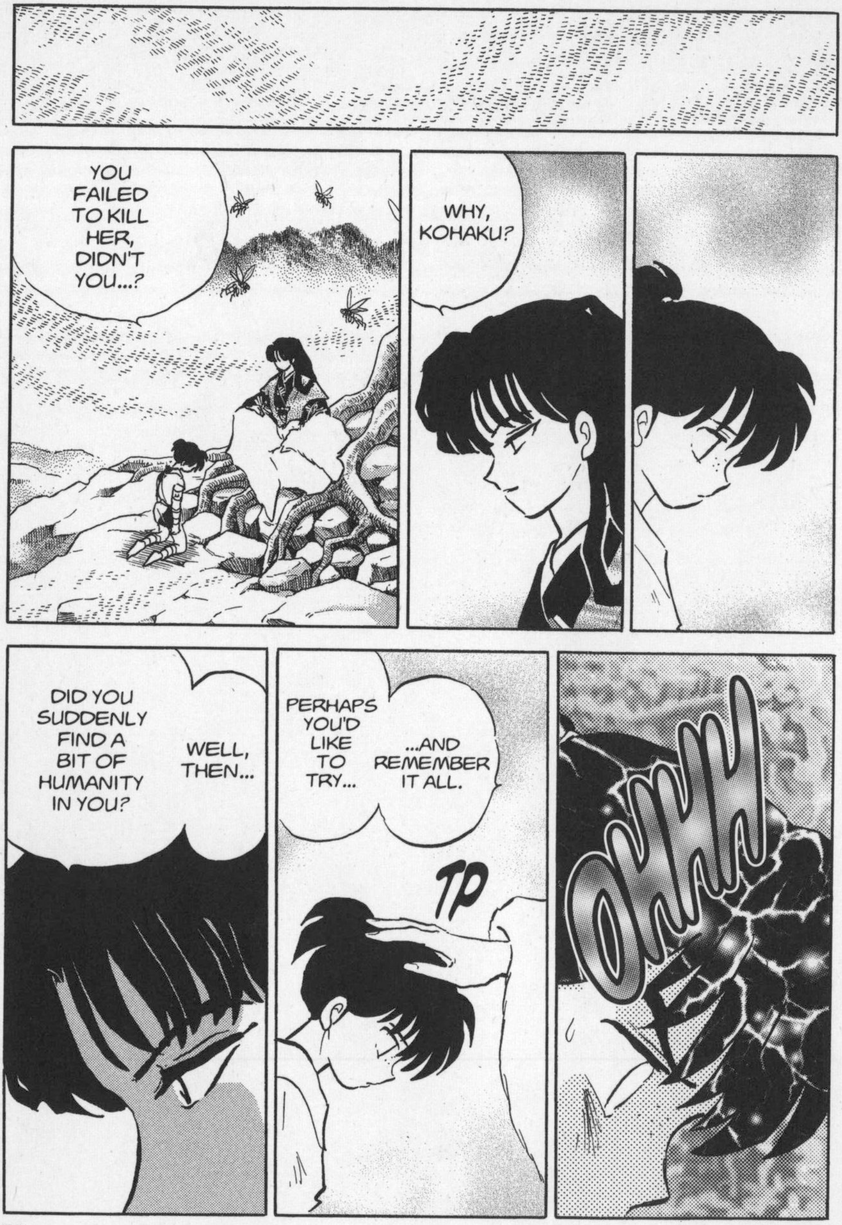
YOU FAILED TO KILL HER, DIDN'T YOU...?
WHY, KOHAKU?
DID YOU SUDDENLY FIND A BIT OF HUMANITY IN YOU?
WELL, THEN...
PERHAPS YOU'D LIKE TO TRY...
...AND REMEMBER IT ALL.
TP
OHHH

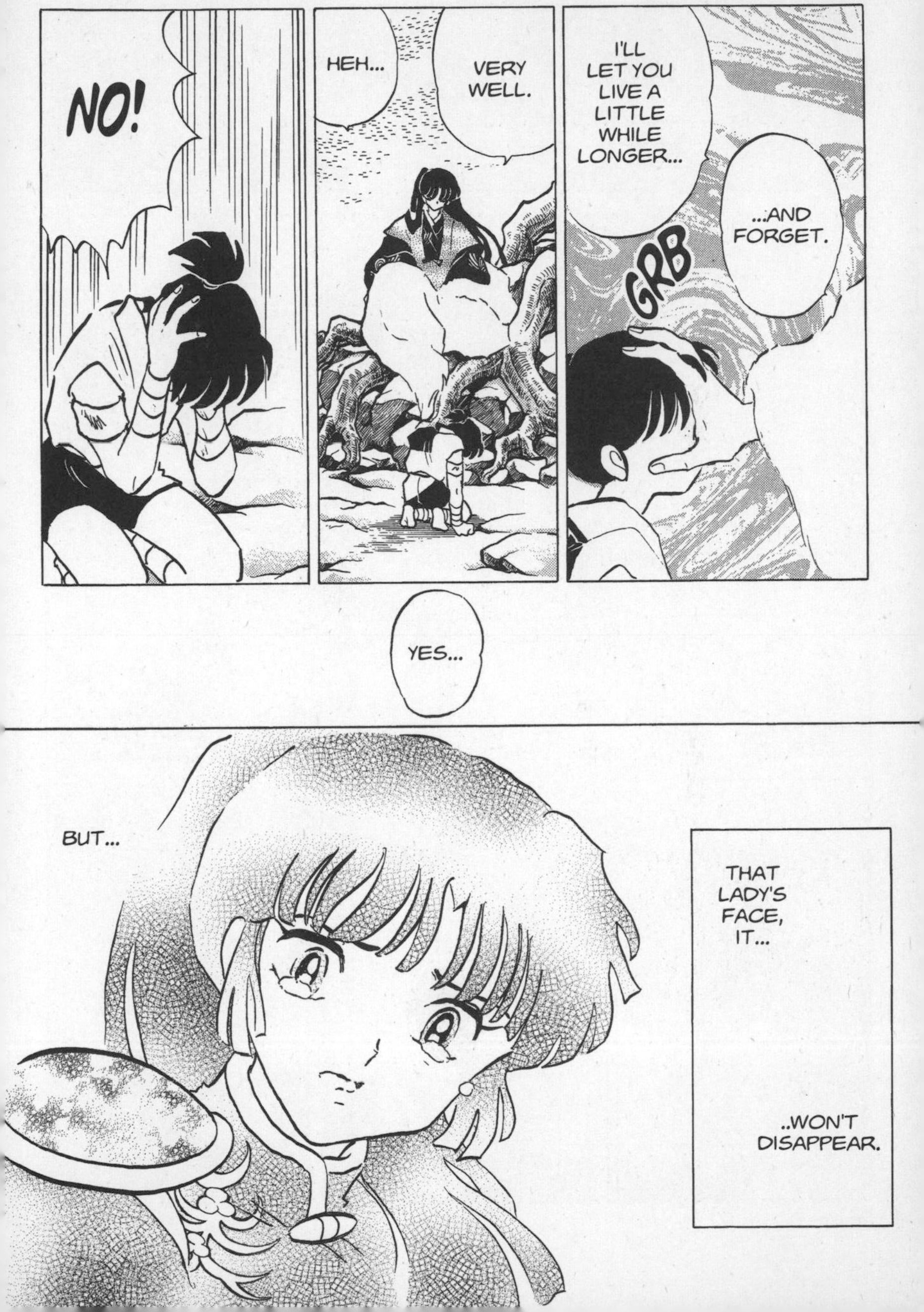
NO!
HEH...
VERY WELL.
I'LL LET YOU LIVE A LITTLE WHILE LONGER...
GRB
...AND FORGET.
YES...
BUT...
THAT LADY'S FACE, IT...
..WON'T DISAPPEAR.

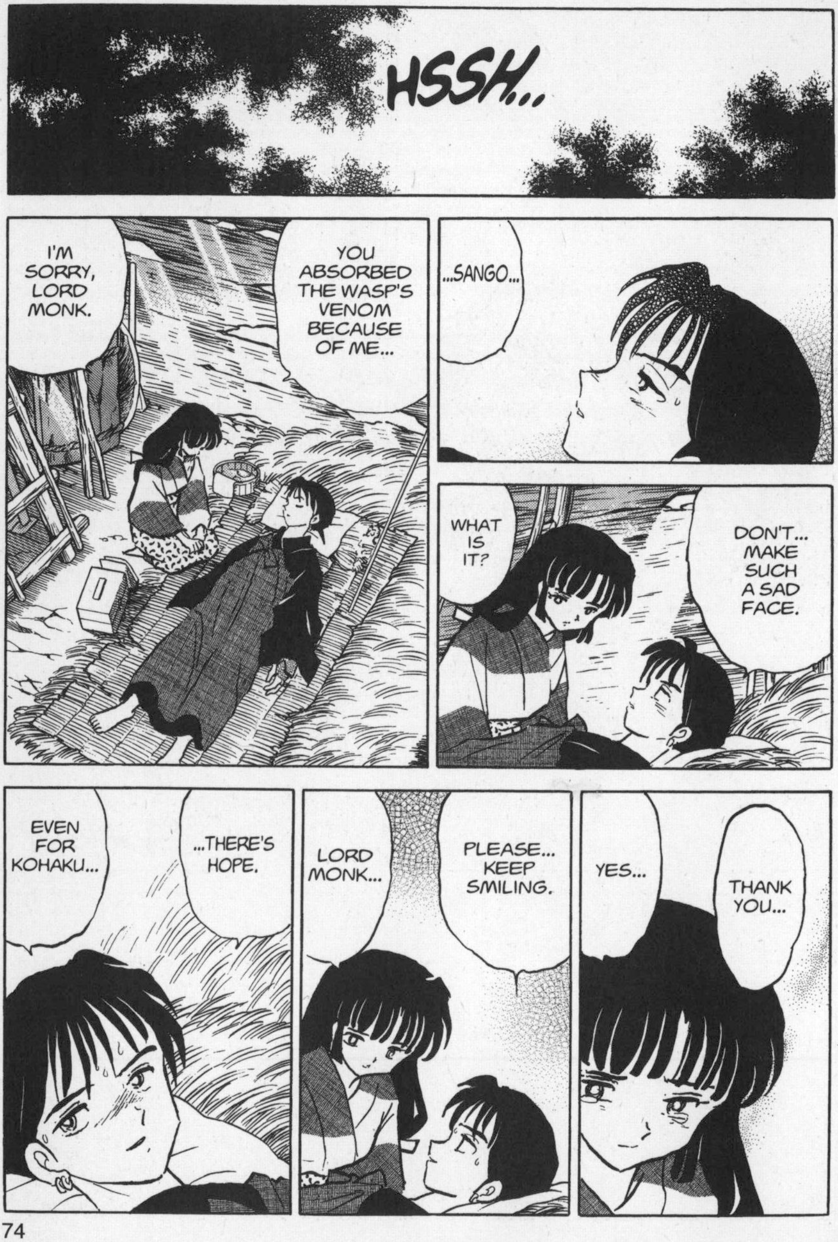
HSSH...
I'M SORRY, LORD MONK.
YOU ABSORBED THE WASP'S VENOM BECAUSE OF ME...
...SANGO...
WHAT IS IT?
DON'T... MAKE SUCH A SAD FACE.
EVEN FOR KOHAKU...
...THERE'S HOPE.
LORD MONK...
PLEASE... KEEP SMILING.
YES...
THANK YOU...

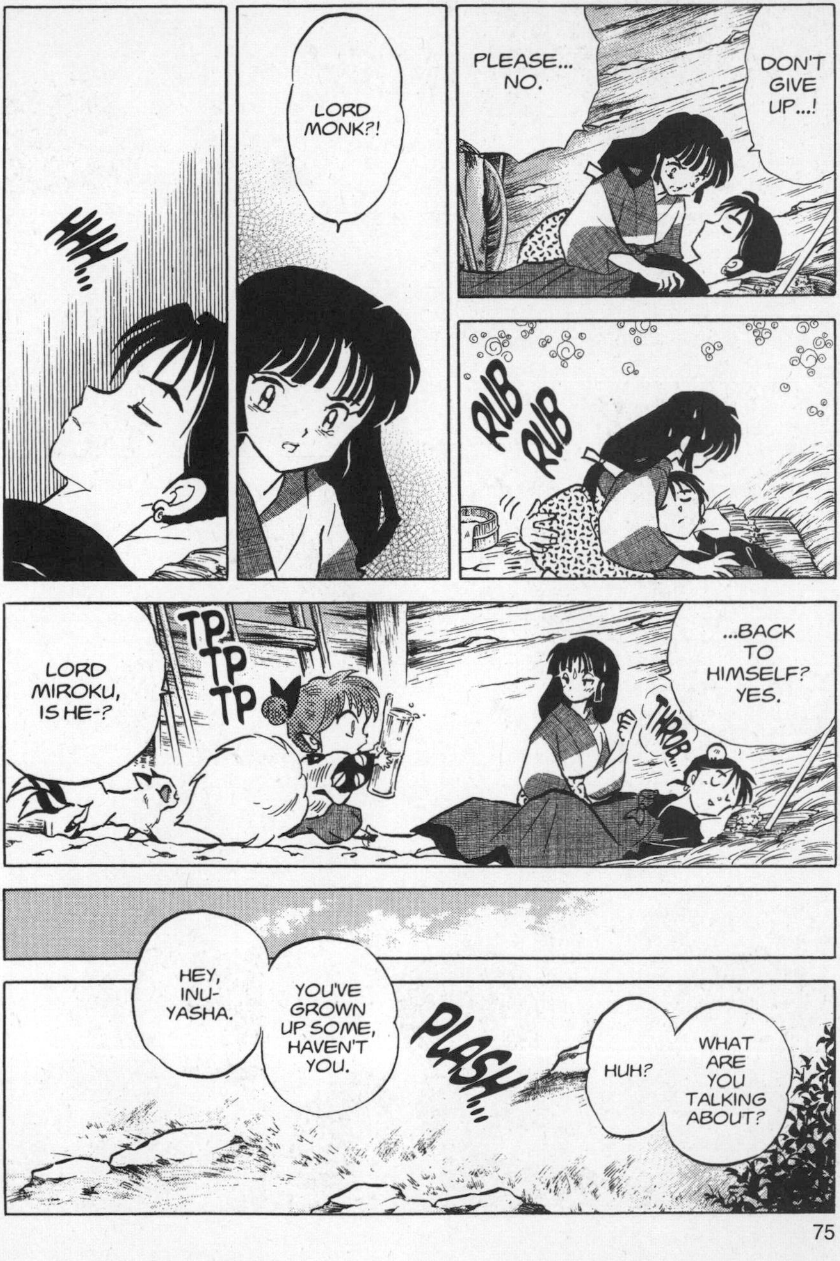
HHH...
LORD MONK?!
PLEASE... NO.
DON'T GIVE UP...!
RUB RUB
LORD MIROKU, IS HE-?
TP TP TP
...BACK TO HIMSELF? YES.
THROB...
HEY, INU-YASHA.
YOU'VE GROWN UP SOME, HAVEN'T YOU.
PLASH...
HUH?
WHAT ARE YOU TALKING ABOUT?

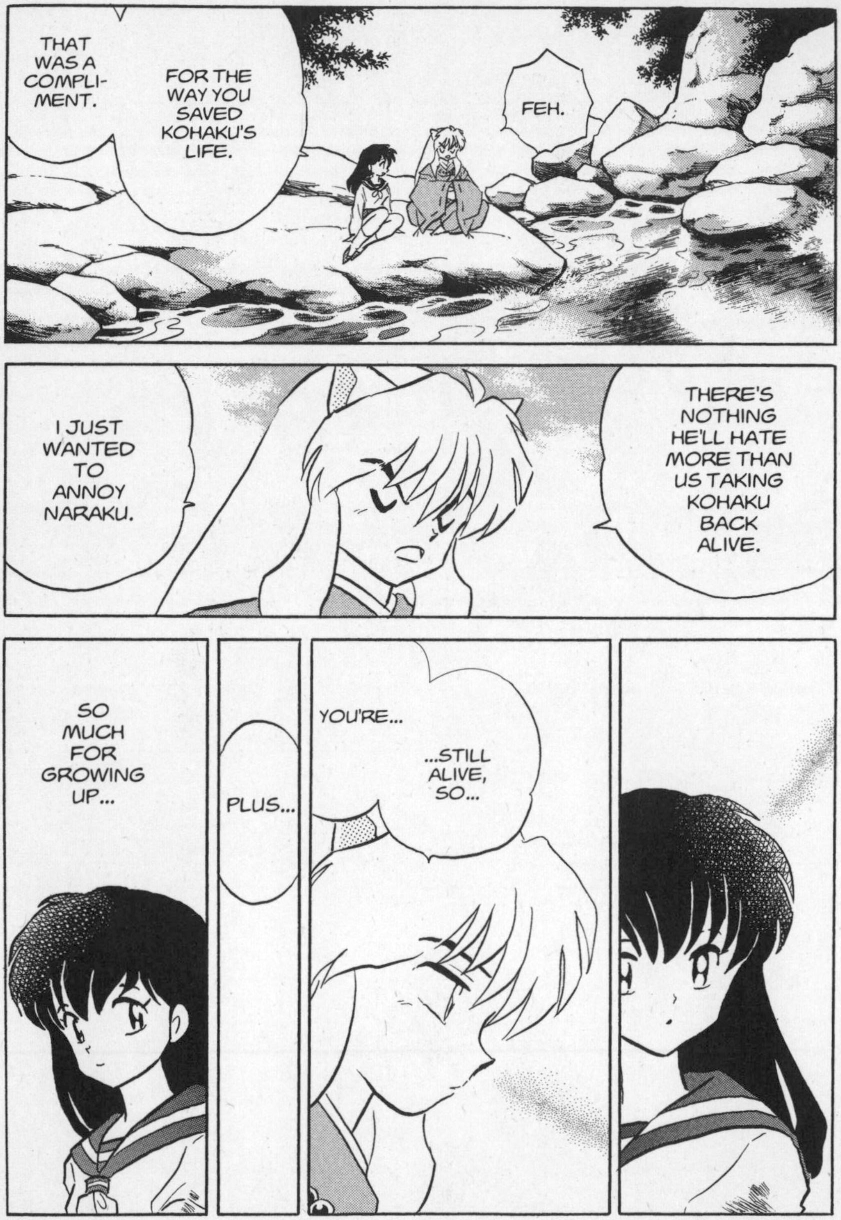
THAT WAS A COMPLIMENT.
FOR THE WAY YOU SAVED KOHAKU'S LIFE.
FEH.
I JUST WANTED TO ANNOY NARAKU.
THERE'S NOTHING HE'LL HATE MORE THAN US TAKING KOHAKU BACK ALIVE.
SO MUCH FOR GROWING UP...
PLUS...
YOU'RE...
...STILL ALIVE, SO...

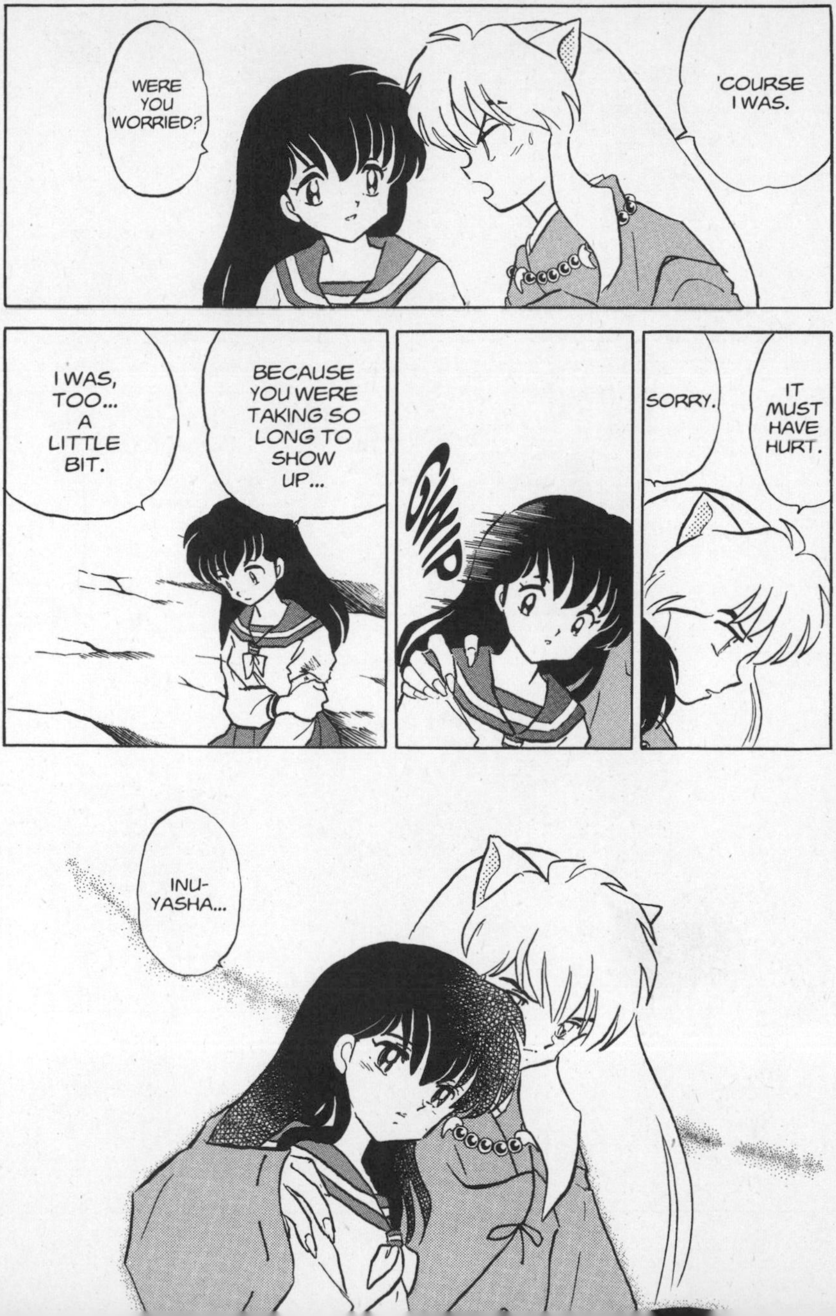
WERE YOU WORRIED?
'COURSE I WAS.
I WAS, TOO... A LITTLE BIT.
BECAUSE YOU WERE TAKING SO LONG TO SHOW UP...
GWIP
SORRY.
IT MUST HAVE HURT.
INU-YASHA...

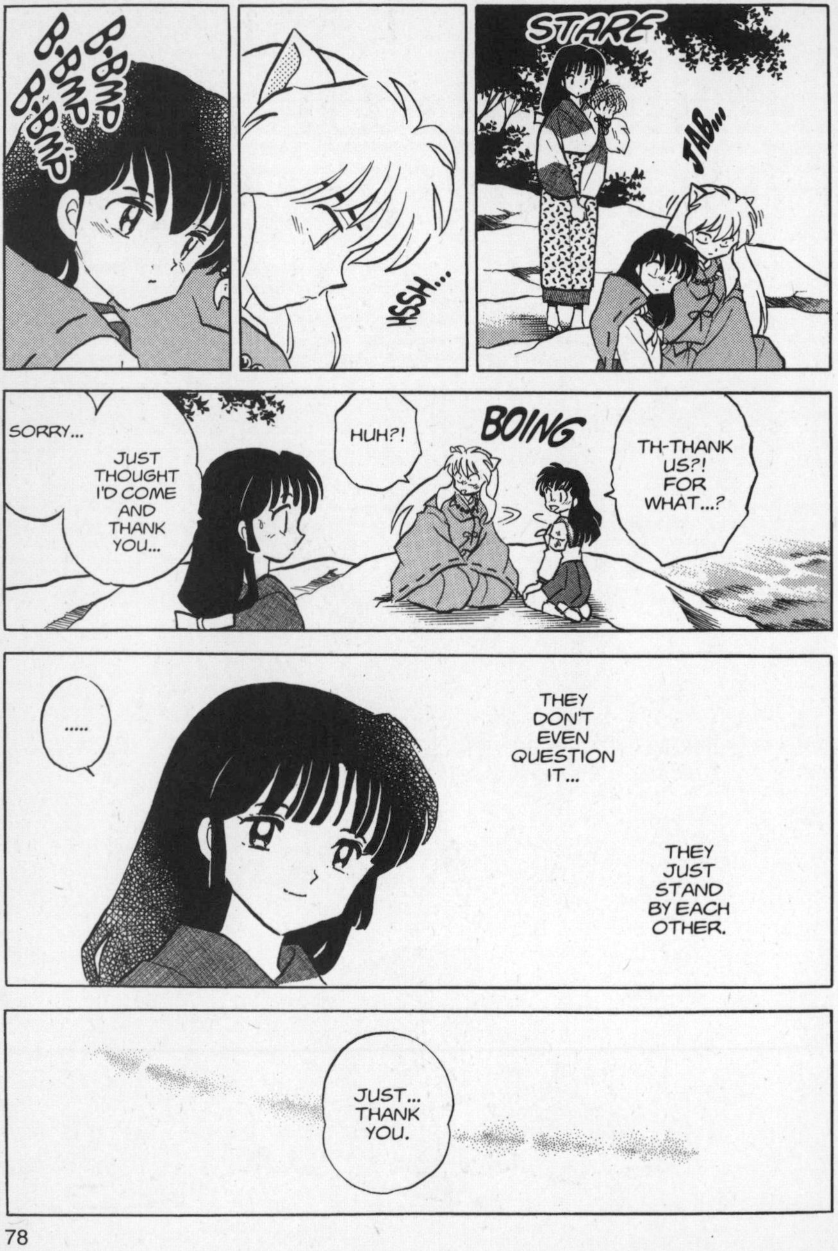
B-BMP B-BMP B-BMP
HSSH...
STARE
JAB...
SORRY...
JUST THOUGHT I'D COME AND THANK YOU...
HUH?!
BOING
TH-THANK US?! FOR WHAT...?
.....
THEY DON'T EVEN QUESTION IT...
THEY JUST STAND BY EACH OTHER.
JUST... THANK YOU.

SCROLL FIVE

SECRET OF THE TRANSFORMATION

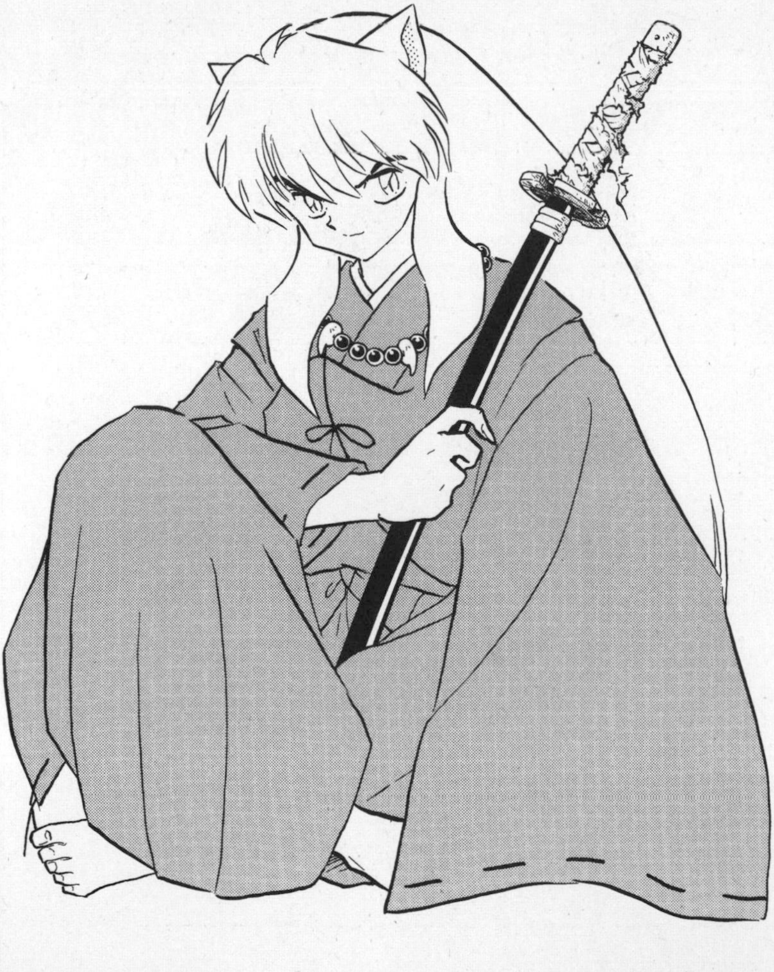

A FRIEND OF YOUR FATHER'S... *HERE,* IN SO REMOTE A FOREST?

.....

ZK

HSSS...

I'VE BEEN THINKING IT WAS TIME YOU CAME FOR A VISIT...

...SESSHŌ-MARU.

A VOICE, FROM UP IN THE SKY...

HMM—?

THERE'S NO ONE AROUND.

YOU KNEW THAT I WOULD COME...

...BOKU-SEN'Ō?

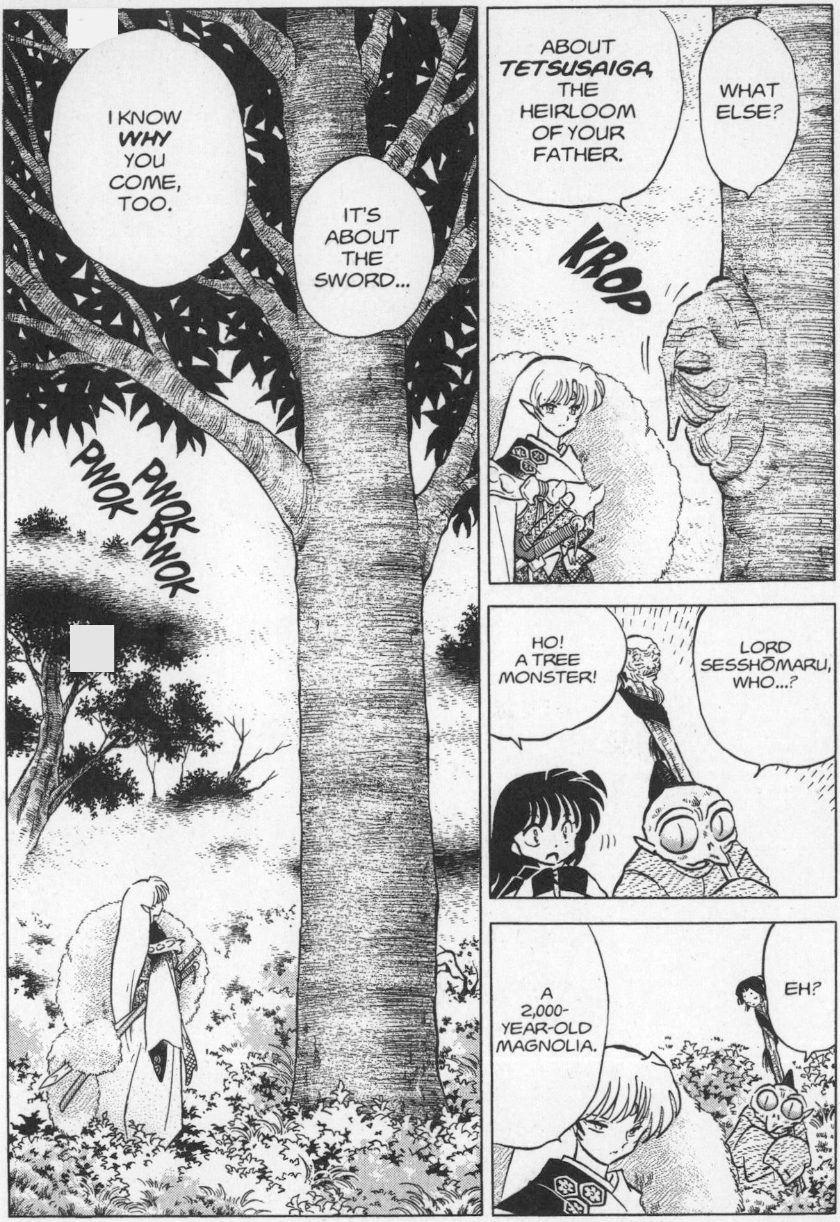
I KNOW WHY YOU COME, TOO.
IT'S ABOUT THE SWORD...
PWOK PWOK
PWOK PWOK
ABOUT TETSUSAIGA, THE HEIRLOOM OF YOUR FATHER.
WHAT ELSE?
KROP
HO! A TREE MONSTER!
LORD SESSHŌMARU, WHO...?
A 2,000-YEAR-OLD MAGNOLIA.
EH?

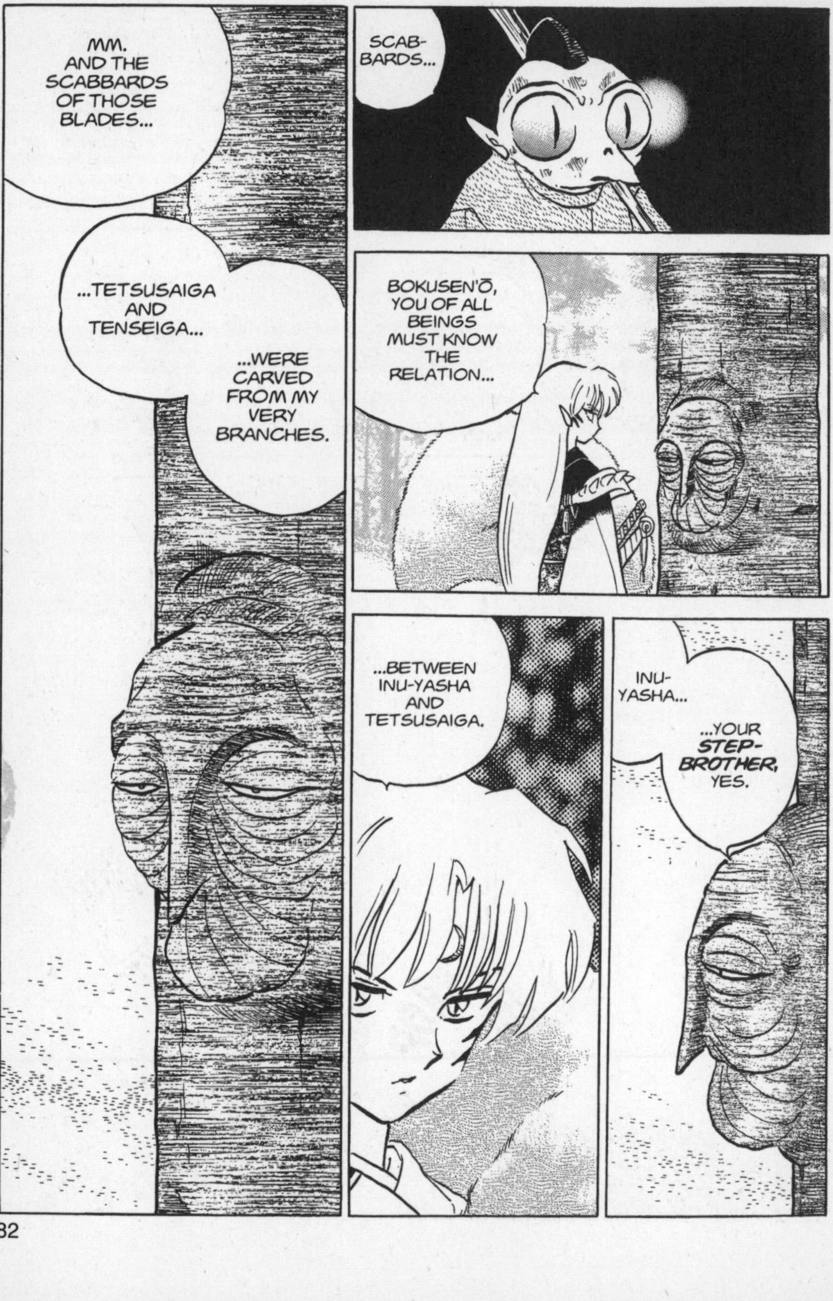
MM. AND THE SCABBARDS OF THOSE BLADES...
...TETSUSAIGA AND TENSEIGA...
...WERE CARVED FROM MY VERY BRANCHES.
SCAB-BARDS...
BOKUSEN'Ō, YOU OF ALL BEINGS MUST KNOW THE RELATION...
...BETWEEN INU-YASHA AND TETSUSAIGA.
INU-YASHA...
...YOUR *STEP-BROTHER*, YES.

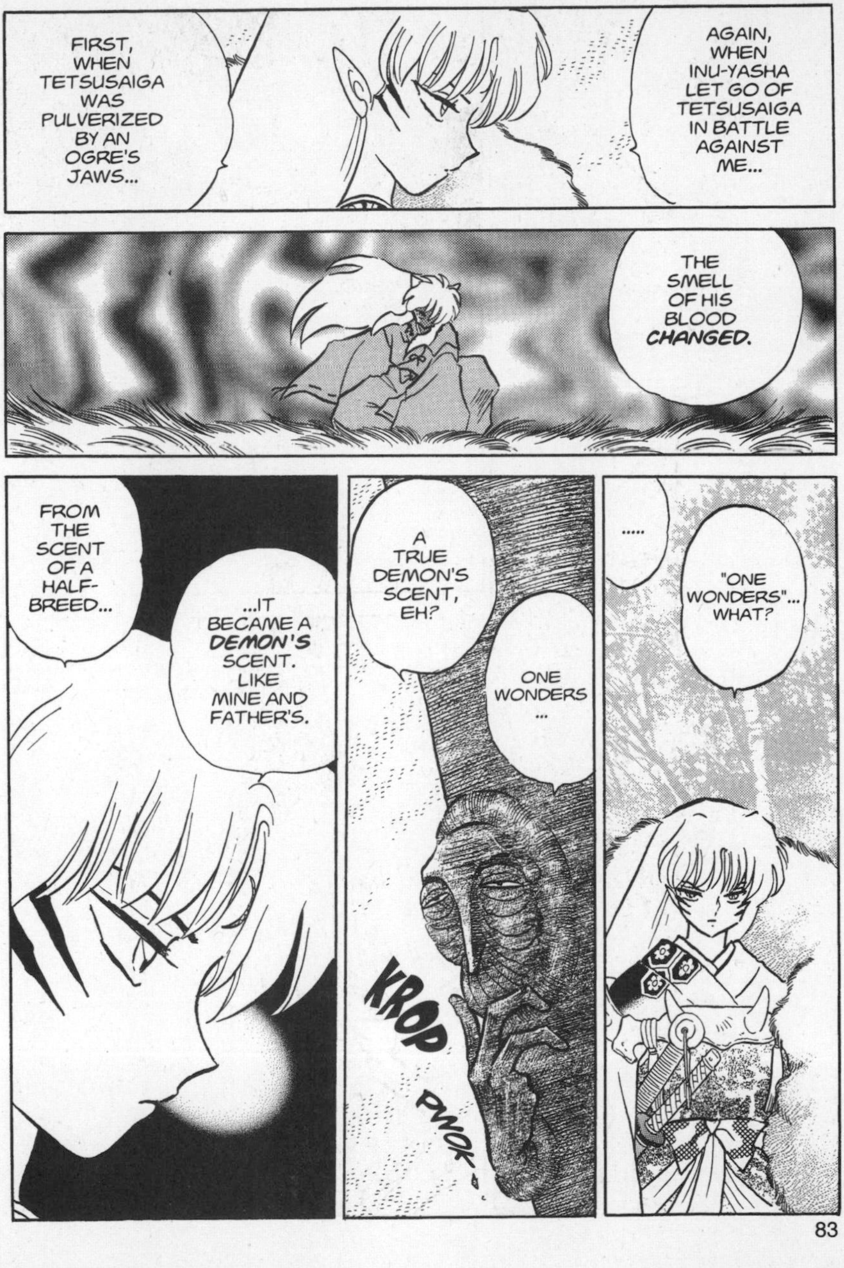
FIRST, WHEN TETSUSAIGA WAS PULVERIZED BY AN OGRE'S JAWS...
AGAIN, WHEN INU-YASHA LET GO OF TETSUSAIGA IN BATTLE AGAINST ME...
THE SMELL OF HIS BLOOD CHANGED.
FROM THE SCENT OF A HALF-BREED...
...IT BECAME A DEMON'S SCENT. LIKE MINE AND FATHER'S.
A TRUE DEMON'S SCENT, EH?
ONE WONDERS ...
KROP
PWOK
.....
"ONE WONDERS"... WHAT?

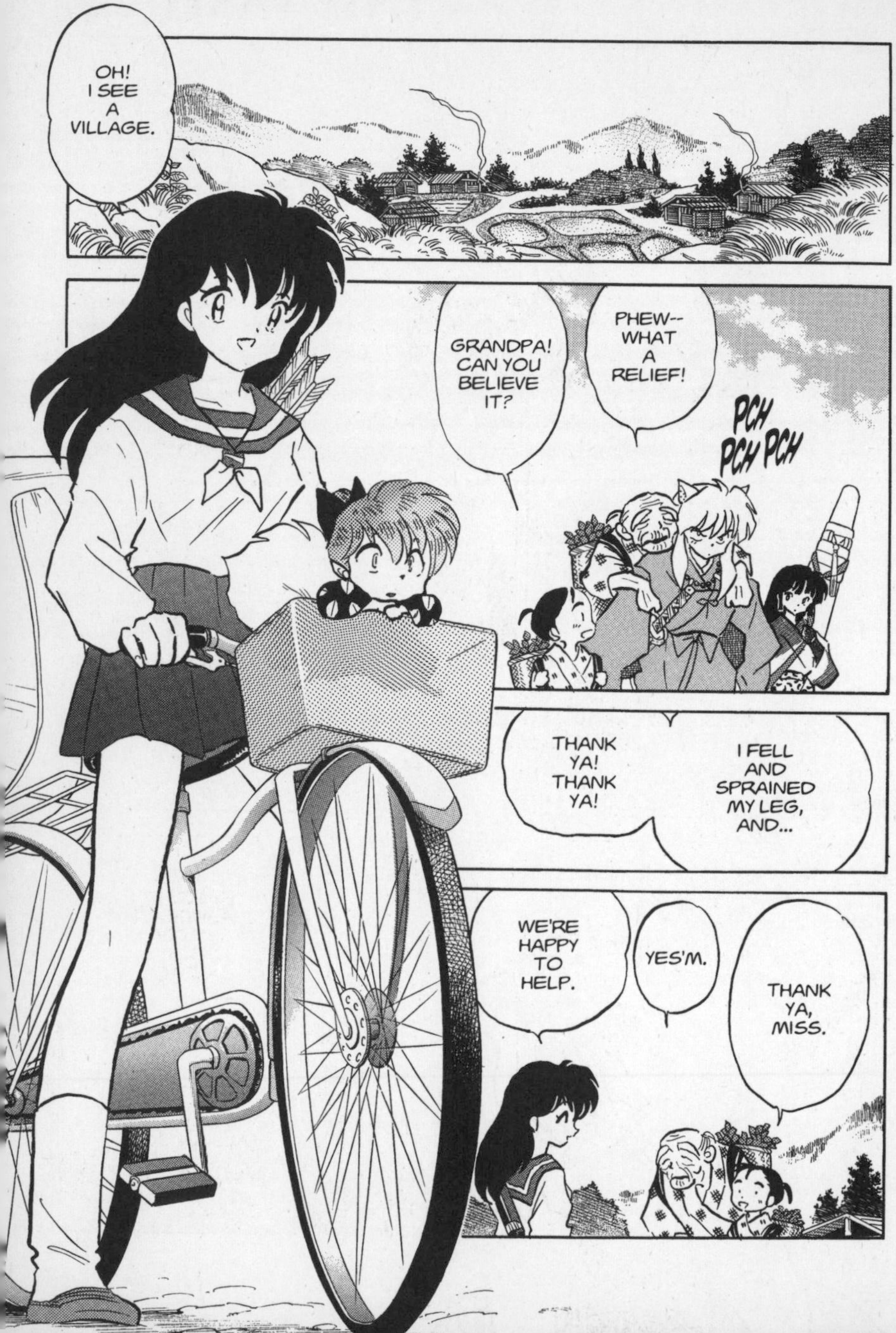
OH! I SEE A VILLAGE.
GRANDPA! CAN YOU BELIEVE IT?
PHEW-- WHAT A RELIEF!
PCH PCH PCH
THANK YA! THANK YA!
I FELL AND SPRAINED MY LEG, AND...
WE'RE HAPPY TO HELP.
YES'M.
THANK YA, MISS.

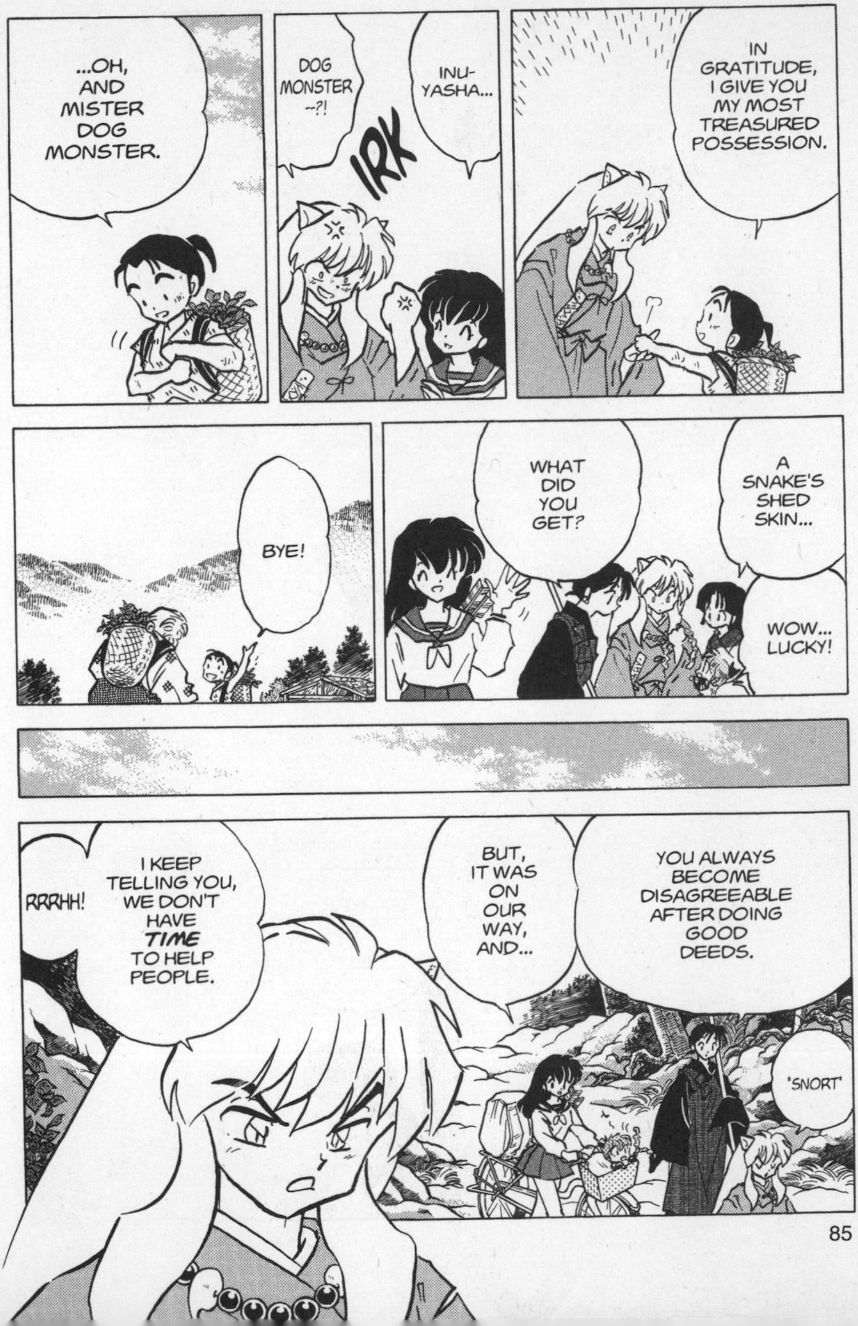
...OH, AND MISTER DOG MONSTER.
DOG MONSTER --?!
INU-YASHA...
IRK
IN GRATITUDE, I GIVE YOU MY MOST TREASURED POSSESSION.
BYE!
WHAT DID YOU GET?
A SNAKE'S SHED SKIN...
WOW... LUCKY!
RRRHH!
I KEEP TELLING YOU, WE DON'T HAVE *TIME* TO HELP PEOPLE.
BUT, IT WAS ON OUR WAY, AND...
YOU ALWAYS BECOME DISAGREEABLE AFTER DOING GOOD DEEDS.
SNORT

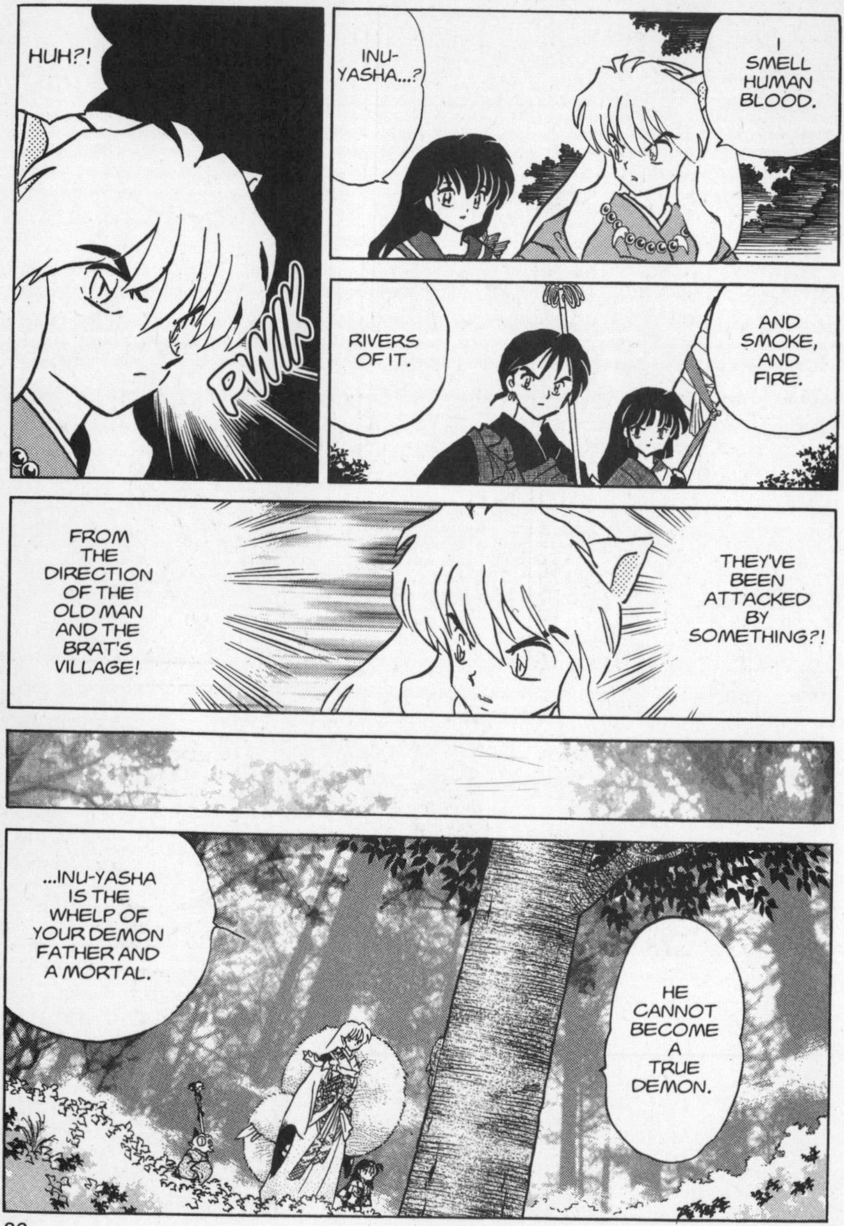
HUH?!
PWIK
INU-YASHA...?
I SMELL HUMAN BLOOD.
RIVERS OF IT.
AND SMOKE, AND FIRE.
FROM THE DIRECTION OF THE OLD MAN AND THE BRAT'S VILLAGE!
THEY'VE BEEN ATTACKED BY SOMETHING?!
...INU-YASHA IS THE WHELP OF YOUR DEMON FATHER AND A MORTAL.
HE CANNOT BECOME A TRUE DEMON.

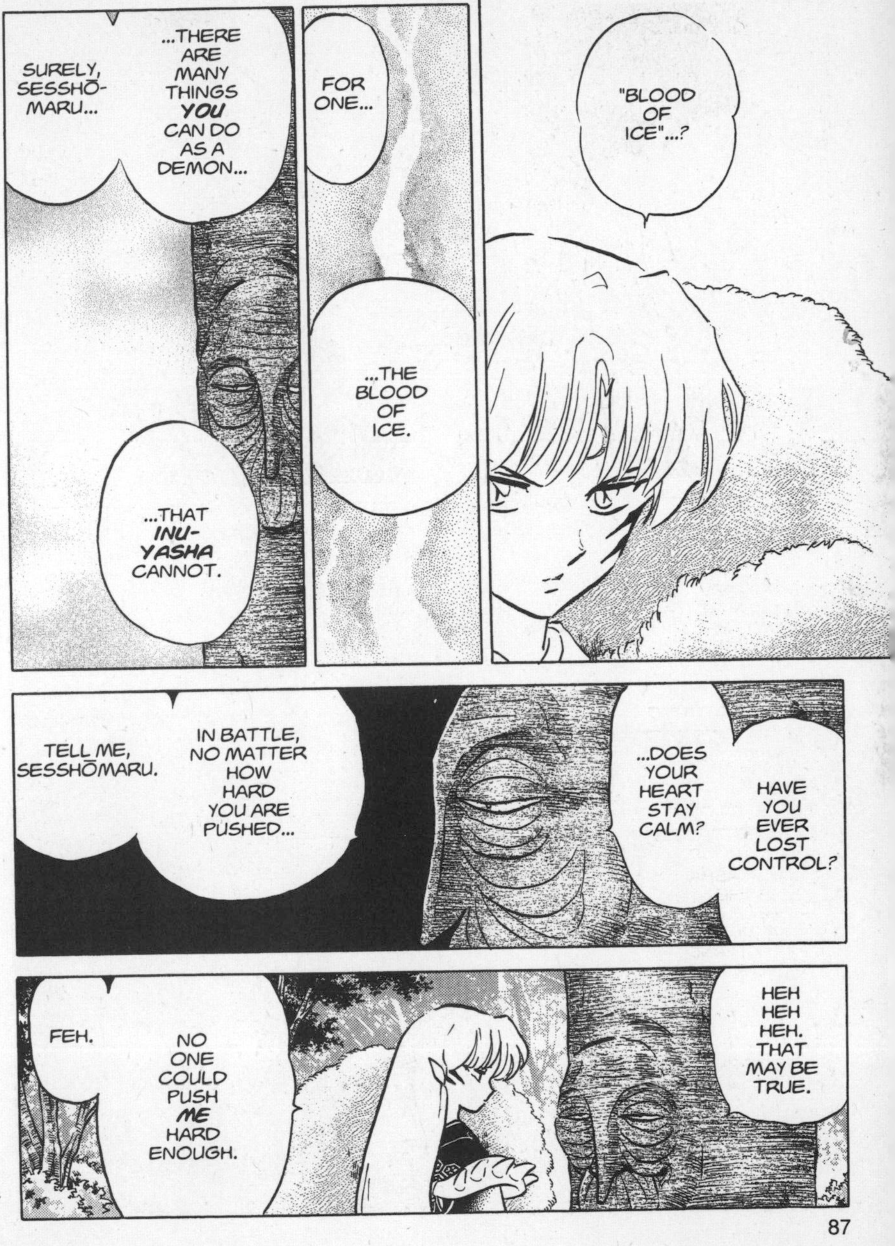
SURELY, SESSHŌMARU...
...THERE ARE MANY THINGS *YOU* CAN DO AS A DEMON...
...THAT *INU-YASHA* CANNOT.
FOR ONE...
...THE BLOOD OF ICE.
"BLOOD OF ICE"...?
TELL ME, SESSHŌMARU.
IN BATTLE, NO MATTER HOW HARD YOU ARE PUSHED...
...DOES YOUR HEART STAY CALM?
HAVE YOU EVER LOST CONTROL?
FEH.
NO ONE COULD PUSH *ME* HARD ENOUGH.
HEH HEH HEH. THAT MAY BE TRUE.

BUT INU-YASHA IS DIFFERENT.

IF HE IS CORNERED, IF HIS *LIFE* IS *ENDANGERED*...

...HIS DEMON-BLOOD TAKES OVER HIS BODY, AND HE TRANSFORMS TO PROTECT HIMSELF.

SO THAT'S WHAT HAPPENED...

BUT THE BLOOD THAT INU-YASHA INHERITED FROM YOUR FATHER...

...IS TOO STRONG FOR HIS HALF-BREED FLESH.

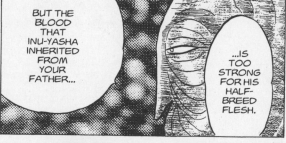

SO WHAT WILL HAPPEN?

PERHAPS...

...HIS HEART WILL BE CONSUMED BY THE DEMON POWER.

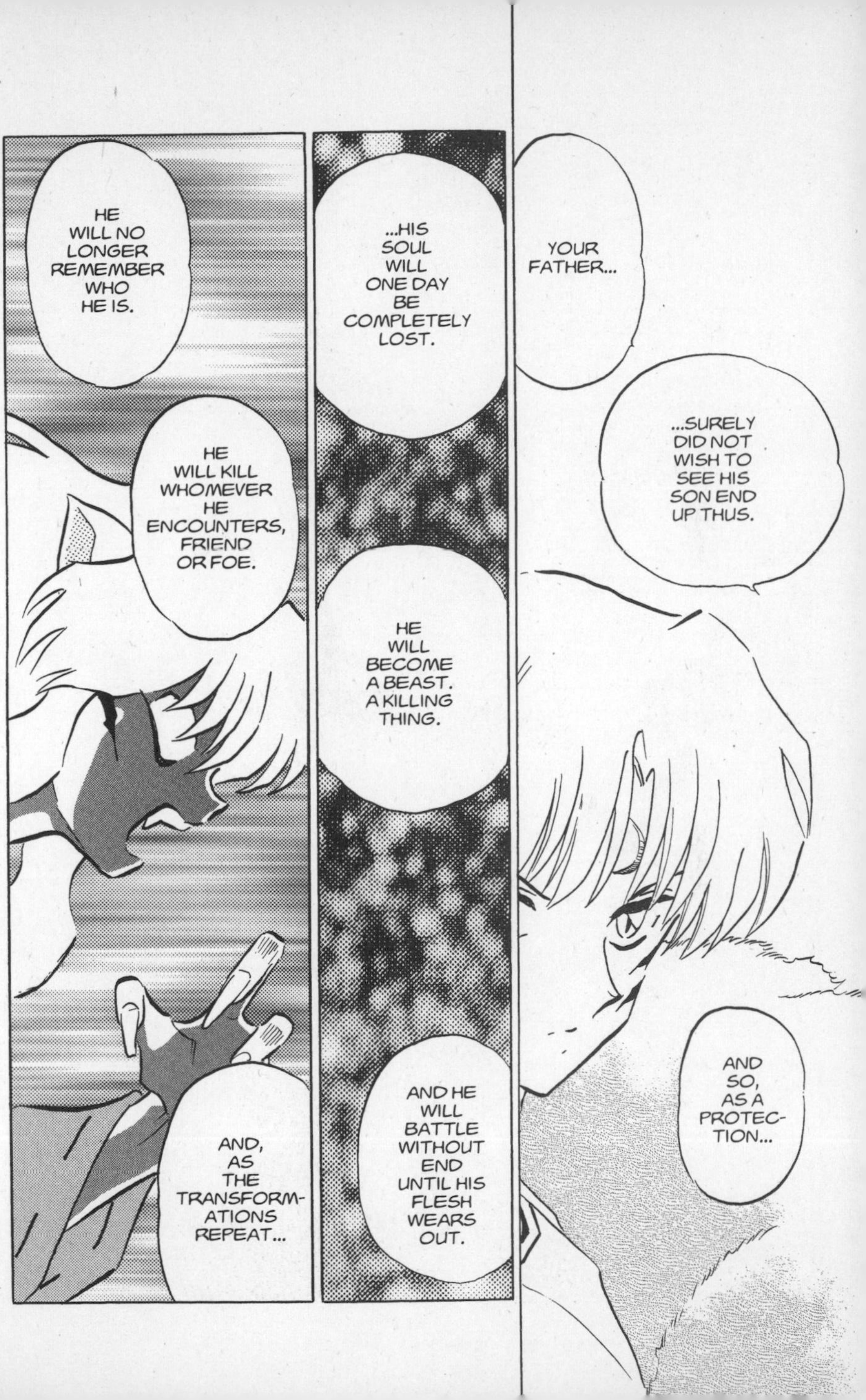
HE WILL NO LONGER REMEMBER WHO HE IS.
HE WILL KILL WHOMEVER HE ENCOUNTERS, FRIEND OR FOE.
AND, AS THE TRANSFORM-ATIONS REPEAT...
...HIS SOUL WILL ONE DAY BE COMPLETELY LOST.
HE WILL BECOME A BEAST. A KILLING THING.
AND HE WILL BATTLE WITHOUT END UNTIL HIS FLESH WEARS OUT.
YOUR FATHER...
...SURELY DID NOT WISH TO SEE HIS SON END UP THUS.
AND SO, AS A PROTEC-TION...

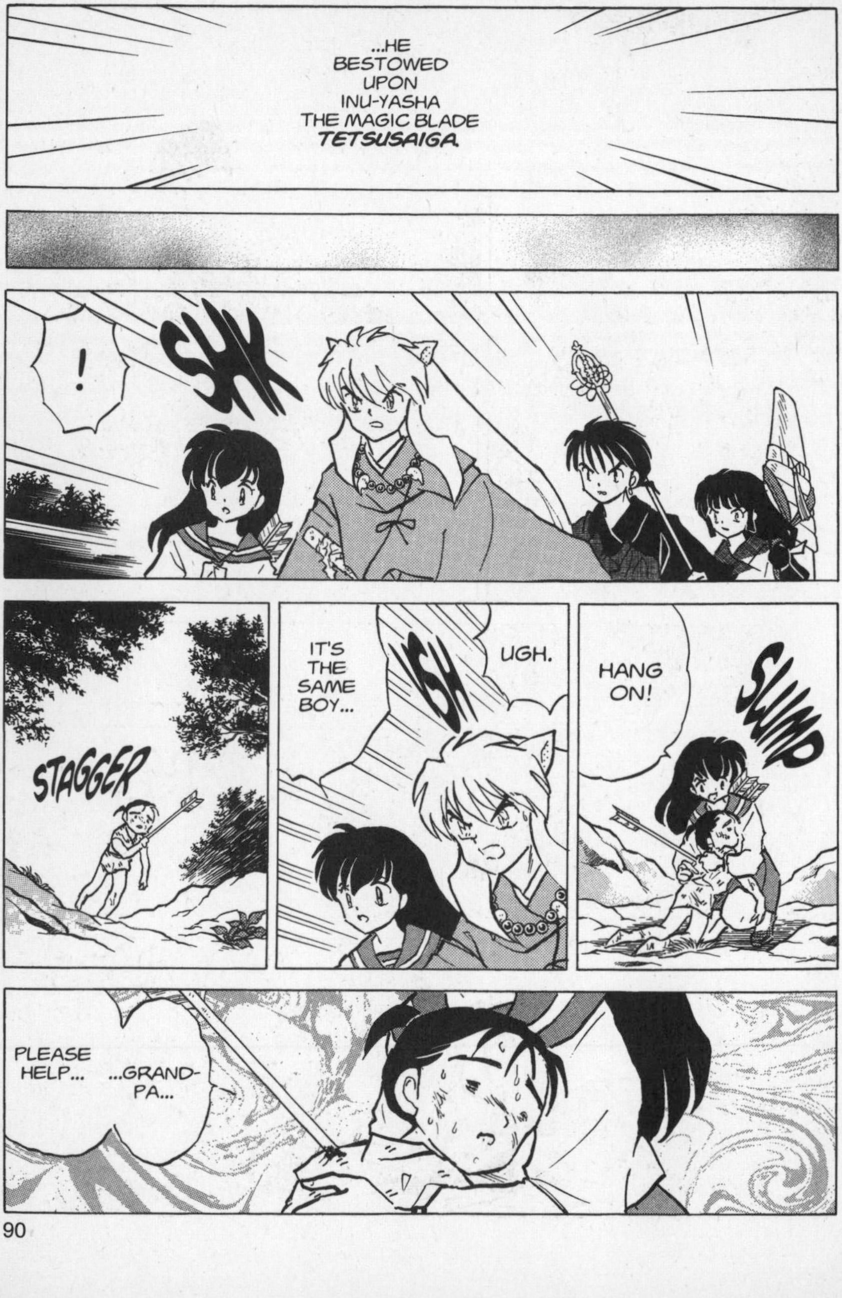
...HE BESTOWED UPON INU-YASHA THE MAGIC BLADE TETSUSAIGA.
!
SHK
STAGGER
IT'S THE SAME BOY...
UGH.
HANG ON!
SLUMP
PLEASE HELP...
...GRAND-PA...

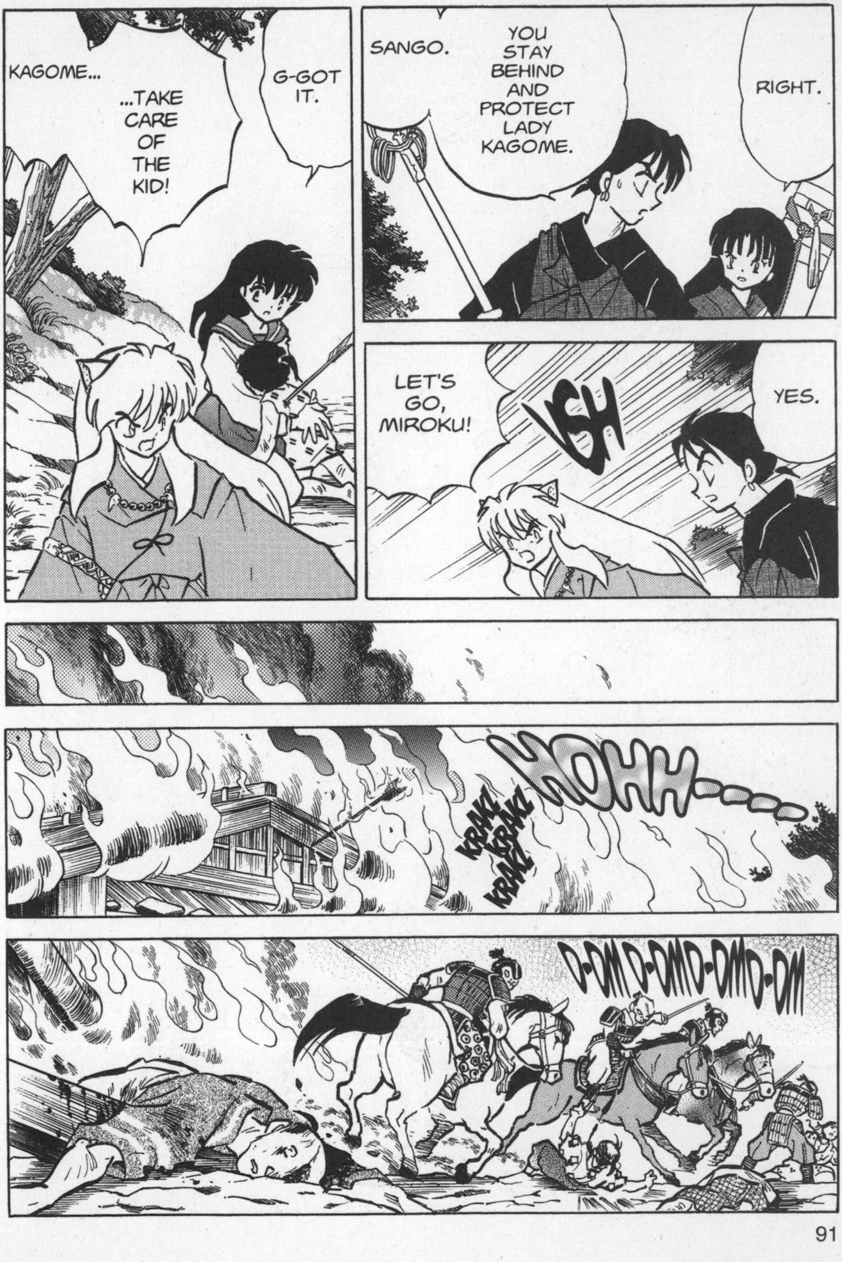
KAGOME...
...TAKE CARE OF THE KID!
G-GOT IT.
SANGO.
YOU STAY BEHIND AND PROTECT LADY KAGOME.
RIGHT.
LET'S GO, MIROKU!
VSH
YES.
KRAK! KRAK! KRAK!
HOHH.....
D-DM D-DM D-DM D-DM

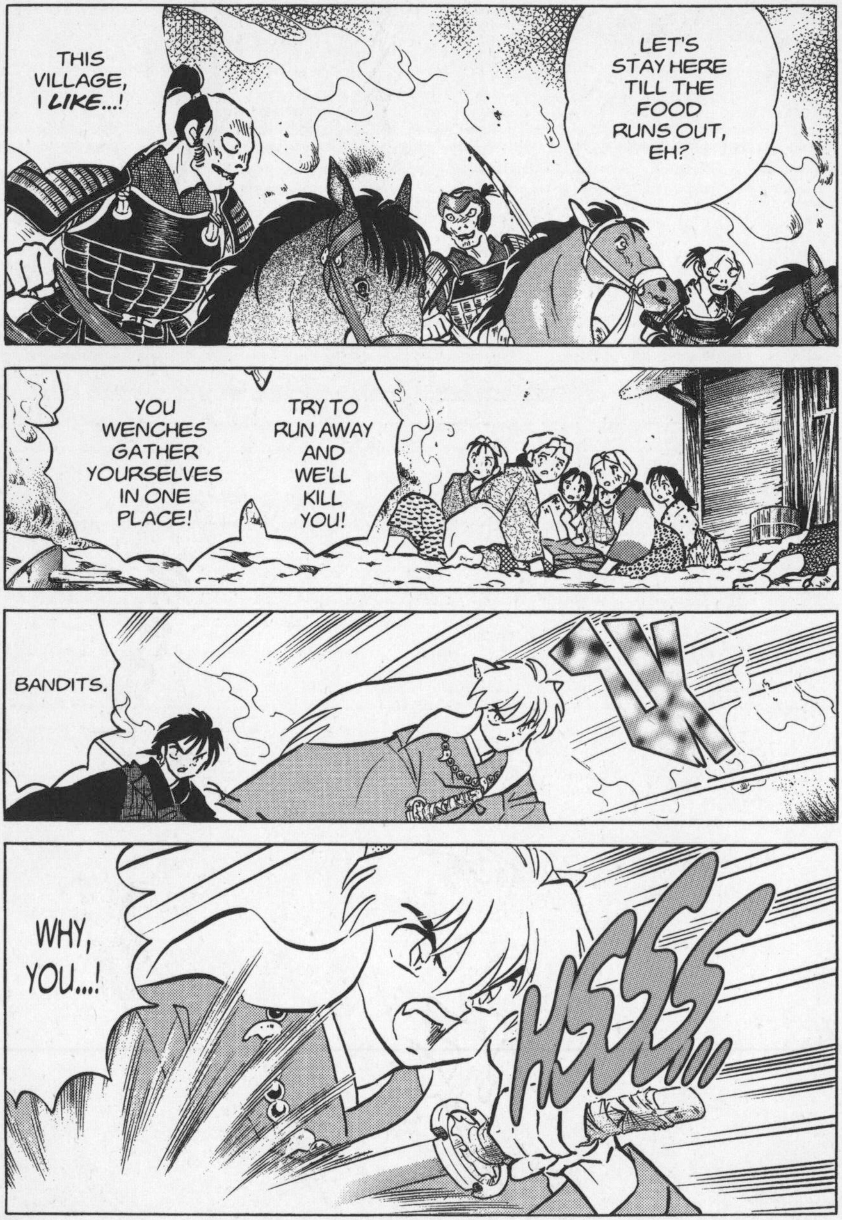
THIS VILLAGE, I **LIKE**...!
LET'S STAY HERE TILL THE FOOD RUNS OUT, EH?
YOU WENCHES GATHER YOURSELVES IN ONE PLACE!
TRY TO RUN AWAY AND WE'LL KILL YOU!
BANDITS.
WHY, YOU...!
HSSS...

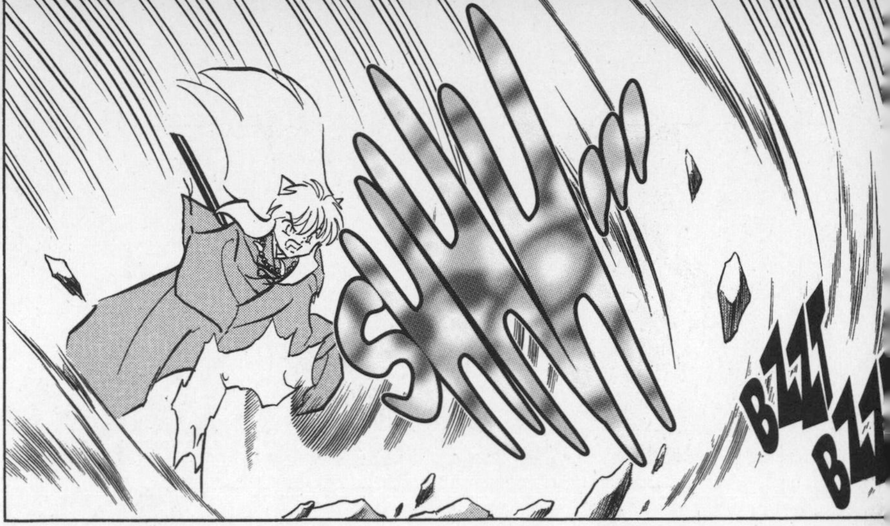
SHH...
BZZT

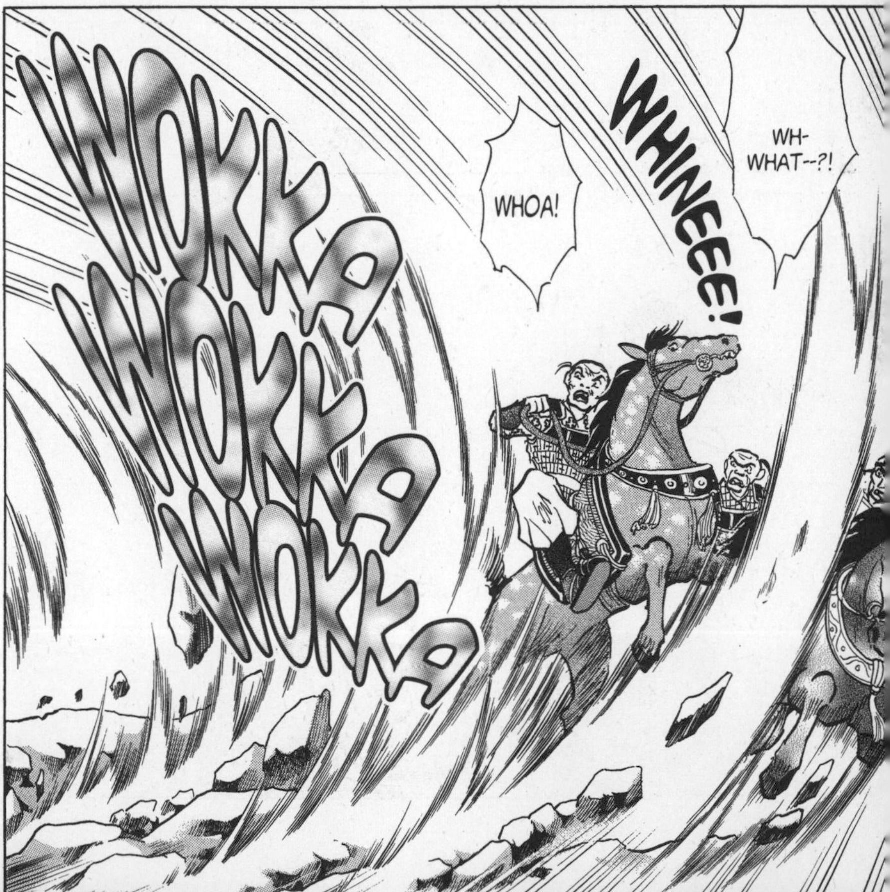
WOKKA
WOKKA
WOKKA
WOKKA
WHOA!
WHINEEE!
WH-
WHAT--?!

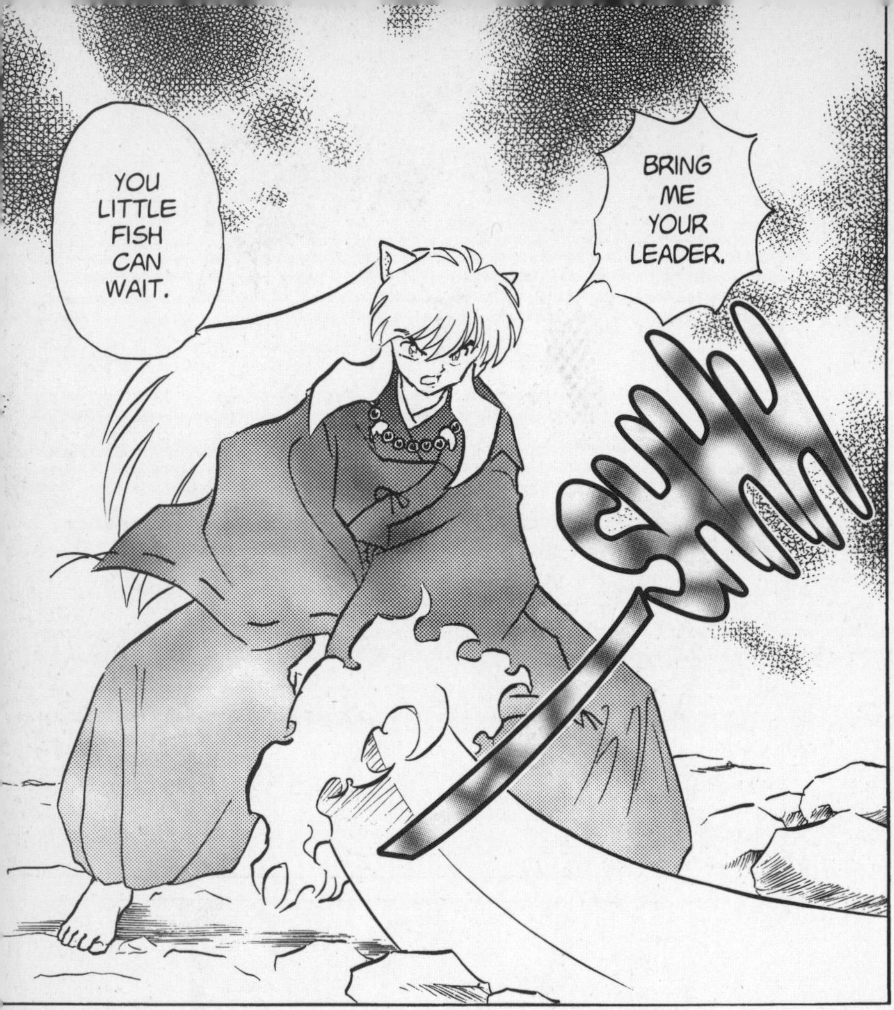
YOU LITTLE FISH CAN WAIT.
BRING ME YOUR LEADER.

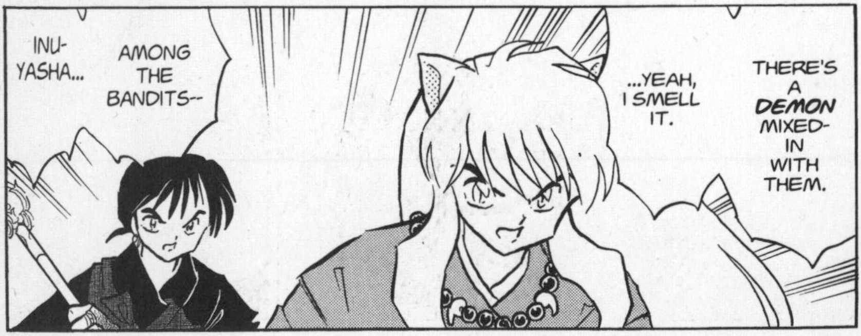
INU-YASHA...
AMONG THE BANDITS--
...YEAH, I SMELL IT.
THERE'S A DEMON MIXED-IN WITH THEM.

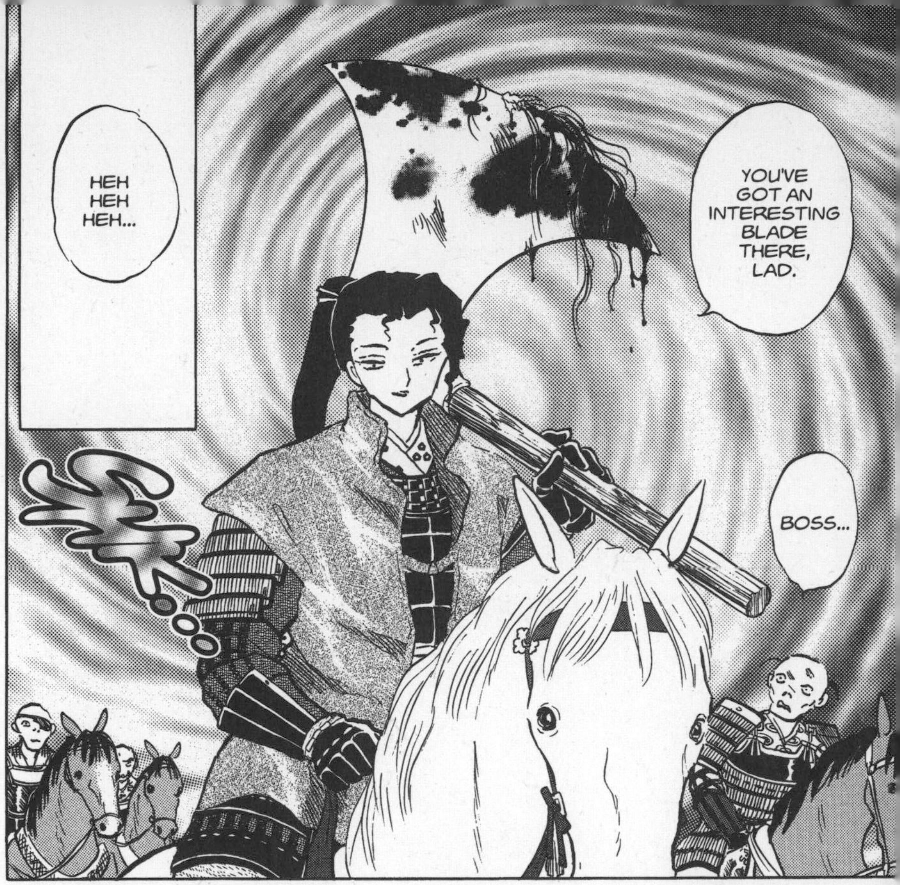
HEH HEH HEH...
YOU'VE GOT AN INTERESTING BLADE THERE, LAD.
BOSS...

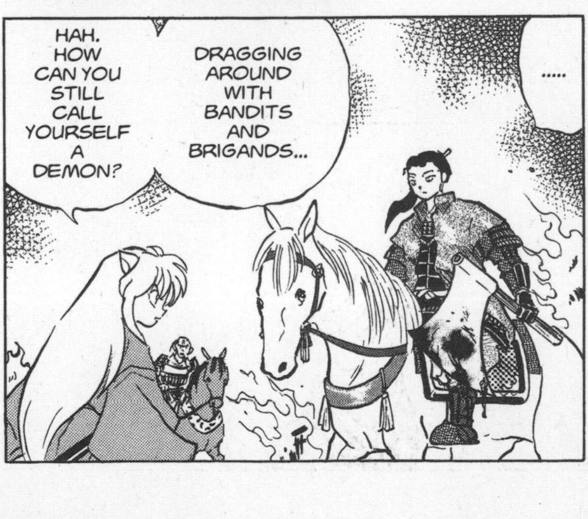
HAH. HOW CAN YOU STILL CALL YOURSELF A DEMON?
DRAGGING AROUND WITH BANDITS AND BRIGANDS...
.....

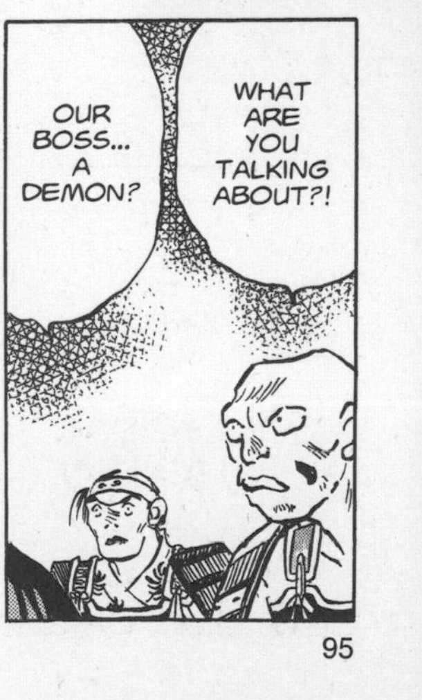
OUR BOSS... A DEMON?
WHAT ARE YOU TALKING ABOUT?!

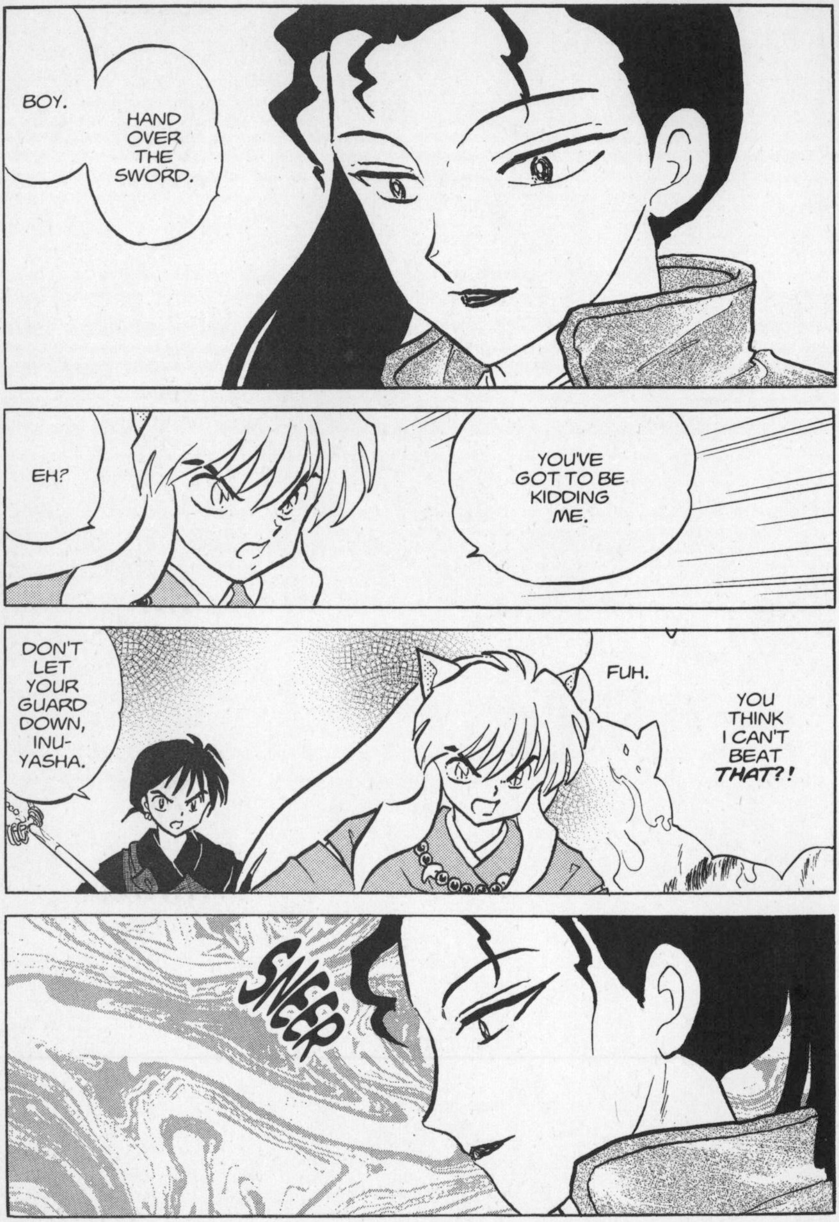
BOY.
HAND OVER THE SWORD.
EH?
YOU'VE GOT TO BE KIDDING ME.
DON'T LET YOUR GUARD DOWN, INU-YASHA.
FUH.
YOU THINK I CAN'T BEAT *THAT?!*
SNEER

SCROLL SIX
THE VENOMOUS COCOON

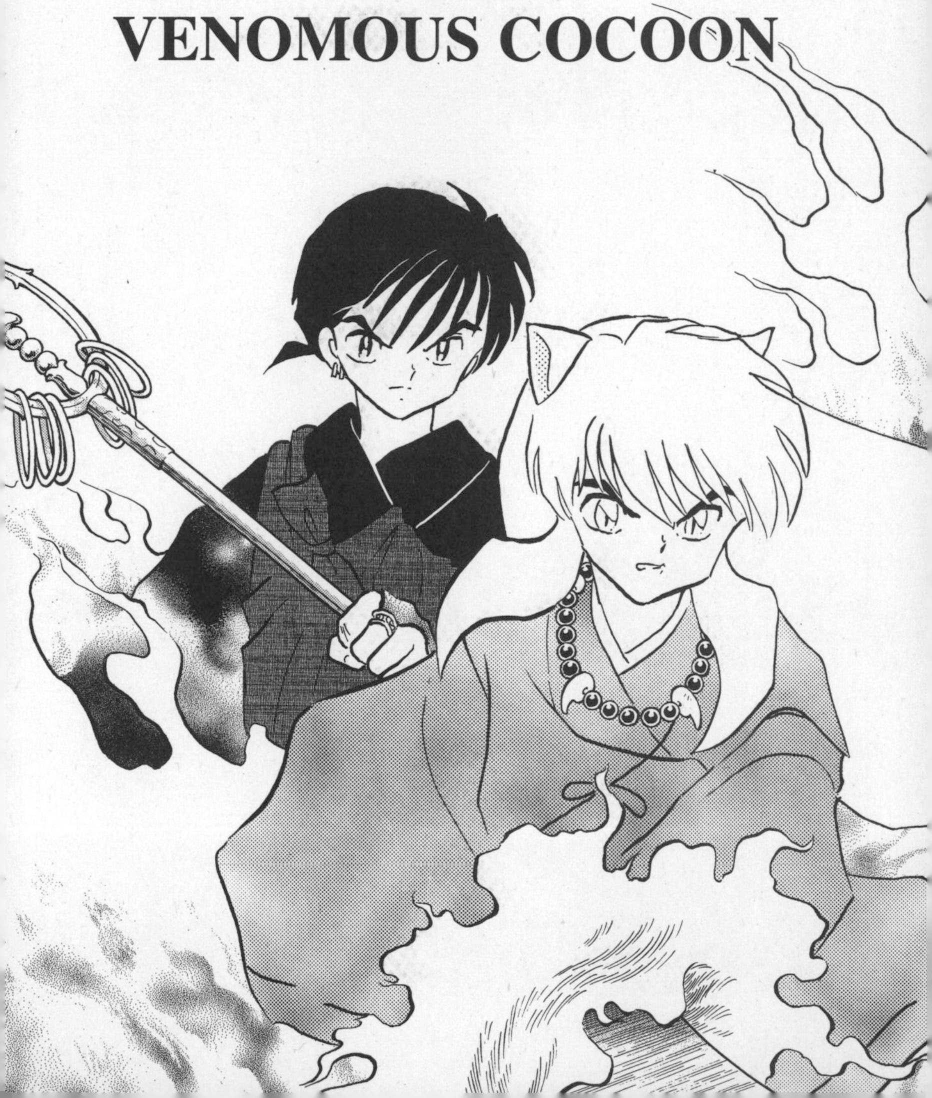

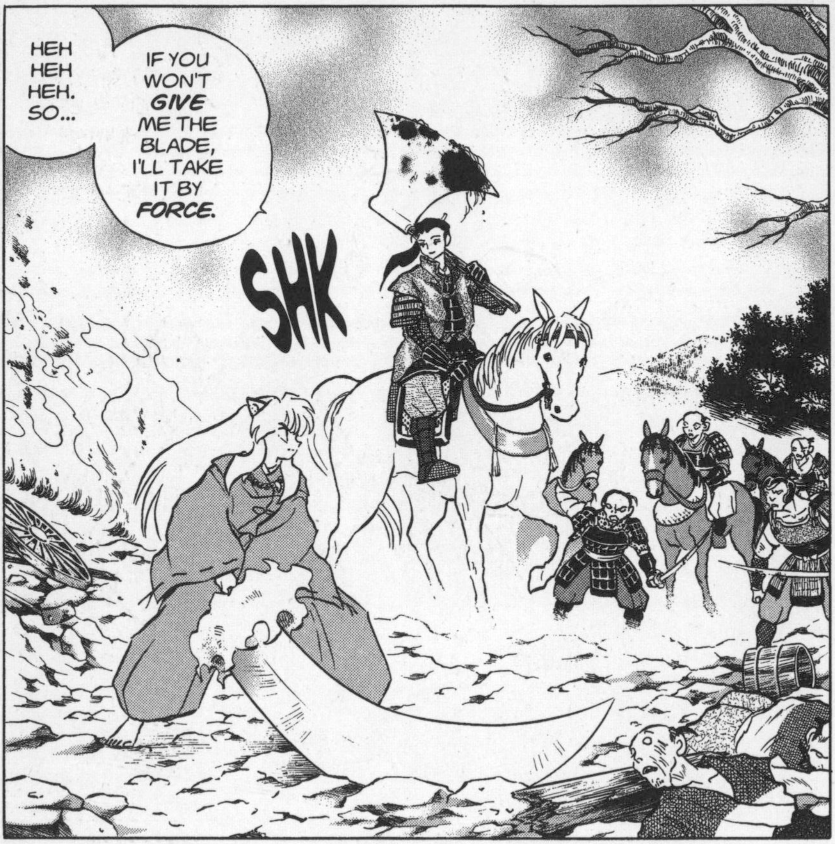
HEH HEH HEH. SO...
IF YOU WON'T GIVE ME THE BLADE, I'LL TAKE IT BY FORCE.
SHK
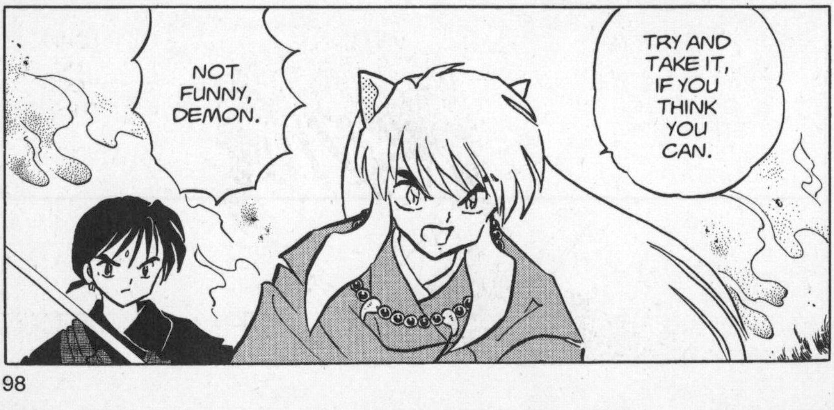
NOT FUNNY, DEMON.
TRY AND TAKE IT, IF YOU THINK YOU CAN.

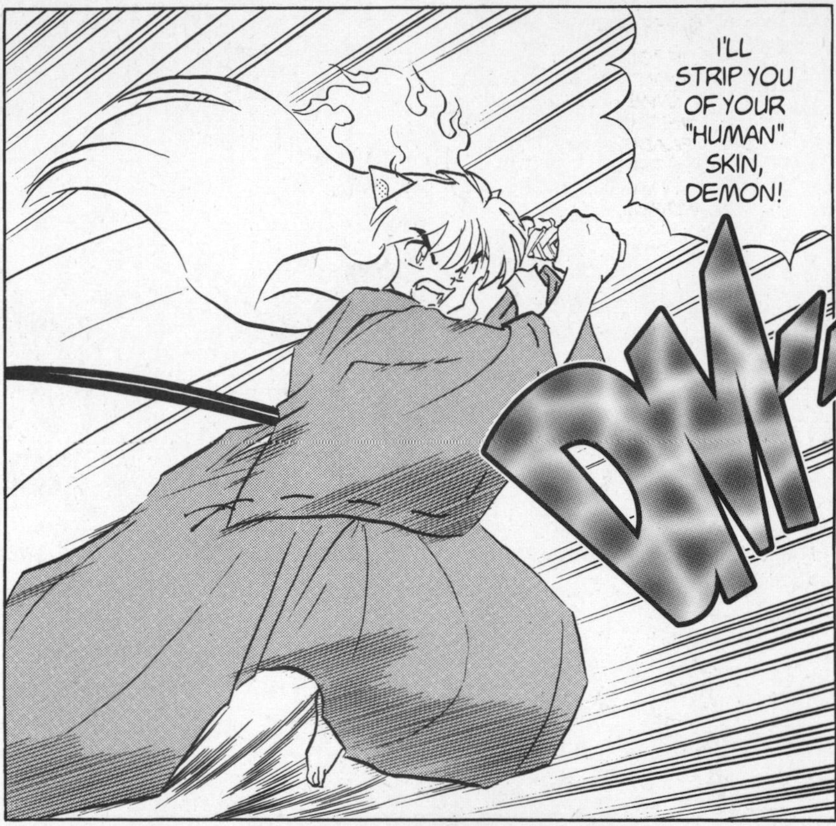
I'LL STRIP YOU OF YOUR "HUMAN" SKIN, DEMON!
DMK!!

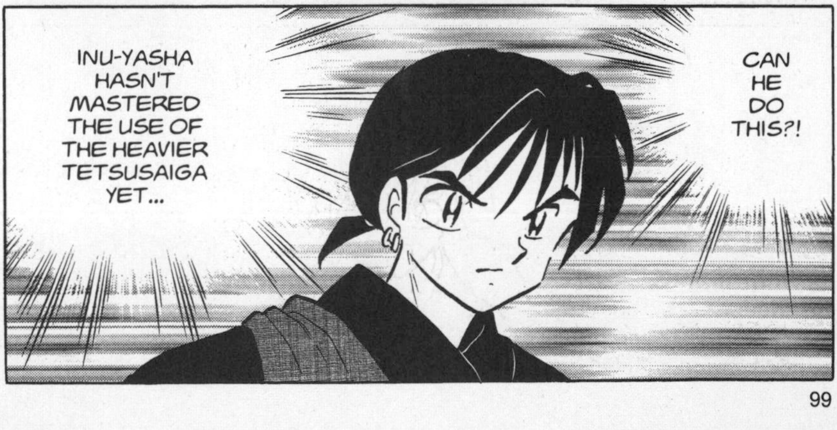
INU-YASHA HASN'T MASTERED THE USE OF THE HEAVIER TETSUSAIGA YET...
CAN HE DO THIS?!

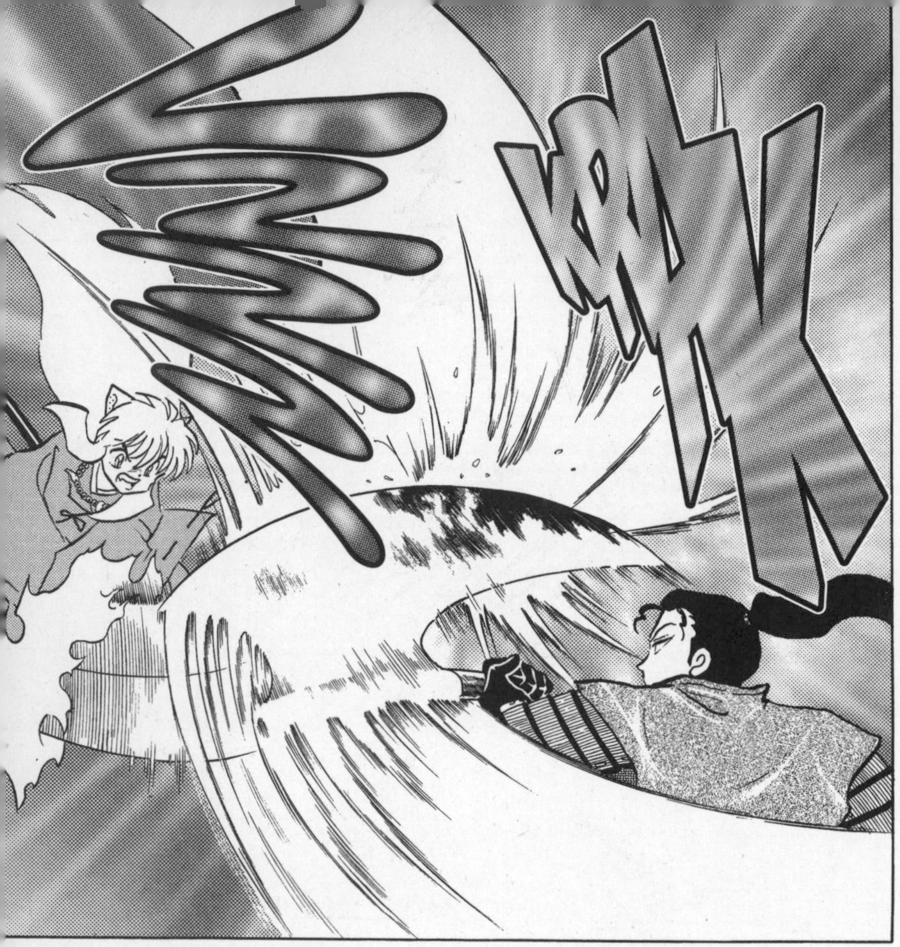

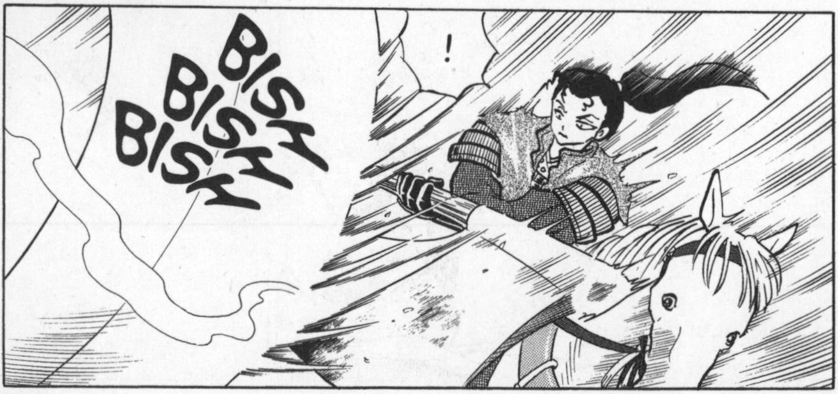
BISH
BISH
BISH
!

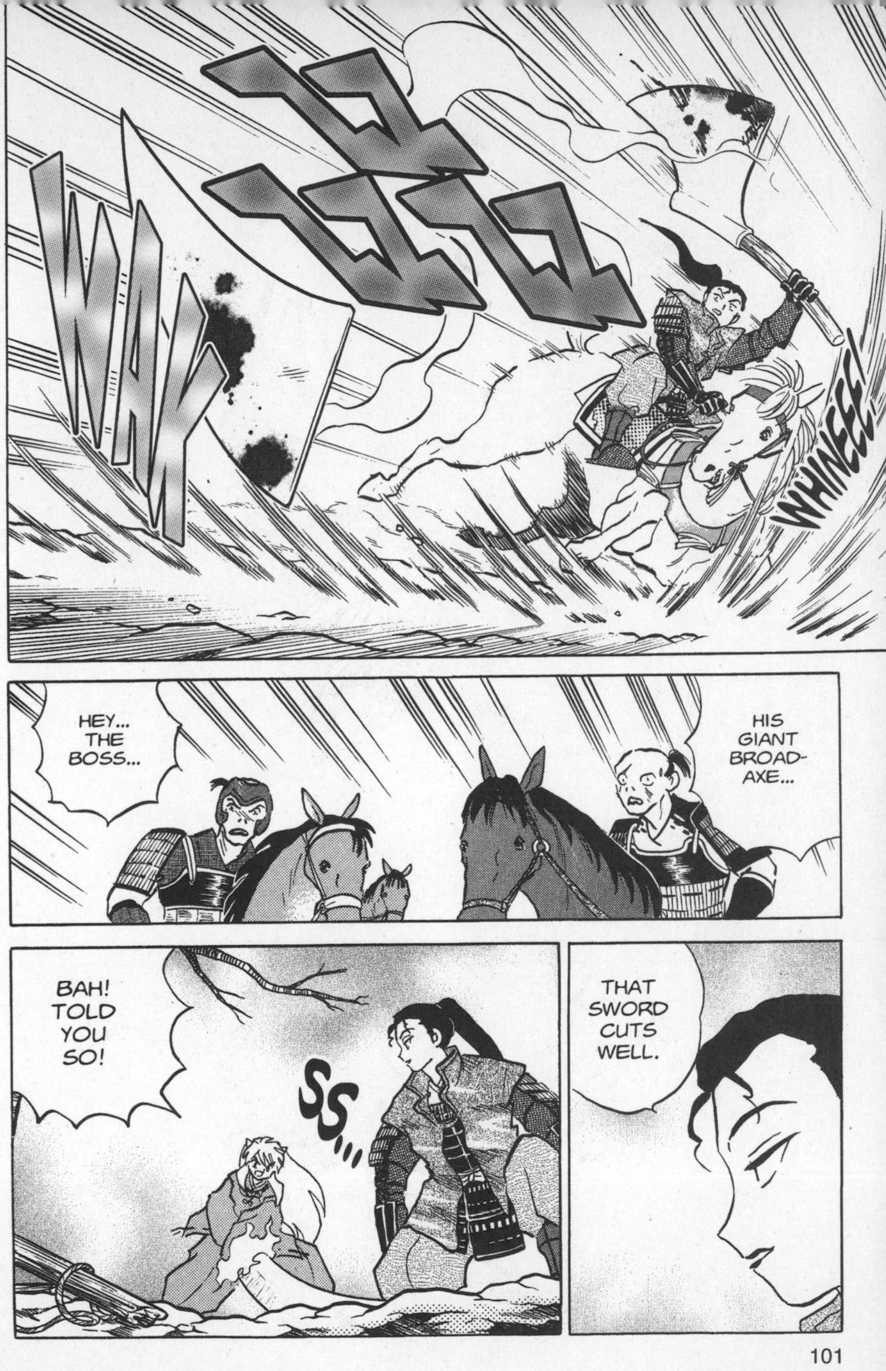
WAK
WHINEEE!
HEY... THE BOSS...
HIS GIANT BROAD-AXE...
BAH! TOLD YOU SO!
SS...
THAT SWORD CUTS WELL.

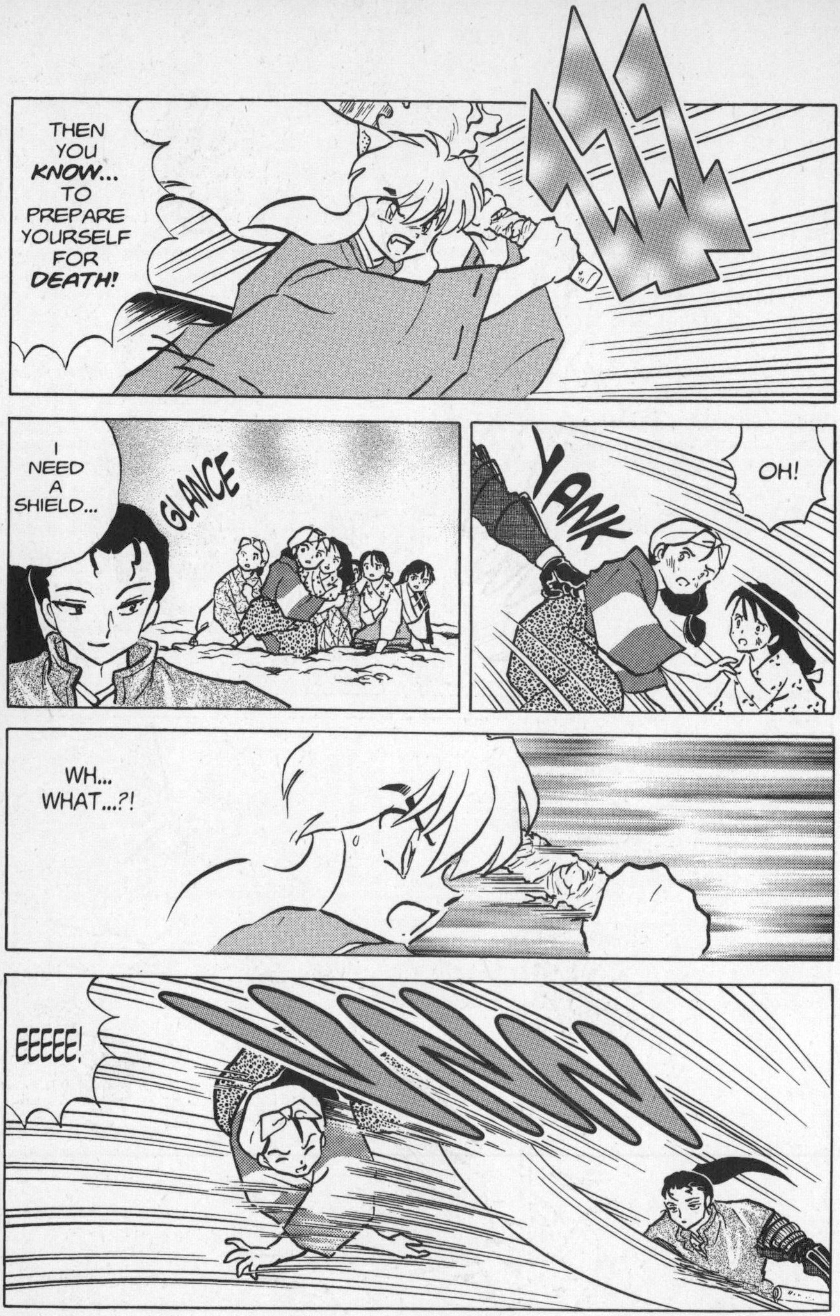

THEN YOU **KNOW...** TO PREPARE YOURSELF FOR **DEATH!**
I NEED A SHIELD...
GLANCE
YANK
OH!
WH... WHAT...?!
EEEEE!

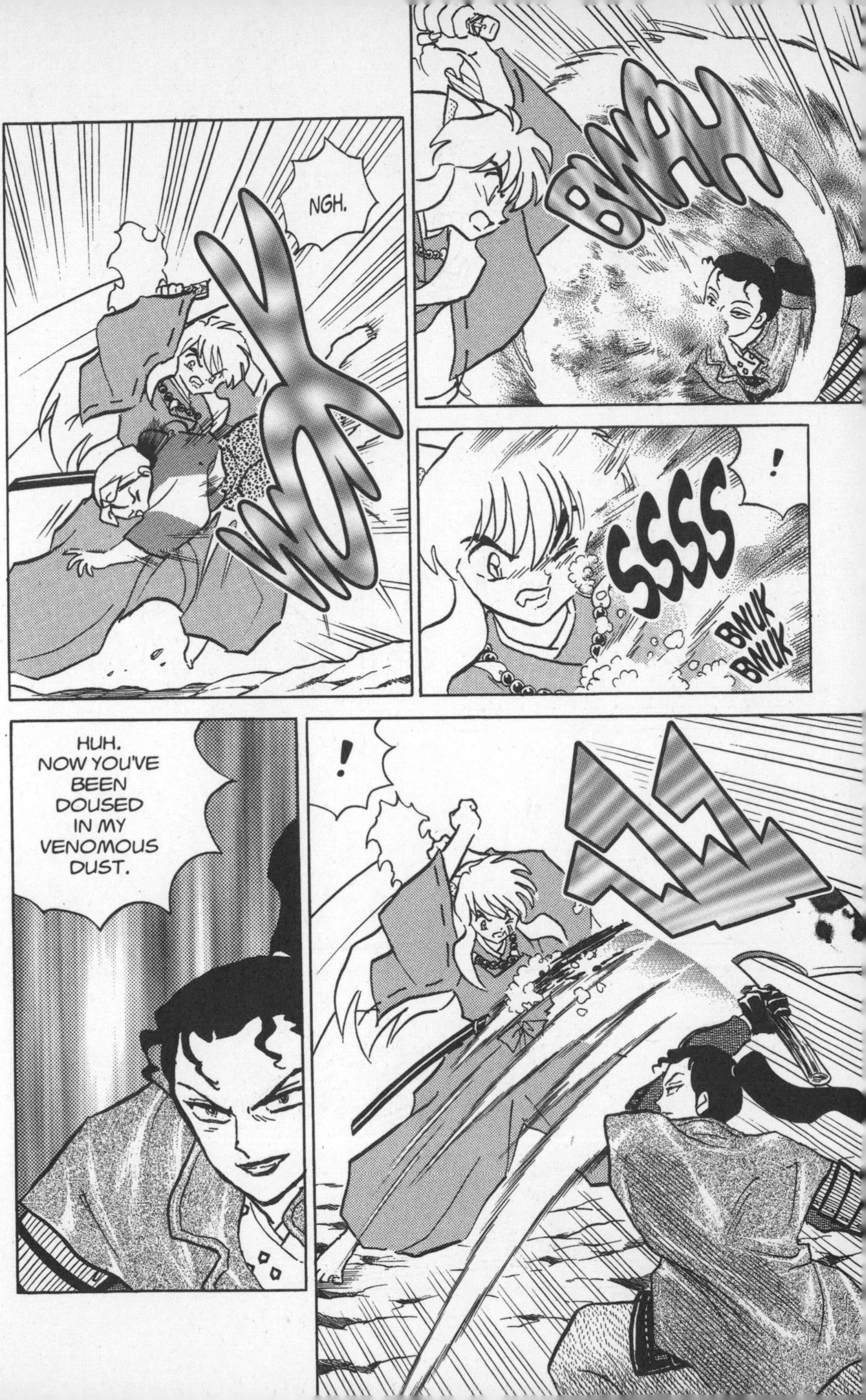
NGH.
BWAH
!
SSSS
BWUK BWUK
HUH. NOW YOU'VE BEEN DOUSED IN MY VENOMOUS DUST.
!

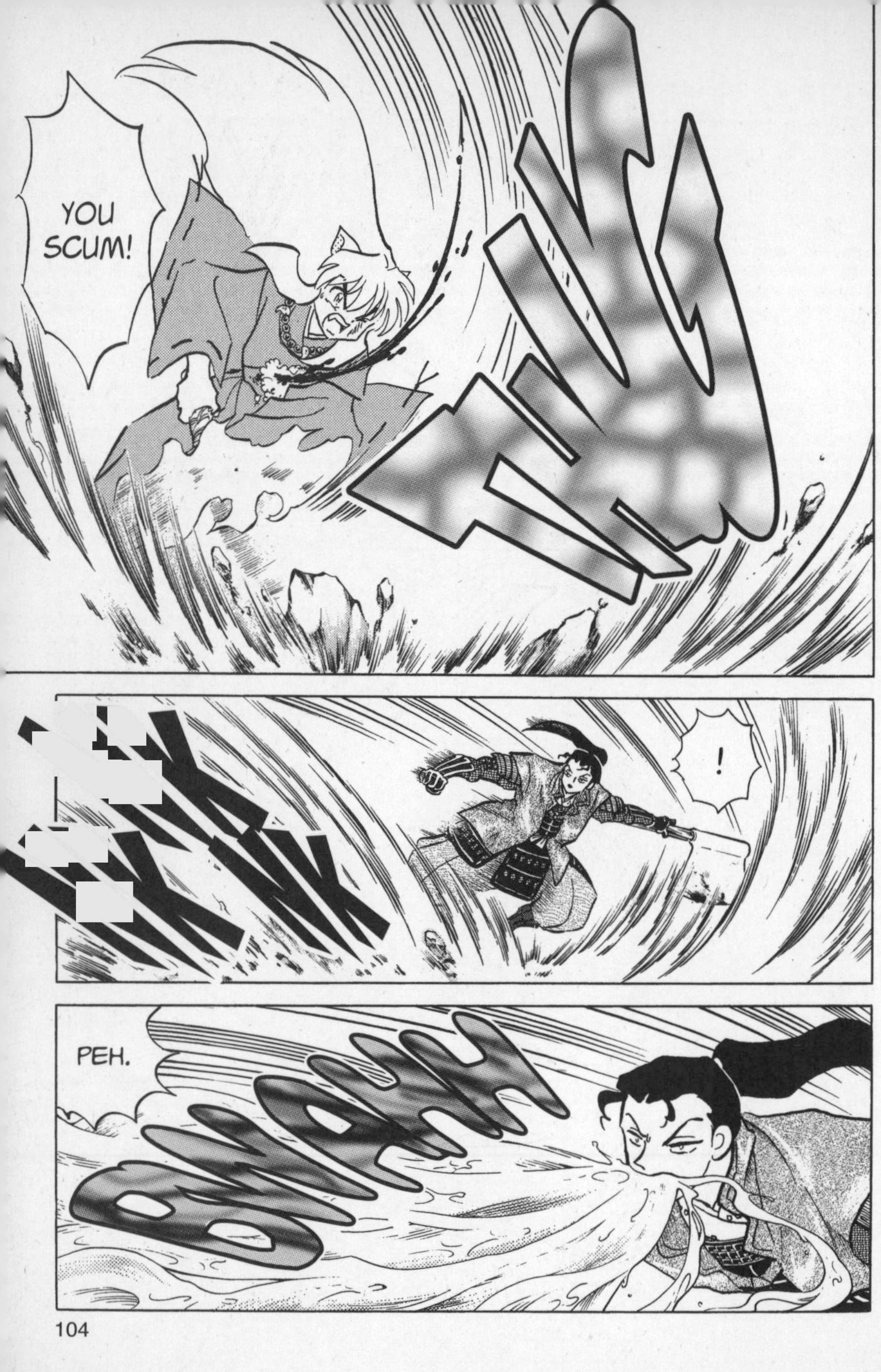
YOU SCUM!
!
PEH.

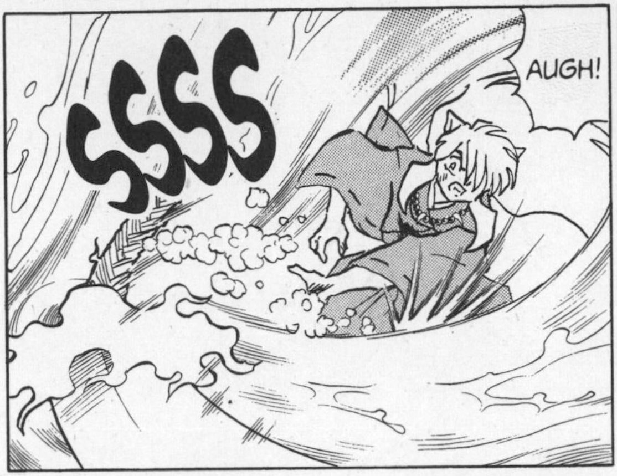
SSSS
AUGH!

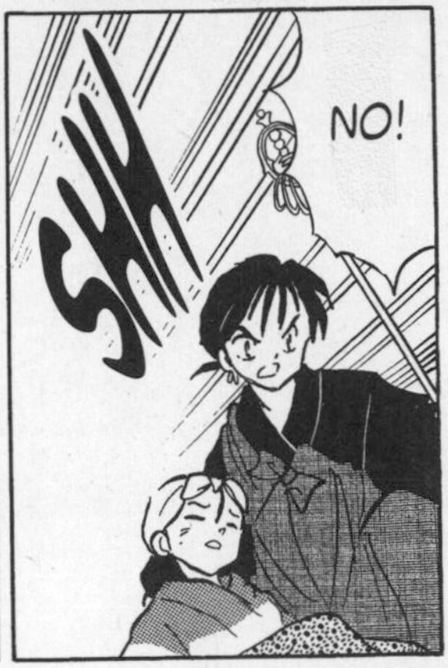
SHH
NO!

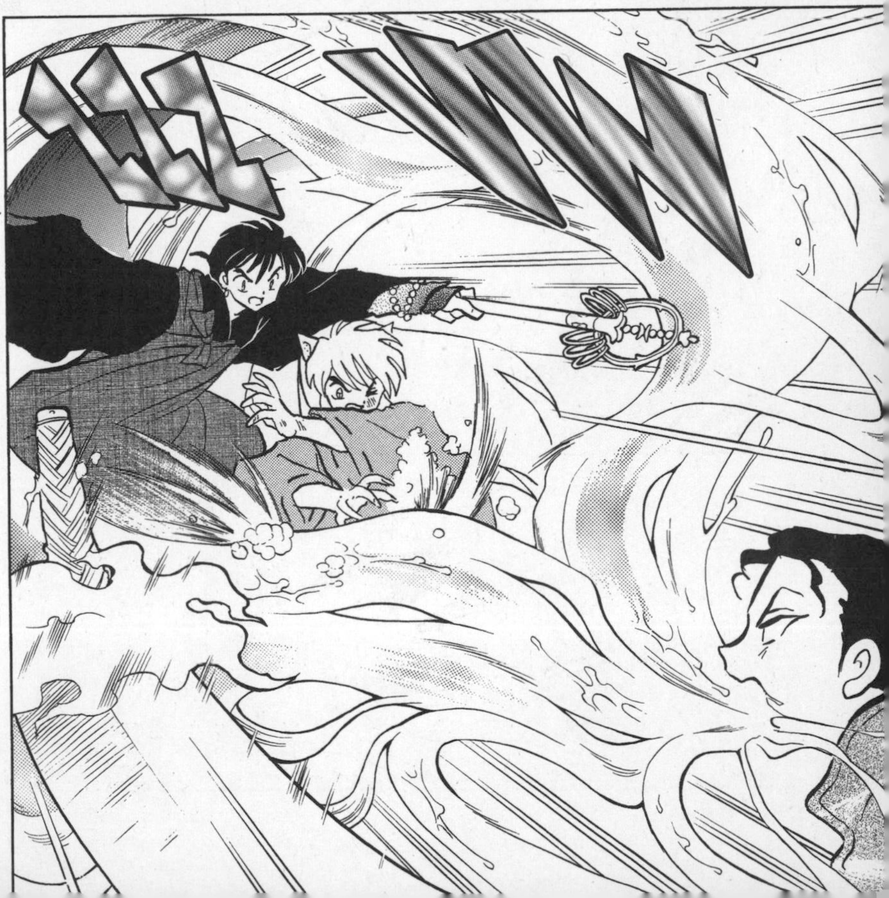

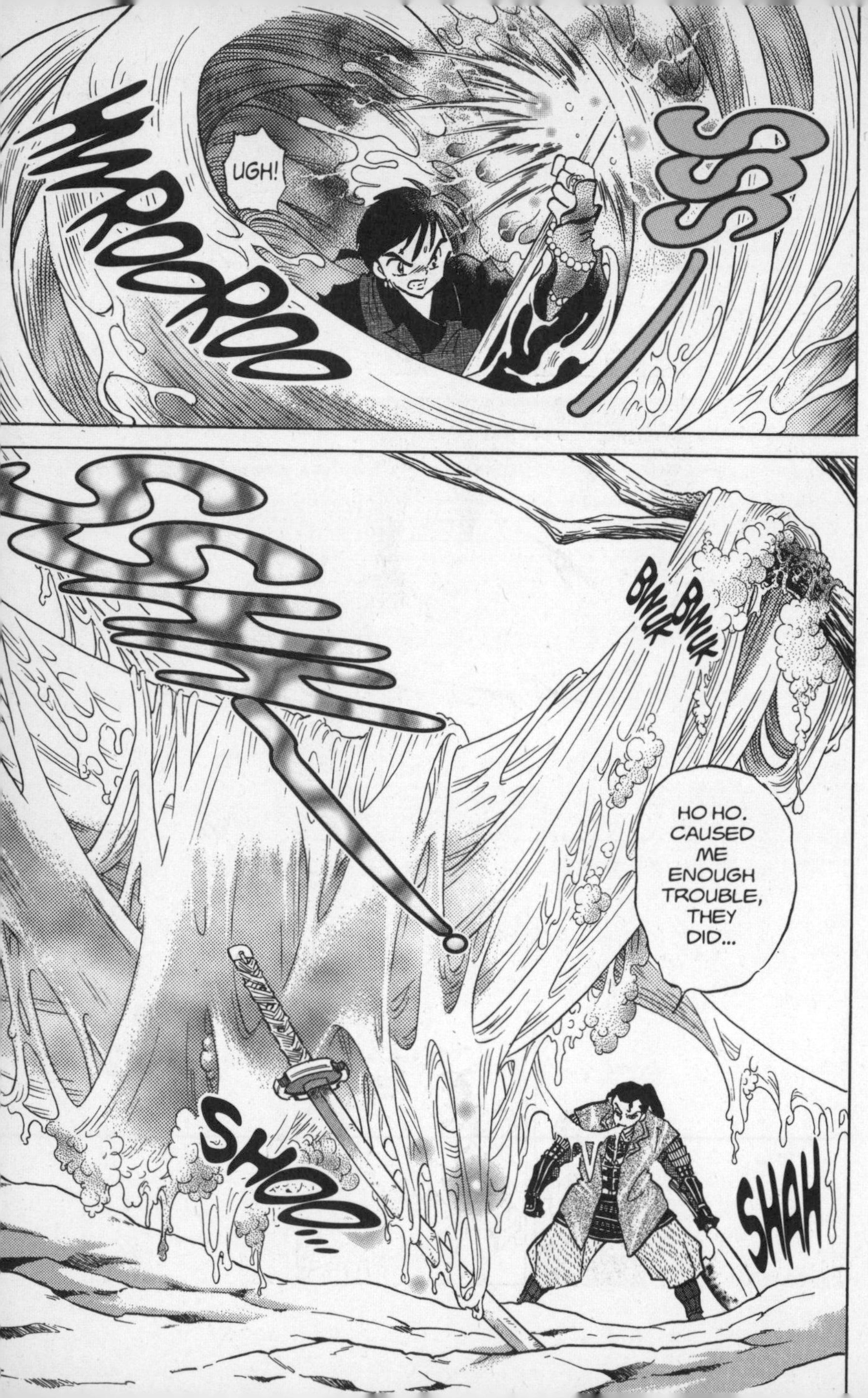
WHROOROO
UGH!
BWUK BWUK
HO HO. CAUSED ME ENOUGH TROUBLE, THEY DID...
SHOO
SHAH

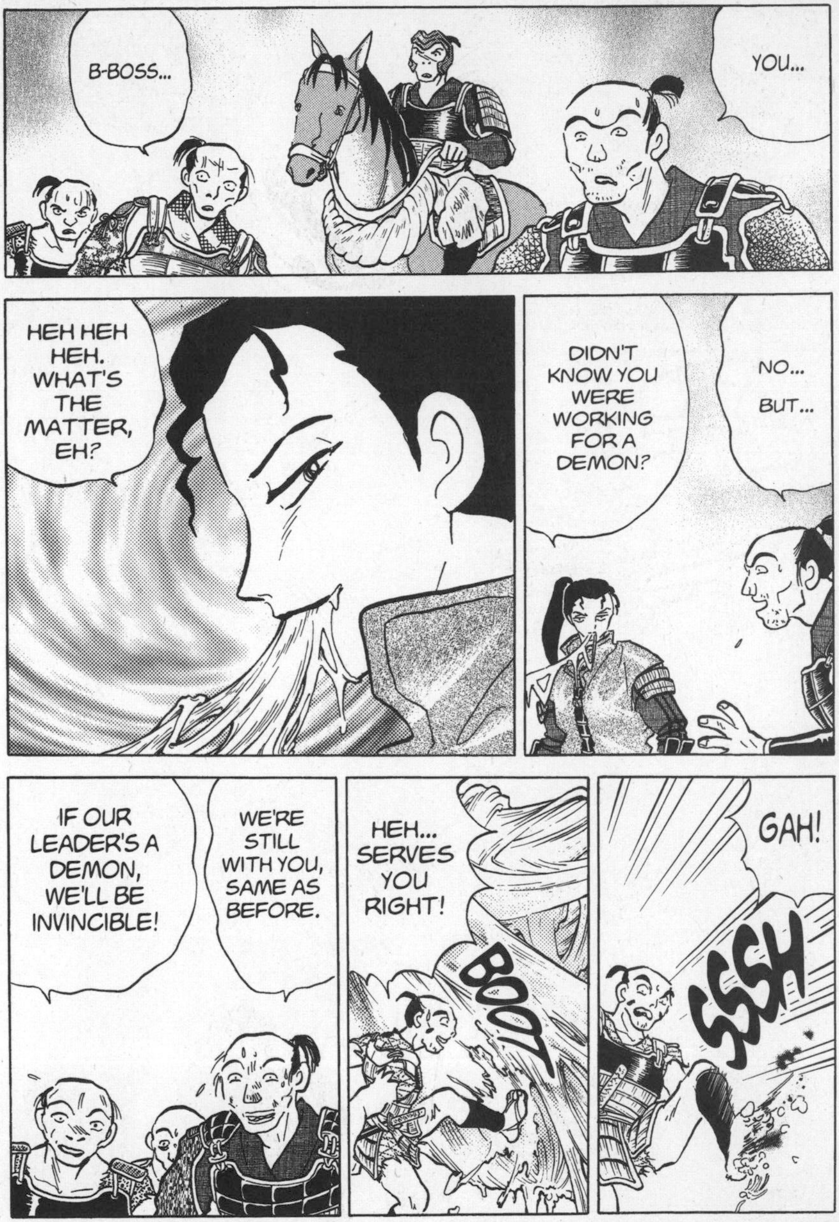
B-BOSS...
YOU...
HEH HEH HEH. WHAT'S THE MATTER, EH?
DIDN'T KNOW YOU WERE WORKING FOR A DEMON?
NO... BUT...
IF OUR LEADER'S A DEMON, WE'LL BE INVINCIBLE!
WE'RE STILL WITH YOU, SAME AS BEFORE.
HEH... SERVES YOU RIGHT!
BOOT
GAH!
SSSH

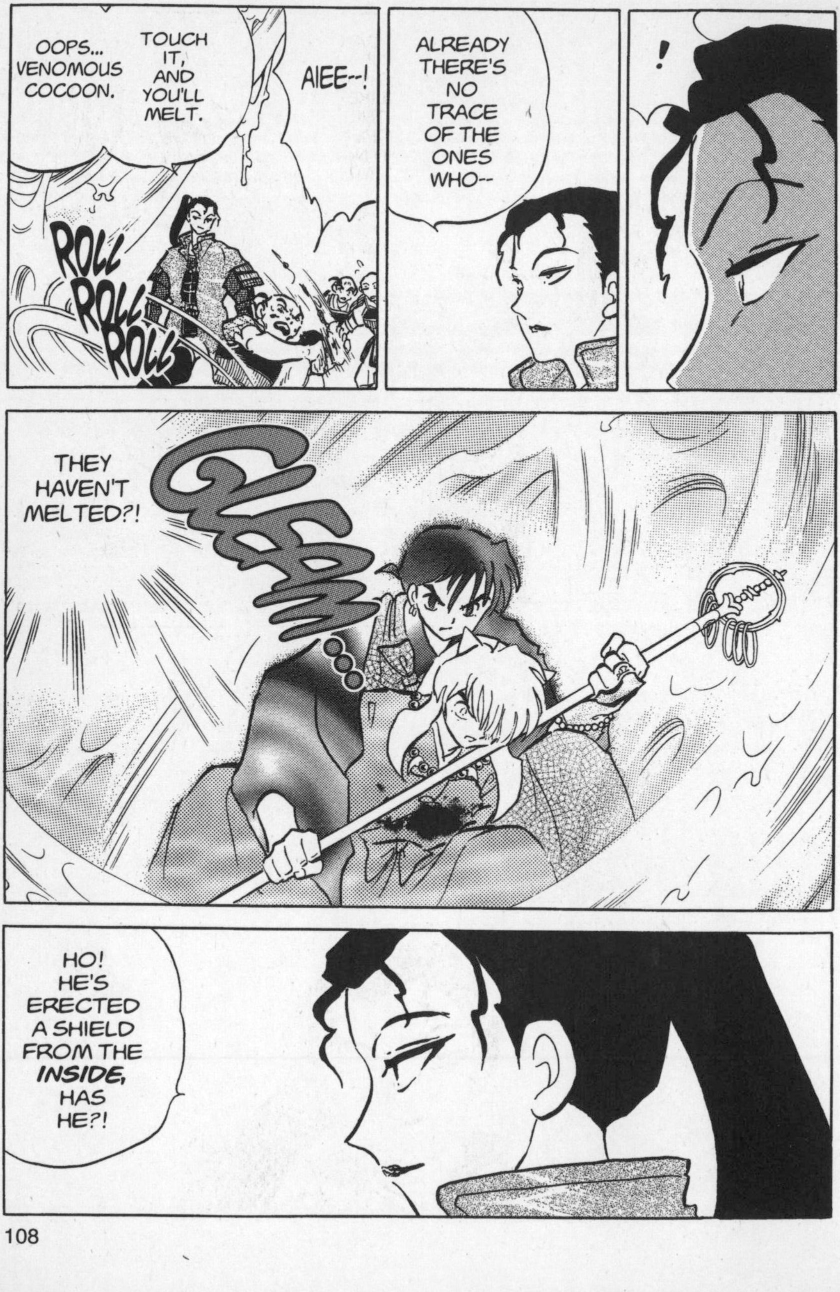
OOPS... VENOMOUS COCOON.
TOUCH IT, AND YOU'LL MELT.
AIEE--!
ROLL ROLL ROLL
ALREADY THERE'S NO TRACE OF THE ONES WHO--
!
THEY HAVEN'T MELTED?!
GLEAM...
HO! HE'S ERECTED A SHIELD FROM THE *INSIDE,* HAS HE?!

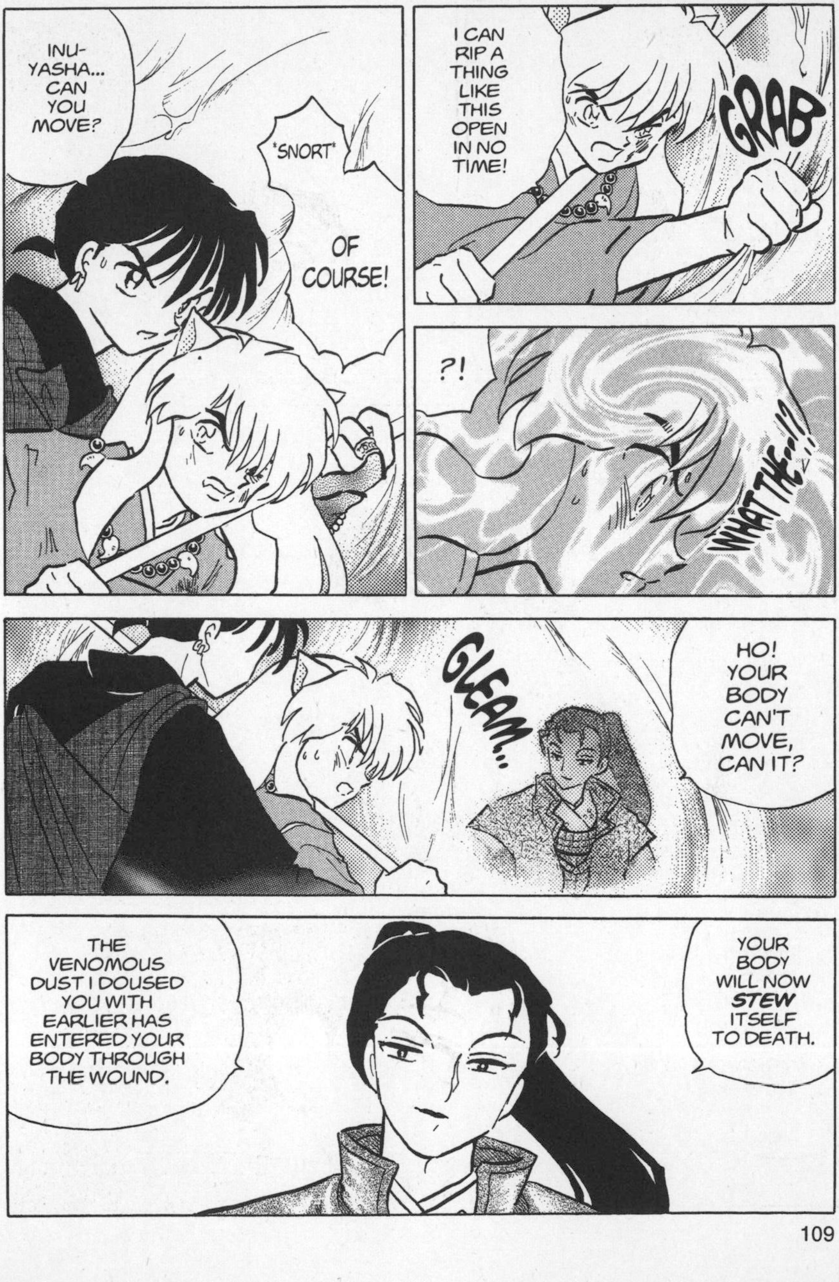
INU-YASHA... CAN YOU MOVE?
SNORT
OF COURSE!
I CAN RIP A THING LIKE THIS OPEN IN NO TIME!
GRAB
?!
WHAT THE...!?
GLEAM...
HO! YOUR BODY CAN'T MOVE, CAN IT?
THE VENOMOUS DUST I DOUSED YOU WITH EARLIER HAS ENTERED YOUR BODY THROUGH THE WOUND.
YOUR BODY WILL NOW STEW ITSELF TO DEATH.

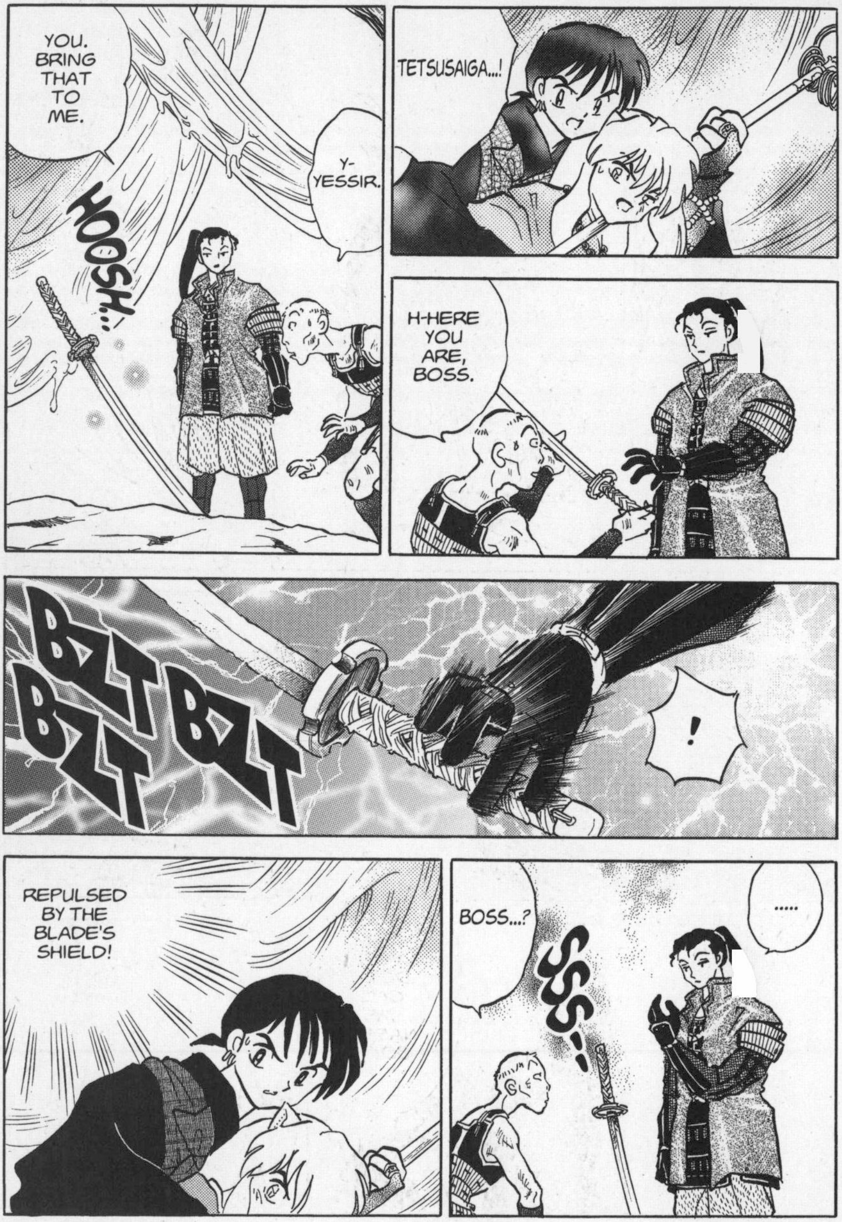
YOU. BRING THAT TO ME.
Y-YESSIR.
HOOSH...
TETSUSAIGA...!
H-HERE YOU ARE, BOSS.
BZLT BZLT BZLT
!
REPULSED BY THE BLADE'S SHIELD!
BOSS...?
.....
SSS...

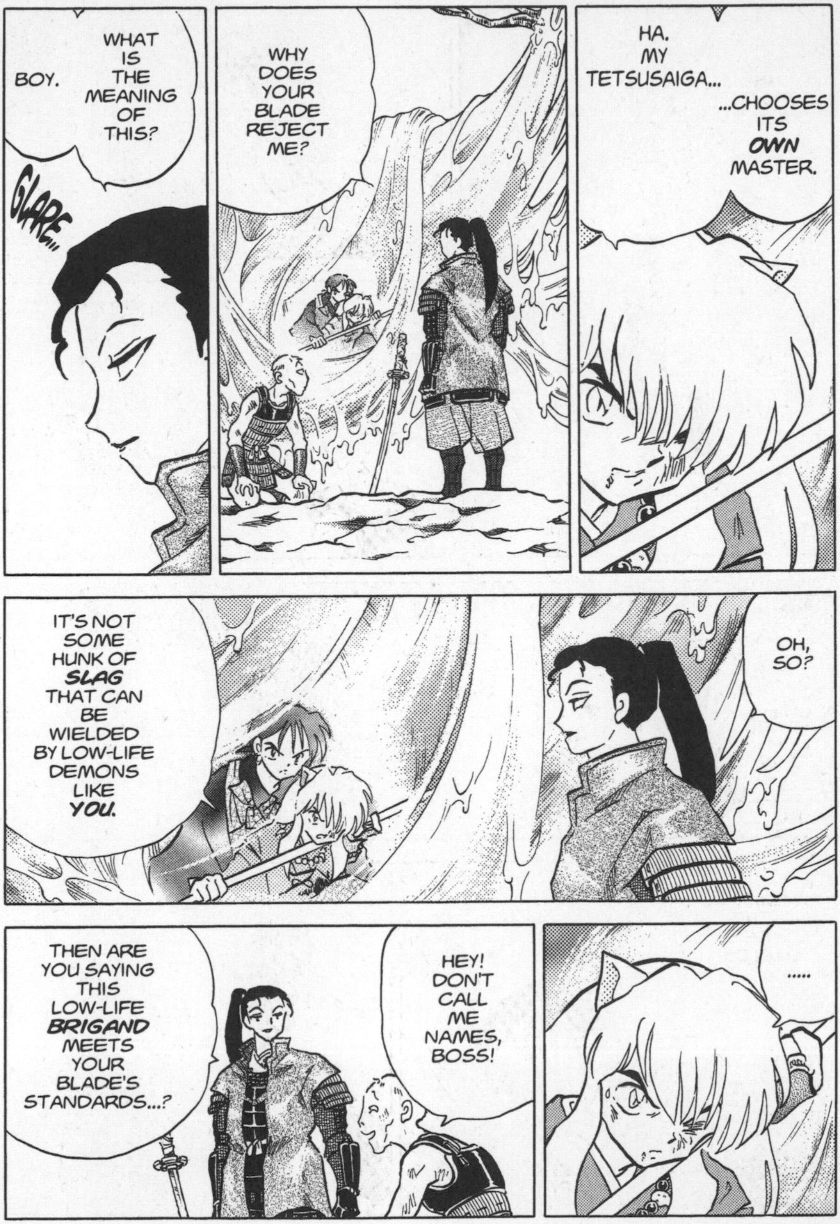
BOY.
WHAT IS THE MEANING OF THIS?
GLARE...
WHY DOES YOUR BLADE REJECT ME?
HA. MY TETSUSAIGA...
...CHOOSES ITS **OWN** MASTER.
IT'S NOT SOME HUNK OF **SLAG** THAT CAN BE WIELDED BY LOW-LIFE DEMONS LIKE **YOU**.
OH, SO?
THEN ARE YOU SAYING THIS LOW-LIFE **BRIGAND** MEETS YOUR BLADE'S STANDARDS...?
HEY! DON'T CALL ME NAMES, BOSS!
.....

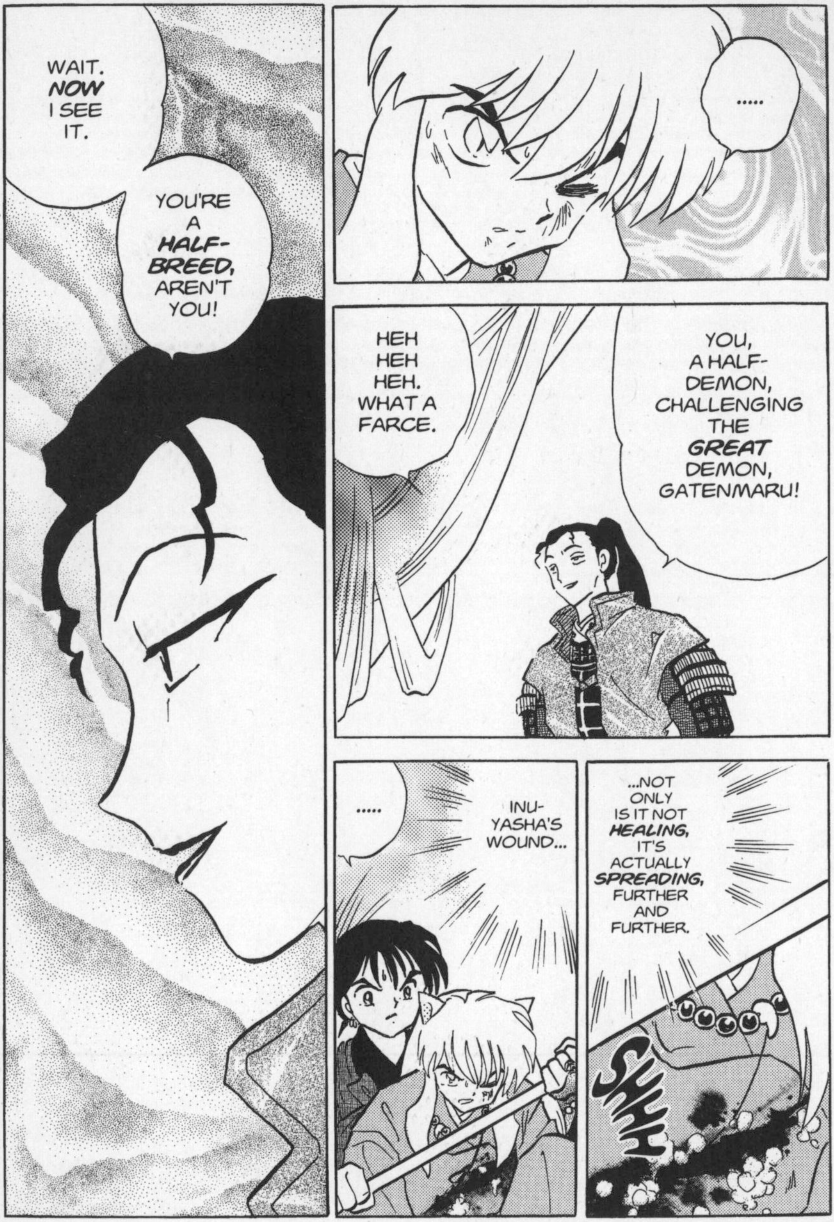
WAIT. NOW I SEE IT.
YOU'RE A HALF-BREED, AREN'T YOU!
.....
HEH HEH HEH. WHAT A FARCE.
YOU, A HALF-DEMON, CHALLENGING THE GREAT DEMON, GATENMARU!
.....
INU-YASHA'S WOUND...
...NOT ONLY IS IT NOT HEALING, IT'S ACTUALLY SPREADING, FURTHER AND FURTHER.
SHHH

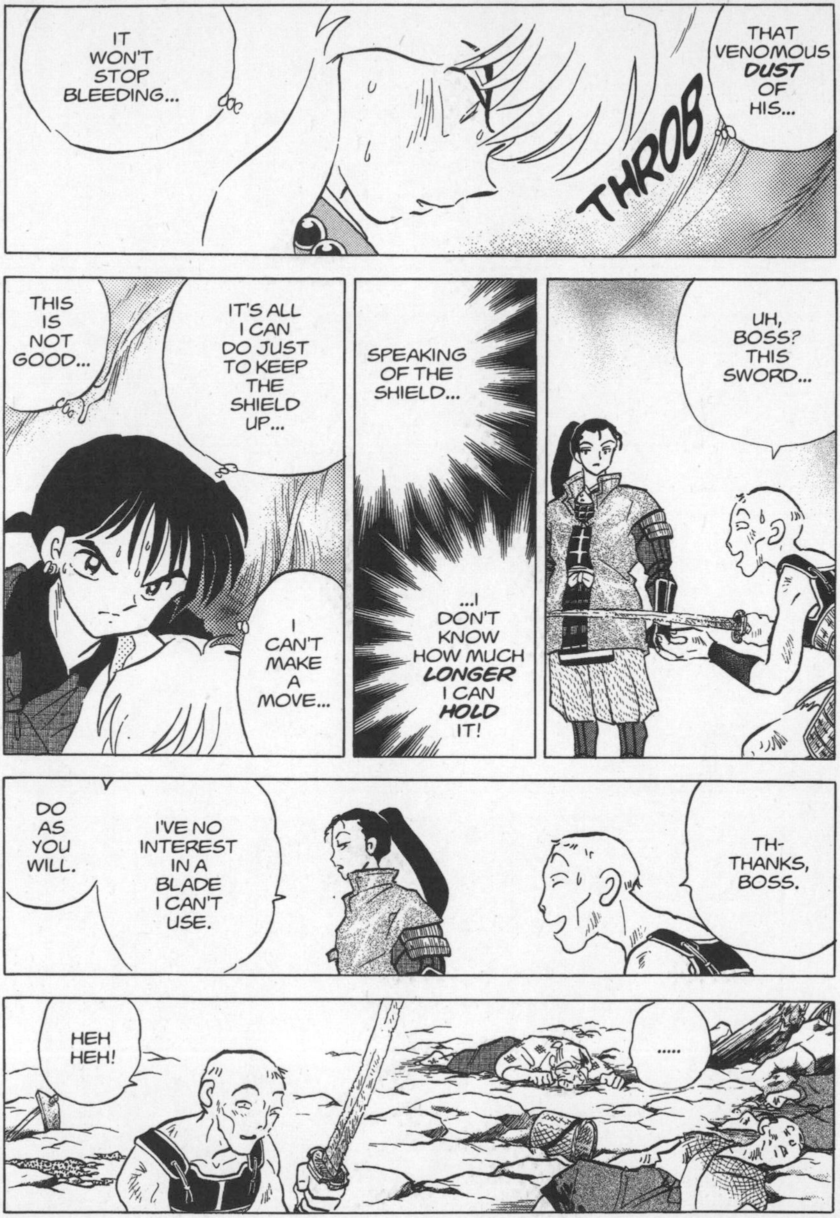
IT WON'T STOP BLEEDING...
THROB
THAT VENOMOUS DUST OF HIS...
THIS IS NOT GOOD...
IT'S ALL I CAN DO JUST TO KEEP THE SHIELD UP...
I CAN'T MAKE A MOVE...
SPEAKING OF THE SHIELD...
...I DON'T KNOW HOW MUCH LONGER I CAN HOLD IT!
UH, BOSS? THIS SWORD...
DO AS YOU WILL.
I'VE NO INTEREST IN A BLADE I CAN'T USE.
TH-THANKS, BOSS.
HEH HEH!
.....

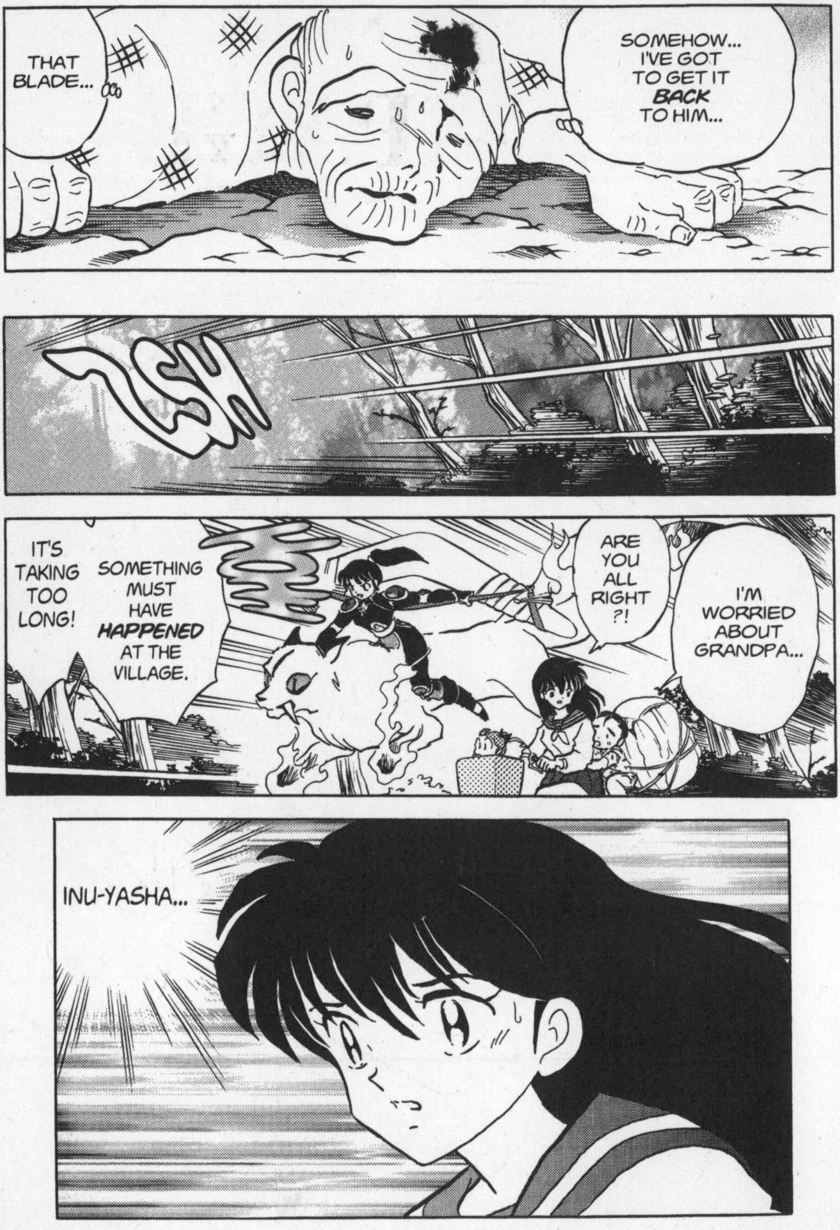
THAT BLADE...
SOMEHOW... I'VE GOT TO GET IT BACK TO HIM...
IT'S TAKING TOO LONG!
SOMETHING MUST HAVE HAPPENED AT THE VILLAGE.
ARE YOU ALL RIGHT ?!
I'M WORRIED ABOUT GRANDPA...
INU-YASHA...

SCROLL SEVEN

RAMPAGE

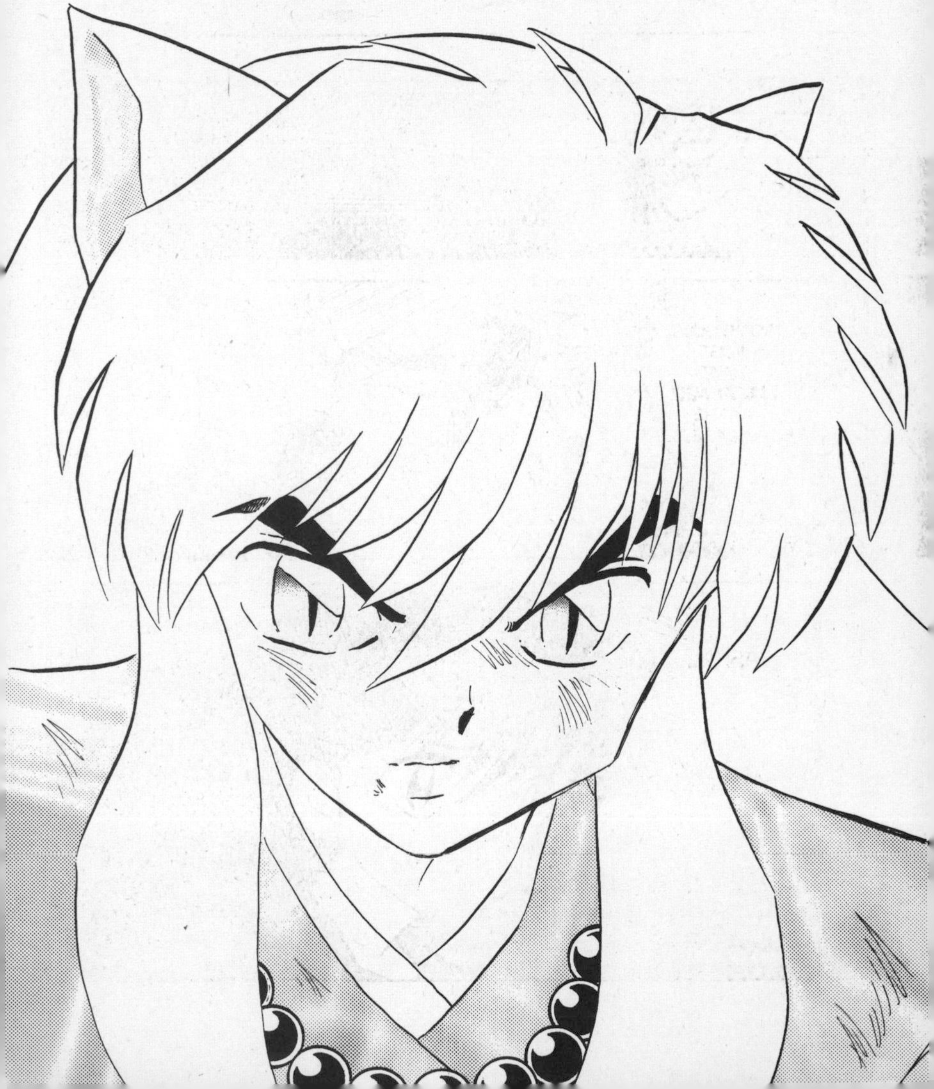

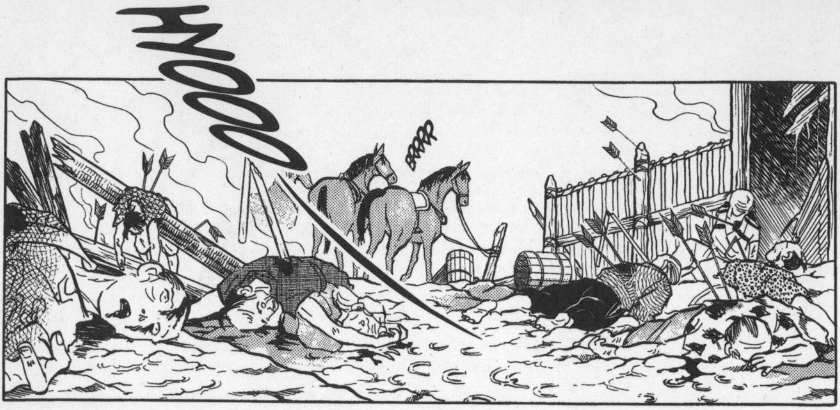
HYOOO
BRRRR

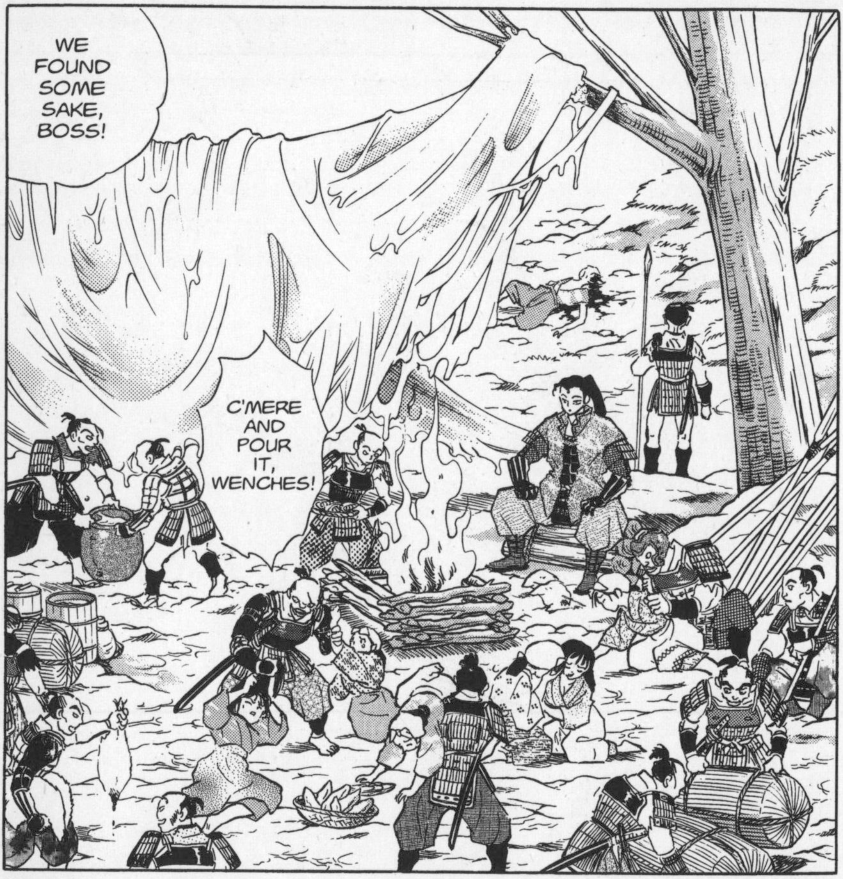
WE FOUND SOME SAKE, BOSS!
C'MERE AND POUR IT, WENCHES!

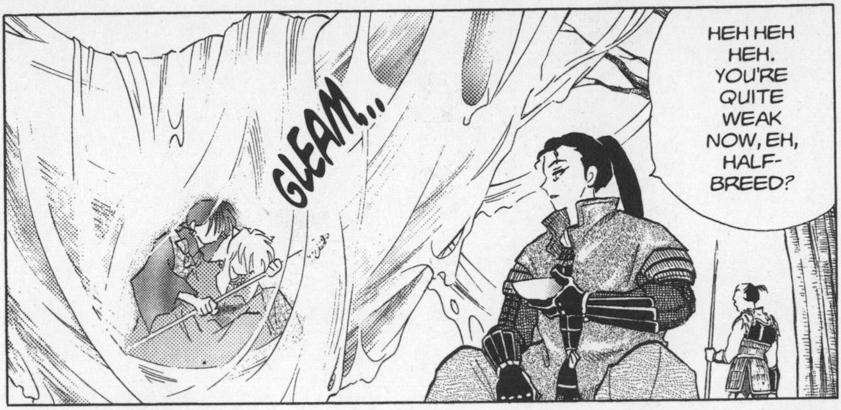
GLEAM...
HEH HEH HEH. YOU'RE QUITE WEAK NOW, EH, HALF-BREED?

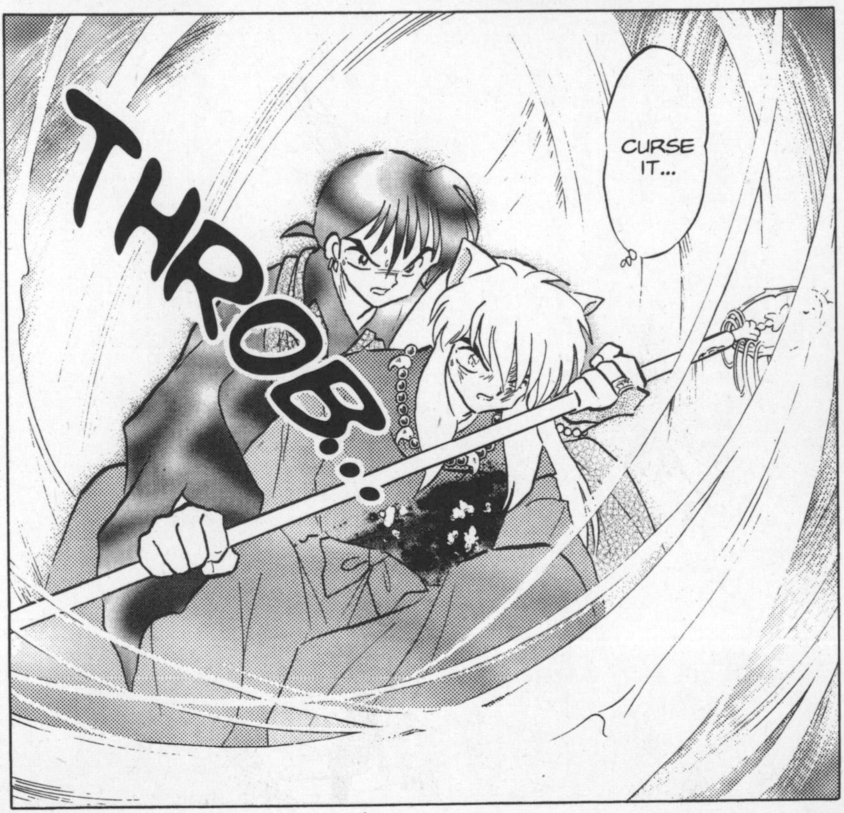
THROB...
CURSE IT...

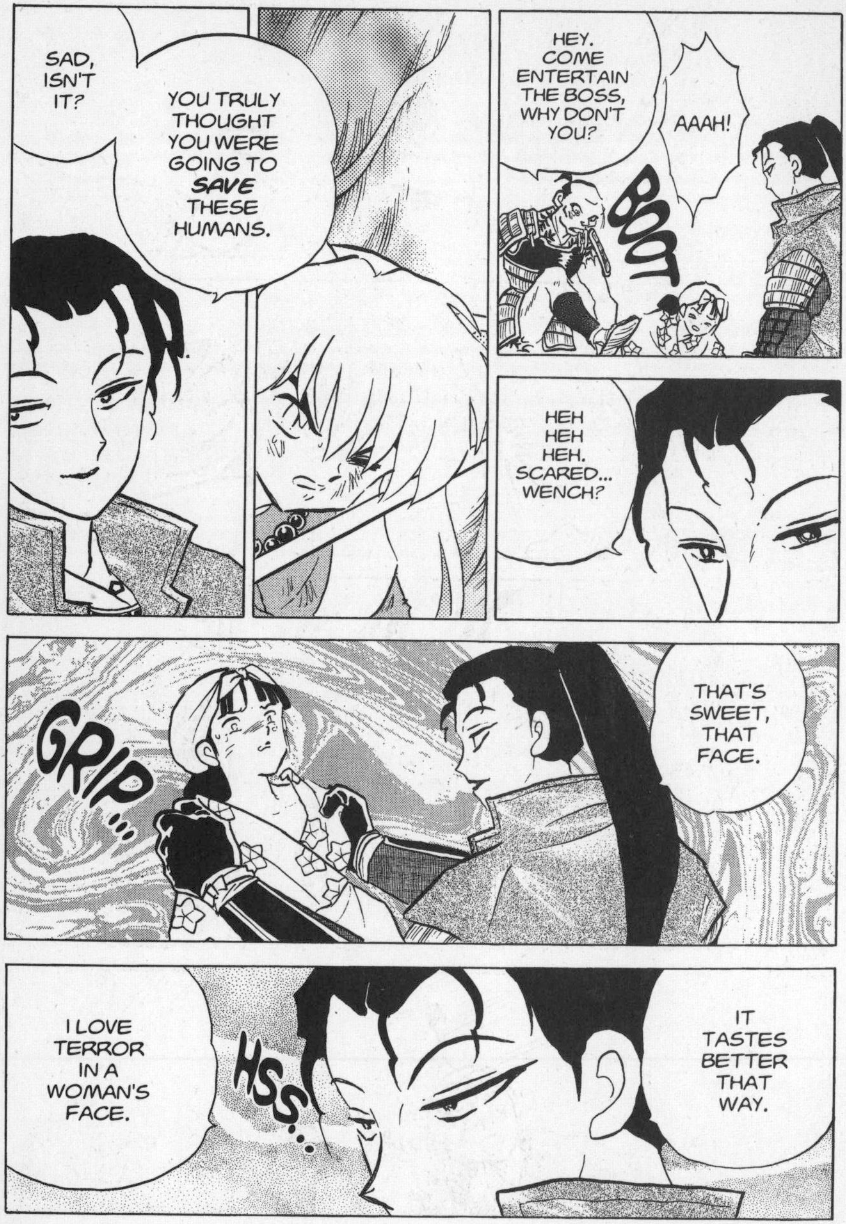
SAD, ISN'T IT?
YOU TRULY THOUGHT YOU WERE GOING TO *SAVE* THESE HUMANS.
HEY. COME ENTERTAIN THE BOSS, WHY DON'T YOU?
AAAH!
BOOT
HEH HEH HEH. SCARED... WENCH?
GRIP...
THAT'S SWEET, THAT FACE.
I LOVE TERROR IN A WOMAN'S FACE.
HSS...
IT TASTES BETTER THAT WAY.

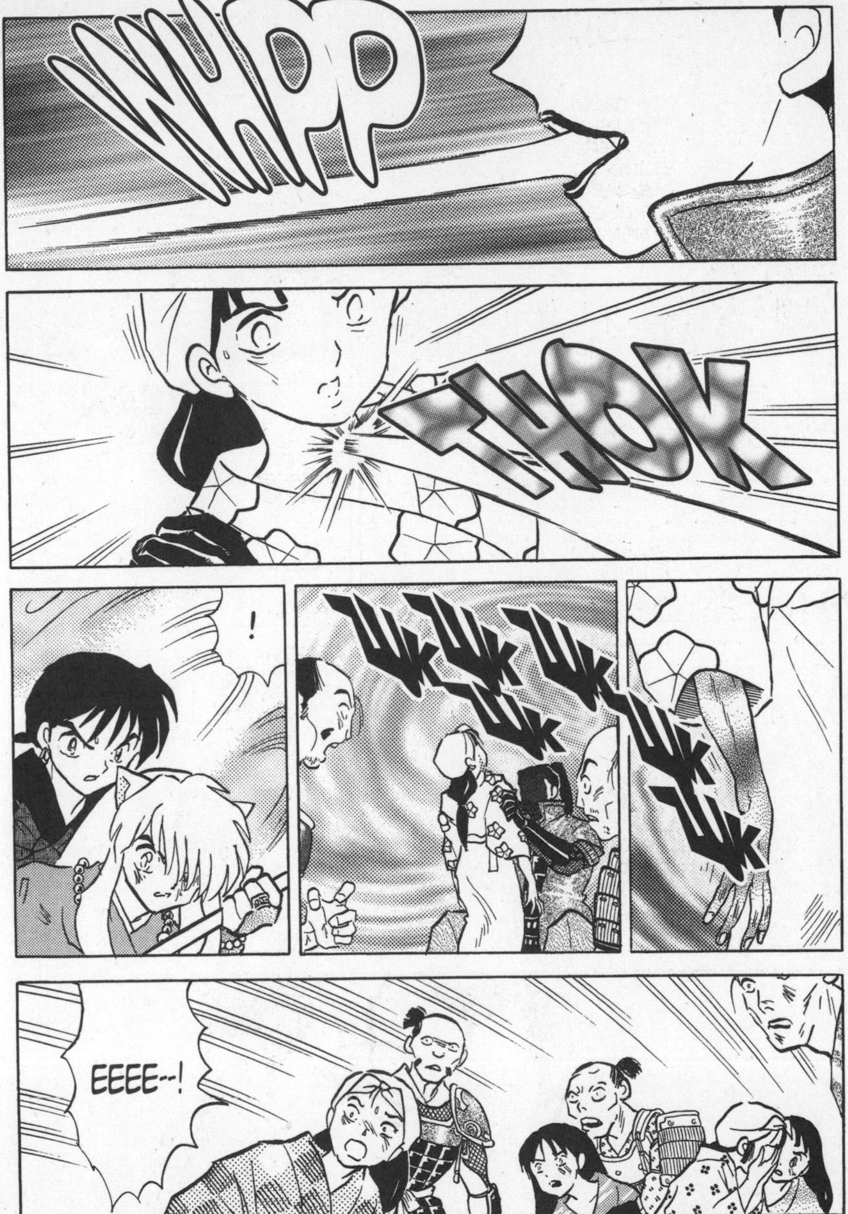
WHPP
THOK
!
TUK TUK TUK TUK TUK TUK TUK
EEEE--!

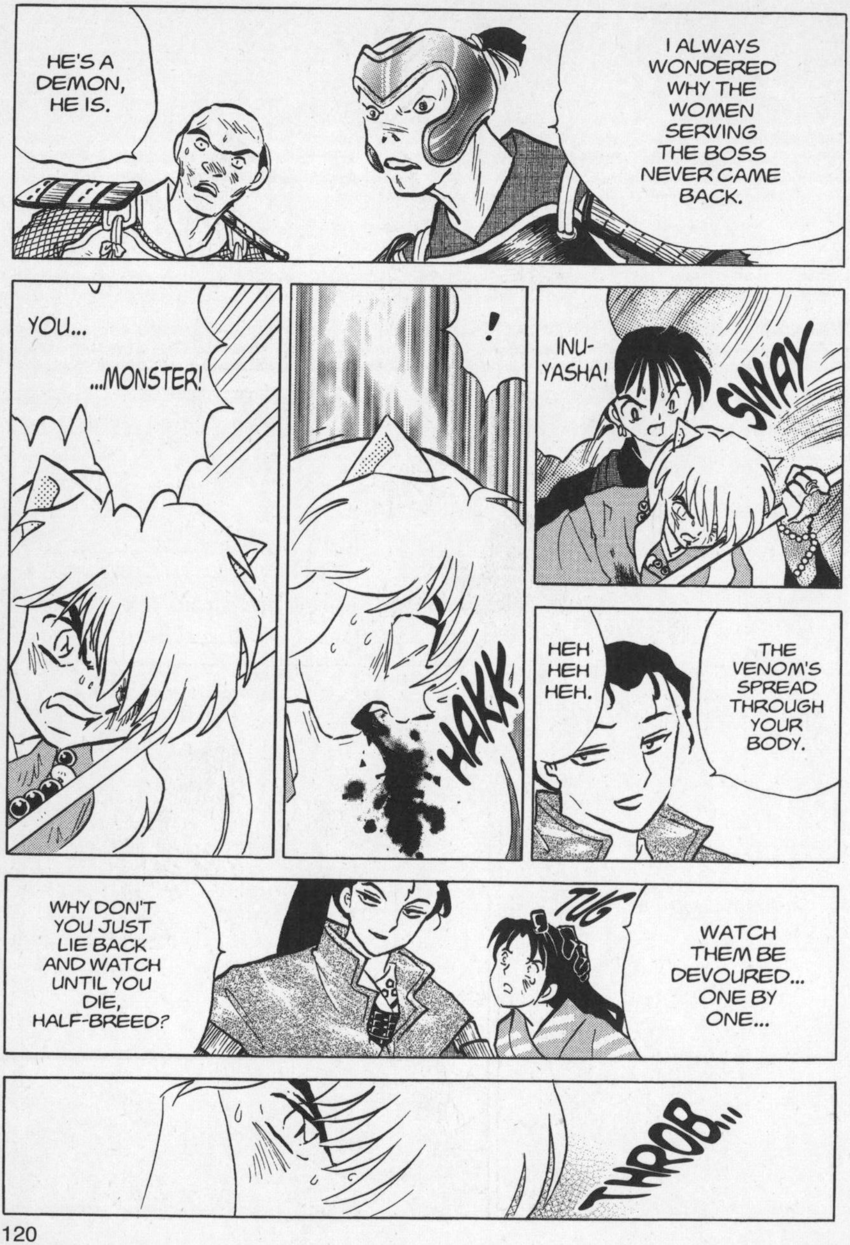
HE'S A DEMON, HE IS.
I ALWAYS WONDERED WHY THE WOMEN SERVING THE BOSS NEVER CAME BACK.
YOU...
...MONSTER!
!
HAKK
INU-YASHA!
SWAY
HEH HEH HEH.
THE VENOM'S SPREAD THROUGH YOUR BODY.
WHY DON'T YOU JUST LIE BACK AND WATCH UNTIL YOU DIE, HALF-BREED?
TUG
WATCH THEM BE DEVOURED... ONE BY ONE...
THROB...

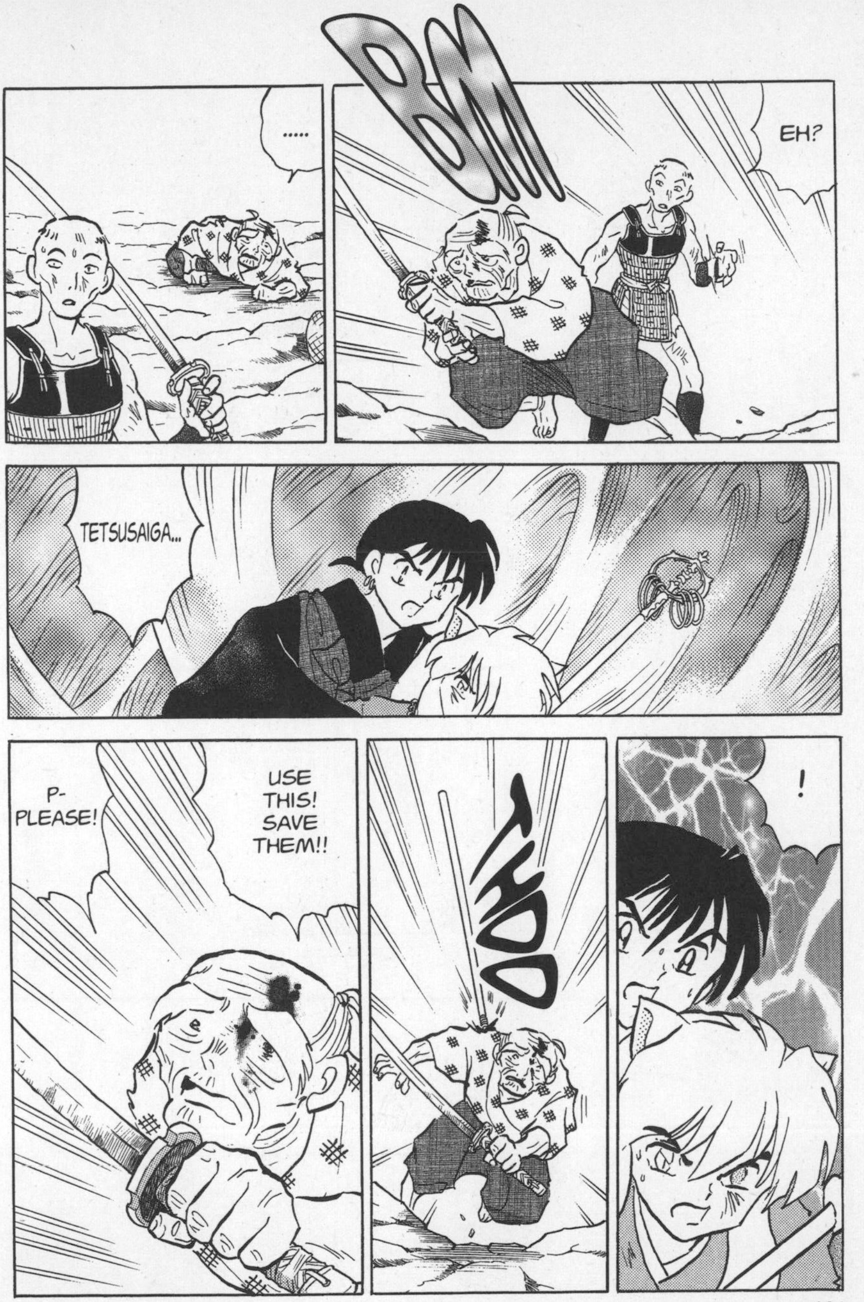

.....
BAM
EH?
TETSUSAIGA...
P-
PLEASE!
USE
THIS!
SAVE
THEM!!
THOO
!

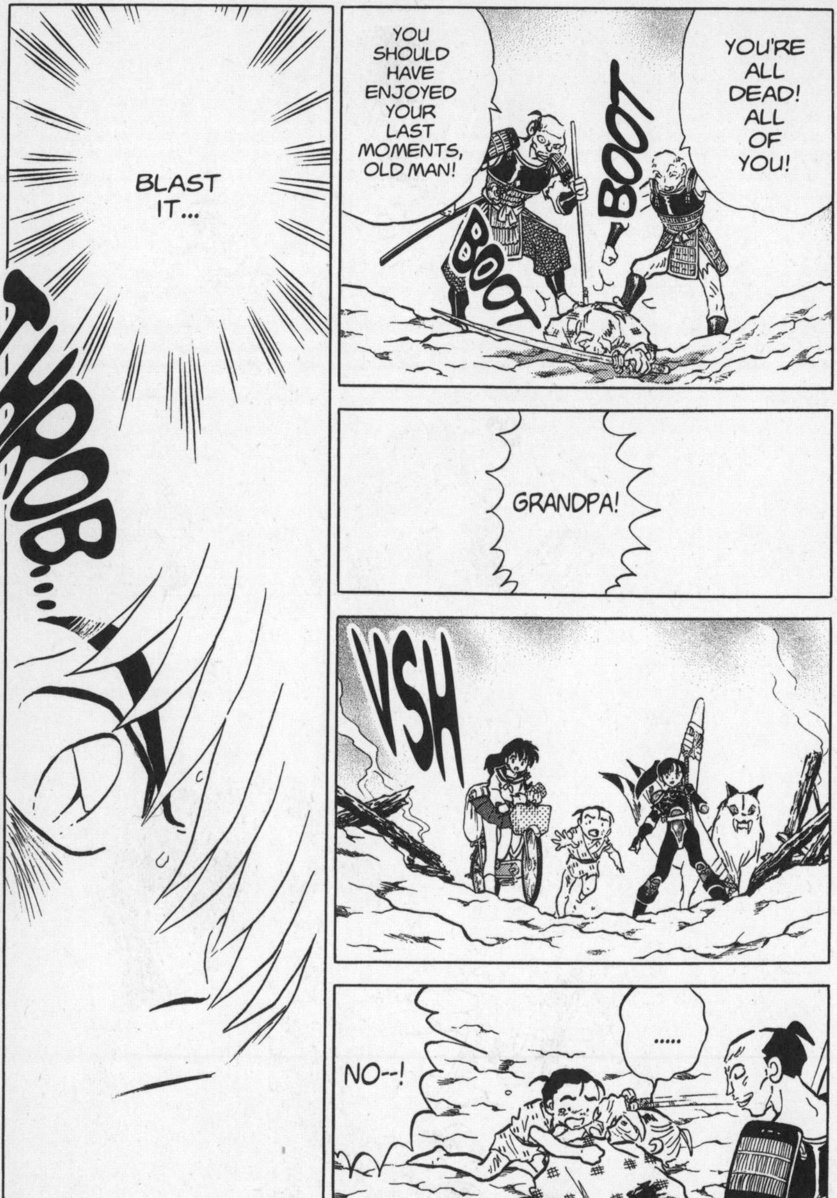
BLAST IT...
THROB...
YOU SHOULD HAVE ENJOYED YOUR LAST MOMENTS, OLD MAN!
BOOT
BOOT
YOU'RE ALL DEAD! ALL OF YOU!
GRANDPA!
VSH
NO--!
.....

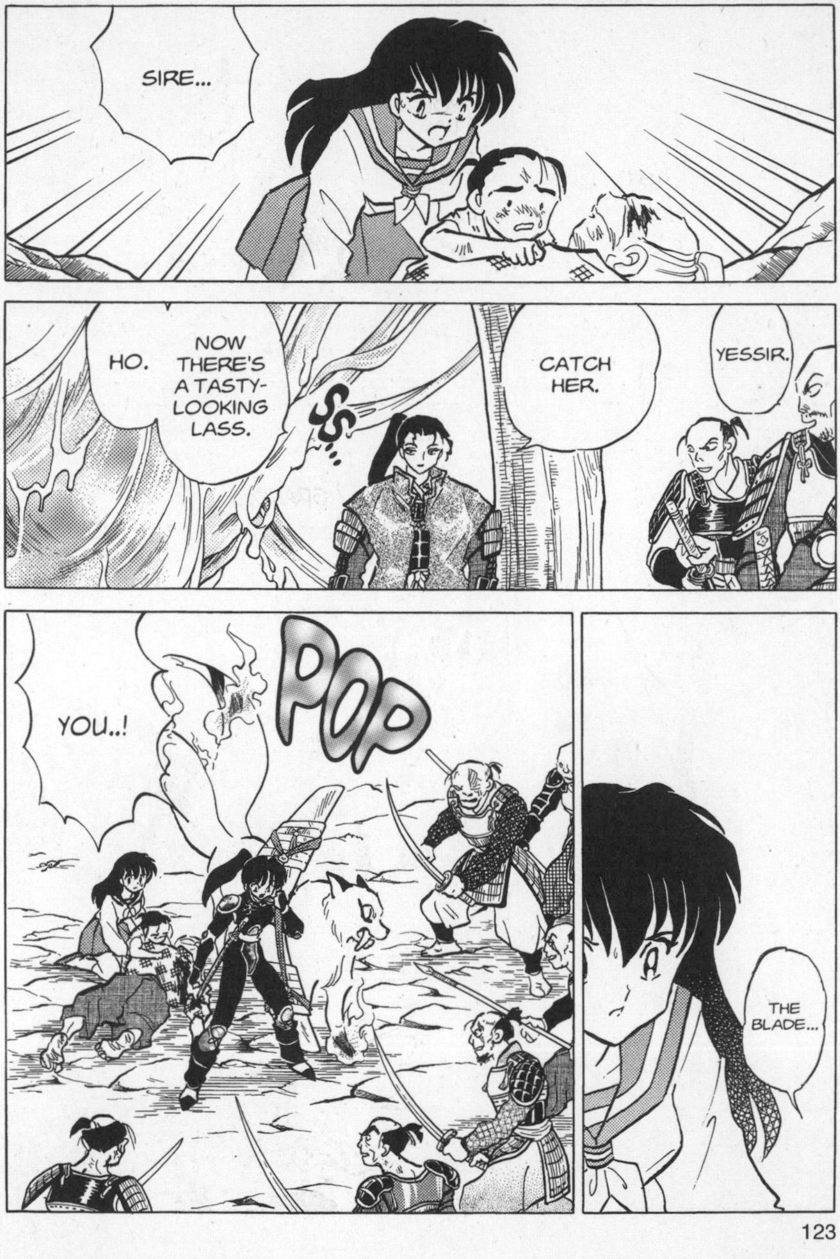
SIRE...
HO.
NOW THERE'S A TASTY-LOOKING LASS.
SS...
CATCH HER.
YESSIR.
YOU..!
POP
THE BLADE...

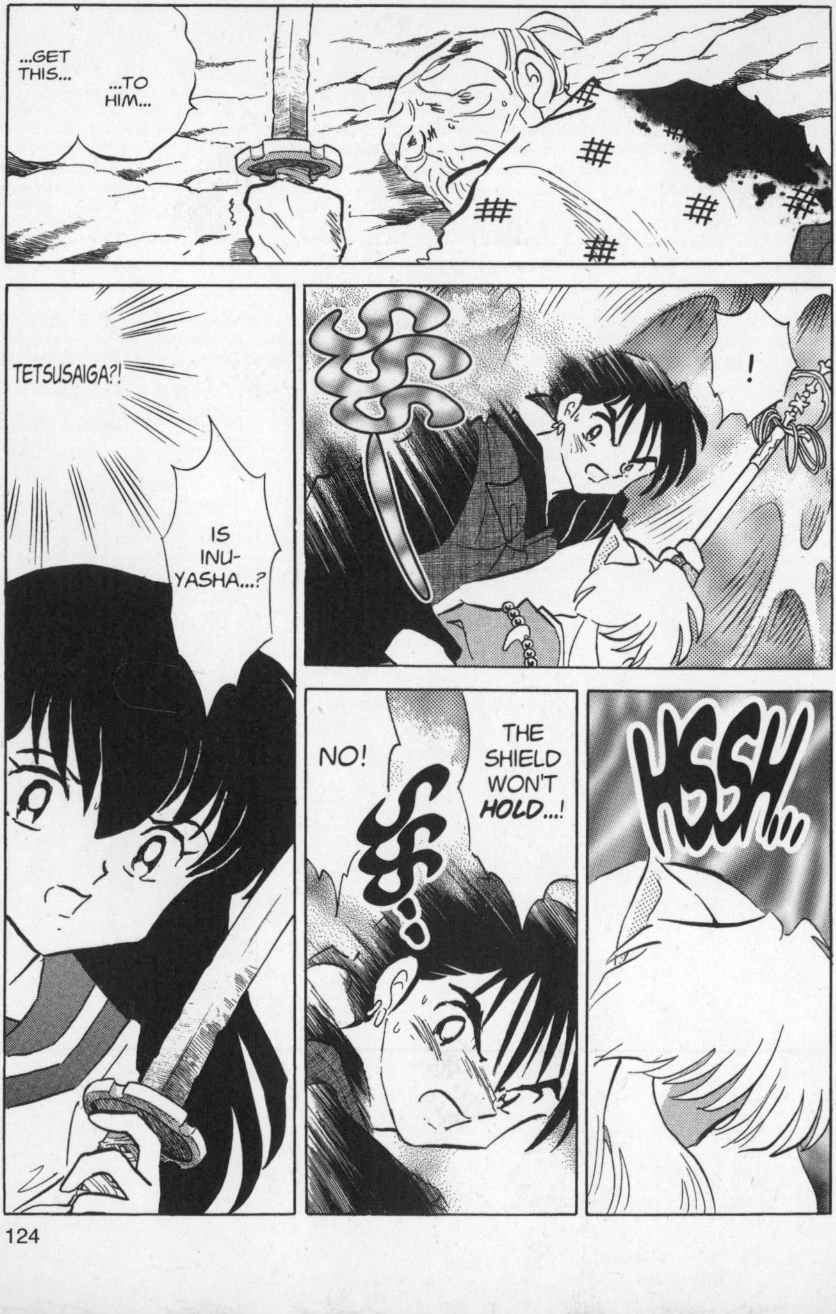

...GET THIS...
...TO HIM...
TETSUSAIGA?!
IS INU-YASHA...?
SSS
!
NO!
THE SHIELD WON'T *HOLD*...!
SSS...
HSSH...

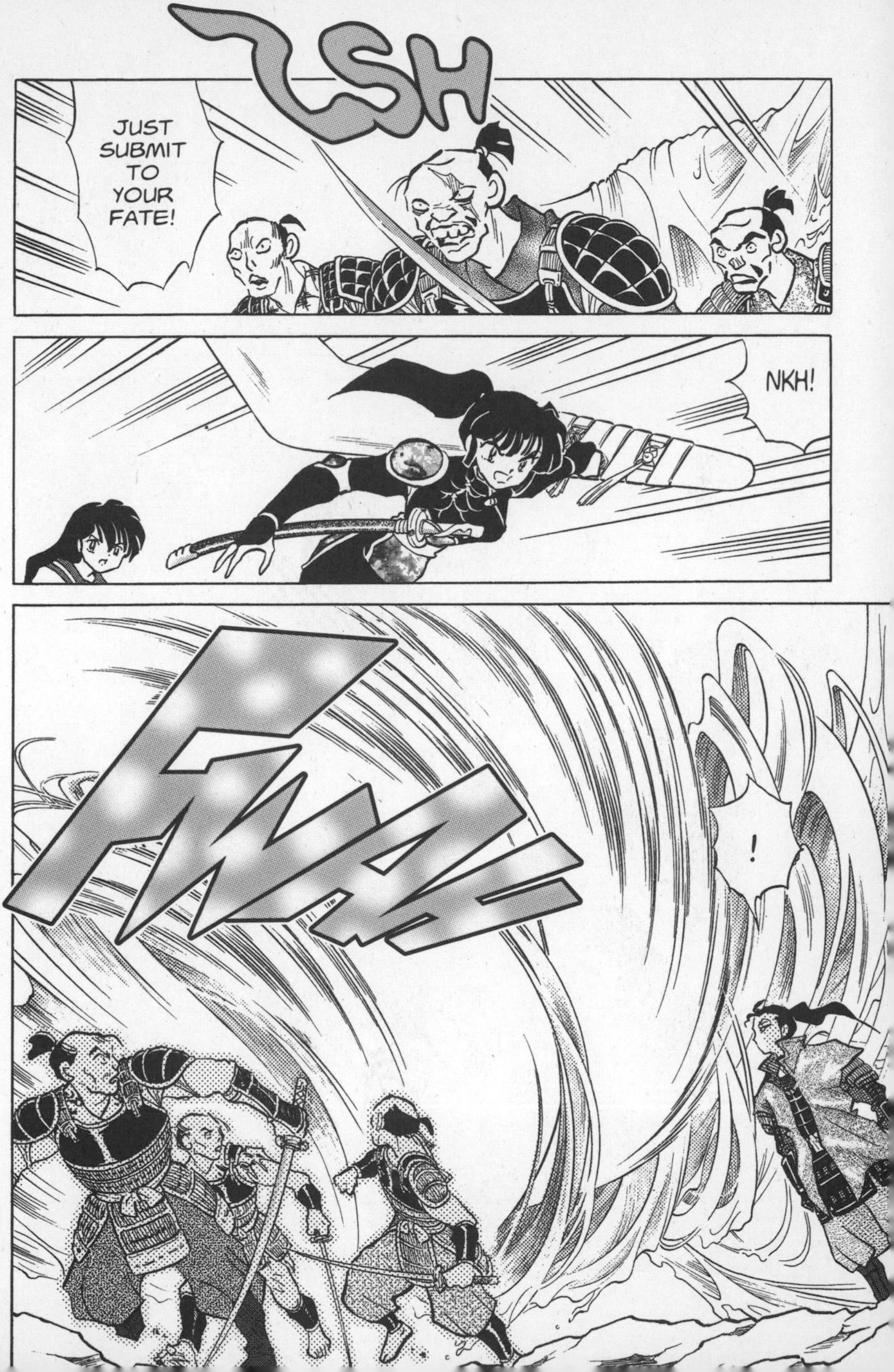
ZSH
JUST SUBMIT TO YOUR FATE!
NKH!
FWAM
!

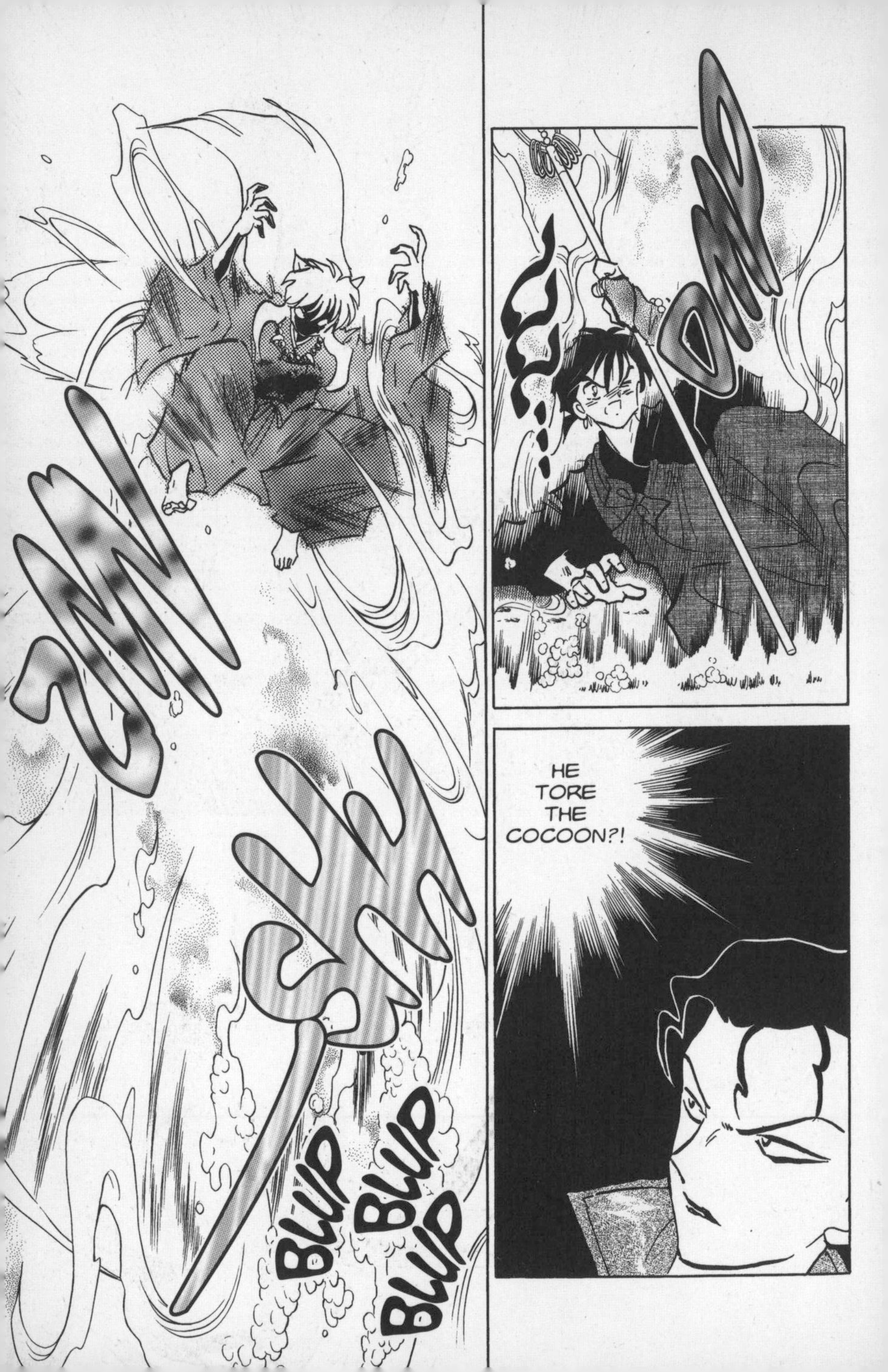
BLUP
BLUP
BLUP
HE TORE THE COCOON?!

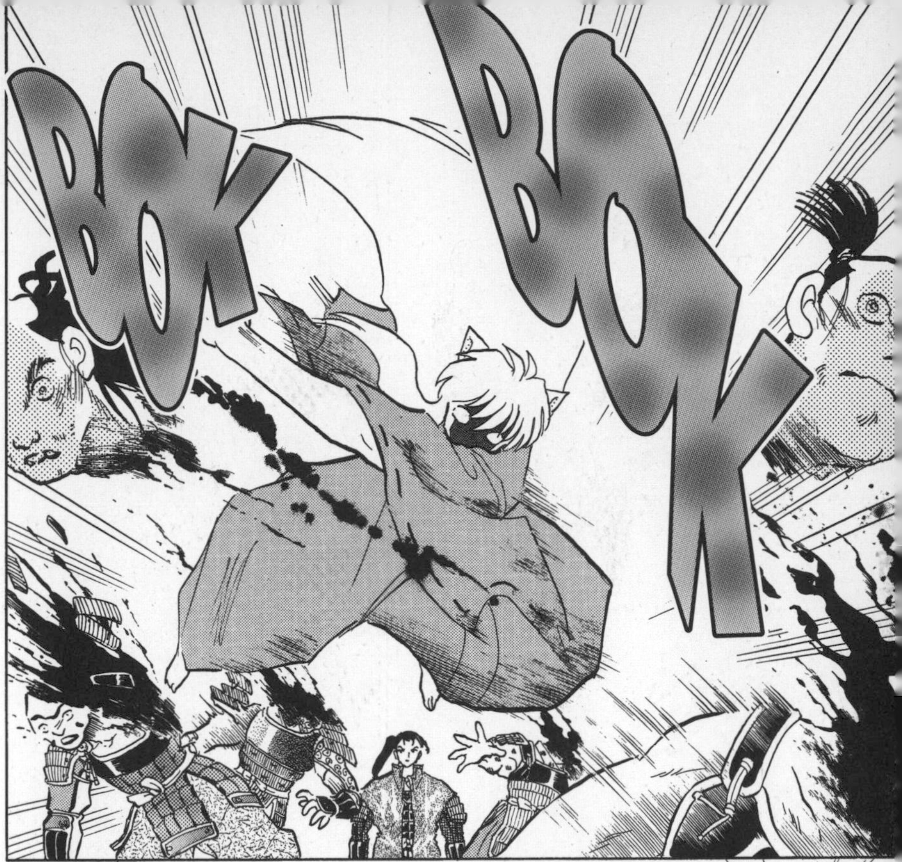
BOK
BOK
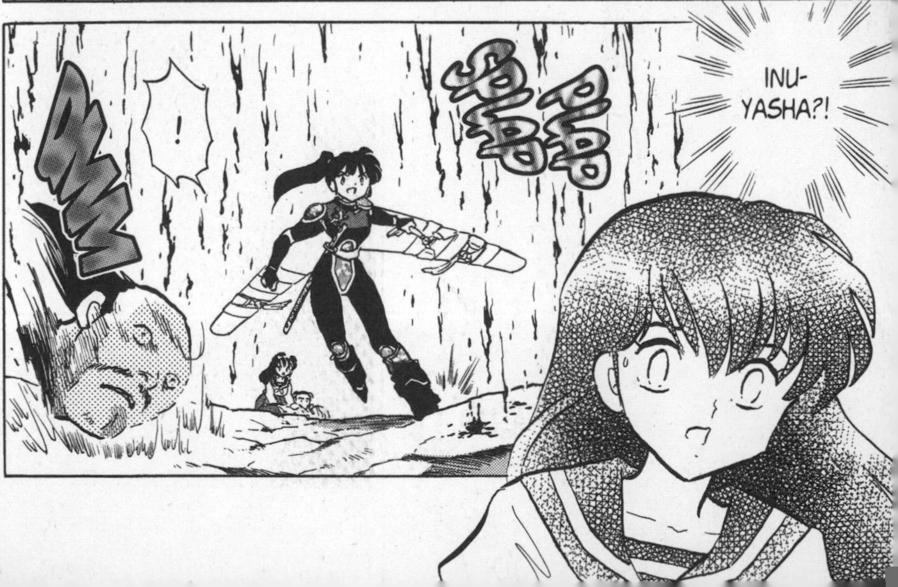
DWM
!
SPLAD
PLAD
INU-
YASHA?!

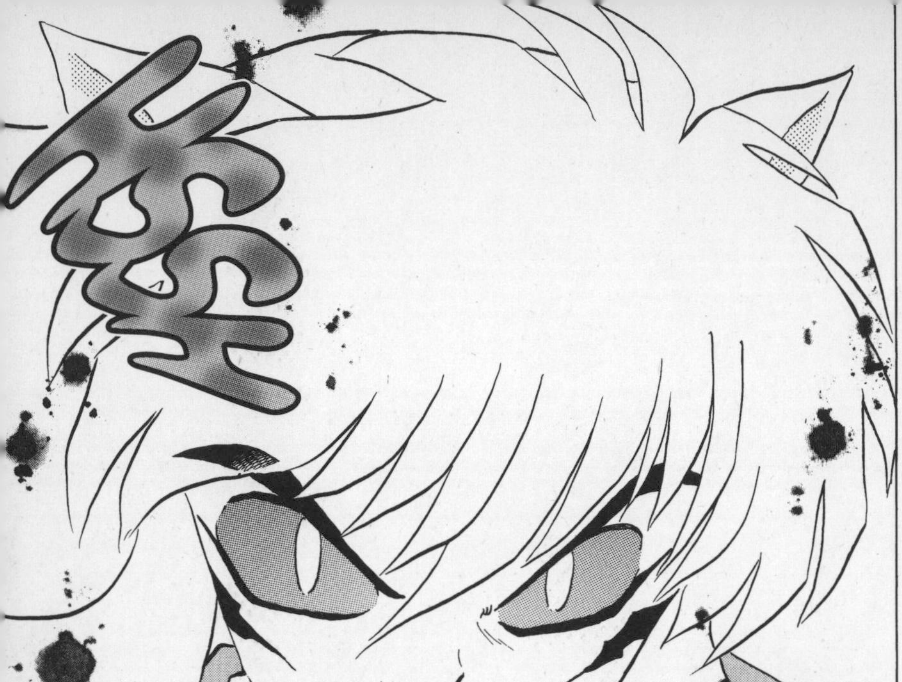

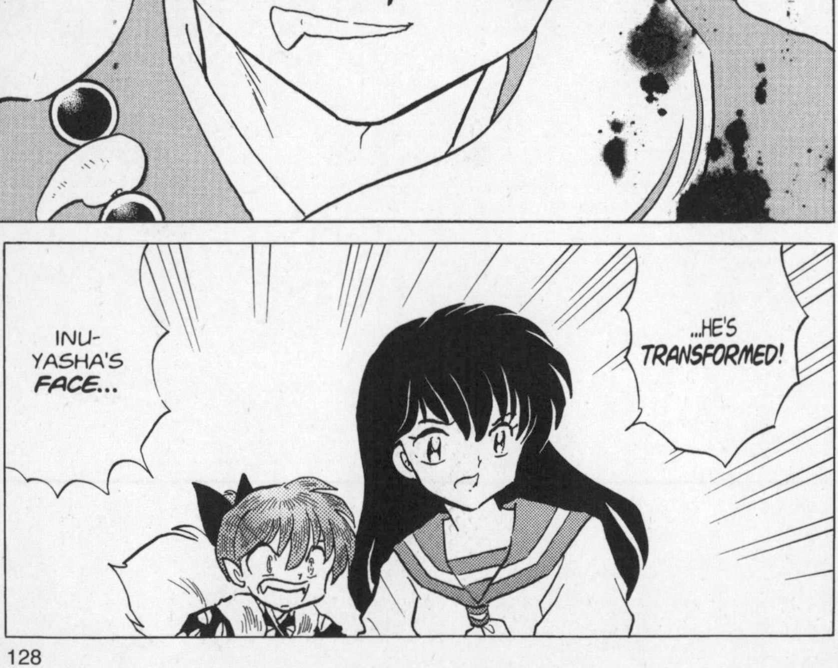
INU-
YASHA'S
FACE...
...HE'S
TRANSFORMED!

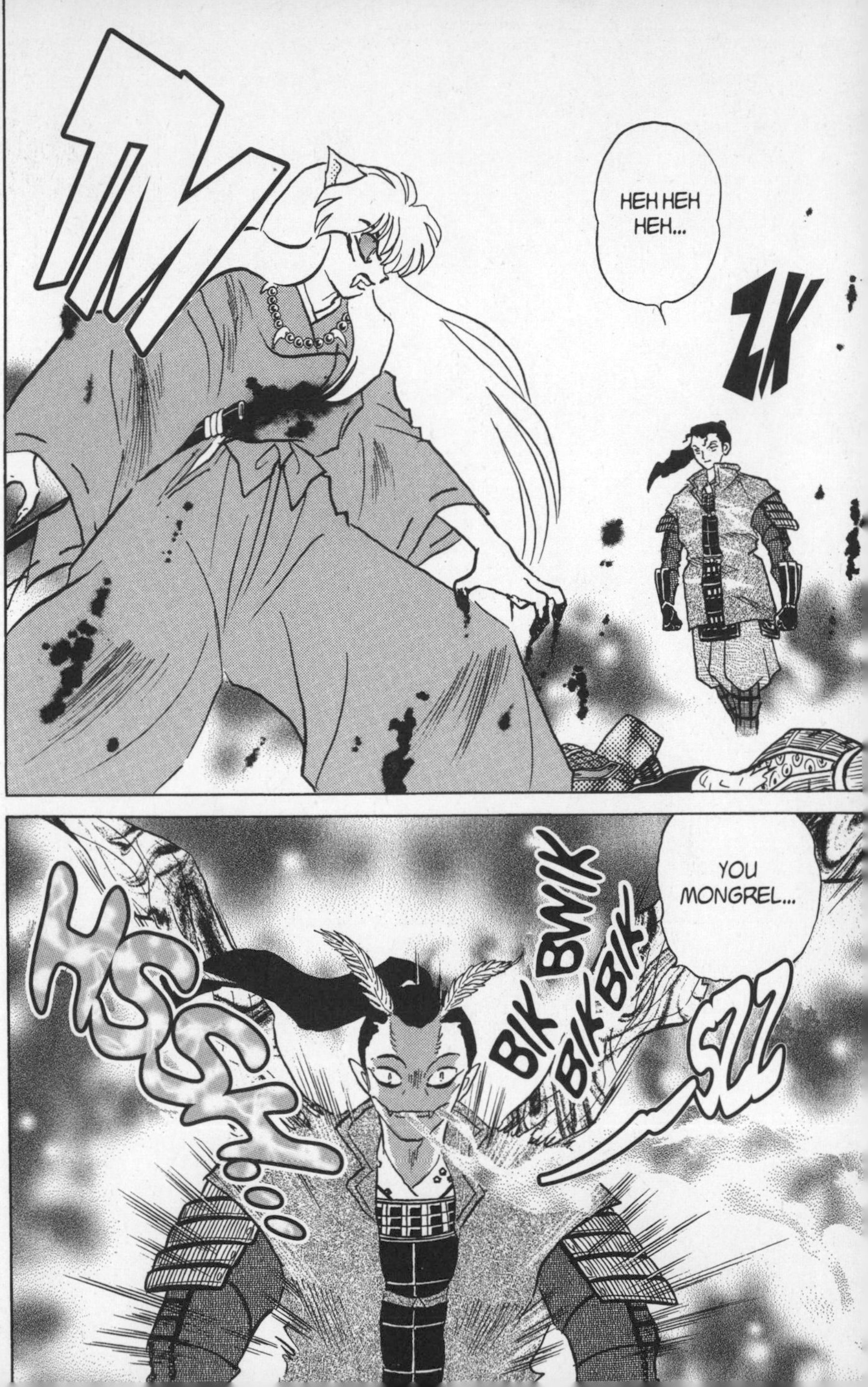
TM
HEH HEH HEH...
ZK
HSSH...
BIK BIK BIK BWIK
YOU MONGREL...
SIZZ

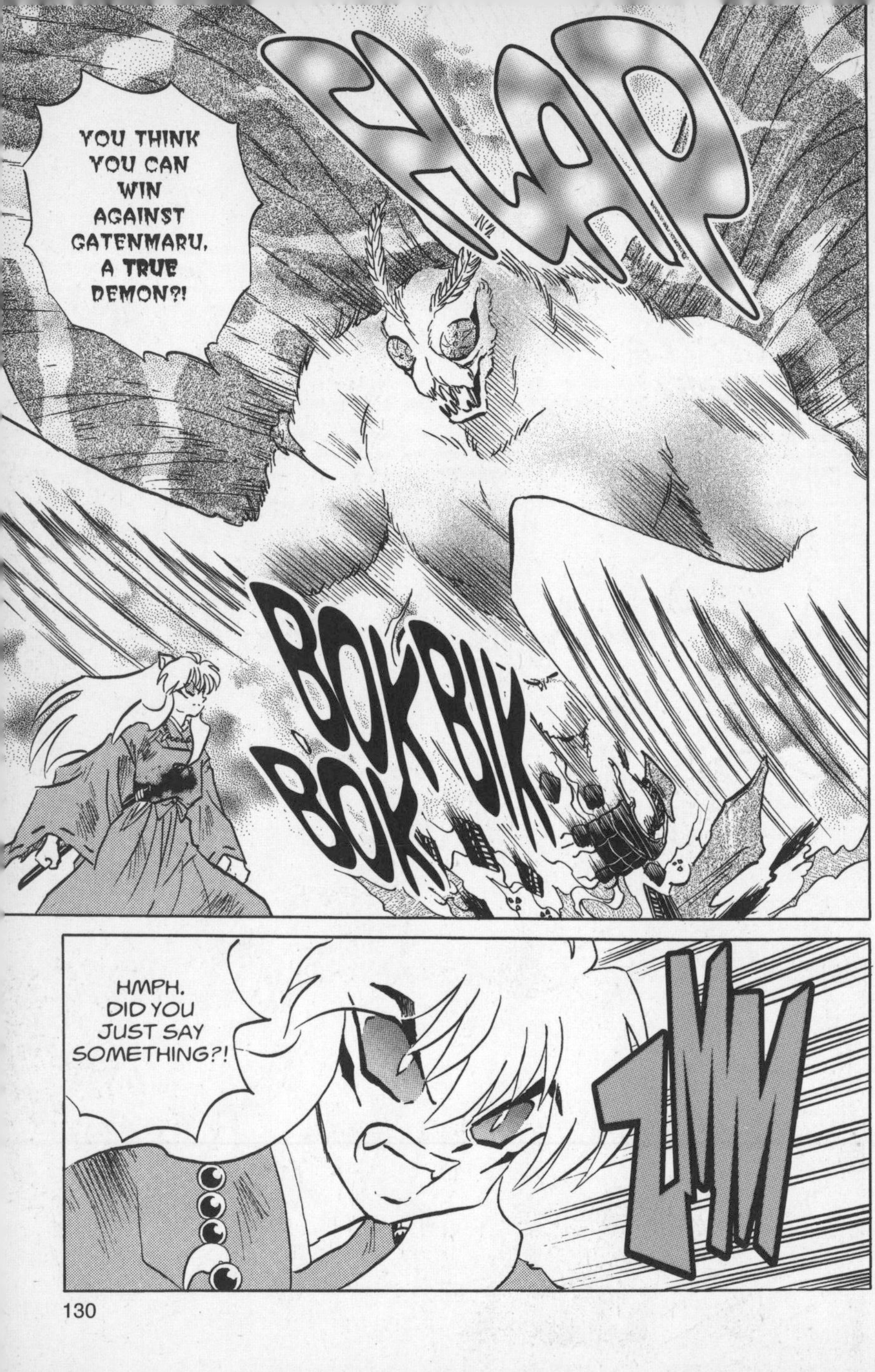
YOU THINK YOU CAN WIN AGAINST GATENMARU, A **TRUE** DEMON?!
BOK BUK BOK BUK
HMPH. DID YOU JUST SAY SOMETHING?!
ZMM

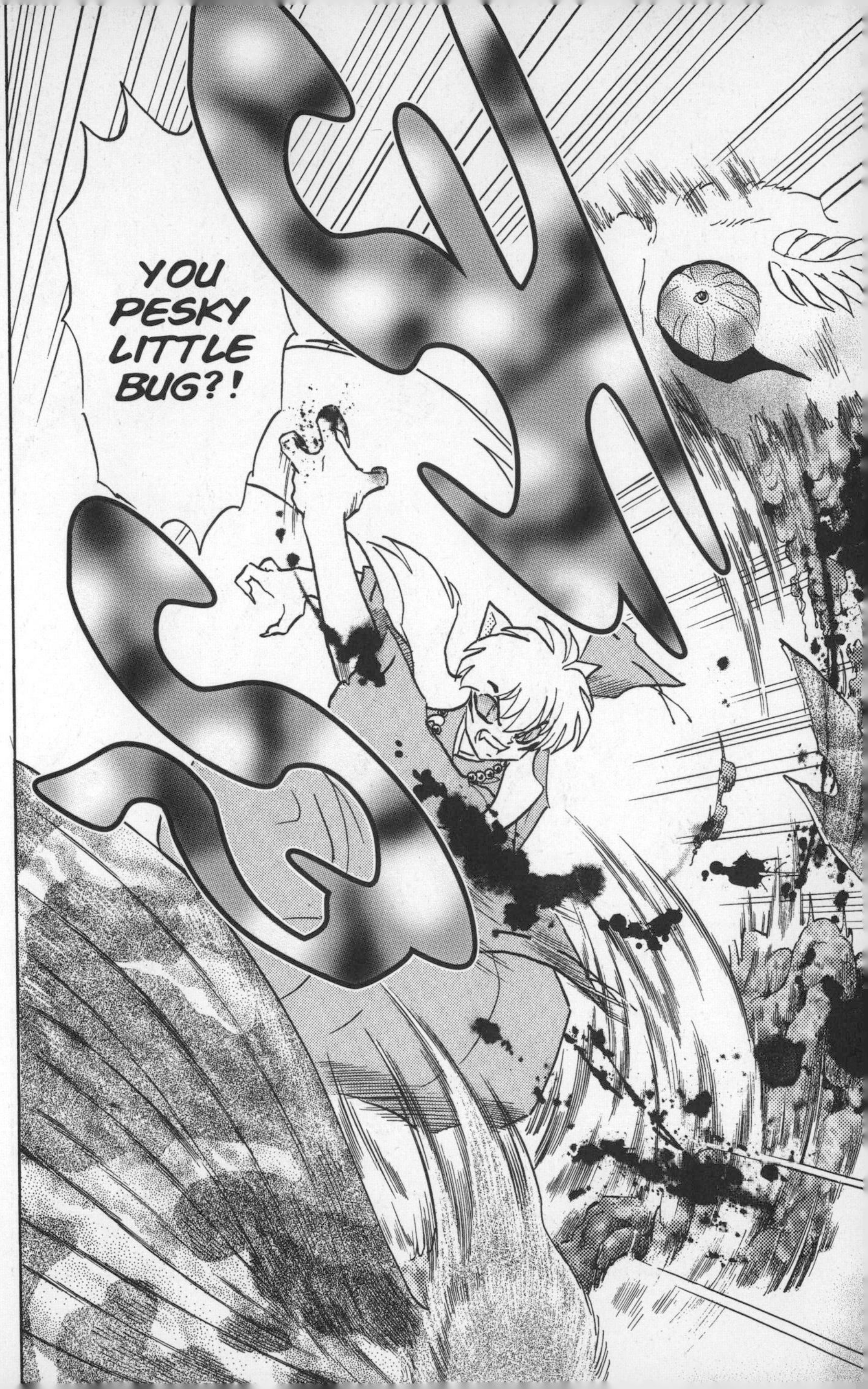
YOU PESKY LITTLE BUG?!

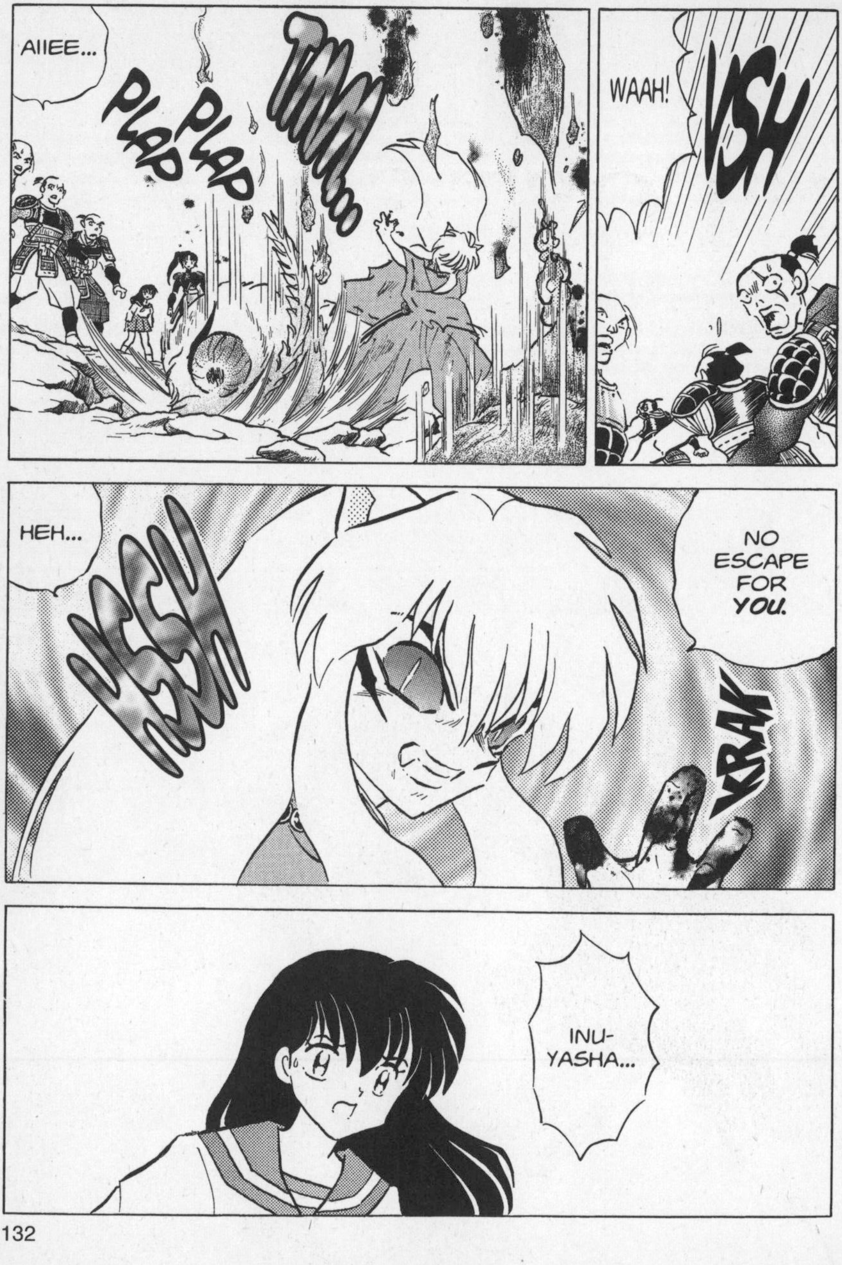
AIIEE...
PLAP PLAP
TMM...
WAAH!
VSH
HEH...
VSSH
NO ESCAPE FOR YOU.
KRAK
INU-YASHA...

SCROLL EIGHT

THE LOST SOUL

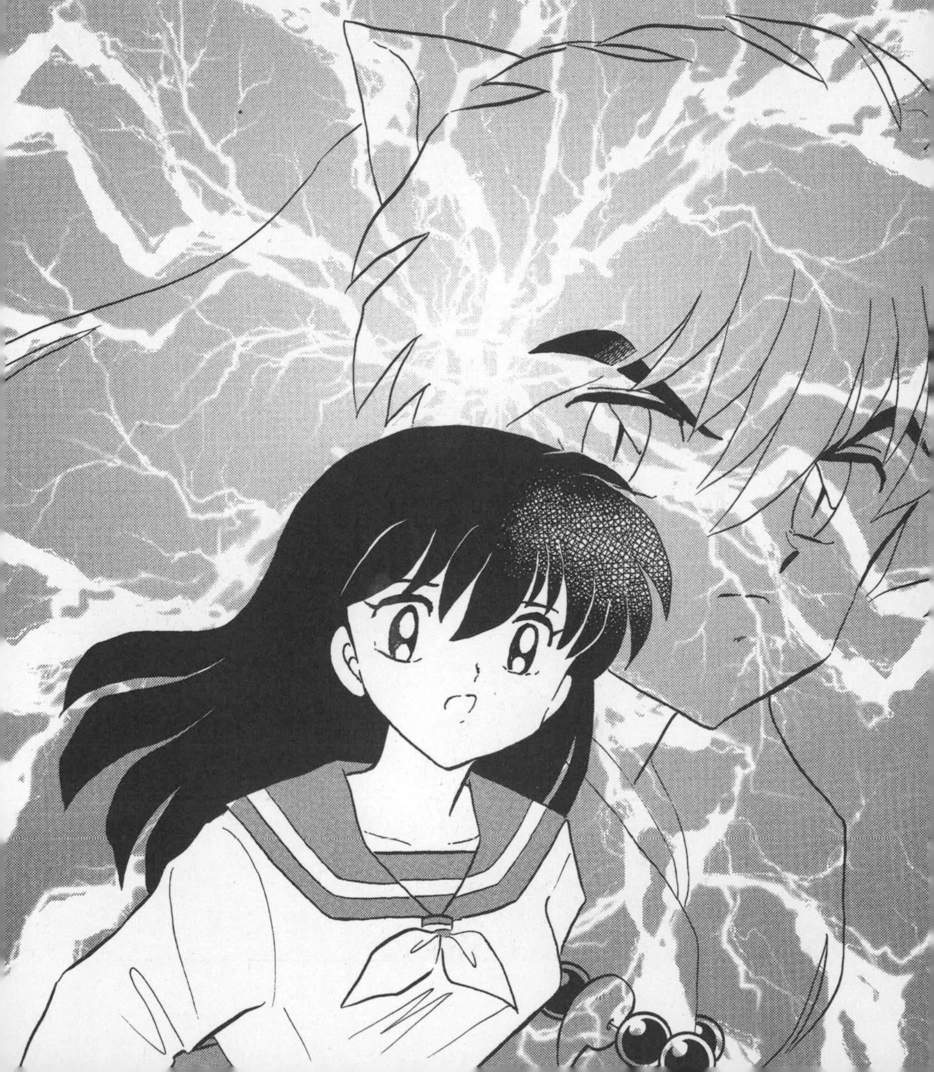

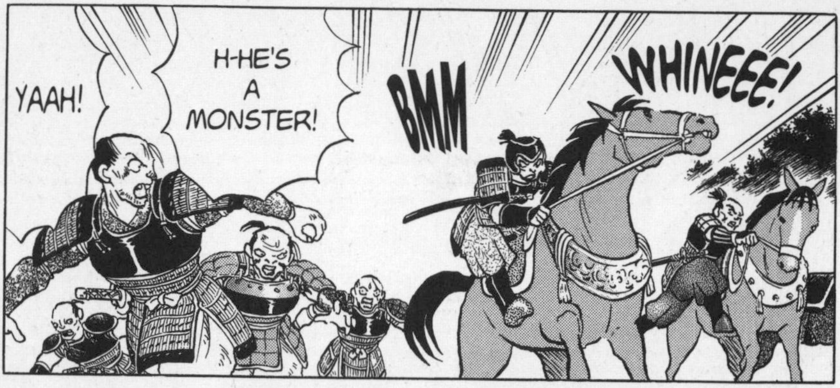
YAAH!
H-HE'S A MONSTER!
BMM
WHINEEE!
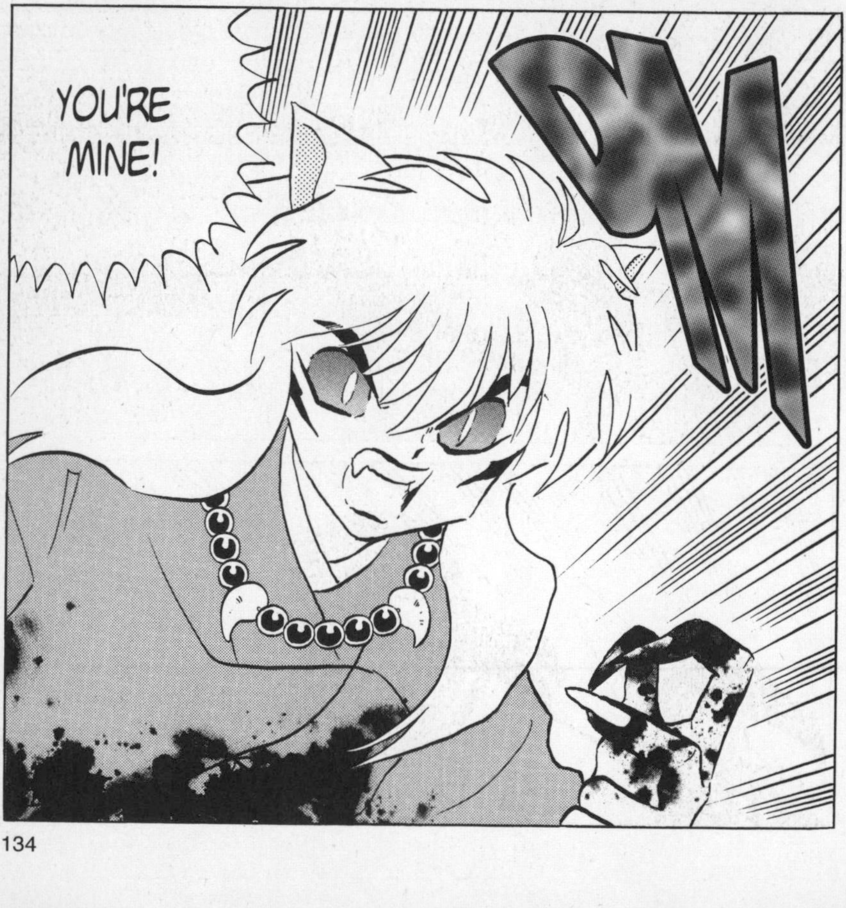
YOU'RE MINE!
DM

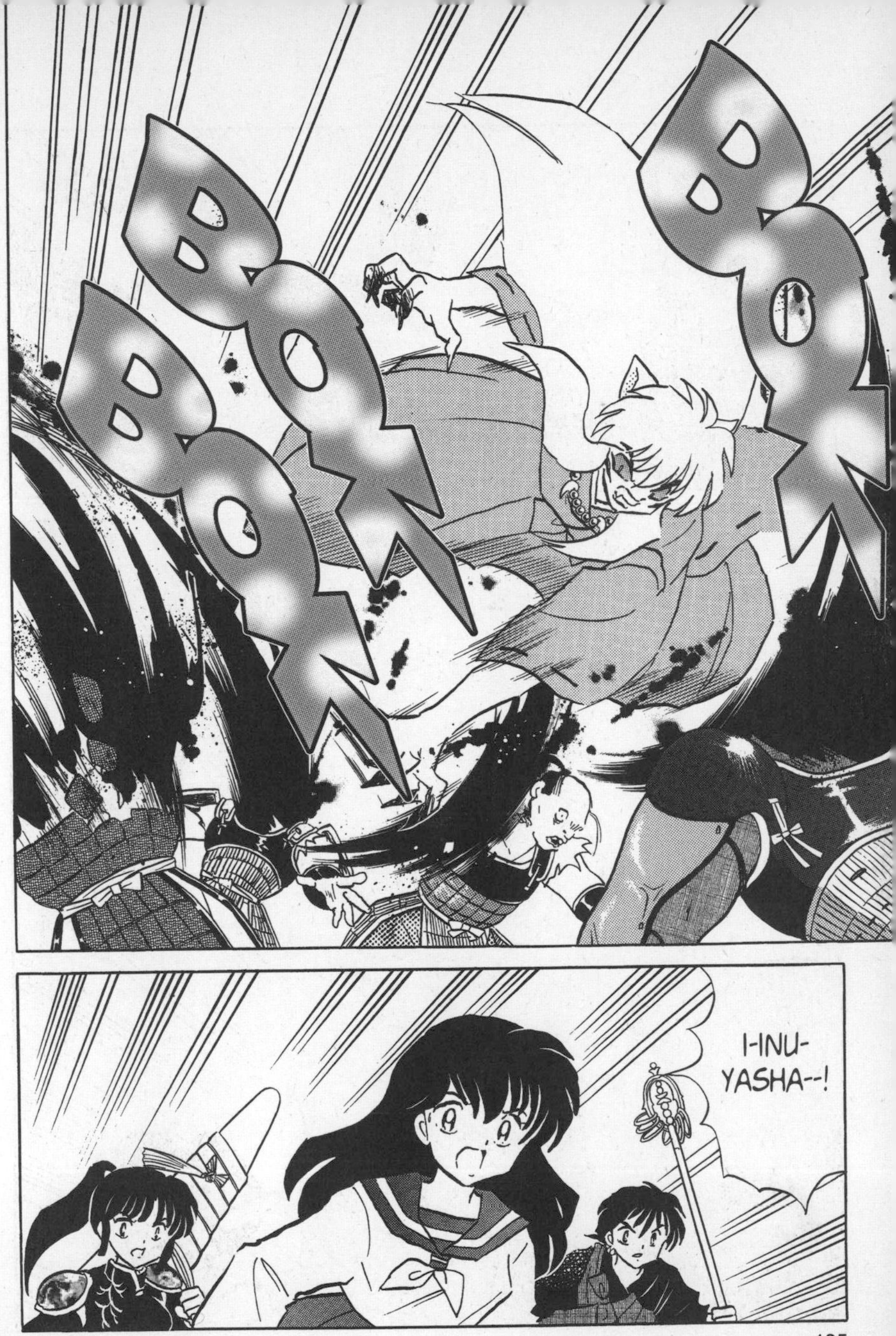
BOOM
BOOM
BOOM
I-INU-YASHA--!

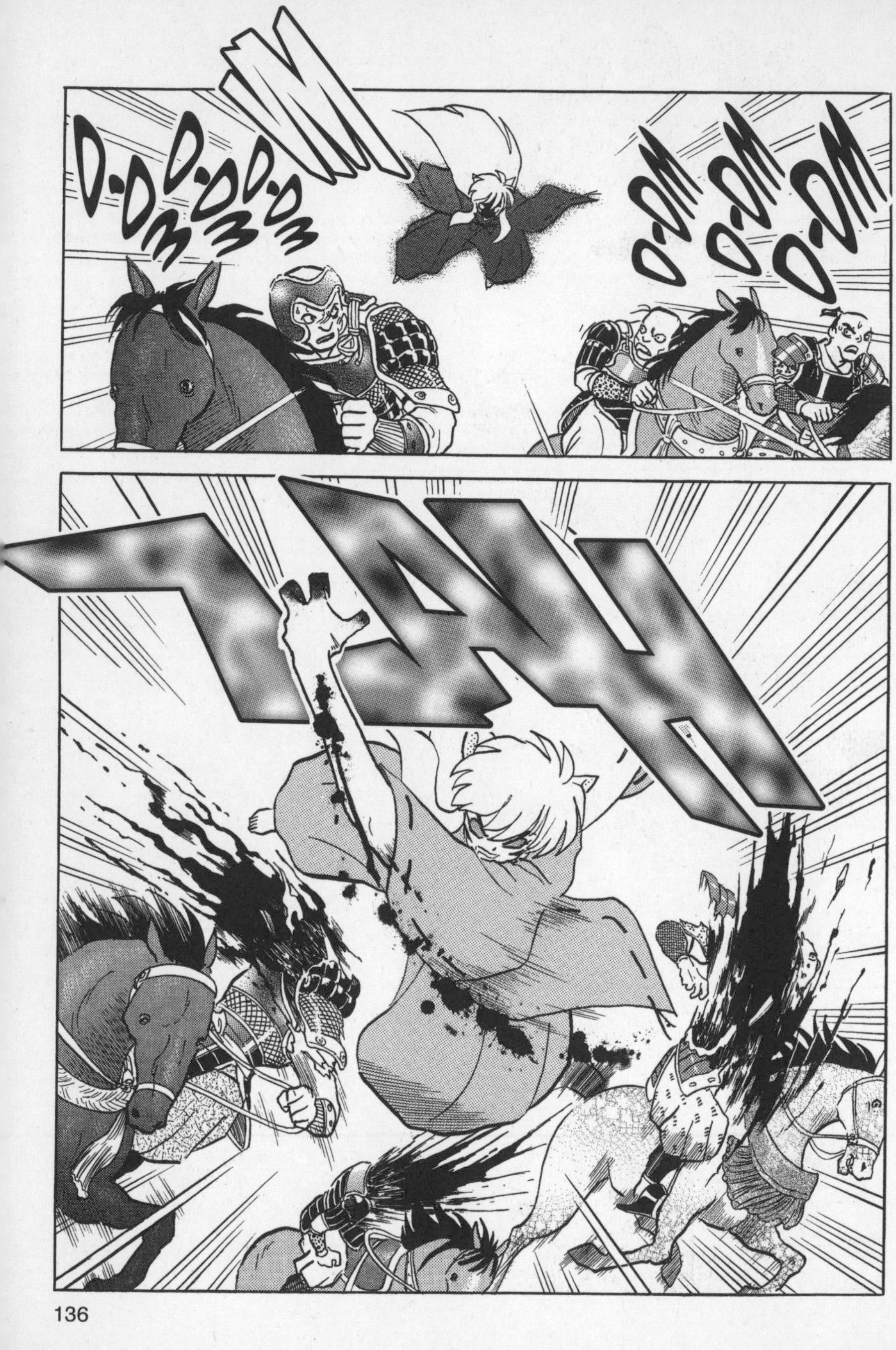

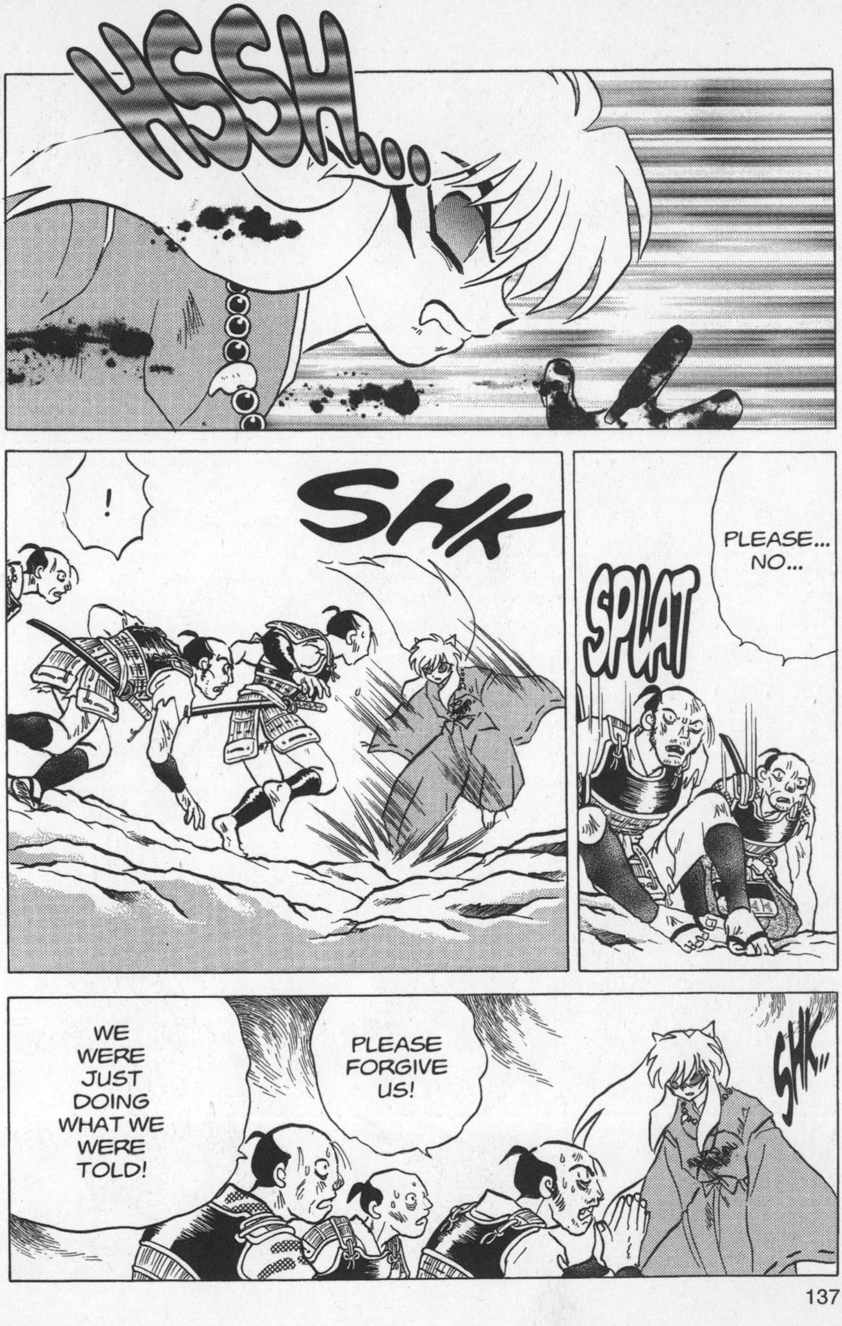
HSSH...
!
SHK
PLEASE... NO...
SPLAT
WE WERE JUST DOING WHAT WE WERE TOLD!
PLEASE FORGIVE US!
SHK...

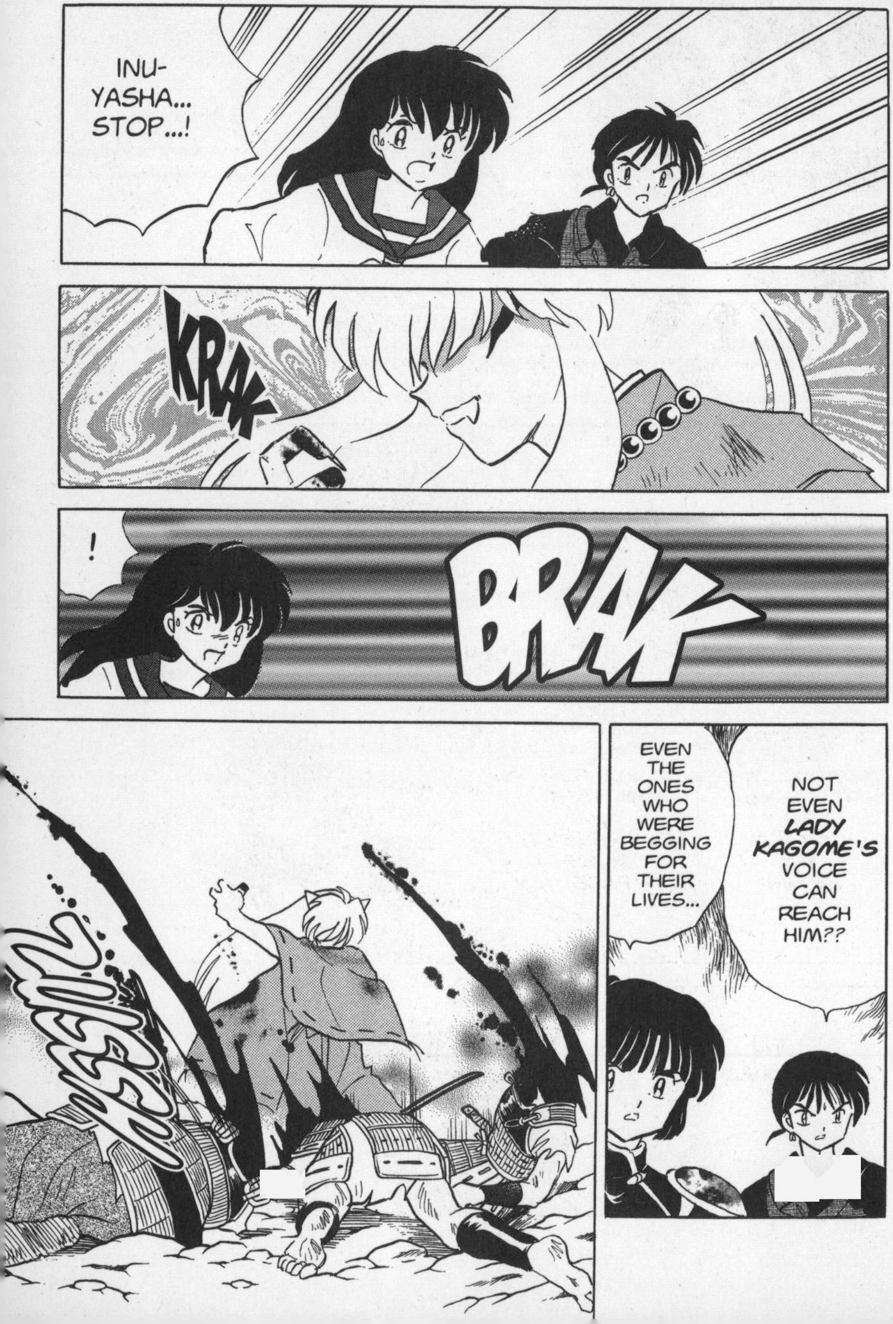
INU-YASHA... STOP...!
KRAK
!
BRAK
EVEN THE ONES WHO WERE BEGGING FOR THEIR LIVES...
NOT EVEN LADY KAGOME'S VOICE CAN REACH HIM??

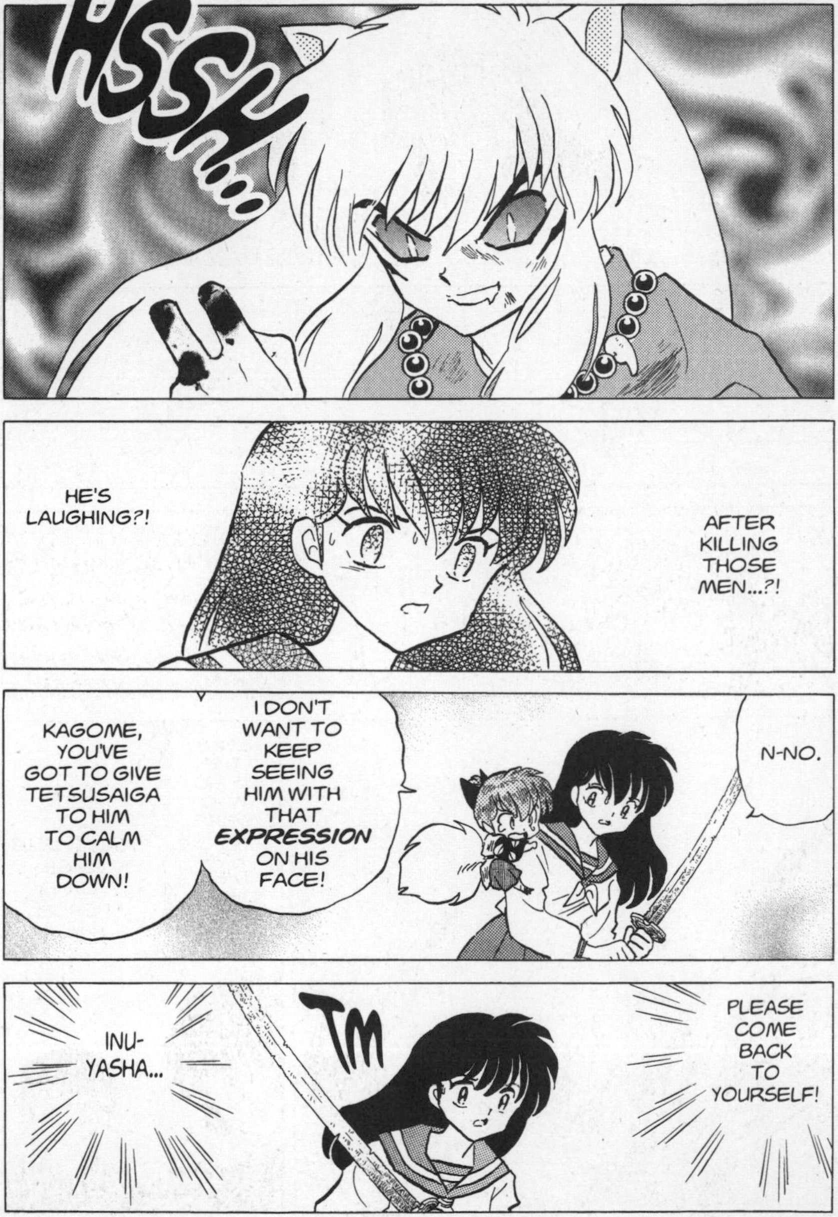
HSSH...
HE'S LAUGHING?!
AFTER KILLING THOSE MEN...?!
KAGOME, YOU'VE GOT TO GIVE TETSUSAIGA TO HIM TO CALM HIM DOWN!
I DON'T WANT TO KEEP SEEING HIM WITH THAT EXPRESSION ON HIS FACE!
N-NO.
INU-YASHA...
TM
PLEASE COME BACK TO YOURSELF!

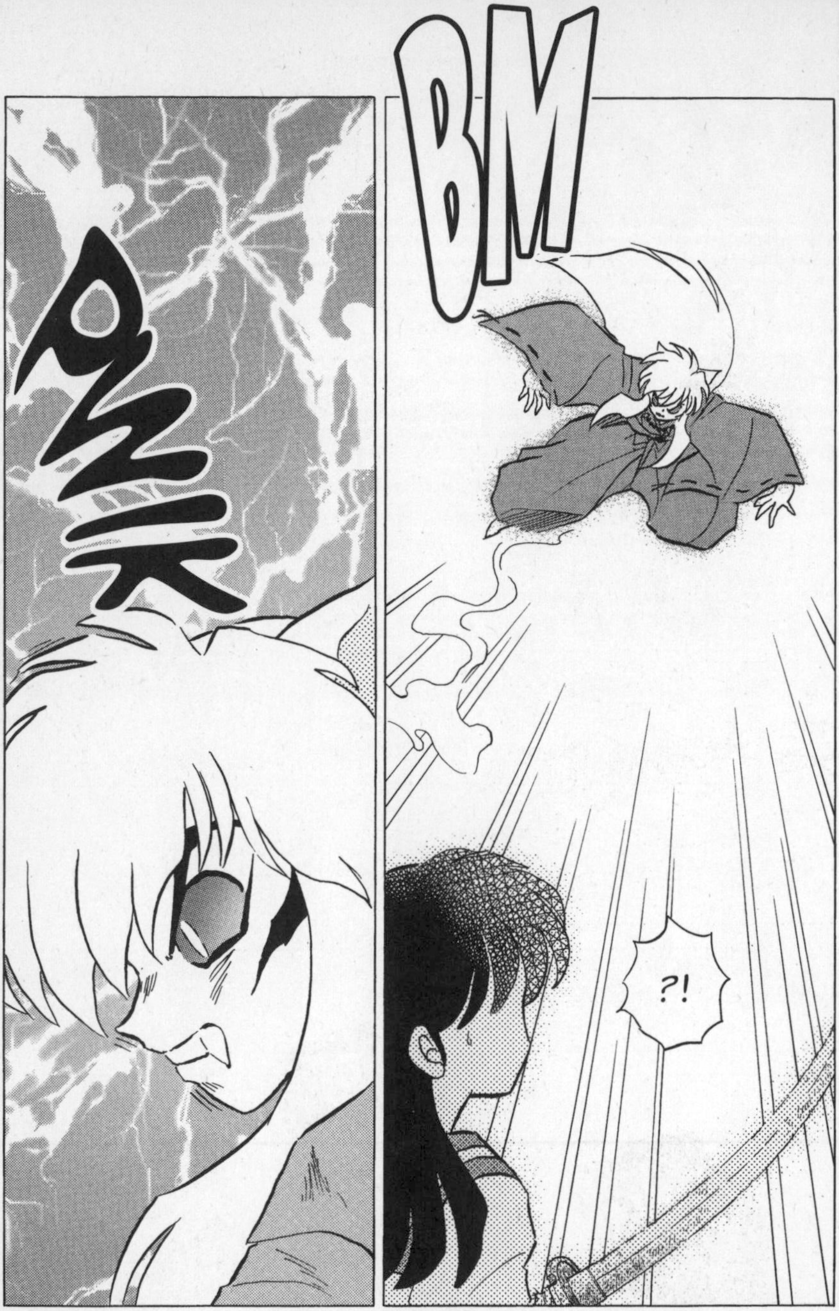
PZZK
BM
?!

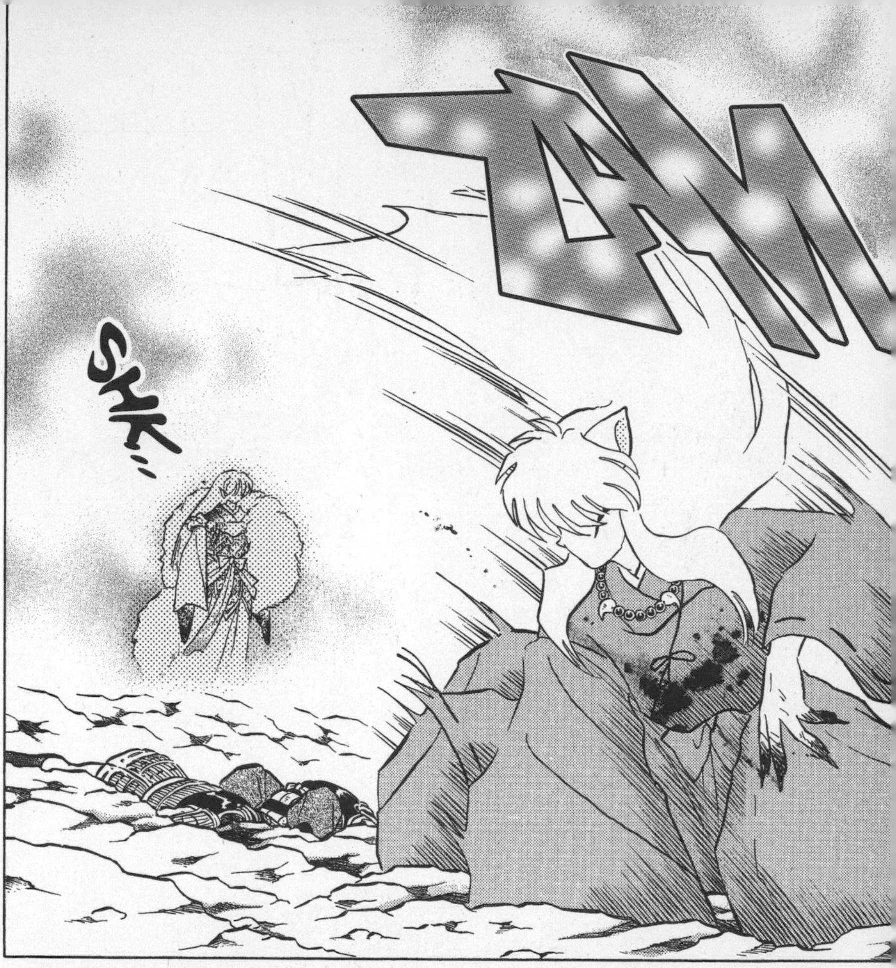
SHK...
TAAN
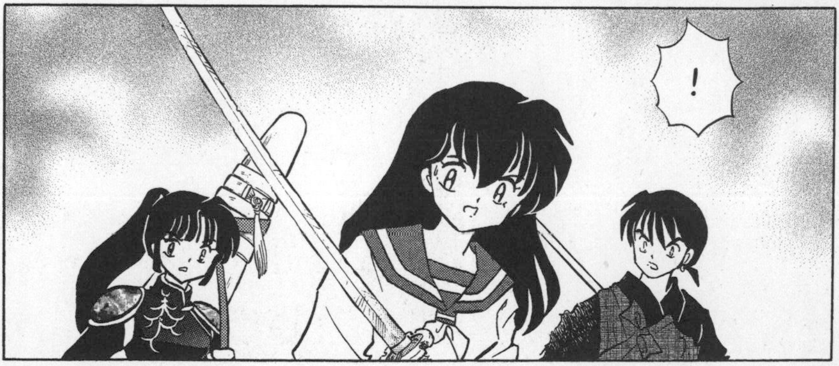
!

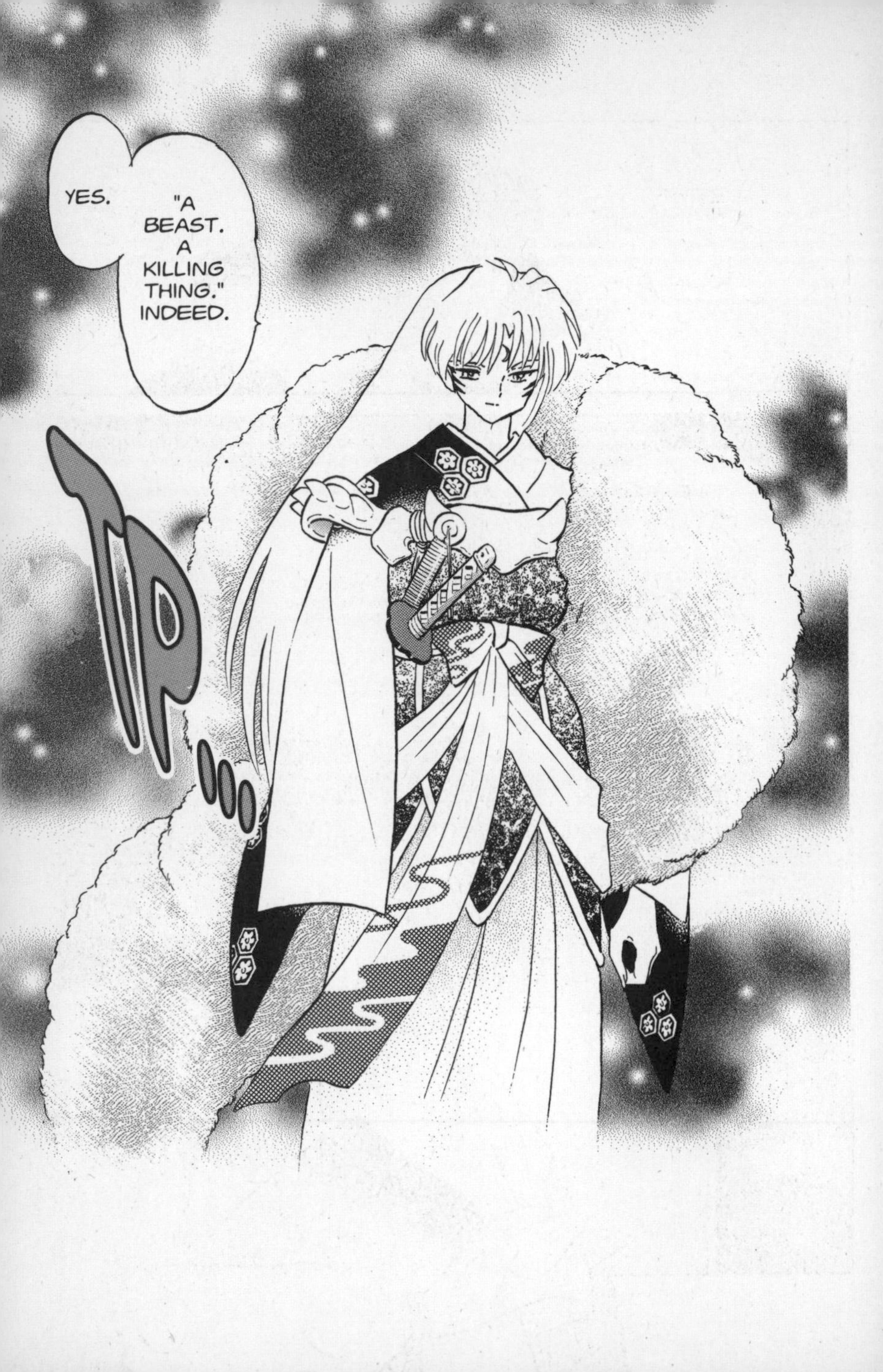
YES. "A BEAST. A KILLING THING." INDEED.
TIP...

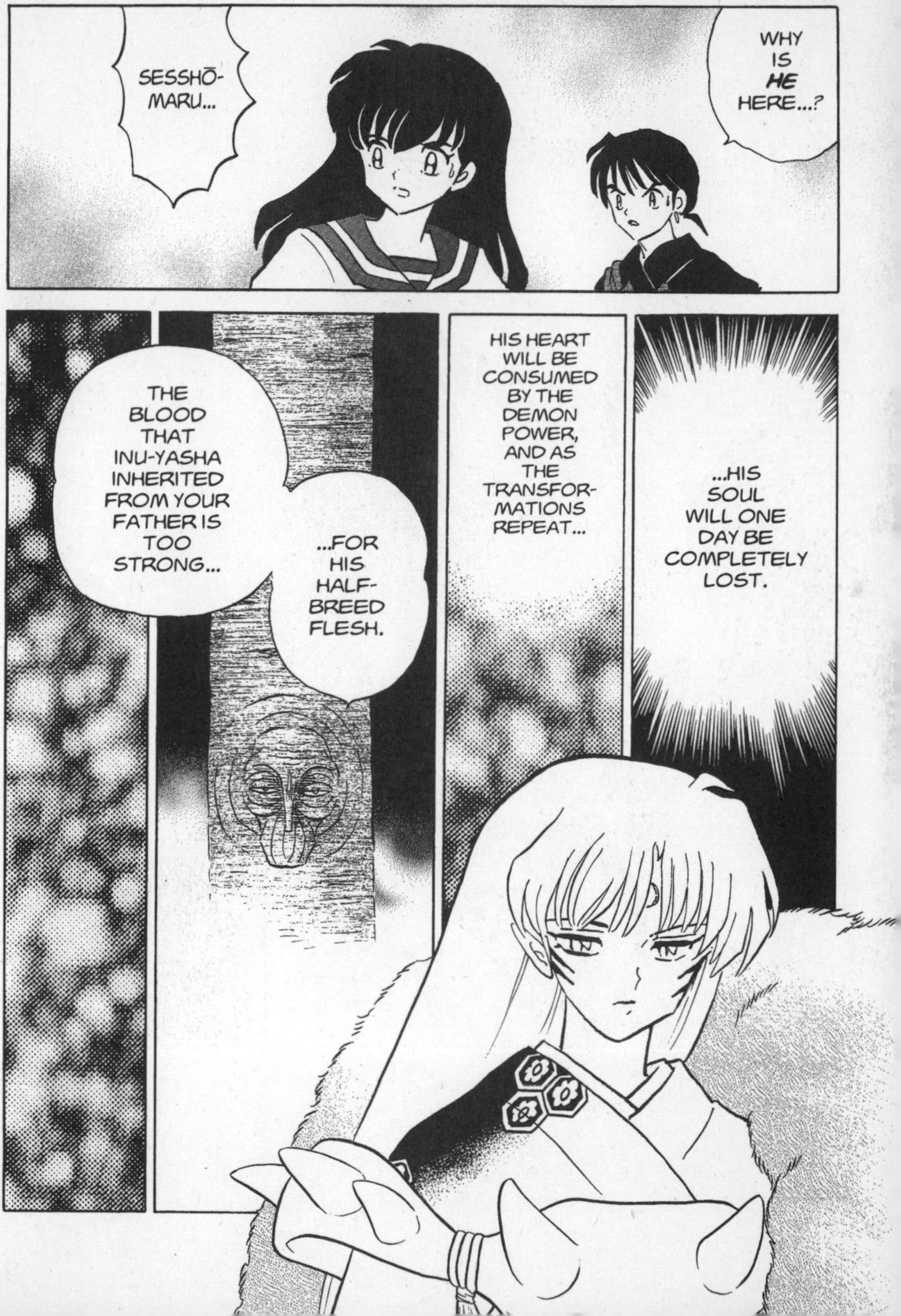
SESSHŌ-MARU...
WHY IS *HE* HERE...?
THE BLOOD THAT INU-YASHA INHERITED FROM YOUR FATHER IS TOO STRONG...
...FOR HIS HALF-BREED FLESH.
HIS HEART WILL BE CONSUMED BY THE DEMON POWER, AND AS THE TRANSFORMATIONS REPEAT...
...HIS SOUL WILL ONE DAY BE COMPLETELY LOST.

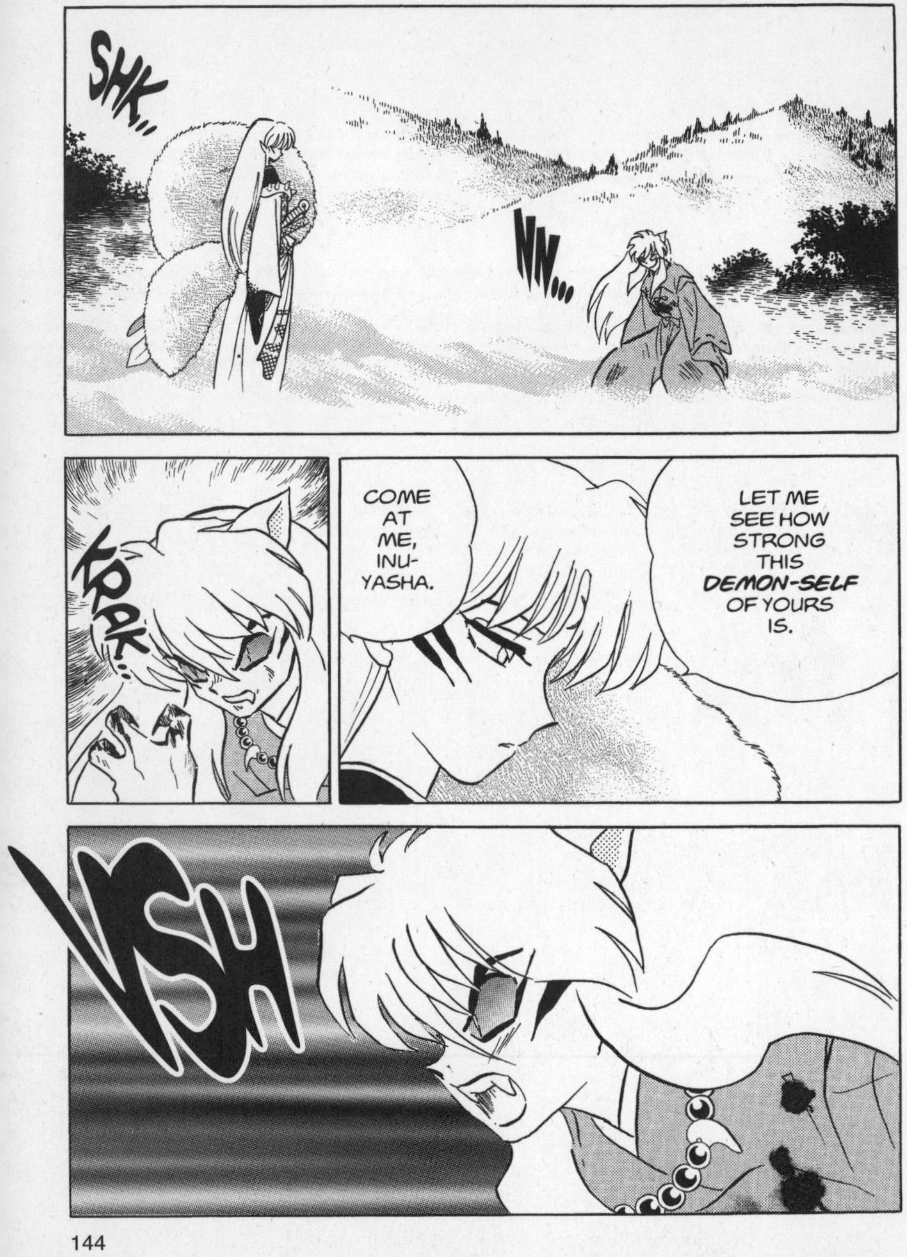
SHK...
NN...
KRAK...
COME AT ME, INU-YASHA.
LET ME SEE HOW STRONG THIS DEMON-SELF OF YOURS IS.
VSH

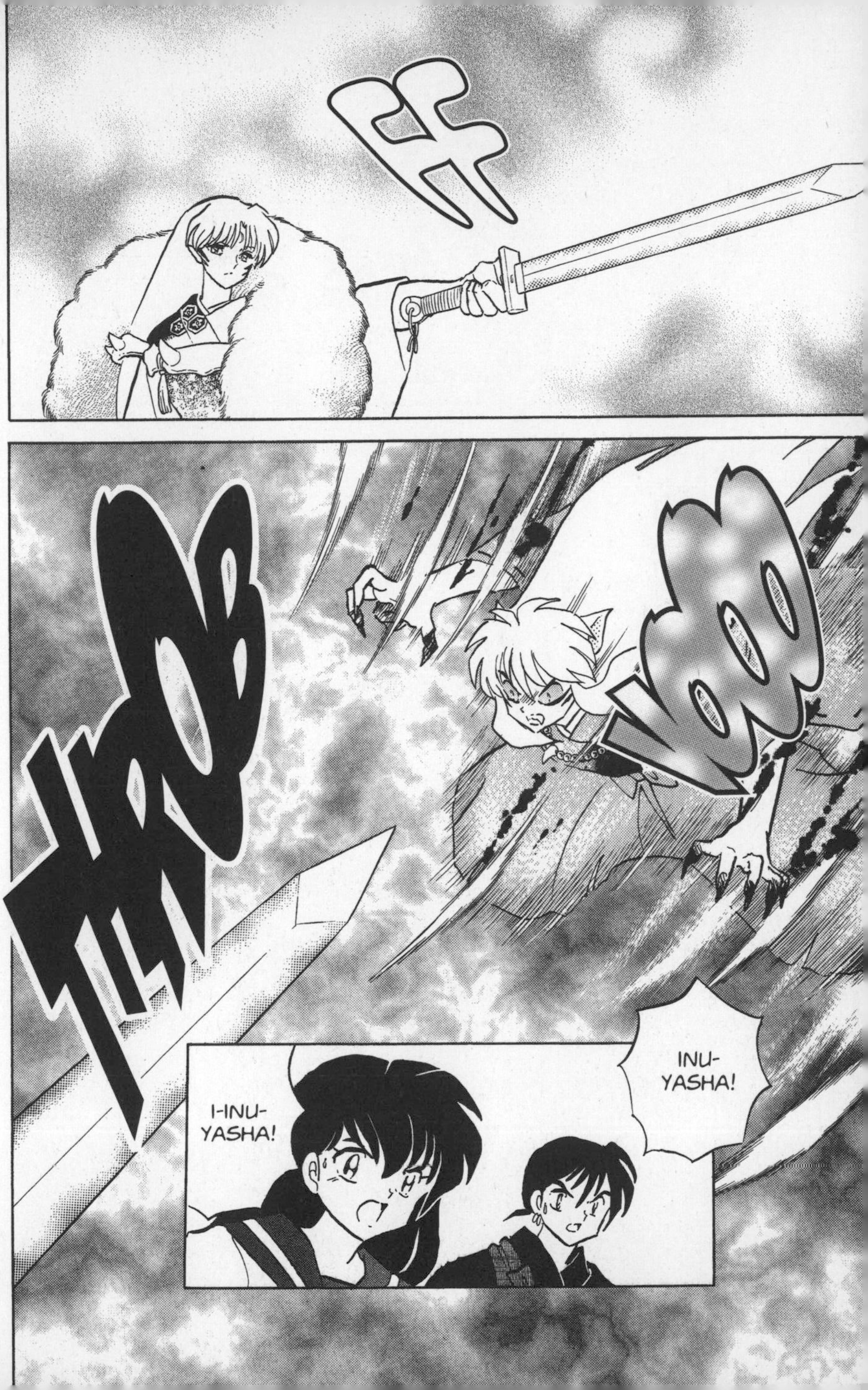
THROB
I-INU-YASHA!
INU-YASHA!

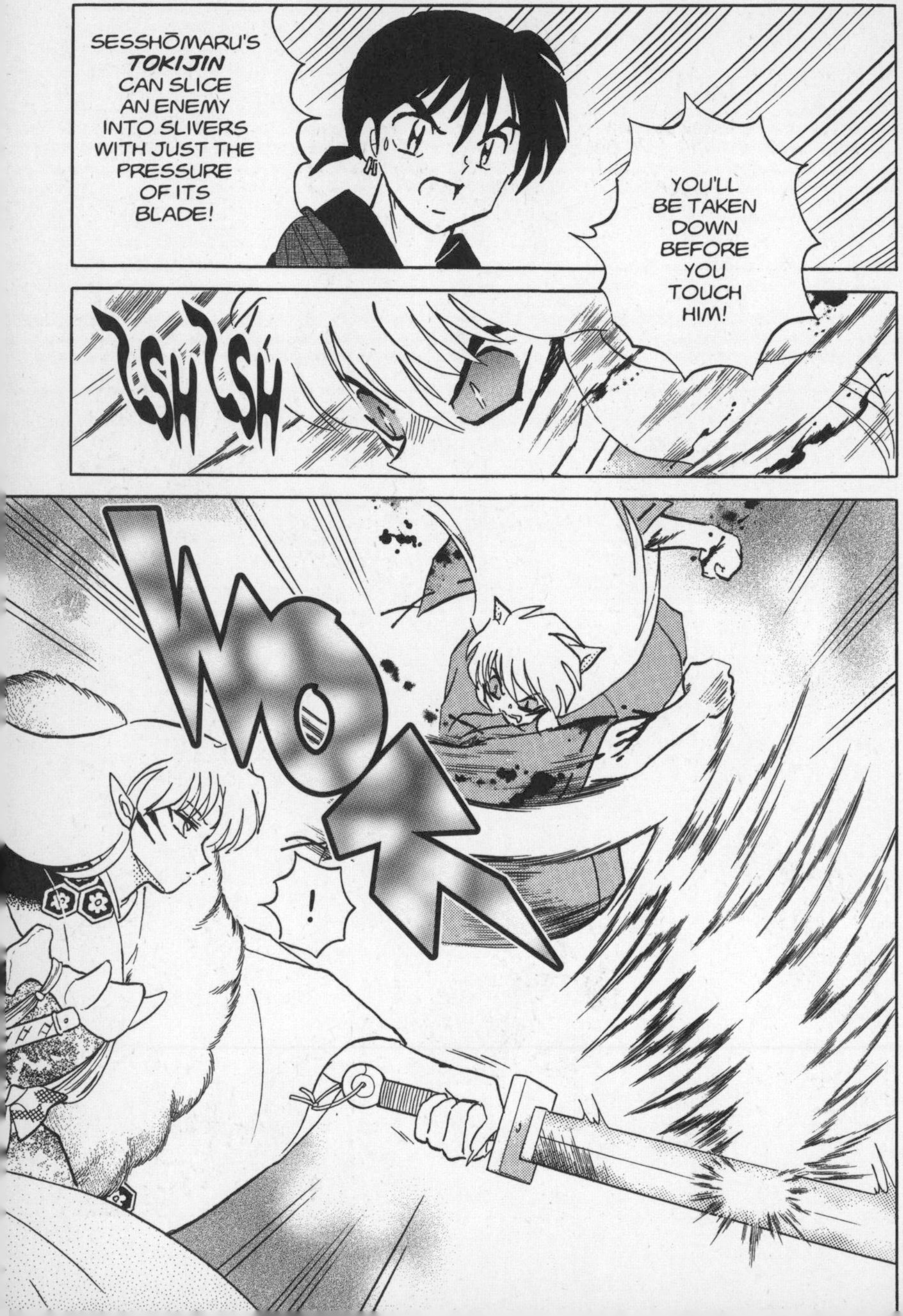
SESSHŌMARU'S ***TOKIJIN*** CAN SLICE AN ENEMY INTO SLIVERS WITH JUST THE PRESSURE OF ITS BLADE!
YOU'LL BE TAKEN DOWN BEFORE YOU TOUCH HIM!
TSH TSH
WOK
!

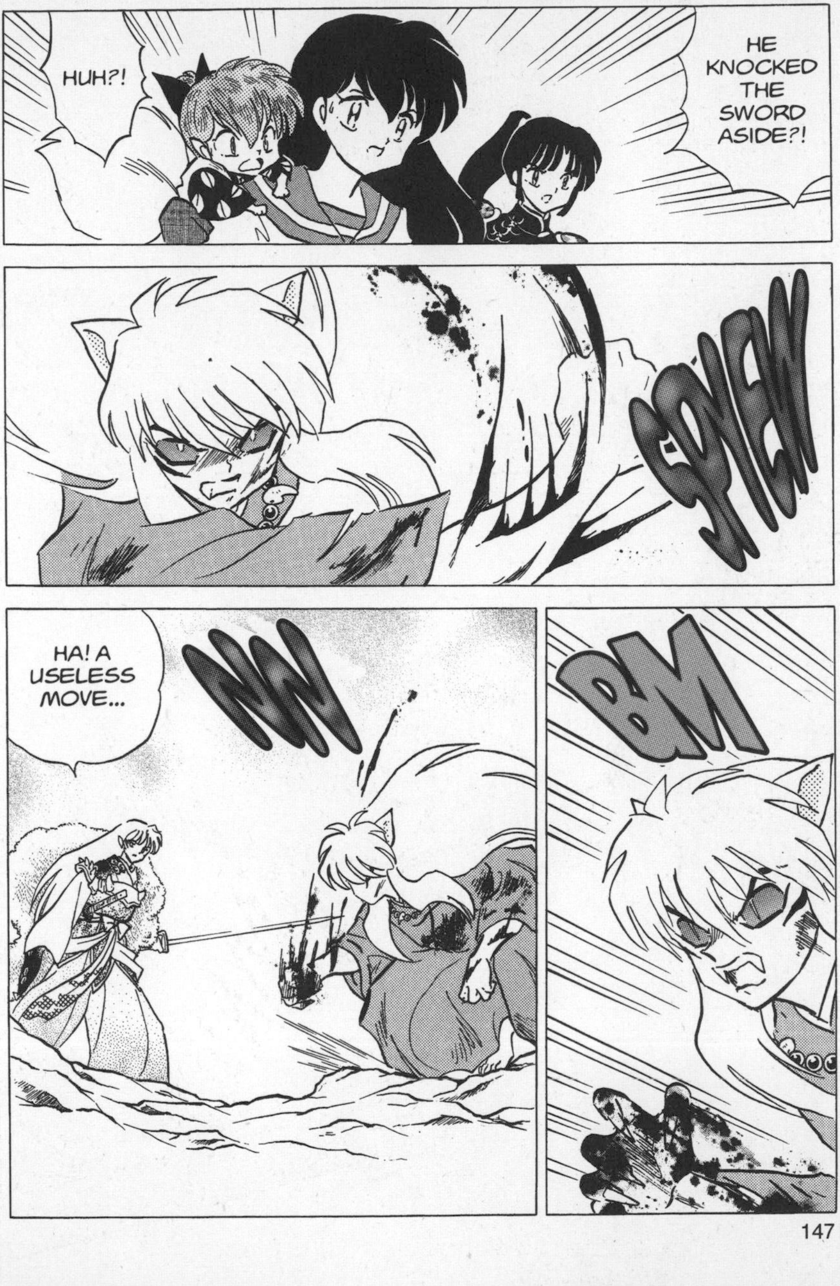
HUH?!
HE KNOCKED THE SWORD ASIDE?!
HA! A USELESS MOVE...
BAM

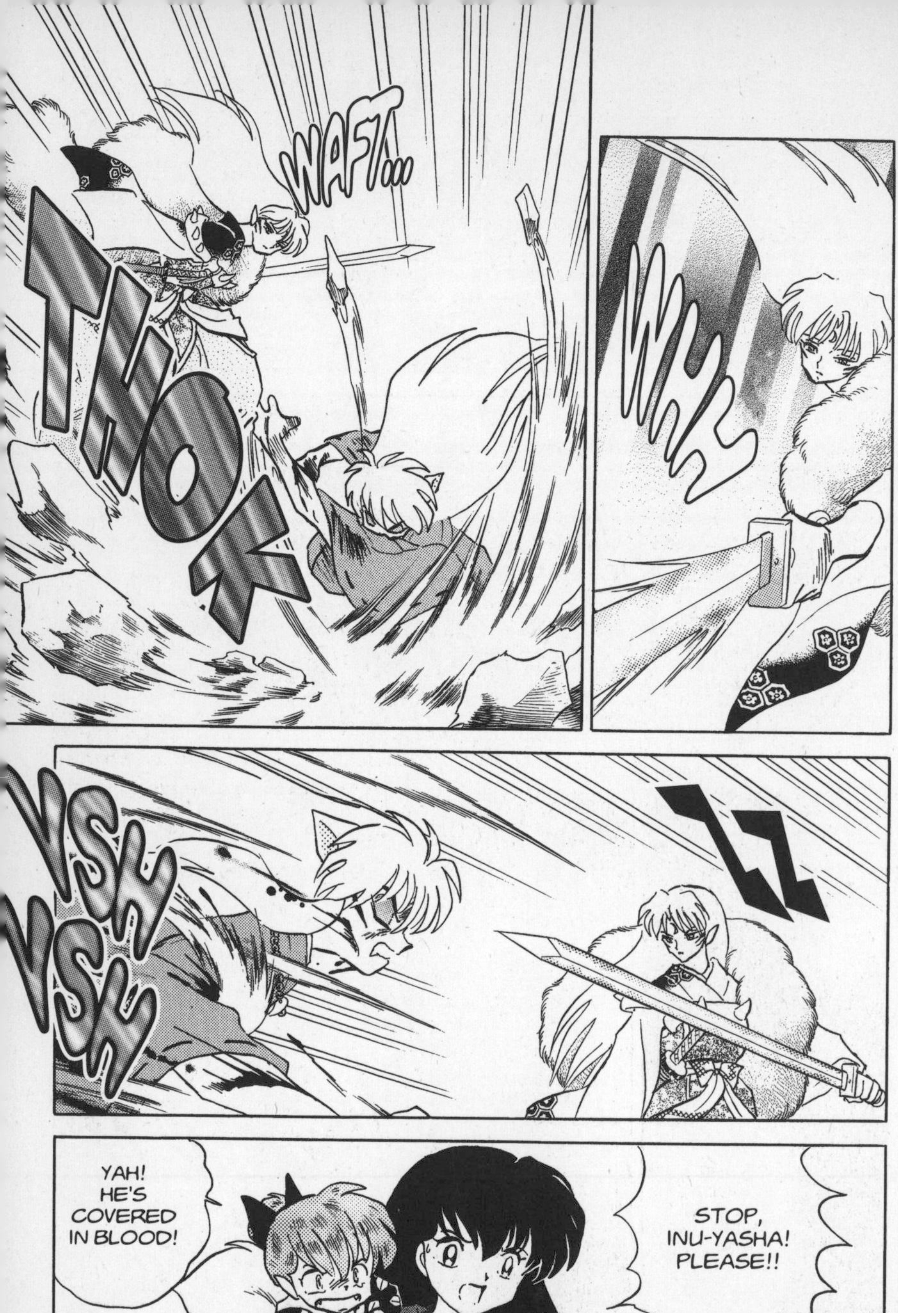
WAFT...
THOK
VSH
VSH
YAH! HE'S COVERED IN BLOOD!
STOP, INU-YASHA! PLEASE!!

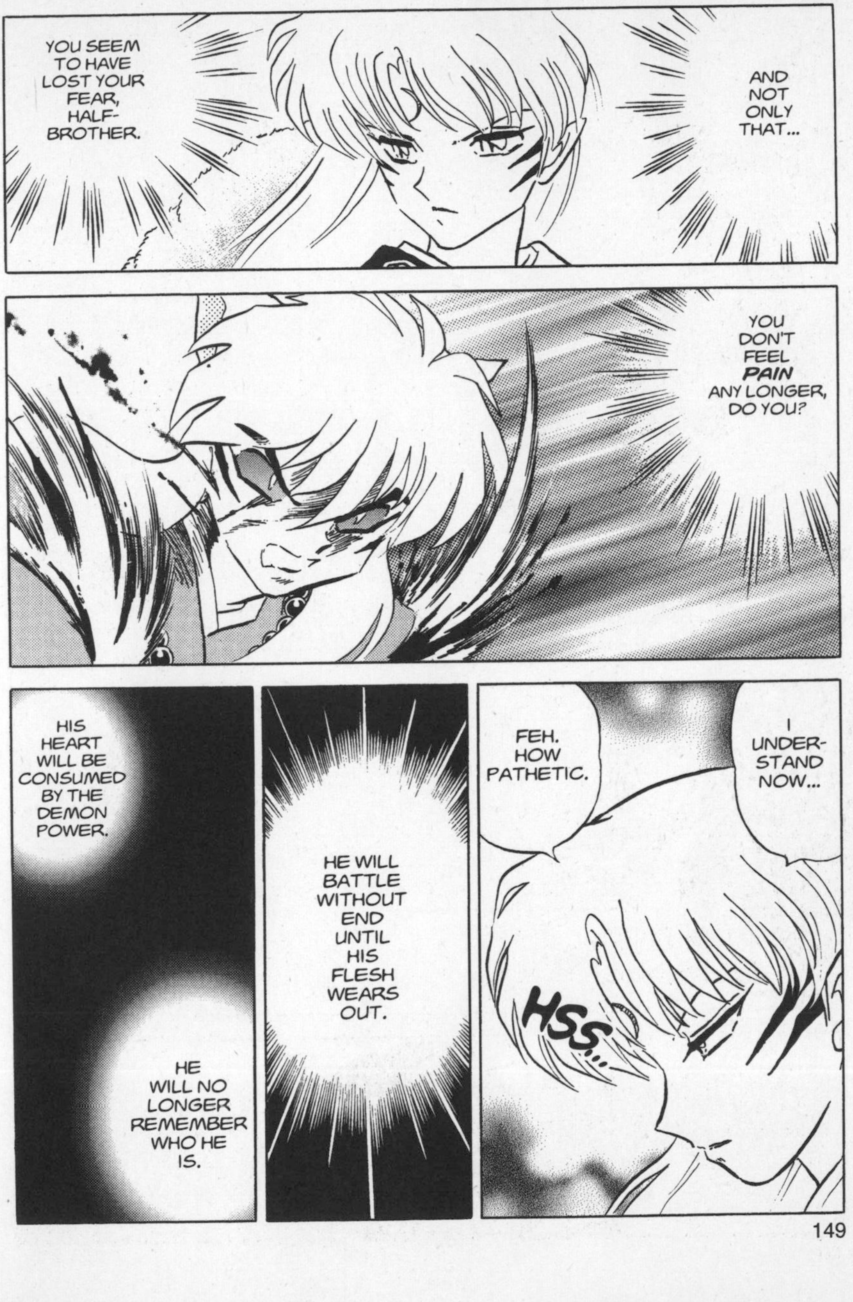
YOU SEEM TO HAVE LOST YOUR FEAR, HALF-BROTHER.
AND NOT ONLY THAT...
YOU DON'T FEEL **PAIN** ANY LONGER, DO YOU?
HIS HEART WILL BE CONSUMED BY THE DEMON POWER.
HE WILL NO LONGER REMEMBER WHO HE IS.
HE WILL BATTLE WITHOUT END UNTIL HIS FLESH WEARS OUT.
FEH. HOW PATHETIC.
I UNDER-STAND NOW...
HSS...

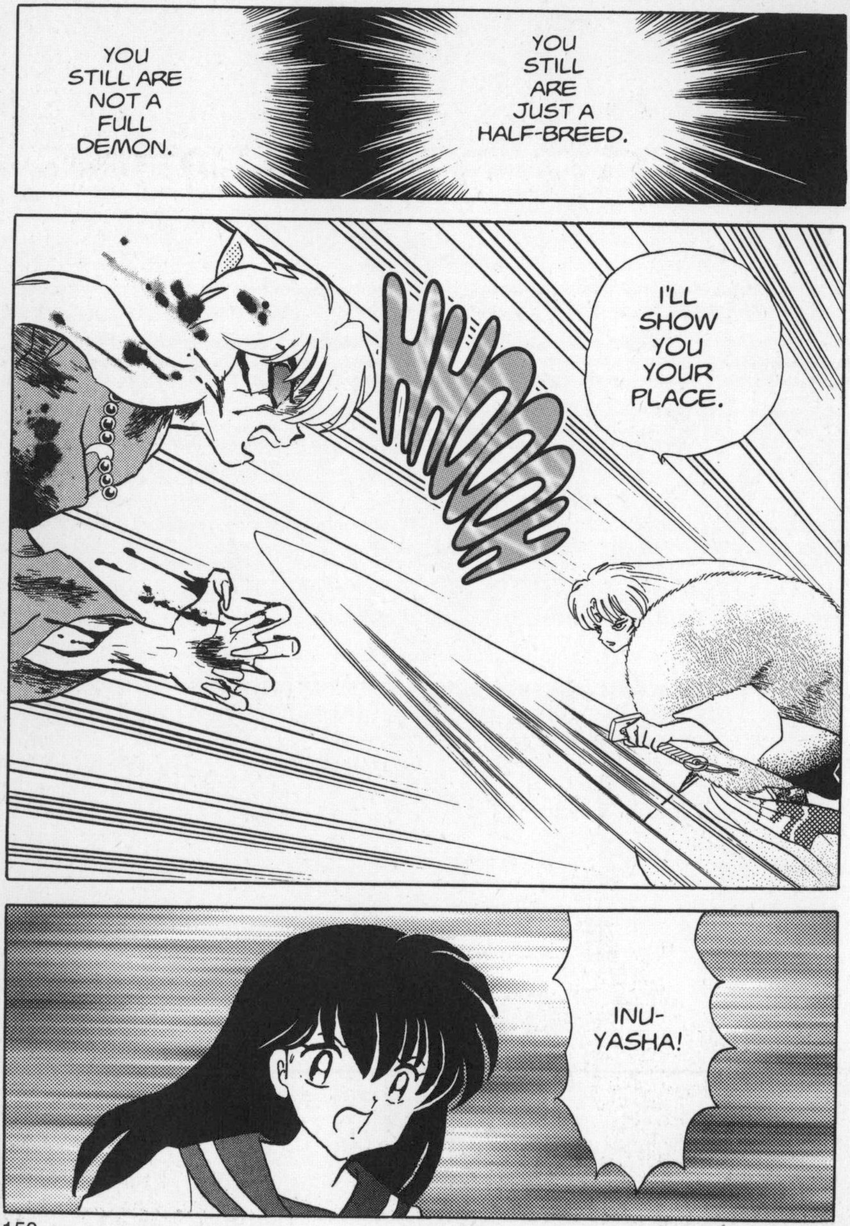
YOU STILL ARE NOT A FULL DEMON.
YOU STILL ARE JUST A HALF-BREED.
I'LL SHOW YOU YOUR PLACE.
INU-YASHA!

SCROLL NINE
BLOOD SOAKED IN

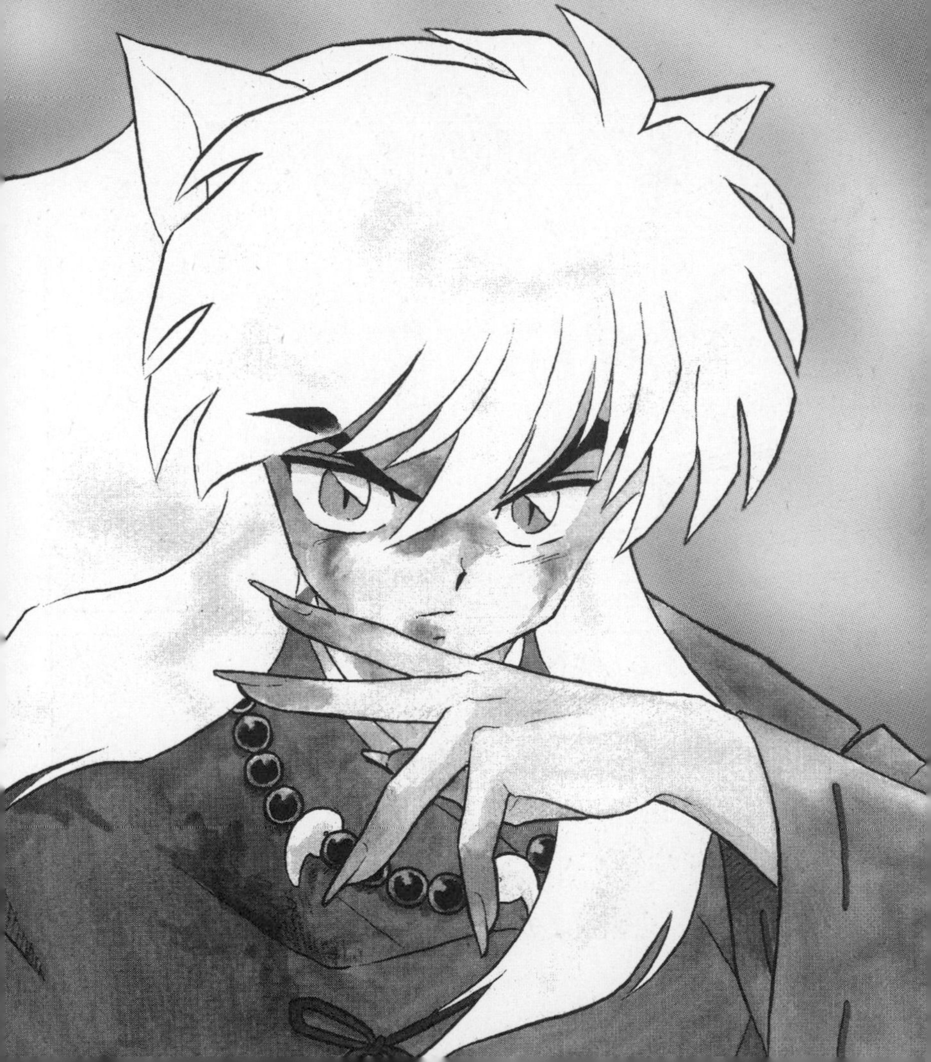

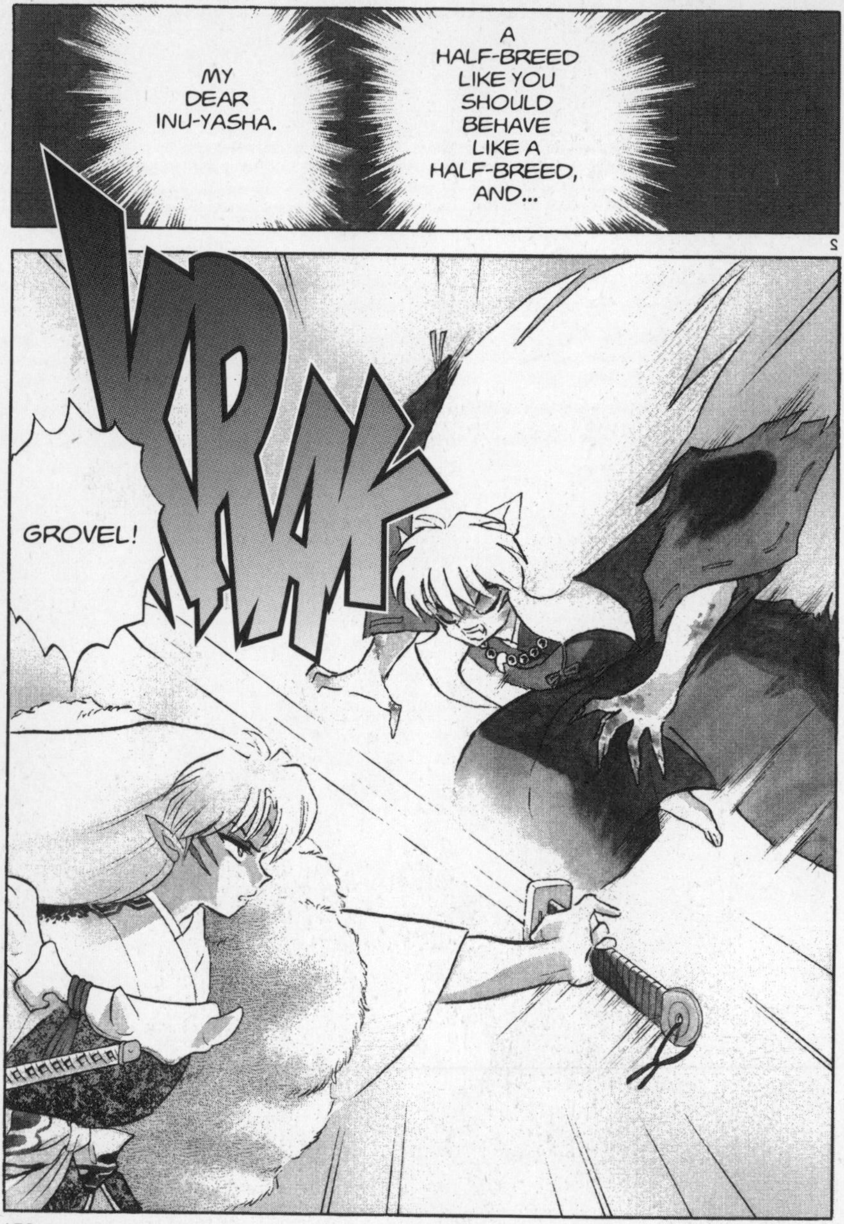
MY DEAR INU-YASHA.
A HALF-BREED LIKE YOU SHOULD BEHAVE LIKE A HALF-BREED, AND...
VRAK
GROVEL!

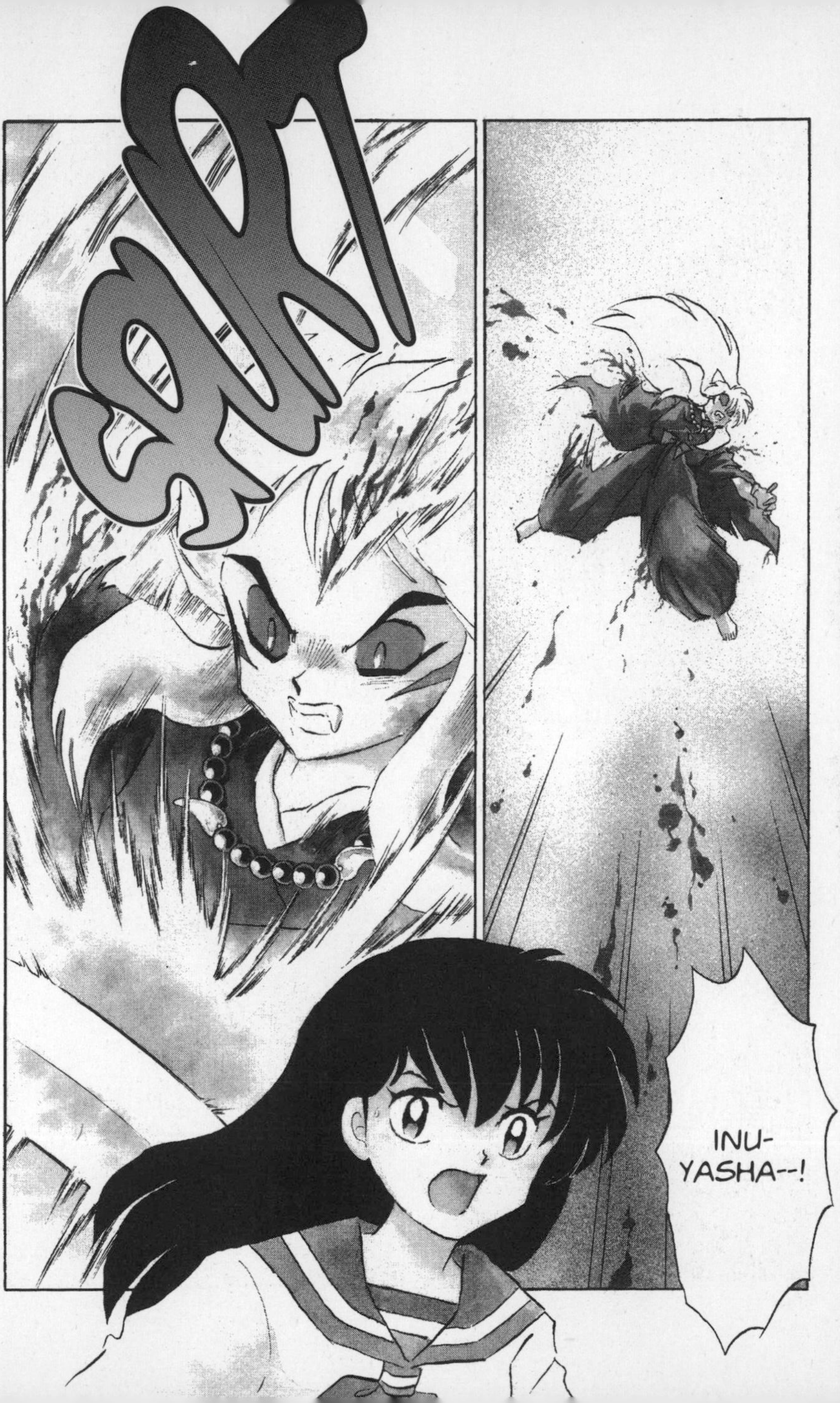
INU-
YASHA--!

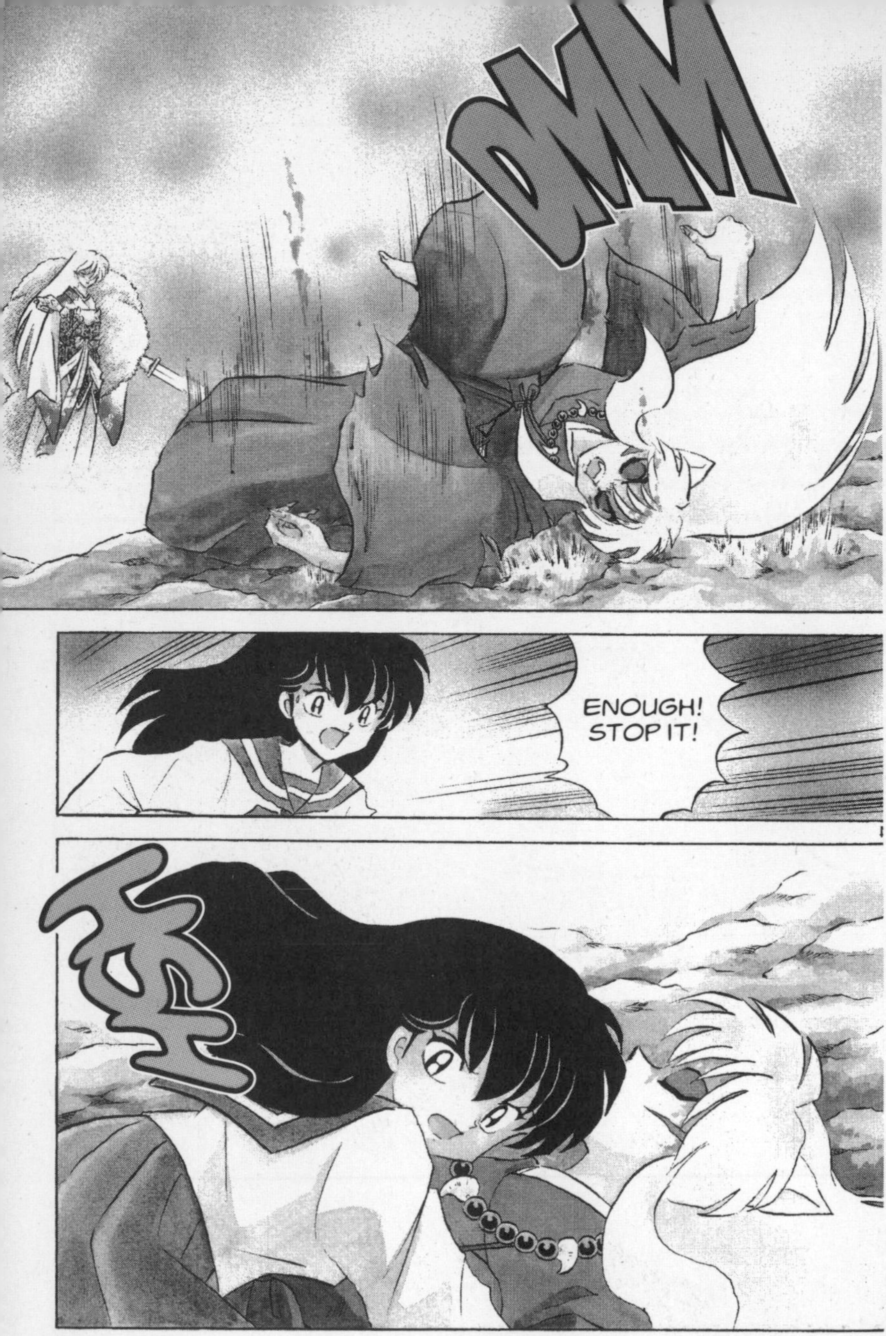
DMM
ENOUGH! STOP IT!

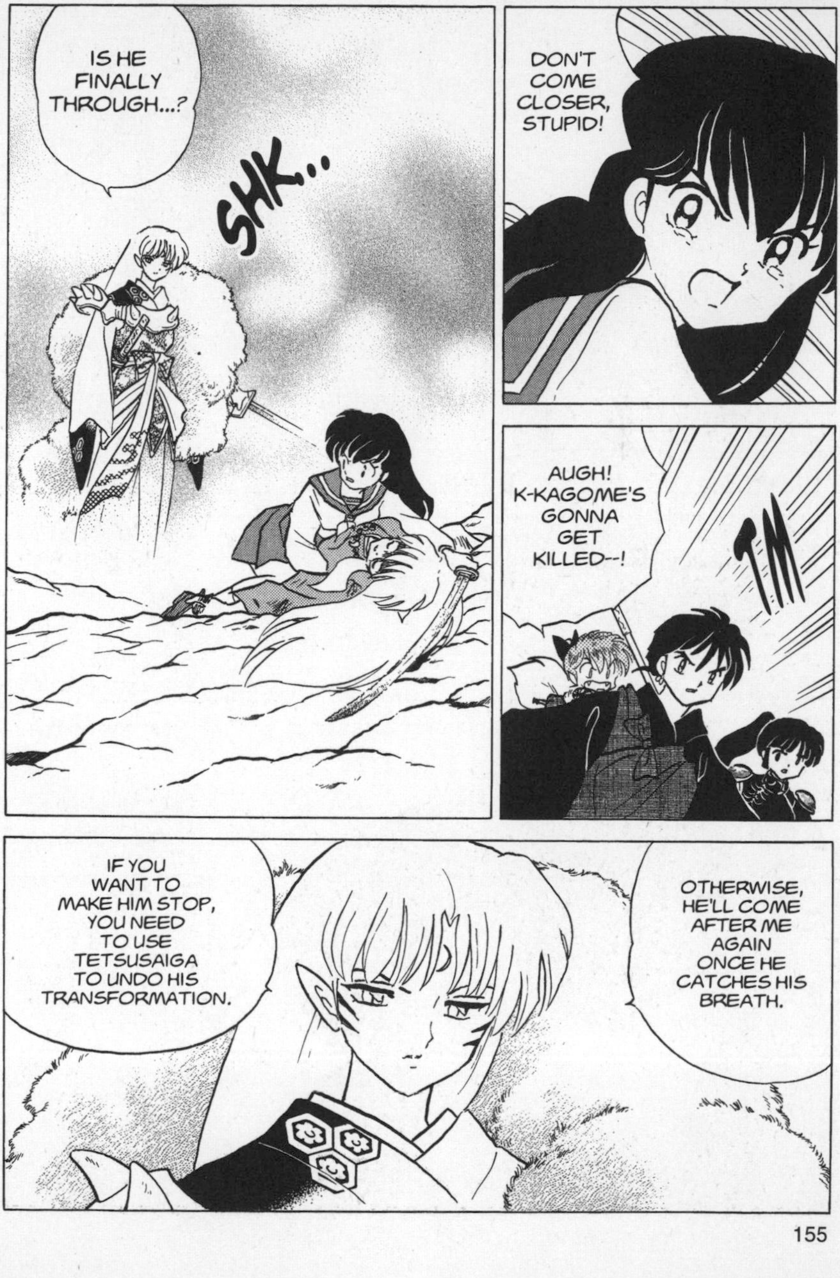
IS HE FINALLY THROUGH...?
SHK...
DON'T COME CLOSER, STUPID!
AUGH! K-KAGOME'S GONNA GET KILLED--!
TM
IF YOU WANT TO MAKE HIM STOP, YOU NEED TO USE TETSUSAIGA TO UNDO HIS TRANSFORMATION.
OTHERWISE, HE'LL COME AFTER ME AGAIN ONCE HE CATCHES HIS BREATH.

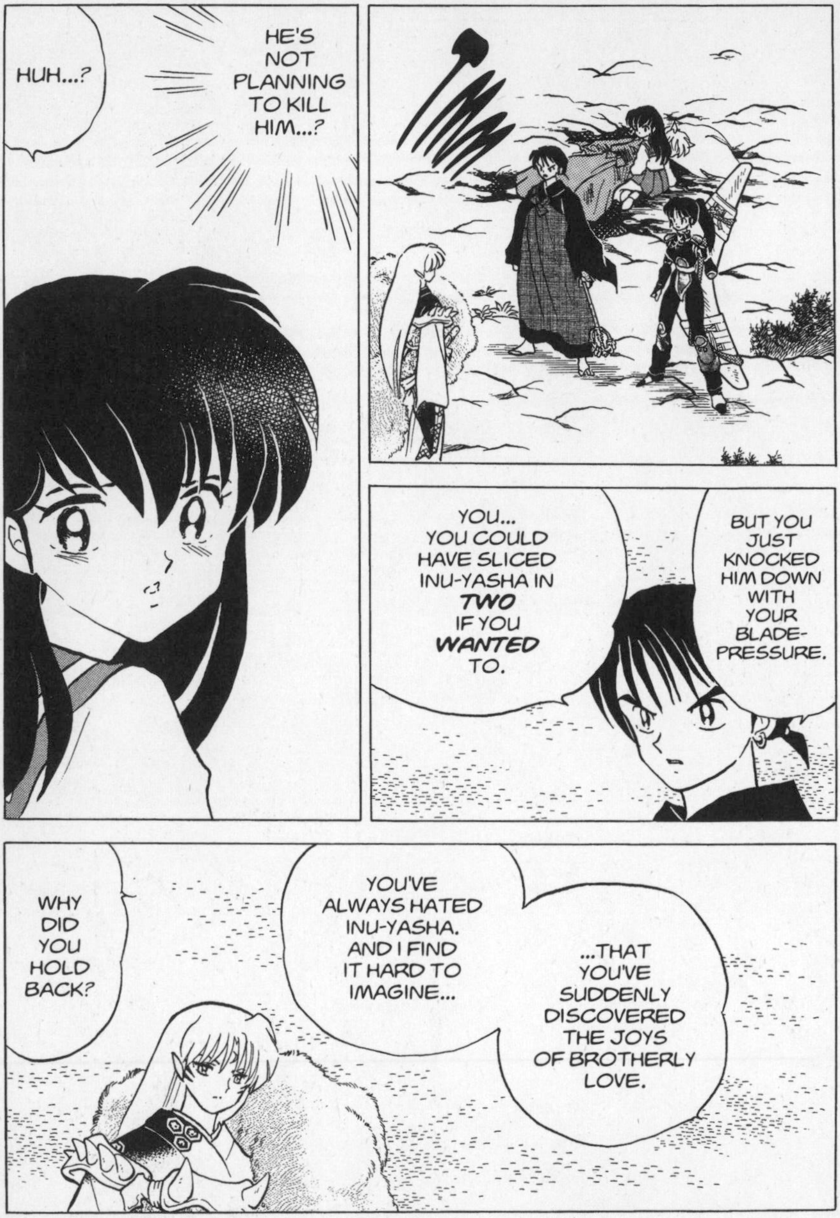
HUH...?
HE'S NOT PLANNING TO KILL HIM...?
YOU... YOU COULD HAVE SLICED INU-YASHA IN **TWO** IF YOU **WANTED** TO.
BUT YOU JUST KNOCKED HIM DOWN WITH YOUR BLADE-PRESSURE.
WHY DID YOU HOLD BACK?
YOU'VE ALWAYS HATED INU-YASHA. AND I FIND IT HARD TO IMAGINE...
...THAT YOU'VE SUDDENLY DISCOVERED THE JOYS OF BROTHERLY LOVE.

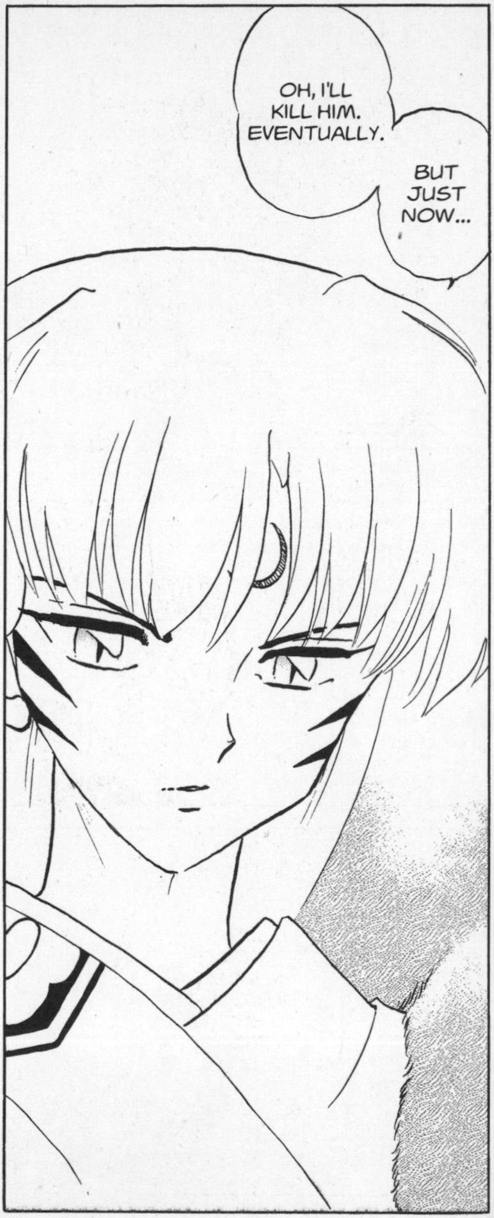
OH, I'LL KILL HIM. EVENTUALLY.
BUT JUST NOW...
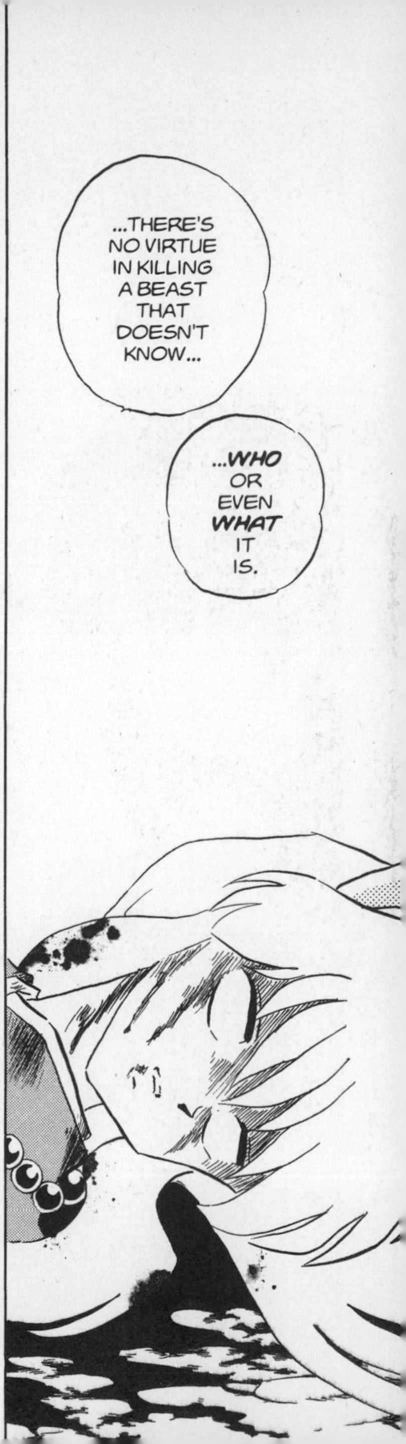
...THERE'S NO VIRTUE IN KILLING A BEAST THAT DOESN'T KNOW...
...**WHO** OR EVEN **WHAT** IT IS.

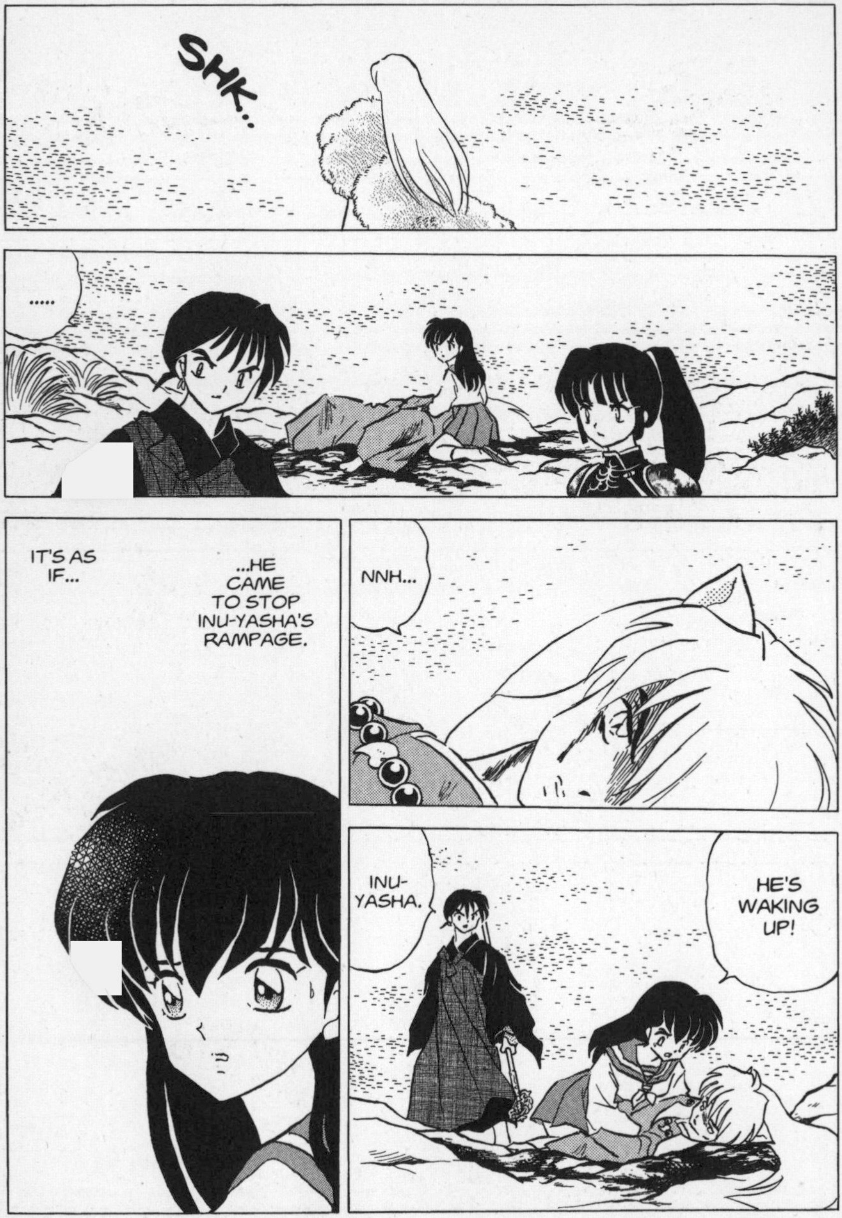
SHK..
.....
IT'S AS IF...
...HE CAME TO STOP INU-YASHA'S RAMPAGE.
NNH...
INU-YASHA.
HE'S WAKING UP!

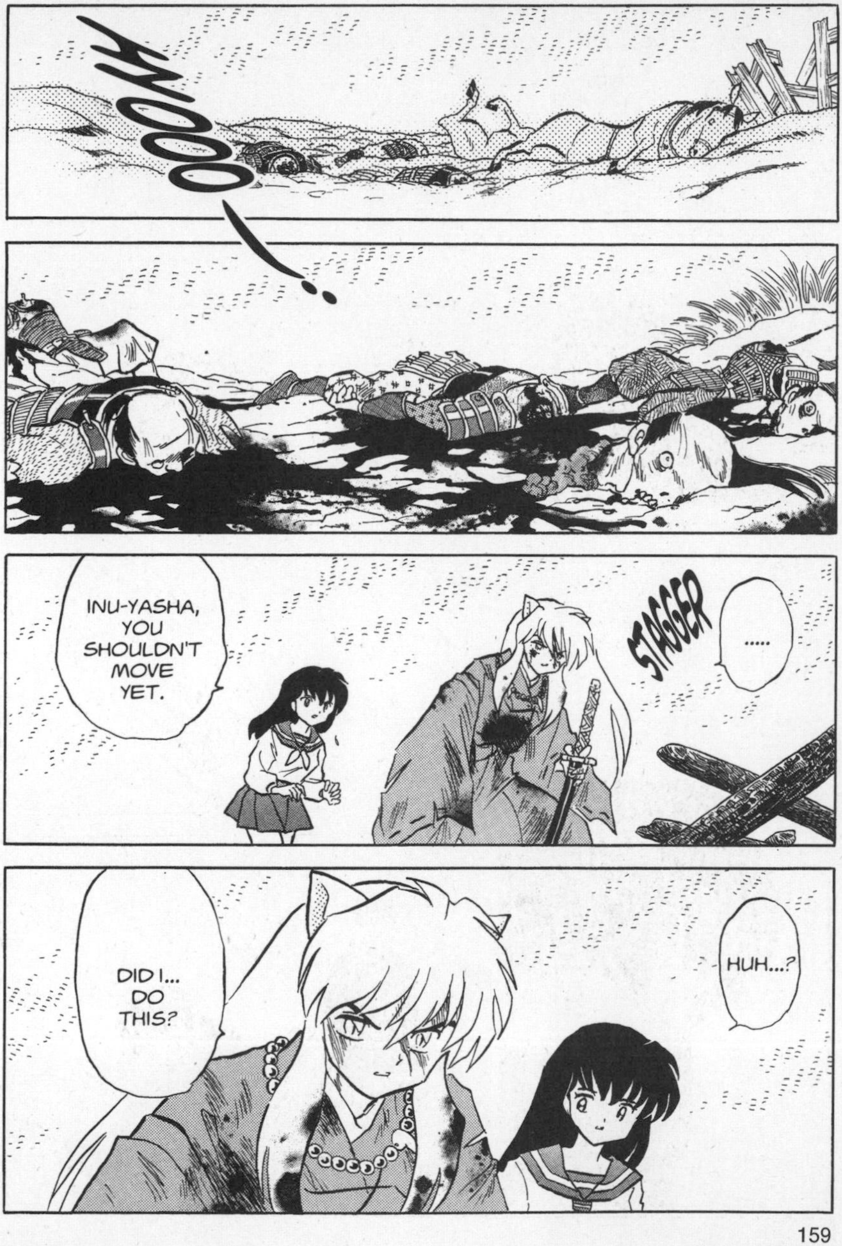
HYOOO!!
INU-YASHA, YOU SHOULDN'T MOVE YET.
STAGGER
.....
DID I... DO THIS?
HUH...?

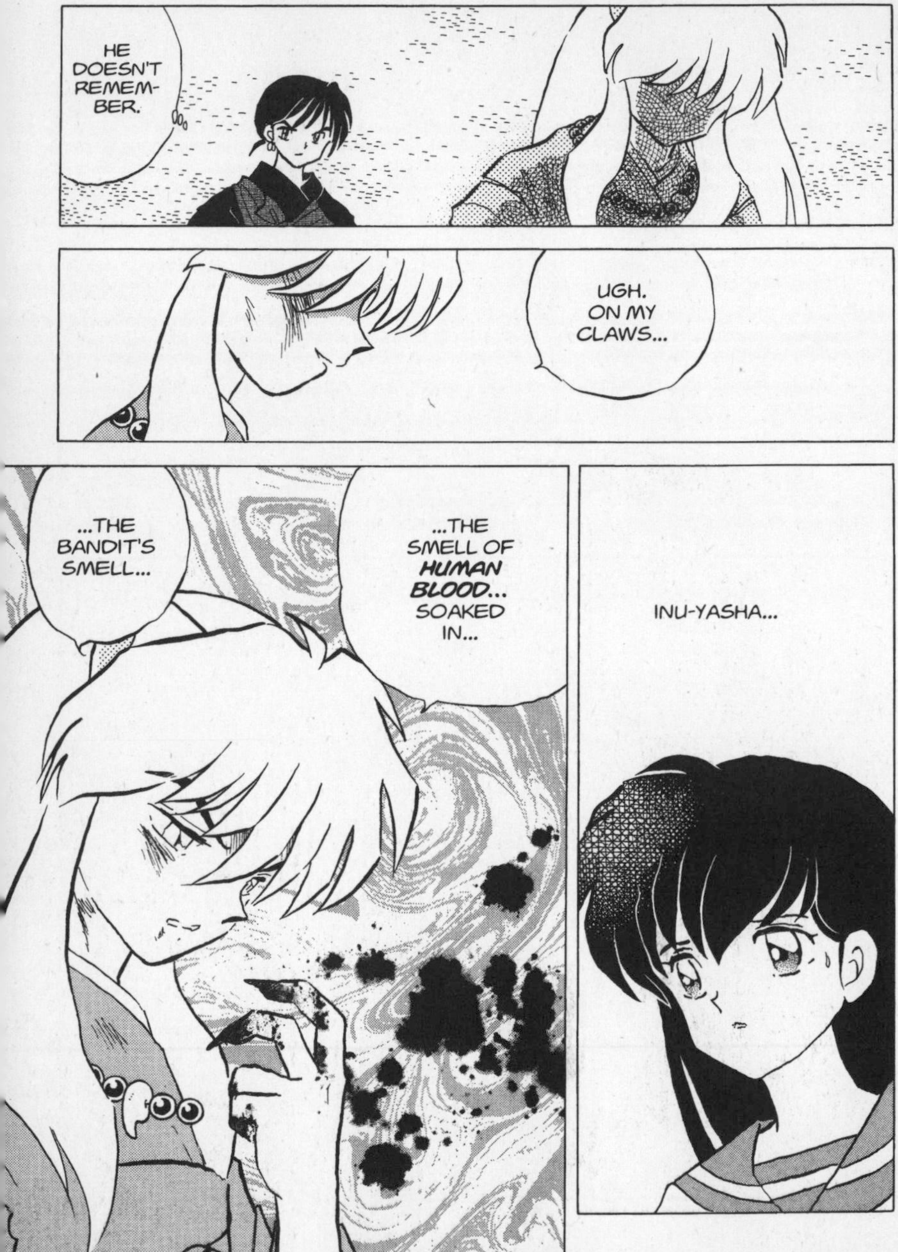
HE DOESN'T REMEMBER.
UGH. ON MY CLAWS...
...THE BANDIT'S SMELL...
...THE SMELL OF HUMAN BLOOD... SOAKED IN...
INU-YASHA...

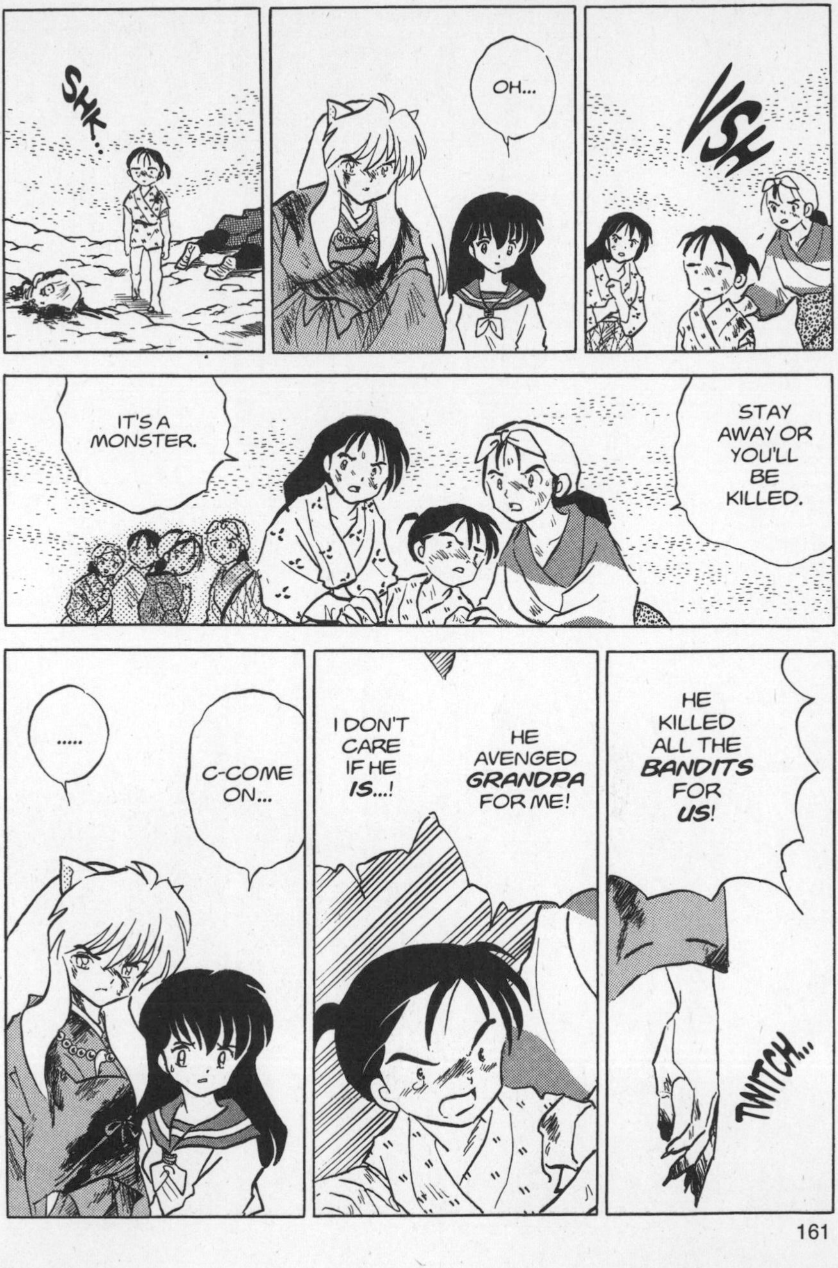
SHK...
OH...
VSH
IT'S A MONSTER.
STAY AWAY OR YOU'LL BE KILLED.
.....
C-COME ON...
I DON'T CARE IF HE *IS*...!
HE AVENGED **GRANDPA** FOR ME!
HE KILLED ALL THE **BANDITS** FOR *US*!
TWITCH...

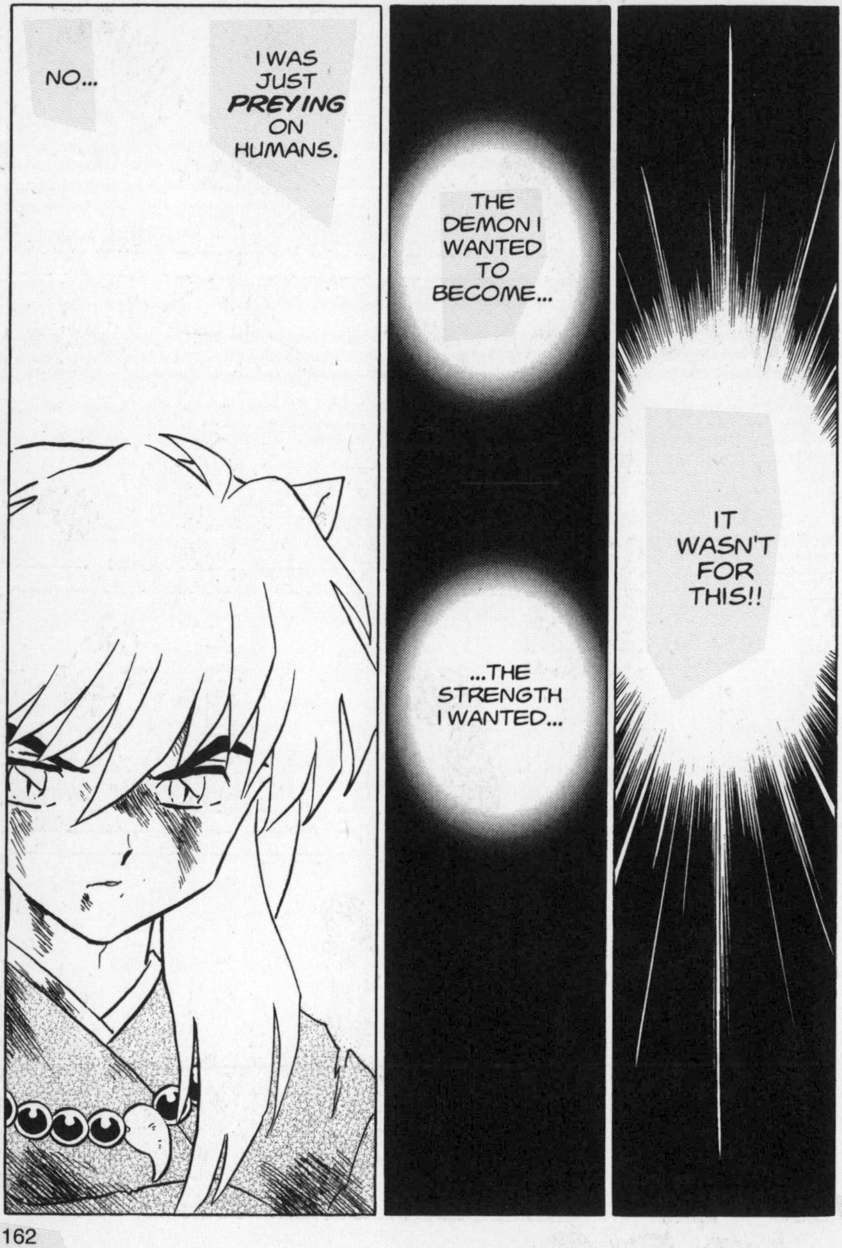
NO...
I WAS JUST PREYING ON HUMANS.
THE DEMON I WANTED TO BECOME...
...THE STRENGTH I WANTED...
IT WASN'T FOR THIS!!

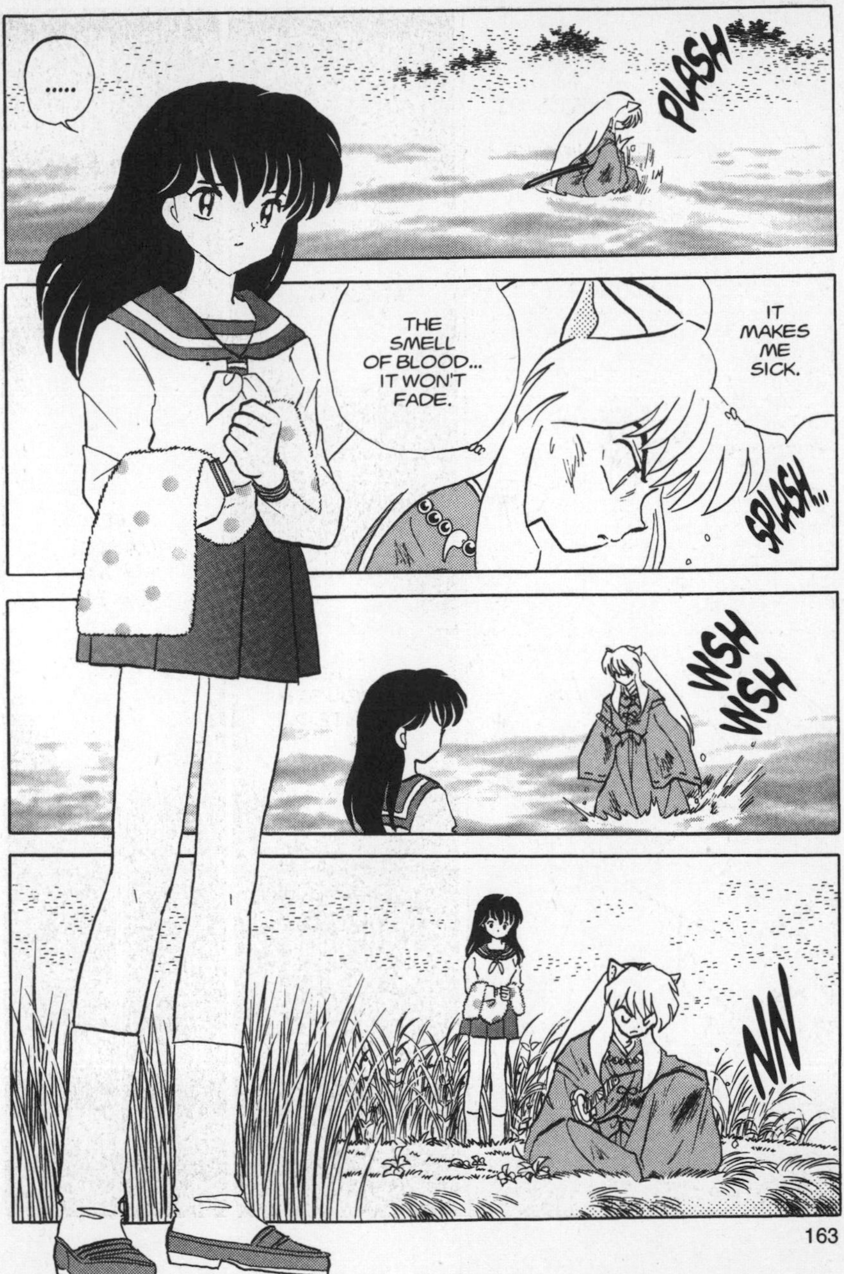
......
PLASH
THE SMELL OF BLOOD... IT WON'T FADE.
IT MAKES ME SICK.
SPLASH...
WSH WSH
NN

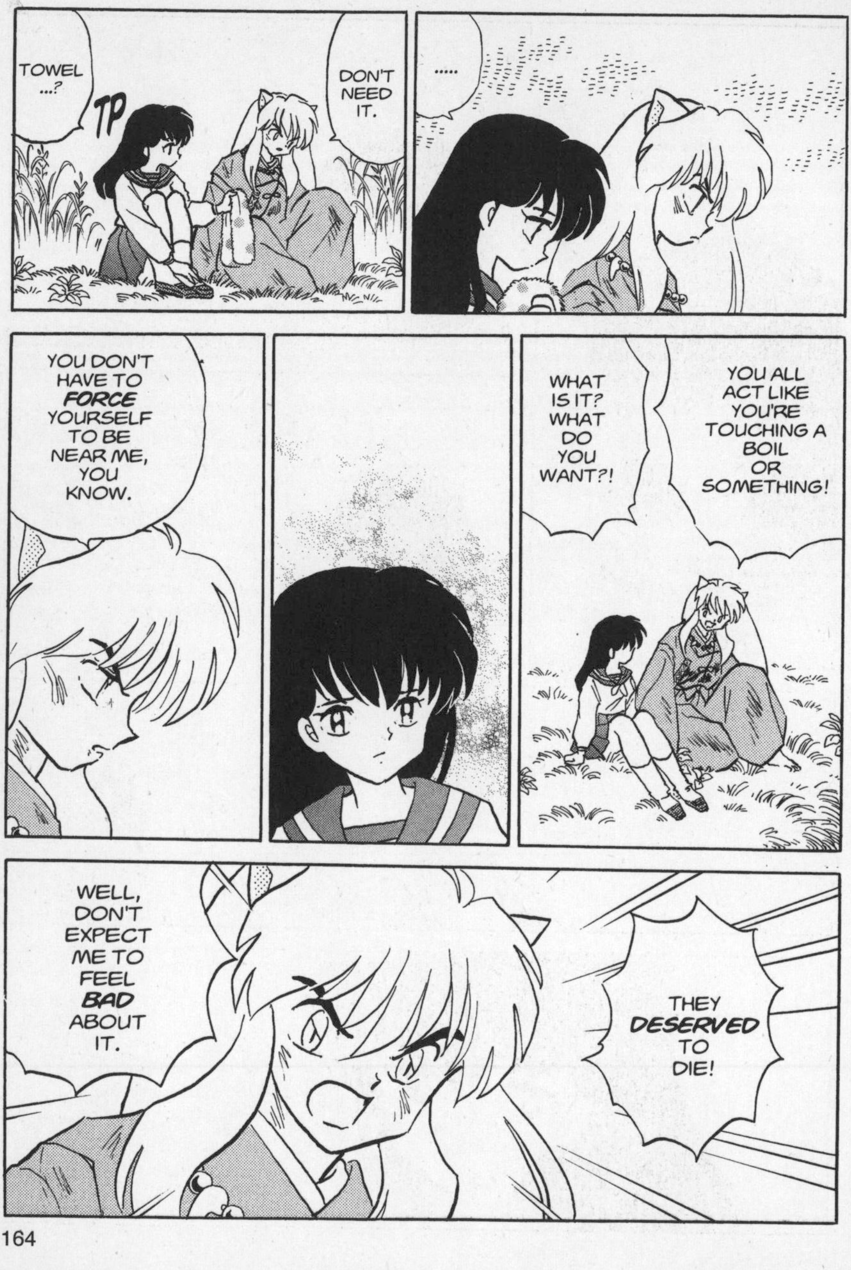
TOWEL ...?
TP
DON'T NEED IT.
.....
YOU DON'T HAVE TO FORCE YOURSELF TO BE NEAR ME, YOU KNOW.
WHAT IS IT? WHAT DO YOU WANT?!
YOU ALL ACT LIKE YOU'RE TOUCHING A BOIL OR SOMETHING!
WELL, DON'T EXPECT ME TO FEEL BAD ABOUT IT.
THEY DESERVED TO DIE!

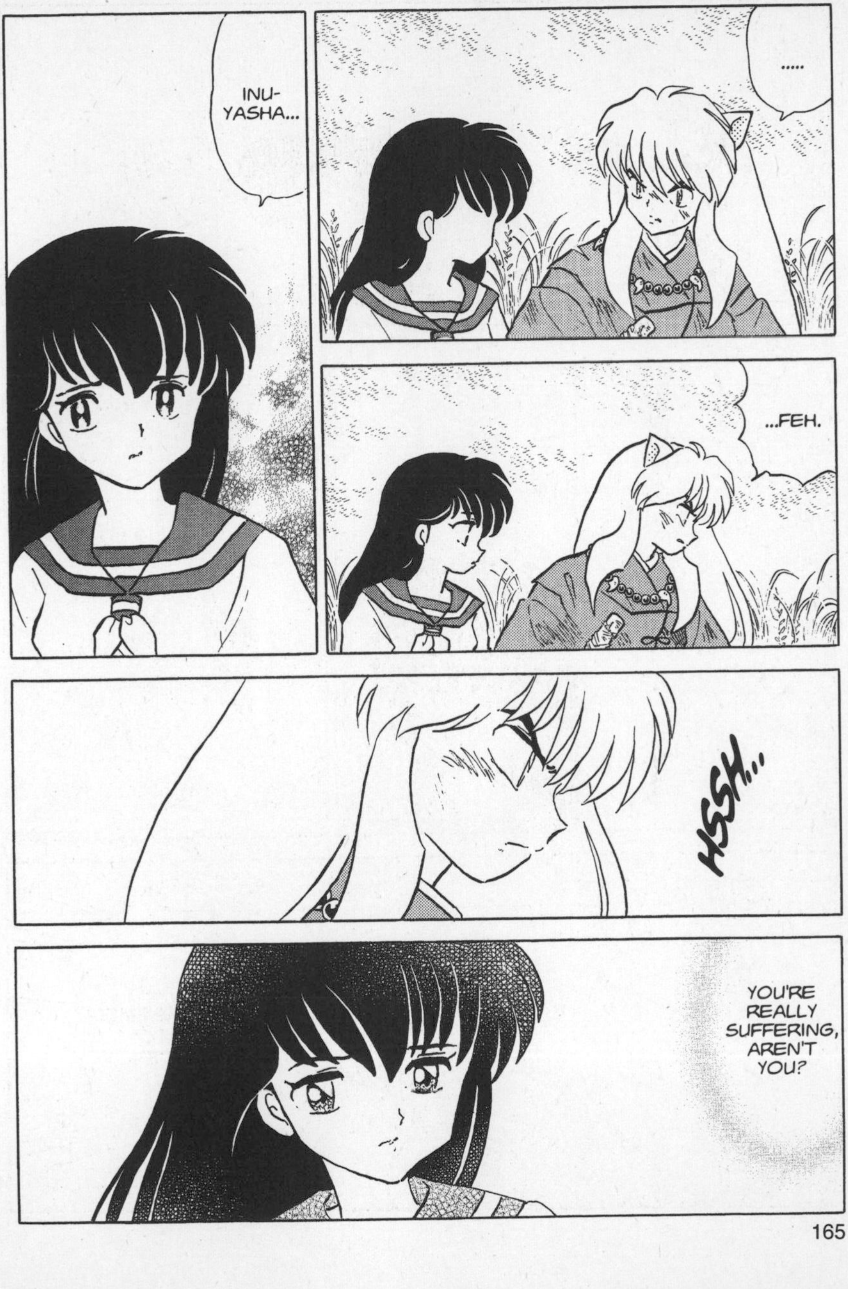
INU-YASHA...
.....
...FEH.
HSSH...
YOU'RE REALLY SUFFERING, AREN'T YOU?

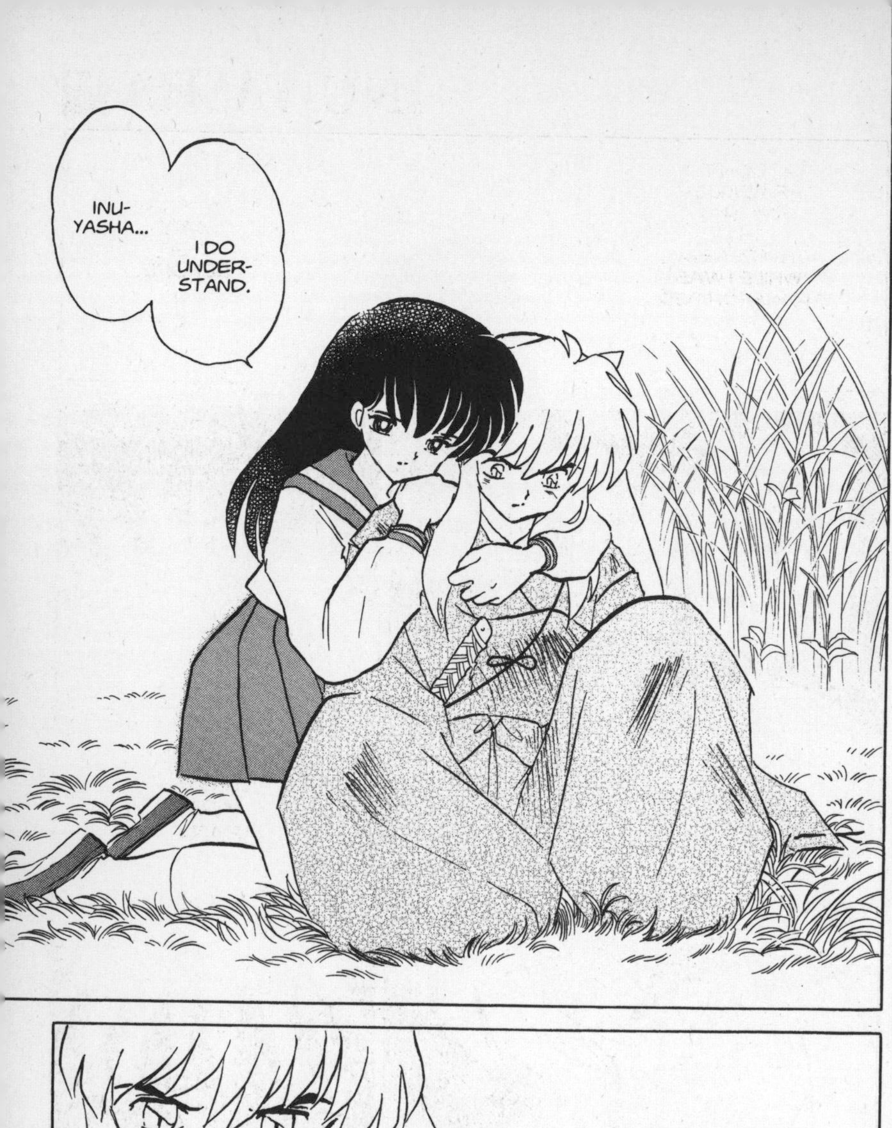
INU-
YASHA...
I DO
UNDER-
STAND.

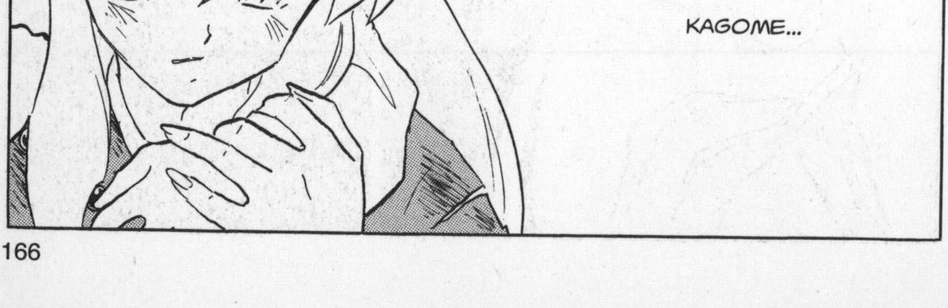
KAGOME...

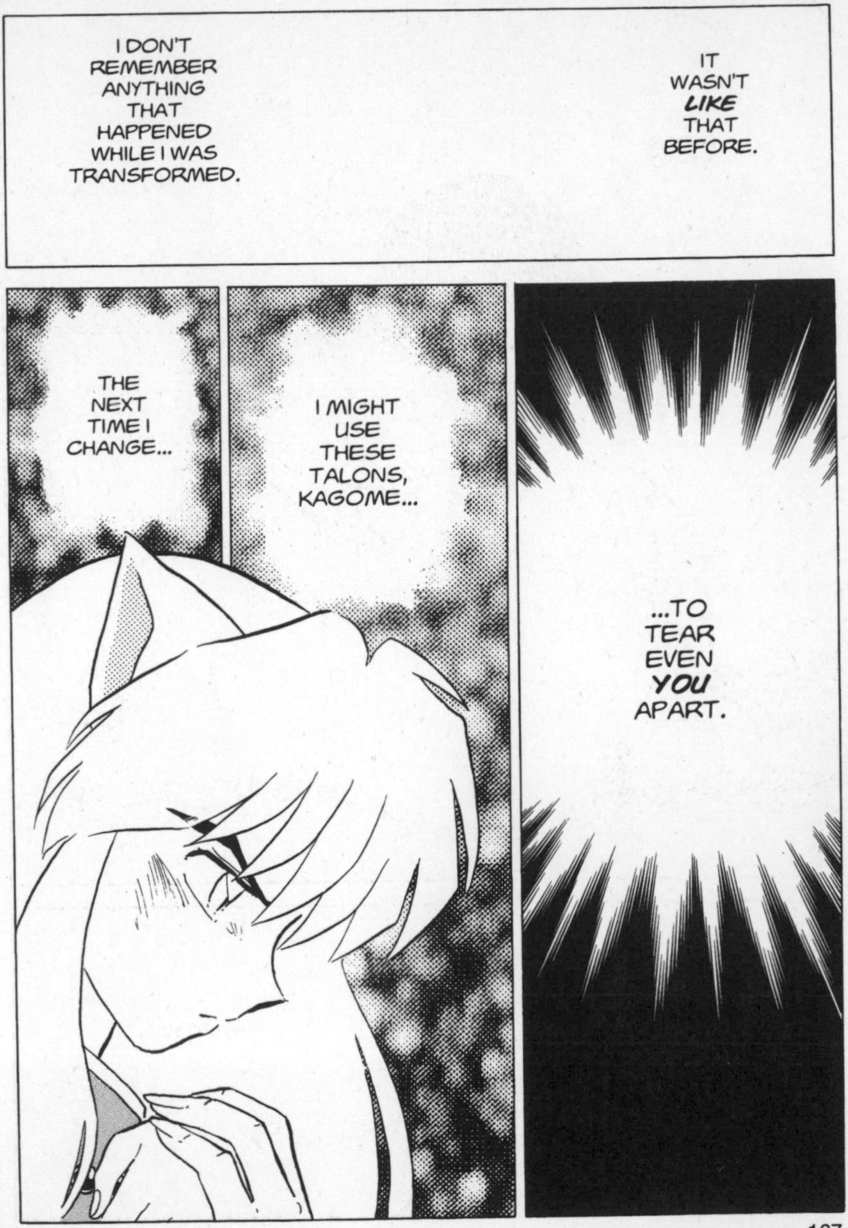
I DON'T REMEMBER ANYTHING THAT HAPPENED WHILE I WAS TRANSFORMED.
IT WASN'T *LIKE* THAT BEFORE.
THE NEXT TIME I CHANGE...
I MIGHT USE THESE TALONS, KAGOME...
...TO TEAR EVEN *YOU* APART.

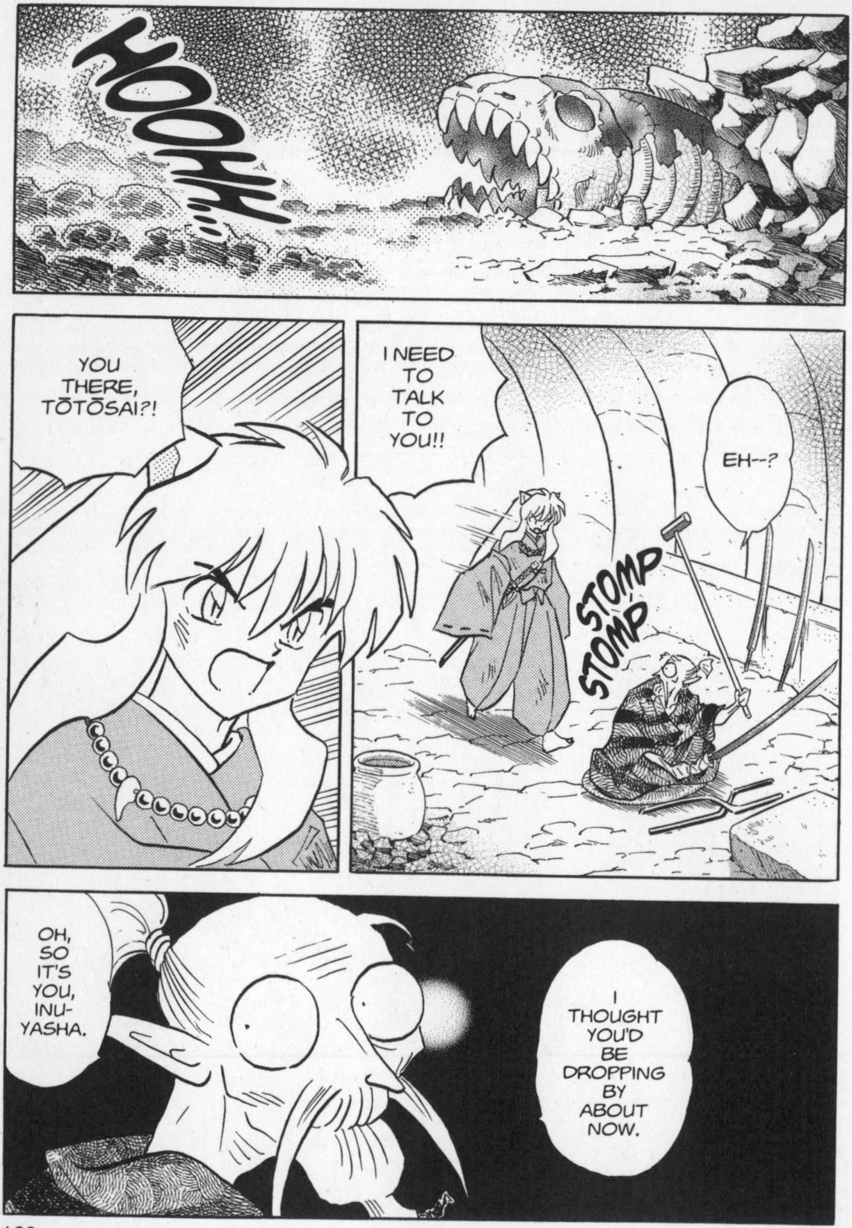
HOOHH...
YOU THERE, TŌTŌSAI?!
I NEED TO TALK TO YOU!!
EH--?
STOMP STOMP
OH, SO IT'S YOU, INU-YASHA.
I THOUGHT YOU'D BE DROPPING BY ABOUT NOW.

SCROLL TEN

THE TALON SHIELD

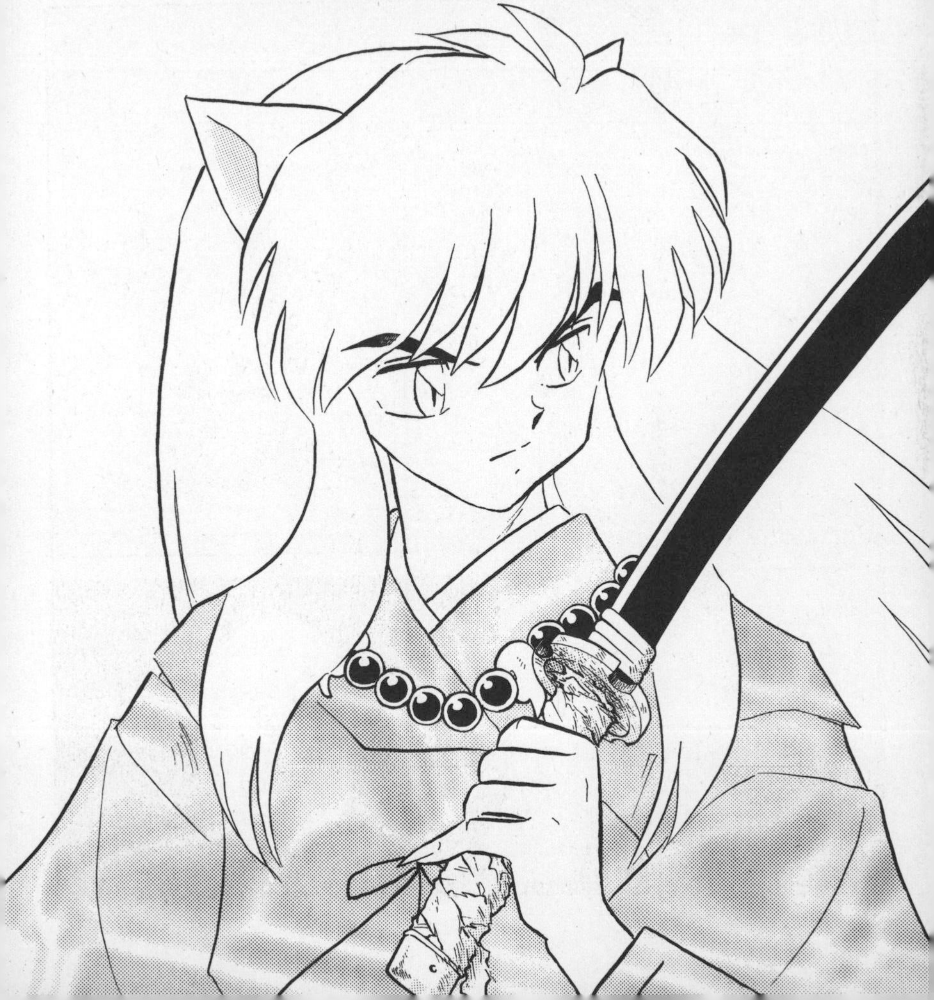

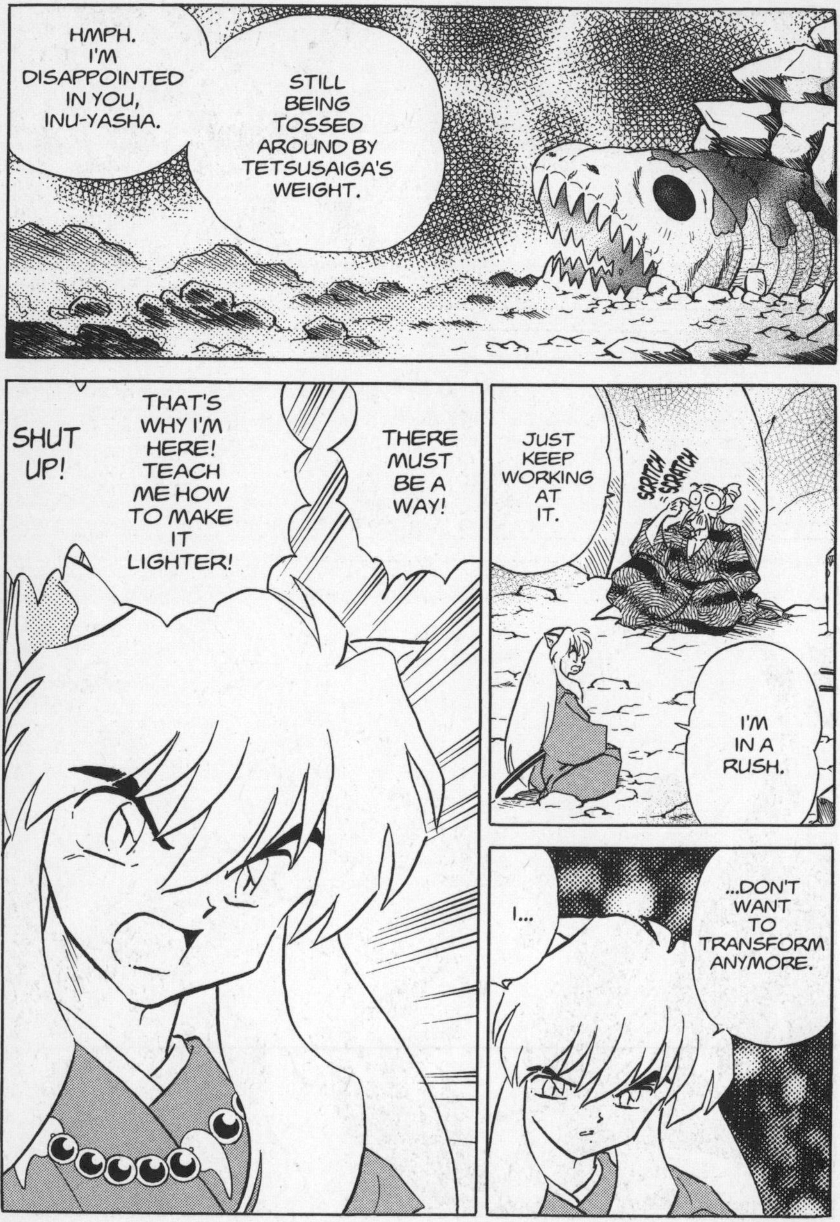
HMPH. I'M DISAPPOINTED IN YOU, INU-YASHA.
STILL BEING TOSSED AROUND BY TETSUSAIGA'S WEIGHT.
SHUT UP!
THAT'S WHY I'M HERE! TEACH ME HOW TO MAKE IT LIGHTER!
THERE MUST BE A WAY!
JUST KEEP WORKING AT IT.
SCRITCH SCRATCH
I'M IN A RUSH.
I...
...DON'T WANT TO TRANSFORM ANYMORE.

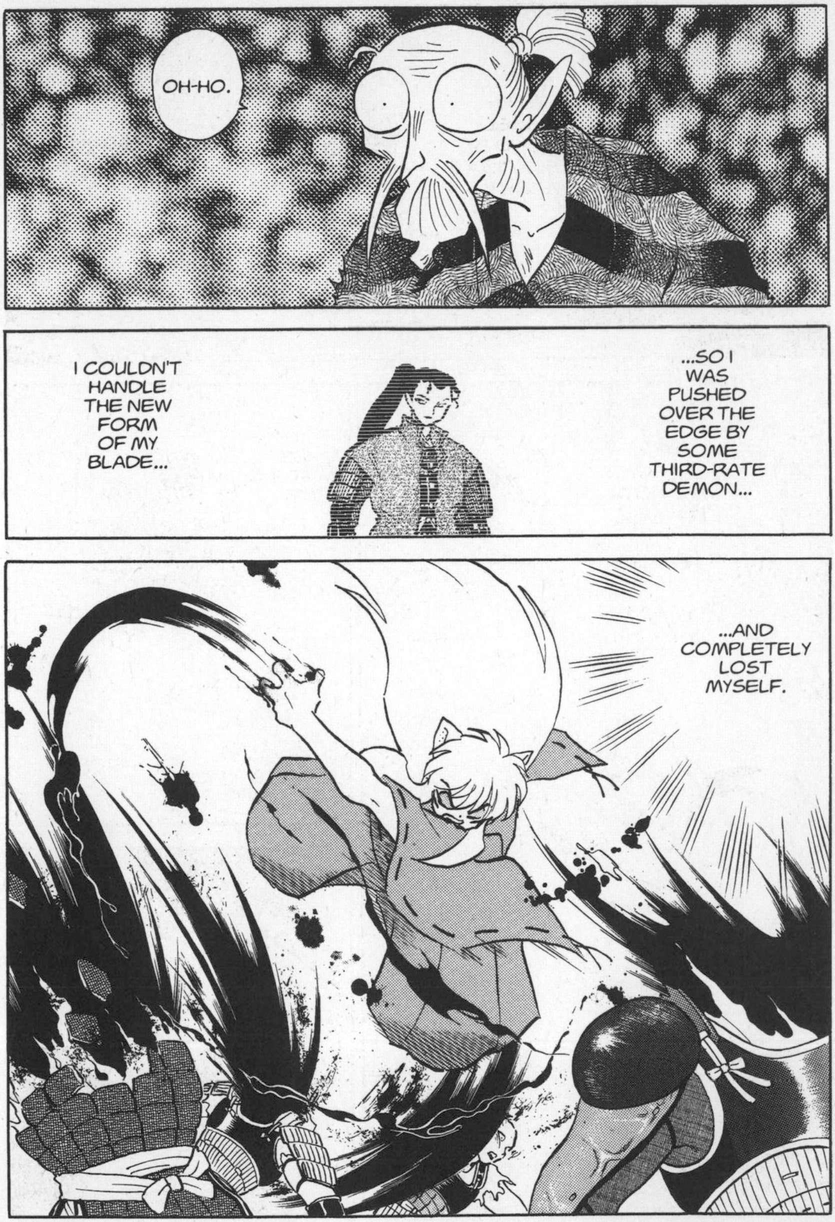
OH-HO.
I COULDN'T HANDLE THE NEW FORM OF MY BLADE...
...SO I WAS PUSHED OVER THE EDGE BY SOME THIRD-RATE DEMON...
...AND COMPLETELY LOST MYSELF.

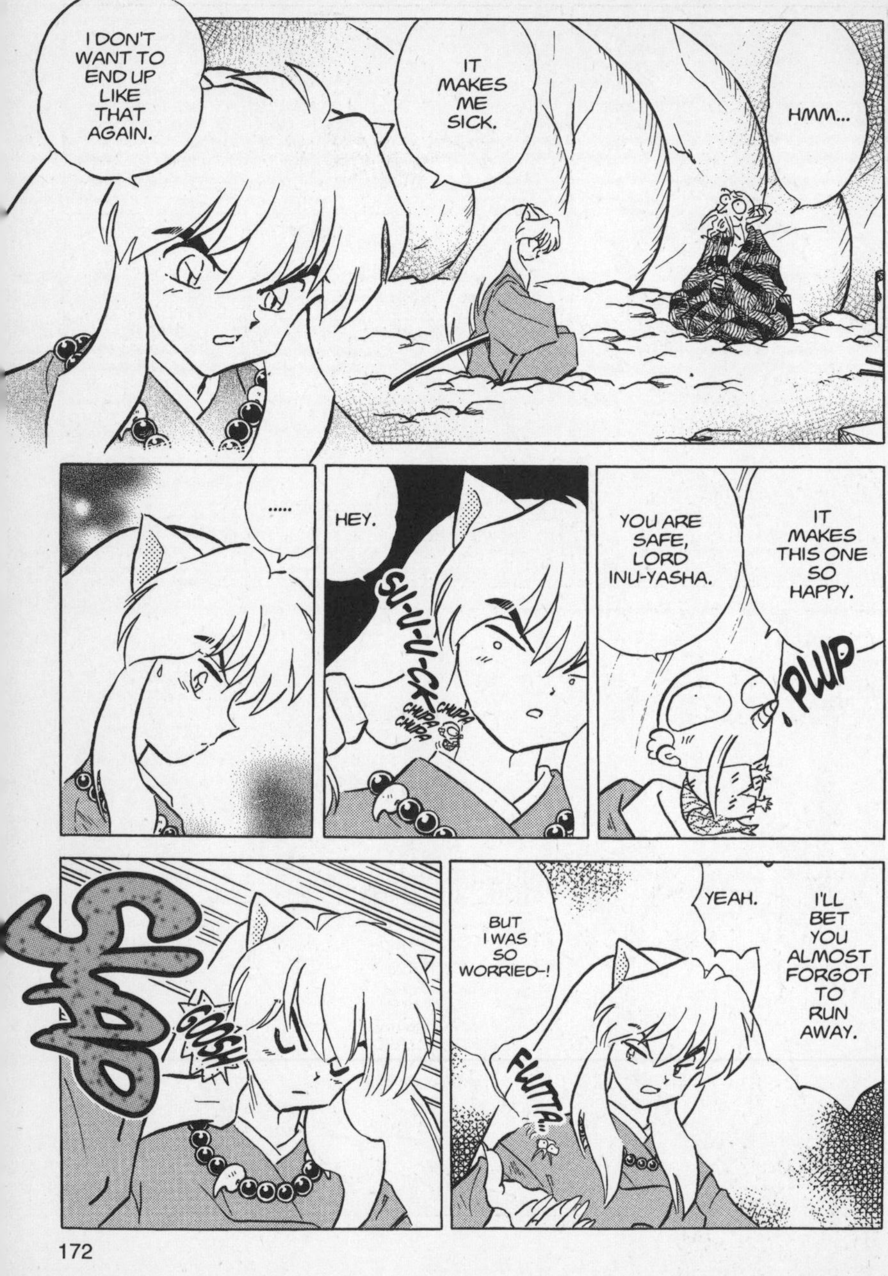
I DON'T WANT TO END UP LIKE THAT AGAIN.
IT MAKES ME SICK.
HMM...
.....
HEY.
SU-U-U-CK
CHUPA CHUPA CHUPA
YOU ARE SAFE, LORD INU-YASHA.
IT MAKES THIS ONE SO HAPPY.
PLUP
SLAP
GOOSH
BUT I WAS SO WORRIED-!
YEAH.
I'LL BET YOU ALMOST FORGOT TO RUN AWAY.
FLUTTA...

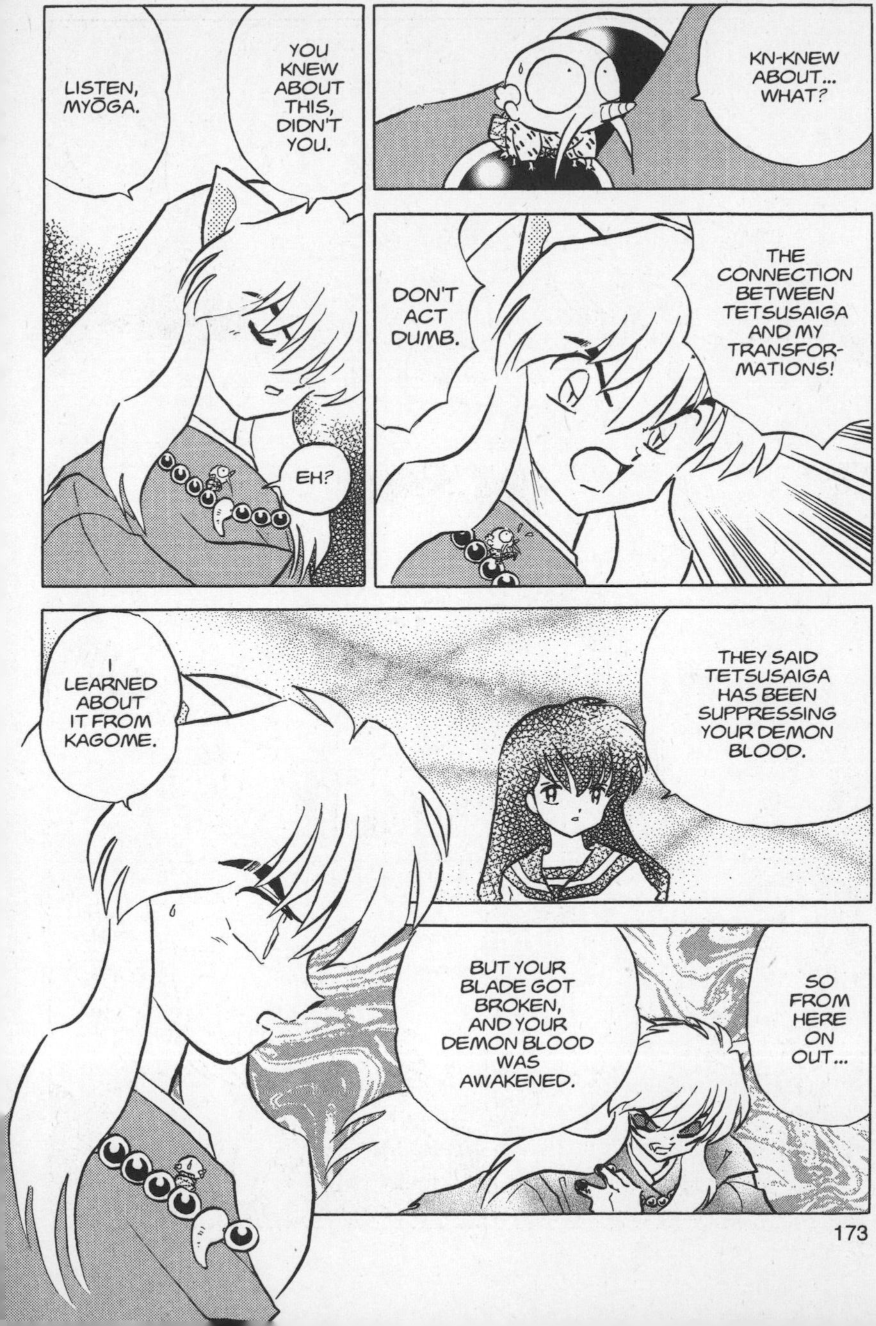
LISTEN, MYŌGA.
YOU KNEW ABOUT THIS, DIDN'T YOU.
EH?
KN-KNEW ABOUT... WHAT?
DON'T ACT DUMB.
THE CONNECTION BETWEEN TETSUSAIGA AND MY TRANSFORMATIONS!
I LEARNED ABOUT IT FROM KAGOME.
THEY SAID TETSUSAIGA HAS BEEN SUPPRESSING YOUR DEMON BLOOD.
BUT YOUR BLADE GOT BROKEN, AND YOUR DEMON BLOOD WAS AWAKENED.
SO FROM HERE ON OUT...

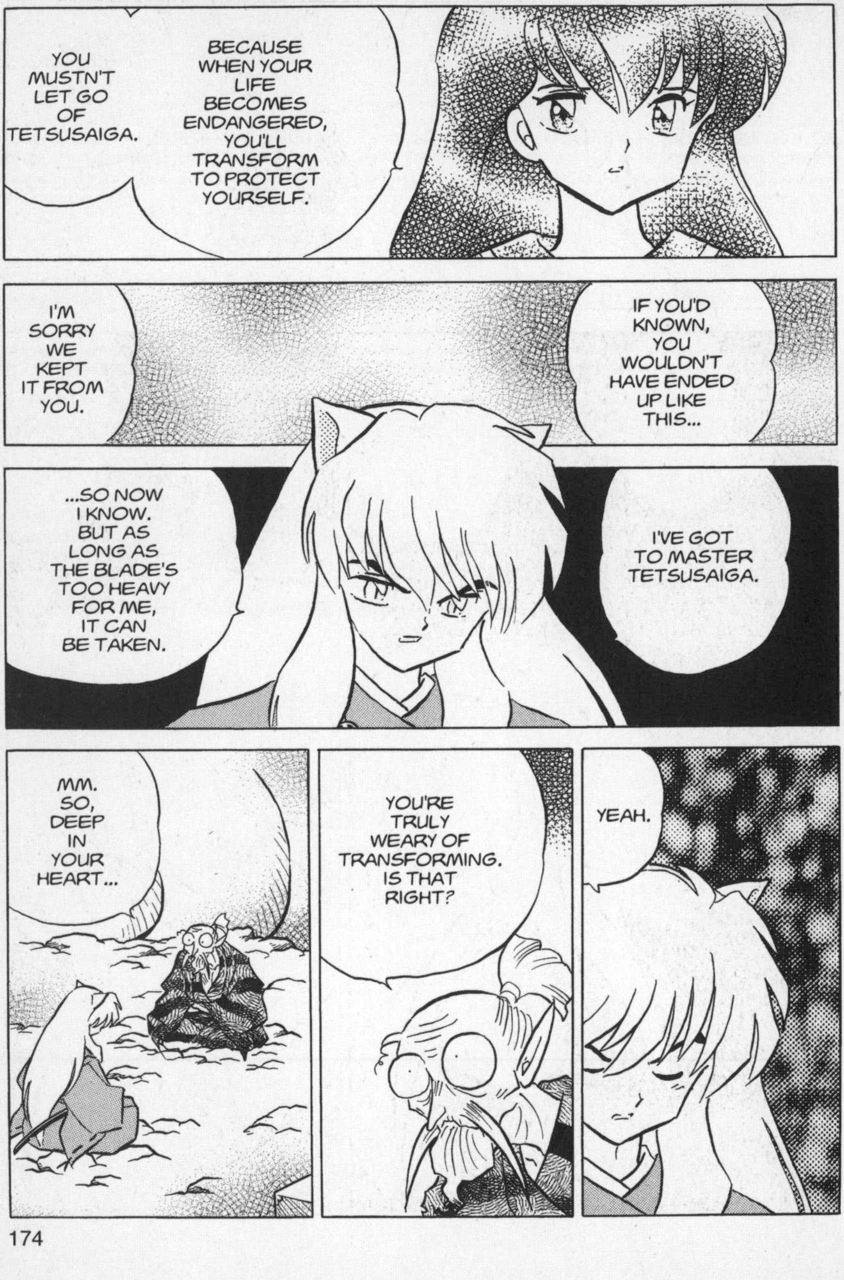
YOU MUSTN'T LET GO OF TETSUSAIGA.
BECAUSE WHEN YOUR LIFE BECOMES ENDANGERED, YOU'LL TRANSFORM TO PROTECT YOURSELF.
I'M SORRY WE KEPT IT FROM YOU.
IF YOU'D KNOWN, YOU WOULDN'T HAVE ENDED UP LIKE THIS...
...SO NOW I KNOW. BUT AS LONG AS THE BLADE'S TOO HEAVY FOR ME, IT CAN BE TAKEN.
I'VE GOT TO MASTER TETSUSAIGA.
MM. SO, DEEP IN YOUR HEART...
YOU'RE TRULY WEARY OF TRANSFORMING. IS THAT RIGHT?
YEAH.

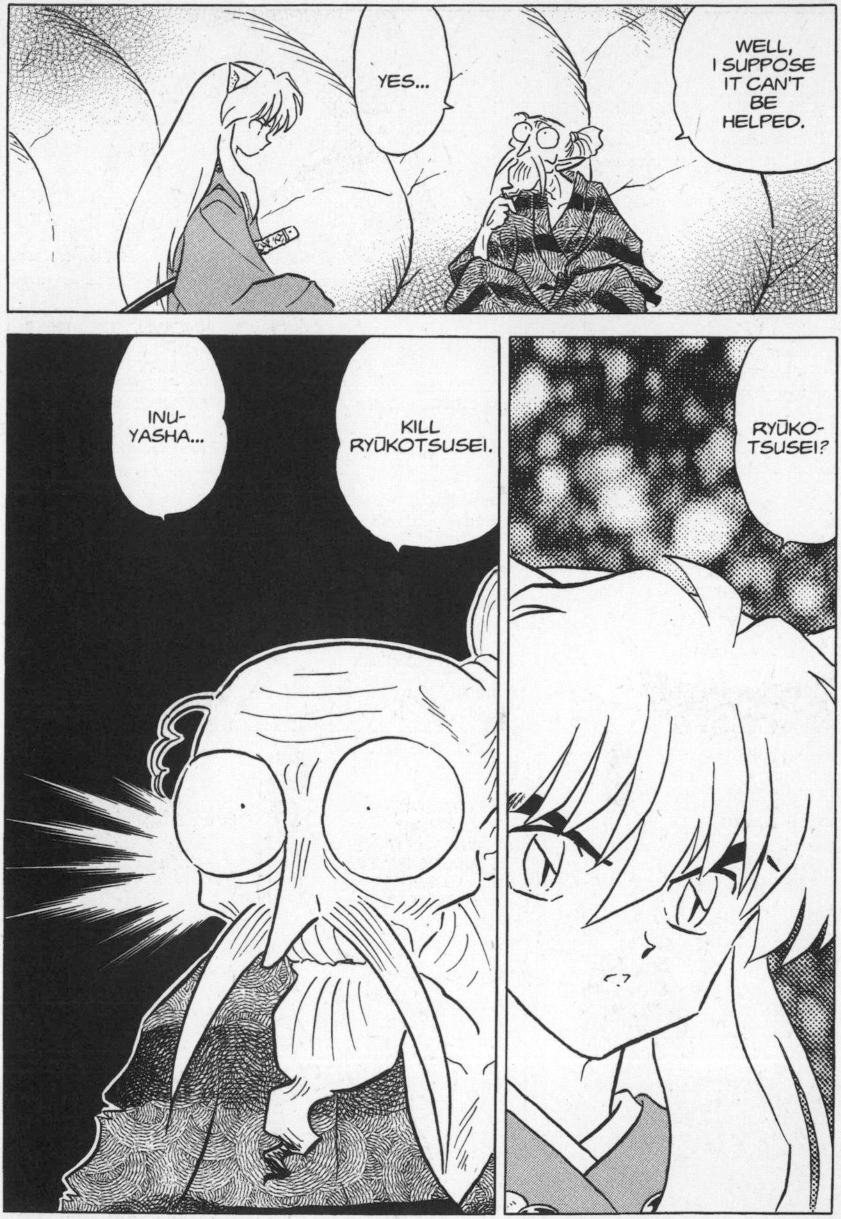
YES...
WELL, I SUPPOSE IT CAN'T BE HELPED.
INU-YASHA...
KILL RYŪKOTSUSEI.
RYŪKO-TSUSEI?

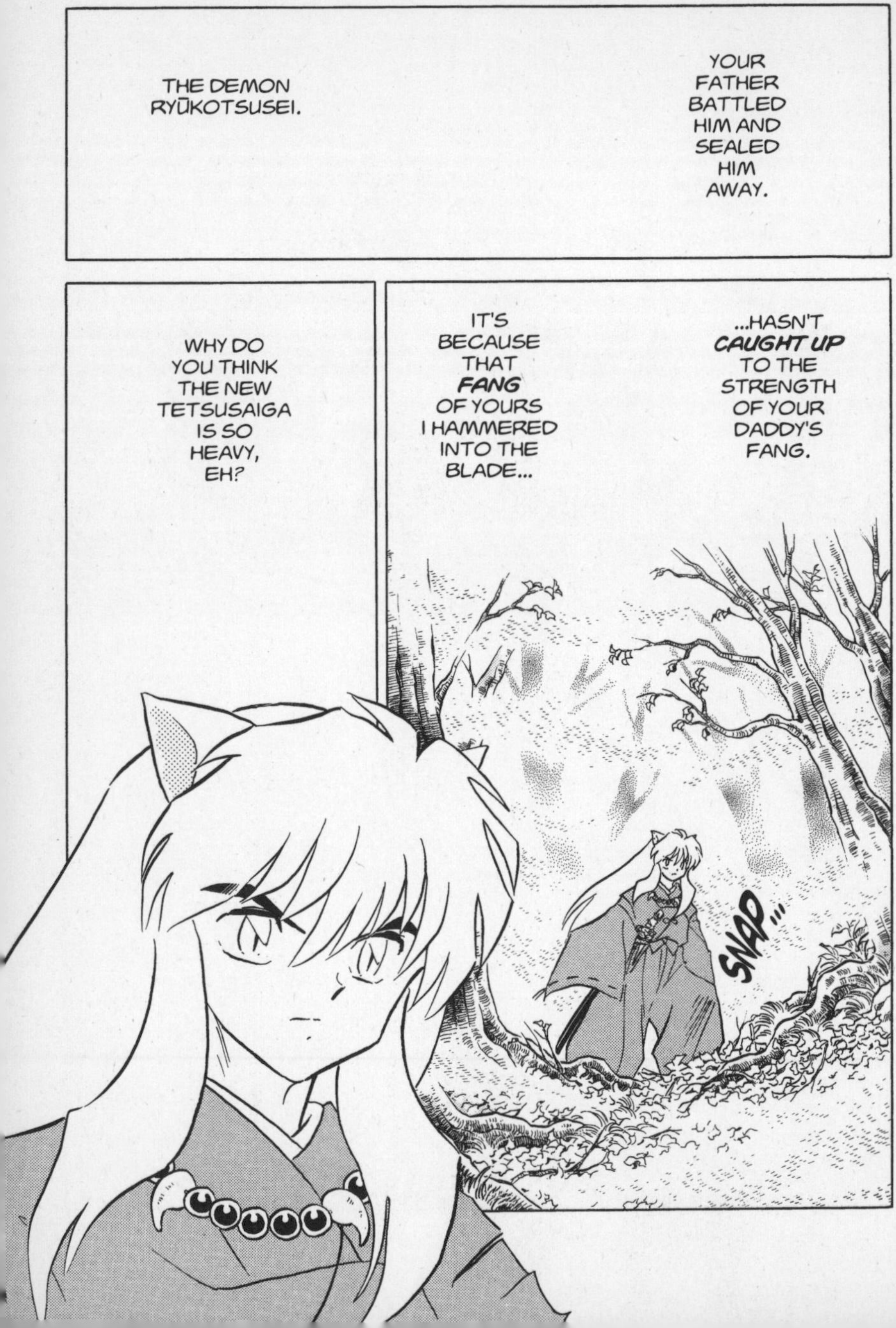
THE DEMON RYŪKOTSUSEI.
YOUR FATHER BATTLED HIM AND SEALED HIM AWAY.
WHY DO YOU THINK THE NEW TETSUSAIGA IS SO HEAVY, EH?
IT'S BECAUSE THAT FANG OF YOURS I HAMMERED INTO THE BLADE...
...HASN'T CAUGHT UP TO THE STRENGTH OF YOUR DADDY'S FANG.
SNAP...

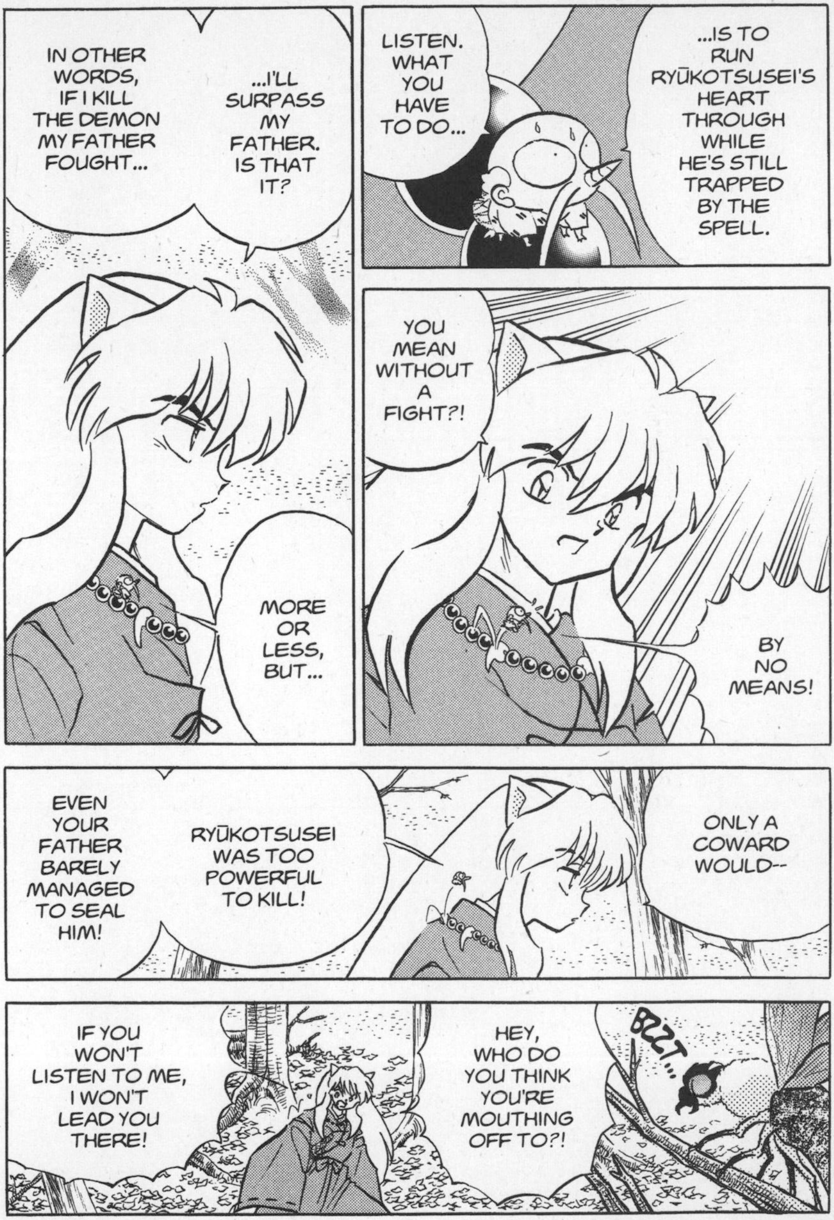
IN OTHER WORDS, IF I KILL THE DEMON MY FATHER FOUGHT...
...I'LL SURPASS MY FATHER. IS THAT IT?
MORE OR LESS, BUT...
LISTEN. WHAT YOU HAVE TO DO...
...IS TO RUN RYŪKOTSUSEI'S HEART THROUGH WHILE HE'S STILL TRAPPED BY THE SPELL.
YOU MEAN WITHOUT A FIGHT?!
BY NO MEANS!
EVEN YOUR FATHER BARELY MANAGED TO SEAL HIM!
RYŪKOTSUSEI WAS TOO POWERFUL TO KILL!
ONLY A COWARD WOULD--
IF YOU WON'T LISTEN TO ME, I WON'T LEAD YOU THERE!
HEY, WHO DO YOU THINK YOU'RE MOUTHING OFF TO?!
BZZT...

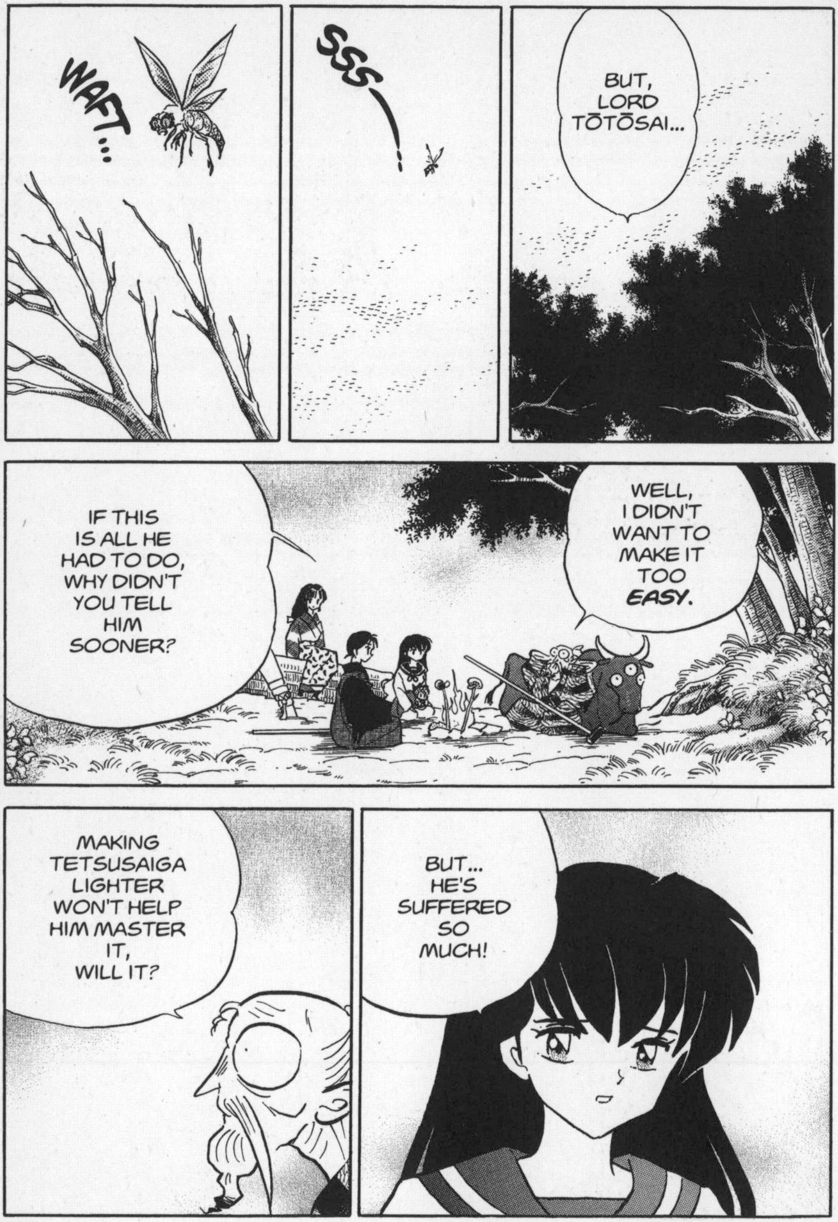
WAFT...
SSS—!
BUT, LORD TŌTŌSAI...
IF THIS IS ALL HE HAD TO DO, WHY DIDN'T YOU TELL HIM SOONER?
WELL, I DIDN'T WANT TO MAKE IT TOO EASY.
MAKING TETSUSAIGA LIGHTER WON'T HELP HIM MASTER IT, WILL IT?
BUT... HE'S SUFFERED SO MUCH!

EVEN IF HIS VICTIMS *WERE* MURDERERS...

...HE STILL HAS *HUMAN BLOOD* ON HIS HANDS!

FUH.

THAT'S WHY I HAD TO TELL HIM.

A BEING WHO KILLS MORTALS WITHOUT A SECOND THOUGHT IS NOT ENTITLED TO WIELD TETSUSAIGA!

HOOO...!

LORD INU-YASHA. OVER THERE.

TK..

RYŪKO-TSUSEI WAS SEALED INTO THAT CLIFF FACE.

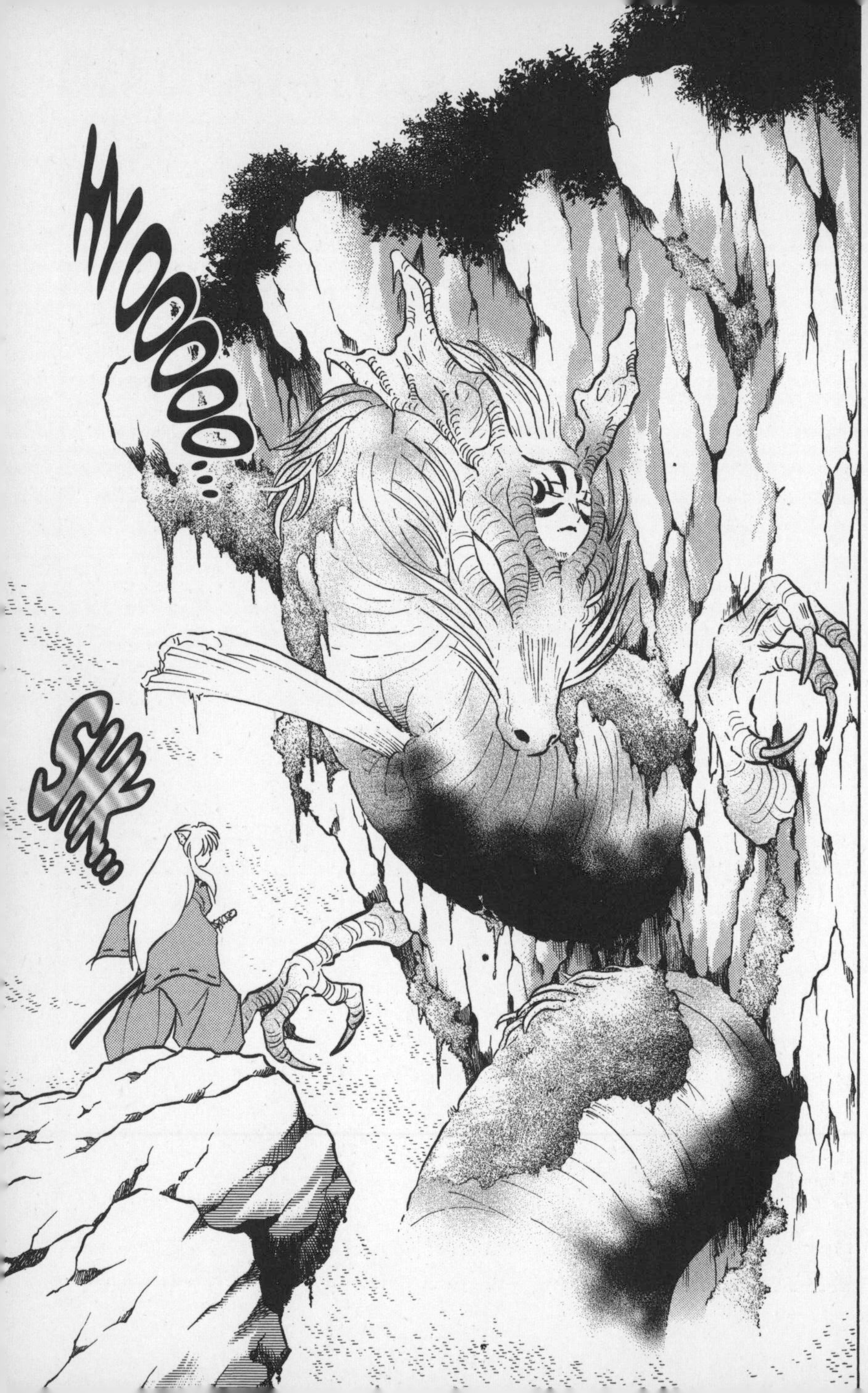
HYOOOOOO...
SHK...

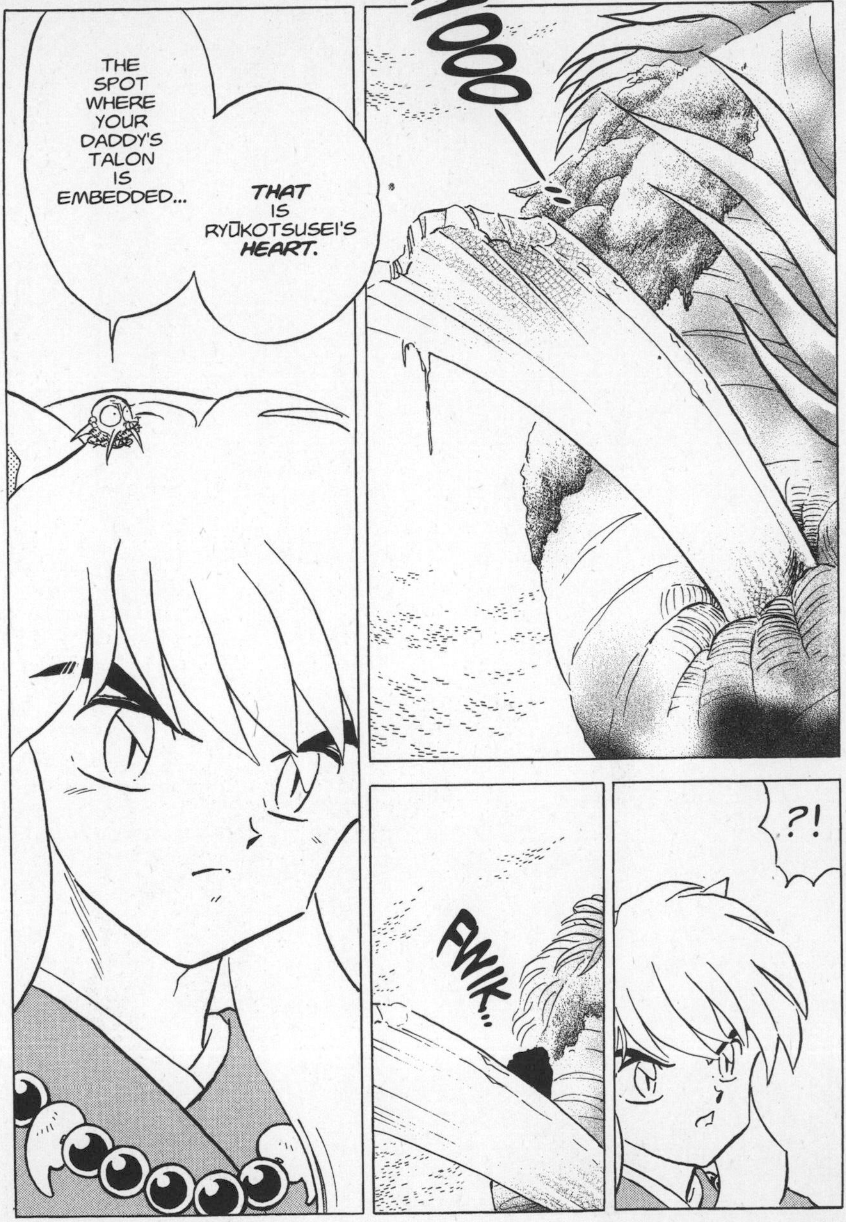
THE SPOT WHERE YOUR DADDY'S TALON IS EMBEDDED...
THAT IS RYŪKOTSUSEI'S HEART.
HYOOO--!!
AWK..
?!

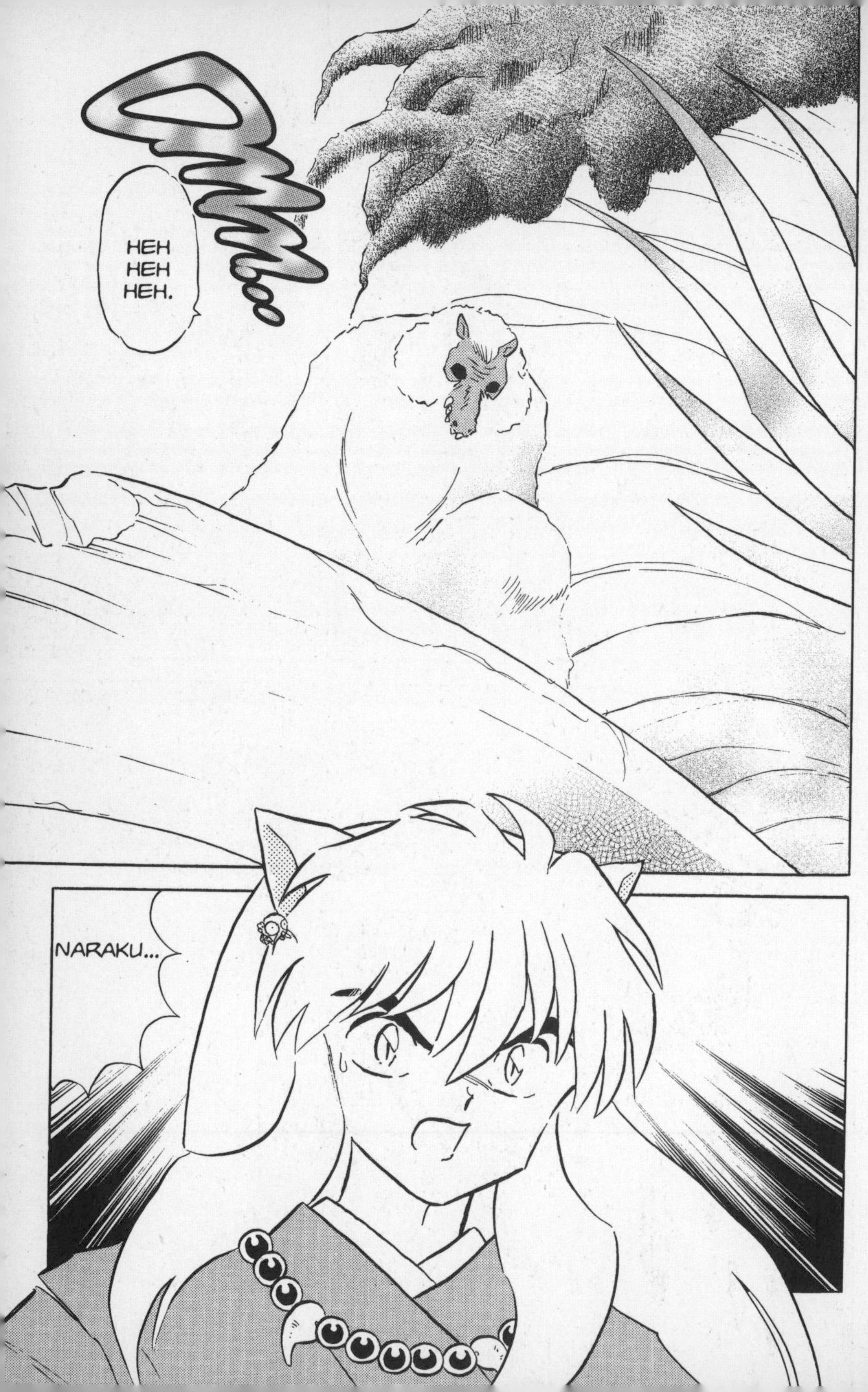
HEH HEH HEH.
NARAKU...

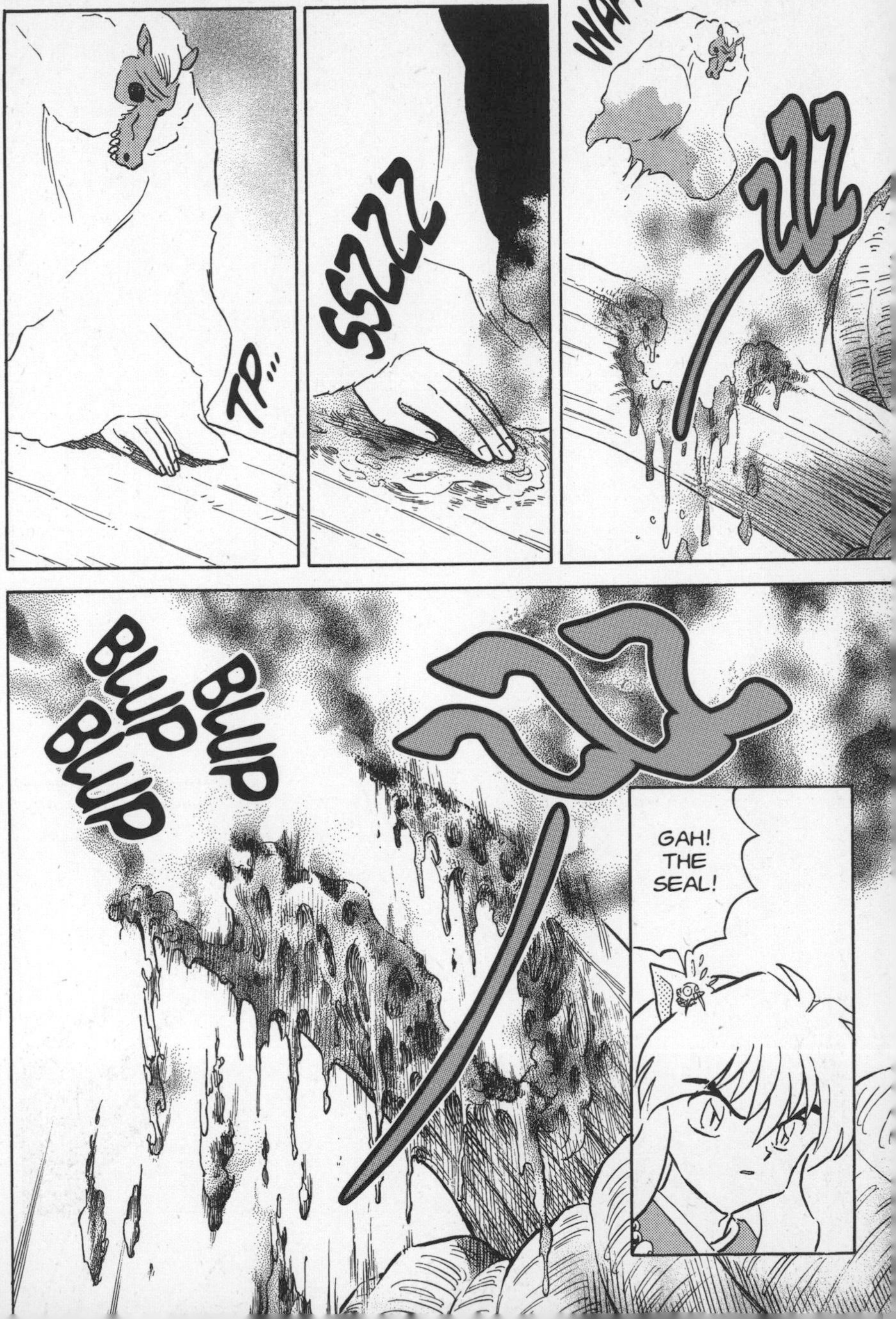
TP...
SSZZZ
WAFT
ZZZ
BLUP
BLUP
BLUP
GAH! THE SEAL!

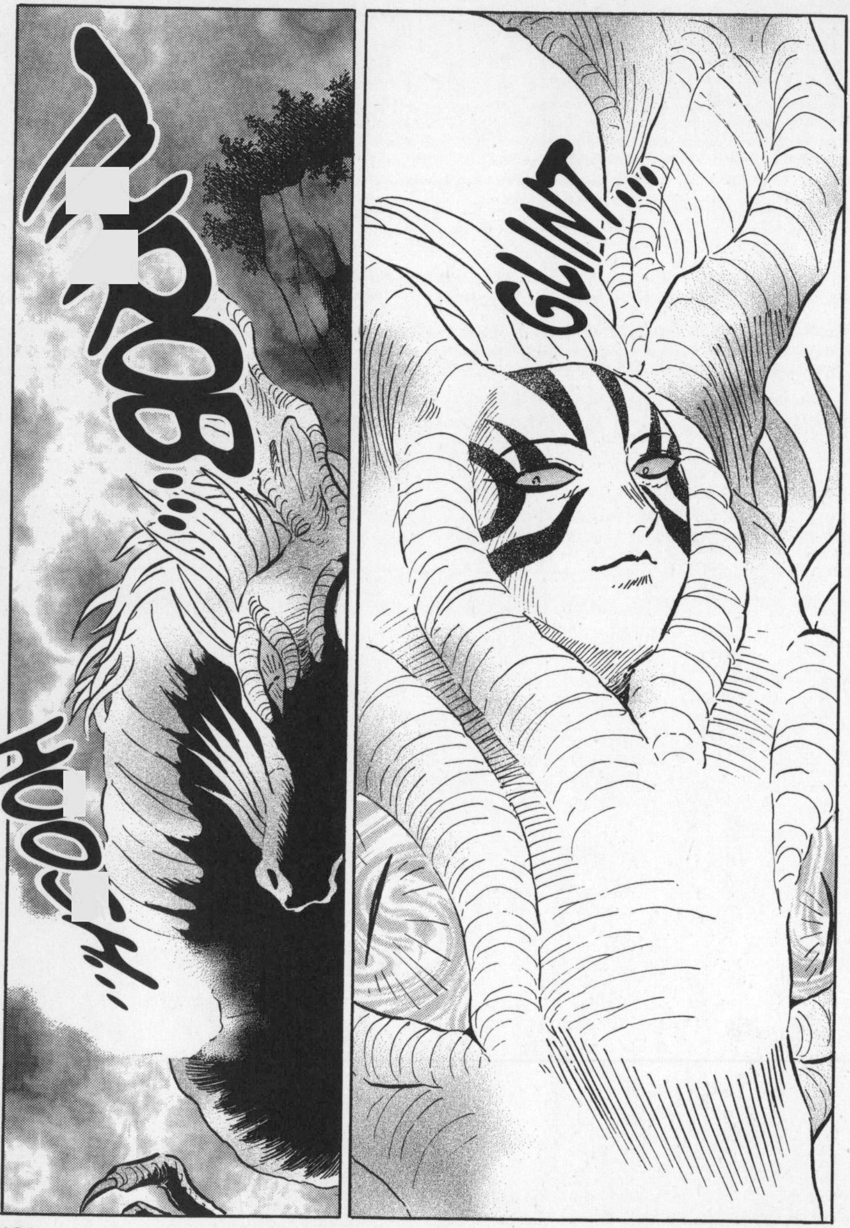
THROB...
HOOSH!!
GLINT...

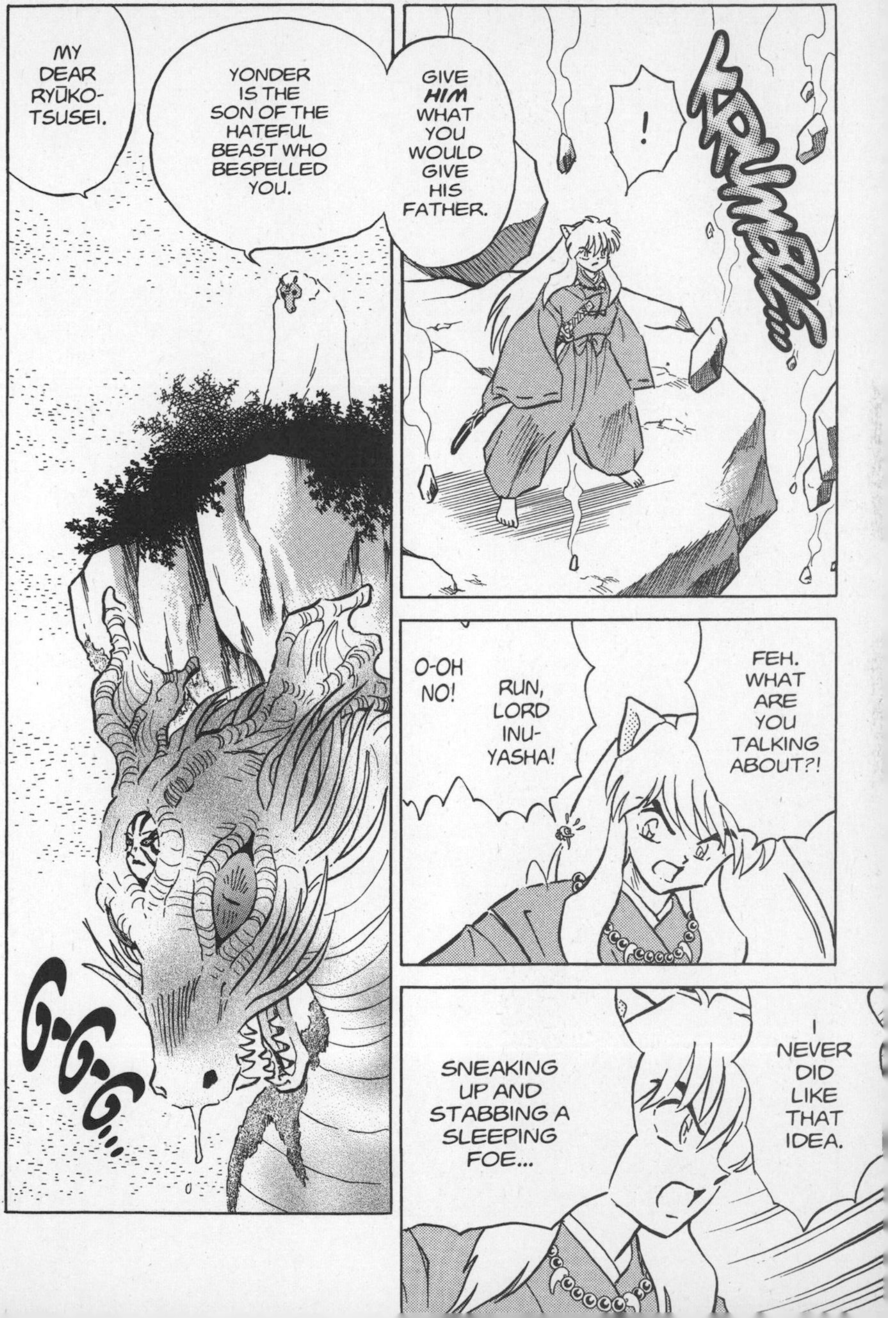
MY DEAR RYŪKO-TSUSEI.
YONDER IS THE SON OF THE HATEFUL BEAST WHO BESPELLED YOU.
GIVE *HIM* WHAT YOU WOULD GIVE HIS FATHER.
G-G-G...
!
KRUMBLE...
O-OH NO!
RUN, LORD INU-YASHA!
FEH. WHAT ARE YOU TALKING ABOUT?!
SNEAKING UP AND STABBING A SLEEPING FOE...
I NEVER DID LIKE THAT IDEA.

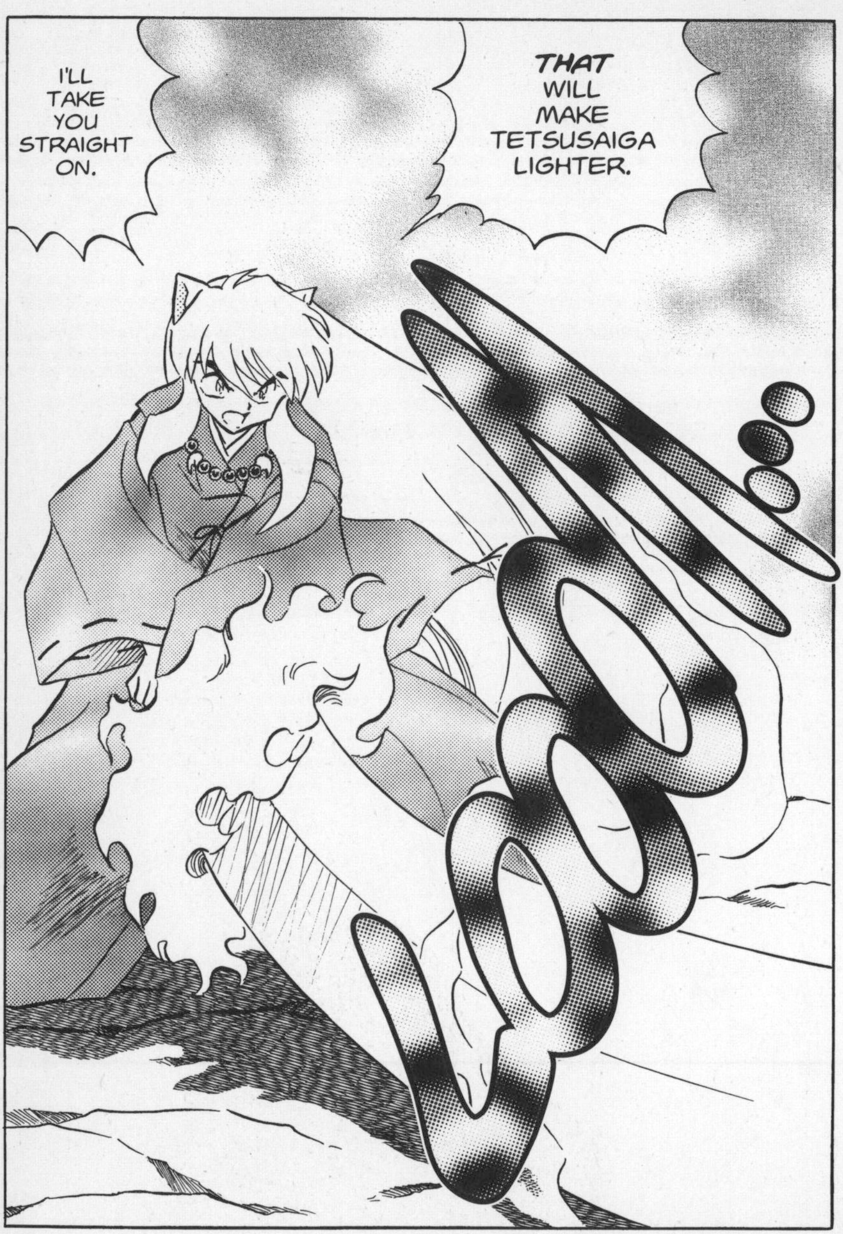
I'LL TAKE YOU STRAIGHT ON.
THAT WILL MAKE TETSUSAIGA LIGHTER.
ZOOM...

TO BE CONTINUED...

About Rumiko Takahashi

Born in 1957 in Niigata, Japan, Rumiko Takahashi attended women's college in Tokyo, where she began studying comics with Kazuo Koike, author of *Crying Freeman*. She later became an assistant to horror-manga artist Kazuo Umezu (*Orochi*). In 1978, she won a prize in Shogakukan's annual "New Comic Artist Contest," and in that same year her boy-meets-alien comedy series *Urusei Yatsura* began appearing in the weekly manga magazine *Shônen Sunday*. This phenomenally successful series ran for nine years and sold over 22 million copies. Takahashi's later *Ranma 1/2* series enjoyed even greater popularity.

Takahashi is considered by many to be one of the world's most popular manga artists. With the publication of Volume 34 of her *Ranma 1/2* series in Japan, Takahashi's total sales passed *one hundred million* copies of her compiled works.

Takahashi's serial titles include *Urusei Yatsura, Ranma 1/2, One-Pound Gospel, Maison Ikkoku* and *InuYasha*. Additionally, Takahashi has drawn many short stories which have been published in America under the title "Rumic Theater," and several installments of a saga known as her "Mermaid" series. Most of Takahashi's major stories have also been animated, and are widely available in translation worldwide. *InuYasha* is her most recent serial story, first published in *Shônen Sunday* in 1996.

EDITOR'S RECOMMENDATIONS

Did you like INUYASHA? Here's what we recommend you try next:

INUYASHA ANI-MANGA

Here's the story you've come to love using actual frames of film in full color from the TV and video series *Inuyasha*.

© 2000 Rumiko Takahashi/Shogakukan, Inc. © Rumiko Takahashi/Shogakukan, Yomiuri TV, Sunrise 2000 Ani-Manga is a trademark of VIZ, LLC

MERMAID SAGA

This is the series Rumiko Takahashi created as her "hobby." Unpressured by editors and deadlines, she lets her creativity flow in this romantic-horror epic. Eating the flesh of a mermaid grants eternal life. But living forever can be a blessing or a curse. Immortal lovers Yuta and Mana are relatively lucky...others who partake of the mermaid's flesh are transformed into savage lost souls!

©1988 Rumiko Takahashi/Shogakukan, Inc.

RANMA 1/2

Rumiko Takahashi's gender-bending martial arts comedy made her famous! Due to an unfortunate accident at a cursed Chinese training ground, when Ranma and his father get splashed with cold water, dad transforms into a giant panda and male Ranma becomes a buxom young girl! Hot water reverses the effect...but only until the next time. Ranma is constantly challenged by battle-crazed martial artists for offenses both real and imagined, and pursued by lovesick suitors of both genders. What's a half-boy, half-girl to do?

©1988 Rumiko Takahashi/Shogakukan, Inc.

COMPLETE OUR SURVEY AND LET US KNOW WHAT YOU THINK!

☐ Please do NOT send me information about VIZ products, news and events, special offers, or other information.

☐ Please do NOT send me information from VIZ's trusted business partners.

Name: _____

Address: _____

City: _____ **State:** _____ **Zip:** _____

E-mail: _____

☐ Male ☐ Female   **Date of Birth** (mm/dd/yyyy): ___ / ___ / ___   (Under 13? Parental consent required)

What race/ethnicity do you consider yourself? (please check one)

☐ Asian/Pacific Islander   ☐ Black/African American   ☐ Hispanic/Latino

☐ Native American/Alaskan Native ☐ White/Caucasian   ☐ Other: _____

What VIZ product did you purchase? (check all that apply and indicate title purchased)

☐ DVD/VHS _____

☐ Graphic Novel _____

☐ Magazines _____

☐ Merchandise _____

Reason for purchase: (check all that apply)

☐ Special offer   ☐ Favorite title   ☐ Gift

☐ Recommendation   ☐ Other _____

Where did you make your purchase? (please check one)

☐ Comic store   ☐ Bookstore   ☐ Mass/Grocery Store

☐ Newsstand   ☐ Video/Video Game Store ☐ Other: _____

☐ Online (site: _____)

What other VIZ properties have you purchased/own? _____

_____

How many anime and/or manga titles have you purchased in the last year? How many were VIZ titles? (please check one from each column)

ANIME
- ☐ None
- ☐ 1-4
- ☐ 5-10
- ☐ 11+

MANGA
- ☐ None
- ☐ 1-4
- ☐ 5-10
- ☐ 11+

VIZ
- ☐ None
- ☐ 1-4
- ☐ 5-10
- ☐ 11+

I find the pricing of VIZ products to be: (please check one)

☐ Cheap   ☐ Reasonable   ☐ Expensive

What genre of manga and anime would you like to see from VIZ? (please check two)

☐ Adventure   ☐ Comic Strip   ☐ Science Fiction   ☐ Fighting

☐ Horror   ☐ Romance   ☐ Fantasy   ☐ Sports

What do you think of VIZ's new look?

☐ Love It   ☐ It's OK   ☐ Hate It   ☐ Didn't Notice   ☐ No Opinion

Which do you prefer? (please check one)

☐ Reading right-to-left

☐ Reading left-to-right

Which do you prefer? (please check one)

☐ Sound effects in English

☐ Sound effects in Japanese with English captions

☐ Sound effects in Japanese only with a glossary at the back

THANK YOU! Please send the completed form to:

NJW Research
42 Catharine St.
Poughkeepsie, NY 12601

All information provided will be used for internal purposes only. We promise not to sell or otherwise divulge your information.